The Political Economy of the American Frontier

This book offers an analytical explanation for the origins of and change in property institutions on the American frontier during the nineteenth century. Its scope is interdisciplinary, integrating insights from political science, economics, law, and history. This book shows how claim clubs – informal governments established by squatters in each of the major frontier sectors of agriculture, mining, logging, and ranching – substituted for the state as a source of private property institutions and how they changed the course of who received a legal title, and for what price, throughout the nineteenth century. Unlike existing analytical studies of the frontier that emphasize one or two sectors, this book considers all major sectors, as well as the relationship between informal and formal property institutions, while also proposing a novel theory of emergence and change in property institutions that provides a framework to interpret the complicated history of land laws in the United States.

Ilia Murtazashvili is currently an assistant professor in the Graduate School of Public and International Affairs, University of Pittsburgh. He holds a PhD in political science and an MA in agricultural and applied economics from the University of Wisconsin–Madison. Murtazashvili's research focuses on political economy and institutional design. He is the co-author, with Donald Alexander Downs, of *Arms and the University: Military Presence and the Civic Education of Non-Military Students* (Cambridge, 2012).

Political Economy of Institutions and Decisions

Series Editors

Stephen Ansolabehere, *Harvard University*
Jeffry Frieden, *Harvard University*

Founding Editors

James E. Alt, *Harvard University*
Douglass C. North, *Washington University of St. Louis*

Other Books in the Series

Alberto Alesina and Howard Rosenthal, *Partisan Politics, Divided Government and the Economy*
Lee J. Alston, Thrainn Eggertsson, and Douglass C. North, eds., *Empirical Studies in Institutional Change*
Lee J. Alston and Joseph P. Ferrie, *Southern Paternalism and the Rise of the American Welfare State: Economics, Politics, and Institutions, 1865–1965*
James E. Alt and Kenneth Shepsle, eds., *Perspectives on Positive Political Economy*
Josephine T. Andrews, *When Majorities Fail: The Russian Parliament, 1990–1993*
Jeffrey S. Banks and Eric A. Hanushek, eds., *Modern Political Economy: Old Topics, New Directions*
Yoram Barzel, *Economic Analysis of Property Rights, 2nd Edition*
Yoram Barzel, *A Theory of the State: Economic Rights, Legal Rights, and the Scope of the State*
Robert Bates, *Beyond the Miracle of the Market: The Political Economy of Agrarian Development in Kenya*
Jenna Bednar, *The Robust Federation: Principles of Design*
Charles M. Cameron, *Veto Bargaining: Presidents and the Politics of Negative Power*
Kelly H. Chang, *Appointing Central Bankers: The Politics of Monetary Policy in the United States and the European Monetary Union*
Peter Cowhey and Mathew McCubbins, eds., *Structure and Policy in Japan and the United States: An Institutionalist Approach*

Continued after the Index

The Political Economy of the American Frontier

ILIA MURTAZASHVILI
University of Pittsburgh

CAMBRIDGE
UNIVERSITY PRESS

CAMBRIDGE
UNIVERSITY PRESS

32 Avenue of the Americas, New York, NY 10013-2473, USA

Cambridge University Press is part of the University of Cambridge.

It furthers the University's mission by disseminating knowledge in the pursuit of education, learning, and research at the highest international levels of excellence.

www.cambridge.org
Information on this title: www.cambridge.org/9781107019126

First published 2013

Printed in the United States of America

A catalog record for this publication is available from the British Library.

Library of Congress Cataloging in Publication Data
Murtazashvili, Ilia, 1975–
The political economy of the American frontier / Ilia Murtazashvili, University of Pittsburgh.
pages cm. – (Political economy of institutions and decisions)
Includes bibliographical references and index.
ISBN 978-1-107-01912-6 (hardback)
1. Land tenure – West (U.S.) – History – 19th century. 2. Land settlement – West (U.S.) – History – 19th century. 3. Land claim associations – West (U.S.) – History – 19th century. 4. Agriculture – Economic aspects – West (U.S.) – History – 19th century. 5. Mines and mineral resources – Economic aspects – West (U.S.) – History – 19th century. 6. Logging – Economic aspects – West (U.S.) – History – 19th century. 7. Ranching – Economic aspects – West (U.S.) – History – 19th century. 8. Frontier and pioneer life – West (U.S.) I. Title.
HD209.M87 2013
333.3'17809034–dc23 2013012346

ISBN 978-1-107-01912-6 Hardback

Contents

List of Maps, Figure, and Tables

MAPS

FIGURE

TABLES

Preface

When I first began studying property institutions on the American frontier, I expected to find that squatters were rugged individualists who sowed the seeds of capitalist development. My thoughts were certainly influenced by neoclassical microeconomics, which generally views entrepreneurs as a source of innovation in the economy. Squatters were archetypical entrepreneurs, occupying and improving land in the major frontier sectors of agriculture, mining, logging, and ranching throughout the nineteenth century even though they lacked formal (legal) authority to do so. My perspective was also shaped by popular accounts of the Wild West, which tend to portray the frontier in an individualistic fashion. Each tradition – neoclassical microeconomics and Hollywood accounts of the Wild West – shares in common emphasis on individuals over groups or governments.

As my search continued, I found that the story of the origins and change of property institutions was much more complicated than I had initially thought. To be sure, my findings revealed that squatters were powerful and profound engines of capitalist development. Indeed, they established informal private property institutions that competed with, and in many ways substituted for, state-backed private property rights. However, they were not successful because they did things on their own. Rather, they were good at working together. And when their interests congealed, it was not always a source of social benefits.

In addition, the means by which squatters managed their affairs did not fit with fables typically told by economists interested in informal order. Indeed, one of the defining features of economic studies of social order is explaining how people succeed without relying on governments or even hierarchy. Although there is some truth to accounts offered by economists, my findings suggest that the truly remarkable feature of frontier development was the ability of squatters to devise their own governments. Their informal associations, which were called claim clubs, typically had all the features of the state – executives, deliberative bodies, a system of administration, judges, and juries – despite operating in the state's often pale shadow.

Despite sharing features in common with the state, claim clubs swept formal governments aside in their effort to provide their own property institutions. Over time, they ensured their members got legal title for free. This is a book about claim clubs and their consequences.

Although my stories emphasize claim clubs, this book is organized around two of the fundamental questions of political economy: where do property institutions come from and why do they change? Despite their importance in the political and economic history of the United States, generalized theories of the origins of property institutions have a limited role for organizations such as claim clubs. Economic studies of the origins of property institutions emphasize highly decentralized processes of emergence of property institutions, such as ownership norms arising through spontaneous order or reputational contracting without considering institutions specifying power relations. In contrast, political theories of property institutions alert us to the role of the state as a source of private property institutions. Despite providing many insights into the origins of property institutions, it is my contention that neither of these disciplinary perspectives provides an analytical framework capable of explaining how governments arise within the state to specify and enforce property institutions. Since claim clubs challenged Leviathan while moving substantially beyond the highly decentralized arrangements of economics, a new analytical framework is necessary to understand them; this book is the first attempt at such a framework.

Once we understand where property institutions come from, the next logical question is why they change. As far as institutional change is concerned, my interest is in the evolution of land laws governing the agricultural, mineral, ranching, and logging sectors throughout the nineteenth century. My initial belief was that squatters were a source of efficiency, or Pareto improvement, in the process of institutional change. This assumption also turned out to be incorrect. Claim clubs, rather than benevolently responding to an environment of bureaucratic and legislative incompetence, were in many ways a source of rather than a solution to transaction costs in the land-allocation process.

My initial mistake was to overlook the state's interest in land. I was so concerned with emergence of private property institutions that I did not anticipate the fiscal consequences of land laws for development of the American state. Later, it became clear to me that the fundamental conflict during this period was not so much about private property rights as much as it was about the price of land. My preoccupation with the origins of private property institutions led me to overlook the fundamental conflict during the nineteenth century, which was a bitter and often bloody struggle over the price of land.

In the simplest sense, conflict over the price of land emerged because the state owned a lot of land that squatters wanted. Competitive auctions of state-owned land would have satisfied the state's interest in revenue to provide public goods, including security, as well as a growing demand for private property. Yet the state's interest in competitive markets for land clashed with the aspirations of distributive-minded claim clubs – and as I found out, clubs were astonishingly successful in getting what they wanted, which was free land. Throughout the nineteenth century, claim clubs harnessed their organizational fury to undermine competitive markets for land at every turn and in the process undercut the state's revenue aspirations.

Despite the importance of price in economics and political economy, existing studies of change in property institutions have not considered explicitly conflict over the price of land during the privatization process. Once we recognize the centrality of conflict over the price of land, a different picture of squatters emerges. Far from an efficient response to poorly designed laws, claim clubs were perhaps the fundamental rent-seeking coalitions of the nineteenth century. Squatters were remarkable in their ability to assign and enforce private property institutions informally as well as a fundamental source of distributive politics; my mistake was to assume that the former implied efficiency in the process of institutional change. As far as institutional change is concerned, my contribution is to explain how claim clubs could be simultaneously a remarkable source of self-governance as well as a source of social costs in the process of formal institutional change.

Today's choices are also informed by history (or at least we hope that they are). My findings also led me to reconsider the conventional wisdom regarding the lessons of the American frontier for today's conflicts over land. Existing studies of the frontier generally infer from experience during the nineteenth century the virtue of formalization of title, praising squatters. My lessons differ in two respects.

First, my account suggests that formalization of informal claims to land is less important than balancing the state's interest in land ownership with the demands of individuals for private property rights. Land reforms often have important fiscal consequences, including consequences for the state's ability to provide public goods such as security. Public policies that fail to consider the fiscal consequences of land laws are incomplete, to say the least; yet few studies of emergence and change in property institutions consider carefully the fiscal consequences of land laws.

Second, my findings suggest that the fundamental political problem during decentralization of ownership is committing credibly to competitive markets for state-owned land. One of the primary mistakes the federal government (repeatedly) made was to believe that it could provide one-time or temporary concessions to squatters. These concessions, by undermining credibility of commitment to state ownership, led to new waves of squatters and ultimately ensured that the state was unable to profit from its vast landholding. Although a logic of credibility of commitment provides a lens to understand key developments on the American frontier, the implications in general are far reaching: a government should be concerned not only with its commitment to protecting private property but also to state ownership if it hopes to ensure an orderly process of decentralization of ownership.

Providing a new analytical framework to interpret the political economy of the American frontier, one that integrates insights from political science, economics, history, and law, is a challenging task. To the extent this book does what it sets out to do, many people deserve credit. My greatest debt is to David Weimer, who read the manuscript in its entirety many times, each time offering detailed comments and suggestions that dramatically improved the clarity of my argument. He has been a wonderful mentor and friend, and a continual source of encouragement and inspiration. I also owe a special debt of gratitude to Daniel Bromley for teaching me institutional economics and for an extremely useful set of comments on an early version of the manuscript that led me to rewrite it in its entirety. Special thanks also go to Scott Gehlbach for dozens of discussions about my theoretical argument and political economy more generally. My intellectual debt to them should be clear in the pages that follow.

Several others offered comments and suggestions that influenced my argument in important ways. Stanley Engerman provided extremely useful suggestions early in the project that set it on a productive path. David Canon and Gerald Gamm, two scholars whose knowledge of Congress far surpasses that of anyone I have ever met, helped me improve my analysis of legislative decision making during the nineteenth century. Pete Karsten offered extremely useful suggestions regarding key works from the discipline of history, as well as shared insight from his own work on the study of institutional change; my only regret is that I did not have the benefit of his advice earlier in the project. My analysis of judicial institutions and legal history benefited greatly from discussions with Donald Downs and Howard Schweber, two people who shaped my understanding of public law. John Coleman helped me better understand how my study relates to the American Political Development (APD) perspective. It is my hope that this book illustrates how we can bridge what is often seen as a divide between APD and new institutional economics. Peter Toumanoff, who introduced me to the property rights approach, transaction costs economics, and new institutional economics as an undergraduate also offered valuable insights when I was writing this book on these same subjects.

Several scholars offered useful comments as well as encouraged me to think about the comparative implications of my study, including Melanie Manion, Aidan Vining, Catherine Boone, Ed Friedman, Aili Tripp, Yoshiko Herrera, Lou Picard, J. David Stanfield, and M. Yasin Safar. Although this book is at its core a study in the American frontier, they ensured that I was continually thinking about current conflicts over land in the developing world. The final section of this book is entitled "Land and the State"; it is meant to be a transition to my next book, which will consider in earnest the political economy of land in the developing world, with emphasis on how land reform can make or break the state. To the extent the transition from American economic history to the current developing world is seamless, they deserve credit for ensuring a comparative book was always on my mind.

The anonymous reviewers for Cambridge University Press provided exceptionally detailed, thoughtful, and precise comments on the entire manuscript at a late stage in its development. They suggested many changes yet also offered insight into how to implement them. Indeed, their comments led to the final comprehensive rewrite of the manuscript. In the end, I adopted nearly all the changes suggested, and this book is much better for it.

The editorial and production team at the Press has been remarkably helpful. Lewis Bateman deserves special thanks for seeing promise in this manuscript and for kind words of encouragement. Anne Lovering Rounds and Shaun Vigil were extremely helpful in preparing the manuscript for production. From the moment I began working on the dissertation that set the foundation for this book, I envisioned it as fitting into a long line of books that I have learned a great deal from in the Political Economy of Institutions and Decisions series, and I was extremely happy when the editors of the series, Stephen Ansolabehere and Jeffry Frieden, chose this book to be a part of it.

My wife, Jennifer, has been an unflinching source of support and encouragement from the moment I began writing about the American frontier. Although she studies a very different part of the world, I have learned more from her about informal governance than anyone. This book would not have been possible without her love, patience, and understanding. This book is dedicated to her, and to our beautiful children, Zoe and Leo. It is amazing how much insight a one- and three-year old provide into the emergence of informal private property rights (as well as the challenge of sustaining a sharing rule).

1

Introduction

Where do private property institutions come from and why do they change? This book considers these general questions of political economy in the context of the American frontier during the nineteenth century, a fundamental period in terms of emergence and change in property rights to land. Although the process of institutional transformation during this period is remarkably complex, this book proposes claim clubs – associations established by squatters in the major frontier economic sectors – as an answer to both of these questions. These private-order associations substituted for an all-powerful state conventionally assumed in political theories of emergence of property institutions as the initial source of constitutional and working rules that governed capitalist development in the major frontier sectors of agriculture, mining, logging, and ranching. Claim clubs also had important distributive consequences, securing free land, through either legislation or coercion, for members in each of the economic sectors under consideration.

Despite their political and economic significance, existing perspectives on property institutions have a limited, if any, role for organizations such as claim clubs. For example, North (1990, 1981) emphasized firms as a source of change in property institutions in an economy without providing much of an explanation of where property institutions themselves come from. Ostrom (2005, 1990) understood the significance of self-governing organizations but confined analysis to collective property institutions, not to the origins of private property institutions. Analyzing change in property rights from a more political perspective, Sened (1997), and Riker and Sened (1991) viewed an all-powerful state as a source of property institutions. These political theories offered a more realistic account of the origins of property institutions than earlier economic studies, yet they did not consider organizations that specify and enforce property institutions within the state. Nor have existing studies considered explicitly the often substantial distributive consequences of private-order property organizations.

As such, each perspective provides an incomplete framework to understand land relations in the United States in the nineteenth century.

The thesis of this book can be stated simply. Claim clubs, rather than spontaneously arising norms or an all-powerful state, were the most important initial source of private property institutions as individuals fanned out across the nation's vast lands during the nineteenth century. Once in place, claim clubs were remarkably successful in securing distributive benefits from various levels of government. These bandits within the state were perhaps the most impressive examples of private-order specification and enforcement of property institutions in the political economic history of the United States, as well as one of the most important examples of rent-seeking organizations of the nineteenth century. In short, this book argues that it is impossible to understand emergence and change in property institutions in the United States without according a starring role to claim clubs. Before providing a more thorough introduction to my argument, I briefly introduce the main features of claim clubs.

CLAIM CLUBS: A FEW EXAMPLES

Many of the people who migrated to lands west of the original thirteen states during the late eighteenth and nineteenth centuries occupied state- and privately owned land without legal title. Yet these "squatters," as they were called, were not the isolated individualists we might have in mind when conjuring up images of settlement of western lands. Rather, they were adept at establishing organizations with features similar to those of governments, balancing frequent use of violence or the threat of it to establish order with deliberative features comparable to the nascent machinery of formal government in nearby towns and cities even though they were not formally part of the state. In fact, these were outlaw organizations.

These intriguing organizational features of claim clubs, which balanced a remarkable capacity for violence with a basic framework of deliberative governance, were rivaled only by their effectiveness in getting what they wanted, which was their self-proclaimed "fair share" of the state's land. And there was a tremendous amount of land that was potentially available for the taking. Between the conclusion of the American Revolution and the mid-nineteenth century, the federal government would eventually acquire over a billion acres of land. As Table 1.1 shows, the federal government acquired nearly sixty-five percent of the land area of the United States for a cost of around $77 million from 1781 to 1853. Using 1840 as a base year, this amounts to only about $2 billion in today's dollars.[1]

[1] Whenever real values are used, they are measured in real prices for an appropriate base year using the "Measuring Worth" service of the Economic History Association: http://www.measuringworth.com/. This service provides a simple and easy way to calculate the value of a dollar then and now.

TABLE 1.1. *Territorial Acquisition by the Federal Government, 1781–1853*

	Total Area of Land (acres)	Percent Total U.S. Land Area	Cost
State Cessions (1781–1802)	233,415,680 (Georgia Cession: 56,689,920)	10.4	6,200,000
Louisiana Purchase (1803)	523,446,400	23.3	23,213,568
Red River Basin (1782–1817)	29,066,880	1.3	0
Cession from Spain (1819)	43342,720	2.0	6,674,057
Oregon Compromise (1846)	180,644,480	8.1	0
Mexican Cession (1850)	334,479,360	14.9	16,295,149
Purchase from Texas (1850)	78,842,880	3.5	15,486,448
Gadsden Purchase (1853)	18,961,920	0.8	10,000,000
Total Public Domain	**1,442,200,320**	**64.3**	**77,879,222**

Sources: U.S. Department of the Interior, Bureau of Land Management, *Public Land Statistics* (2011); see also Robbins (1942) and Donaldson (1884).

Territorial acquisition would ultimately provide a foundation for economic development of the nation. Yet interests conflicted from the outset over the price of land. Opportunity-seeking squatters had their eyes on the land, while the federal government had other designs for it, namely allocating land through competitive auctions.[2] The government had good reason to allocate land competitively, such as acquiring revenue to pay down debt, funding infrastructure development in new states (roads and schools), subsidizing development of railroads, and ensuring land promised to veterans maintained its value.[3] In fact,

[2] The concept of selling public land to finance government expenditures and pay down debt became institutionalized during the Articles of Confederation, in particular from 1784 through 1787 through a series of land ordinances, the most famous of which is the Northwest Ordinance – a law that established a framework for self-governance in the territories, prohibited slavery in new states, as well as created a bill of rights for new states. These ordinances, as well as other major laws enacted during the Articles of Confederation, which existed from 1781 to 1787, are found in the *Journal of the Continental Congress*. On the importance of the Northwest Ordinance for economic and political development, see especially North and Rutten (1987).

[3] Grubb (2010, 2007a,b) considers carefully the political economy of revenue from public land during the founding period, providing precise estimates of the value of land compared with the value of debt. According to these estimates, the value of public land was quite substantial, enough to cover the nation's debt at the dawn of the nineteenth century.

TABLE 1.2. *Public Land Survey System*

	Dimension (miles)	Dimension ($mile^2$)	Area (acres)	Notes
Township (36 sections)	6 by 6	36	23,040	A section was usually reserved for public purpose, such as schools
Section	1 by 1	1	640	Initial lots size under the auction system of Northwest Ordinance
Half-section	1 by 1/2	1/2	320	Some claim clubs allowed this many acres
Quarter Section	1/2 by 1/4	1/4	160	Size used for preemption and homestead
Quarter of quarter section	1/4 by 1/4	1/16	40	Size used for freed slaves and on Bureau of Indian Lands

by 1785, the Confederate Congress created a survey system to facilitate decentralization of land ownership through competitive markets. The Public Land Survey System (PLSS) allocated land in townships of thirty-six sections of a square mile each, with sections that could be further subdivided in rectangular lots of 160 acres, which was a standard size for a farm.

The PLSS, the basic features of which are summarized in Table 1.2 to get an idea what different acreages meant in terms of square miles, would eventually be used to survey and allocate essentially all of the lands acquired by the federal government. Although the federal government would eventually give its land to squatters in amounts of 160 acres, the initial plan circa 1785 was to competitively allocate land in 640-acre sections. Eventually, some groups would receive fewer than 160 acres (such as freed slaves and Indians on government reservations), although many claim clubs would eventually allow members to claim more than the 160-acre limit allowed by the federal government.

The tremendous increase in landholding coincided with an important jurisdictional divide in terms of authority to allocate land. In a division of authority that continues to present times, the state governments control public-land policy in the original thirteen states, Kentucky, Tennessee, Texas, Alaska, and Hawaii. These are state-land states, so-called because the state government rather than Congress has primary authority to distribute public land. In all other states, the federal government has the authority to decide how to allocate public land, including decisions about the price of land. These states for which Congress decides how to allocate public land are known as public-land states. Accordingly, in any of the public-land states, squatters were in a standoff with the federal government itself. Map 1.1 provides an idea of just how much land

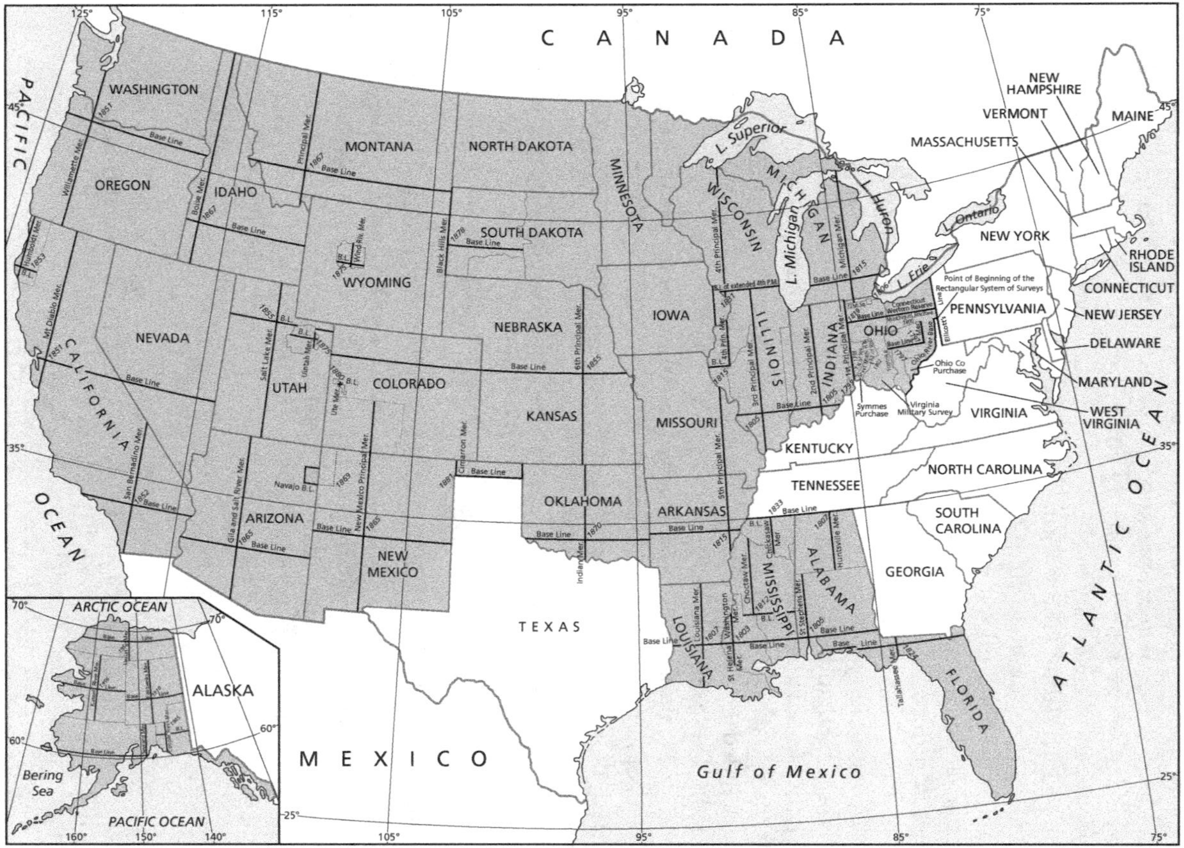

MAP 1.1. Jurisdictional authority over public land in the United States. *Source:* Redrawn from United States Department of the Interior, Bureau of Land Management.

the federal government would eventually control. Shaded areas are the states in which Congress controls disposition of public land.

The PLSS set up a quite rational system to measure, divide, and subdivide land, as well as a way for the government to attain revenue from its vast landholding. These auctions provided the government with a revenue resource in a period in which it had essentially no ability to tax citizens directly. Yet, as we will see, clubs ensured that the American state rarely controlled, and hence seldom profited from, land it formally owned.

Farmers were the first group to develop claim clubs, although miners, loggers, and ranchers would each develop similar organizations. Agricultural claim clubs had a similar constitution even through these clubs would be used by farmers in different time periods and regions. For example, though the first clubs convened on disputed Indian Territory in Pennsylvania around the time of the Revolutionary War, similar ones later sprang up in Indiana in the 1810; in Illinois, Iowa, and Wisconsin in the 1830s and 1840s; and in Colorado in late 1850s. In each situation, when farmers conjured up a club, they wrote down their "rights" and rules for claiming land in a constitution that typically included an eloquent preamble justifying their claim to the land they occupied.[4] These clubs, which were typically called "farmers' protective associations" (or a name along those lines), generally operated at the county level, consisting of hundreds of members each claiming land in amounts from 160 to 320 acres despite the fact that the land they occupied was typically owned by the government (and in some cases, other citizens who purchased land legally). The clubs typically convened shortly after regions became territories of the federal government, although squatters sometimes jumped the gun, drawing up boundaries on land even before treaties extinguished Indian claims to land.

As the empirical studies will show, these clubs were remarkably effective in establishing private property institutions. Of course, because the state formally owned the land they occupied, members had to defend their interests against various outsiders, including federal land agents and marshals. It turned out they were effective in this regard – sometimes frighteningly so. Anyone challenging a member of a club often faced the fury of a collective body, as illustrated by

4 These were not property rights in a strict sense. As Bromley (2006) explains, the content of a right is the ability to call on the state to enforce it. It is only meaningful to call something a property right when the state agrees to protect what one claims to own from others who may covet it or otherwise interfere with its use. Barzel (2002) makes a similar distinction between legal and economic rights. Legal rights are delineated by the state. Economic rights, in contrast, are not backed by the state, although they influence individuals' ability to consume or exchange commodities. Claim clubs were a source of private property *institutions*, as their claims were often effective on each dimension of a property system even if they were not a source of private property *rights*. For this reason, when referring to systems of ownership within a club, I refer to them as private property institutions rather than private property rights.

the following account of the activities of one of Nebraska's clubs during the 1850s (Dick 1954: 24–5):

> Claim-jumping, like horse stealing, was regarded on the frontier as a crime of the highest order. When a man settled on a piece of land claimed by a club member, the latter immediately carried the matter to the club "court." The decision, once handed down, was executed to the discomfort of the jumper... The offender was required to relinquish all claim to the land in question. Failing to heed the warning, he was beaten, his property destroyed, or his life made miserable in various other ways. The penalty of obstinate and unyielding disobedience was "removal from the territory" or, in the language of the day, he was "put over the river." In extreme cases "over" did not mean to reach the other side. Few had the hardihood and persistence to resist judgment for long, for it was well known that persistent offenders would be so effectually removed that they would cause no more trouble.

It is important to keep in mind that the people who were run out of town in this example had legally purchased land. Indeed, throughout the nineteenth century, the federal government set up land auctions in order to provide people with opportunities to acquire western lands. Yet the fact that people legally purchased land mattered little to members of a club. Indeed, clubs viewed a *legal* purchase by anyone who was not a member as antisocial behavior! They doggedly imposed their will on any outsiders, which variously included speculators, other squatters who arrived late to a region, and even federal agents.

These clubs, despite their sometimes violent tactics, had less in common with a mob than with local governments of the nineteenth century. To be certain, they were not formal democracies. Rather, they were perhaps best described as *frontier* democracies – not always democratic and deliberative, yet fairly close in terms of representational features to the actual governments of the day. Members wrote down their rights, often publishing their constitutions in local papers, as well as established a basic machinery of governance, including judges and juries. In other words, these gangs were deliberative. Several provisions from a claim club that came together in 1845 at Sun Prairie, Wisconsin, shows their key features (Hibbard 1905: 96):

> **Resolved**, That in case any person or persons shall purchase land in this vicinity at the time occupied by claimants; that they shall be disregarded as neighbors, and that no dealings of any kind be had with them. That we will neither lend to them, nor visit them, nor act with them in any capacity whatsoever.
>
> **Resolved**, That we will protect each other in the claim of a quarter section, admitting that it should embrace no more than forty acres of grove timber.
>
> **Resolved**, That in case any person or persons should violate the sense of this meeting and deprive claimants of their just expectations, that we will not fail to rebuke his conduct with such severity as has been common in the settlement of Western country.

The constitution of the Sun Prairie claim club went on to establish a full-fledged property system that governed property relations until its members secured legal title within a few years. It was both a property system and the first local government in this region.

This example also illustrates that members recognized that writing down rules would not have amounted to much without the threat of violence. Their willingness to use force will ultimately be quite important in interpreting claim clubs from a political economy perspective. As Thomas Hobbes famously observed in *Leviathan*, "And Covenants, without the Sword, are but words, and no strength at all to secure a man." Recently, it has become fashionable to point out how order arises without coercion of this sort.[5] Perhaps most famously, Ostrom (2005, 1990) stresses the importance of covenants without swords in analyzing self-governance of natural resources.

Although there is much to be learned from these studies of order without the sword, it will become clear that violence undergirded the major political, economic, and social institutions on the American frontier.[6] Claim club constitutions were covenants guaranteed by the sword, and it was the sword that made these informal property arrangements effective. Yet they were not part of an all-powerful Leviathan, but rather challenged the state. Nor were clubs confined to the agricultural sector. One of the remarkable features of claim clubs was their ubiquity across economic sector, time, ideology, and geography.[7] Miners in the American West called their claim clubs "mining districts," and they performed the same essential functions as agricultural claim clubs. During the gold rush in California, which began in the late 1840s, and Nevada's mining boom of the 1850s, the first prospectors typically proceeded to dig for gold in small groups, often sharing in the fruit of their labor – namely, whatever nuggets of value they found. These small groups were known as mining camps. They usually consisted of fewer than ten people and often allocated the fruit of their labor based on some type of sharing rule (Clay and Wright 2010, 2005; Zerbe and Anderson 2001).

[5] See, for example, Ellickson (1991), who provides a rich empirical study of spontaneously arising norms that are enforced without much in the way of violence. Sugden (2004, 1986) provides an excellent theoretical account of spontaneous order.

[6] Knight (1992) makes a similar point in observing that theories of spontaneous order, which seek to understand order without much in the way of conscious design or even enforcement, do not have any real role for bargaining power and hence have serious drawbacks as a generalized theory of institutional change. This book provides additional evidence of the limits of spontaneous order explanations, using evidence from the American frontier to illustrate the importance of considering the role of organizational conflict in the process of institutional change.

[7] For an example, during the violent conflict over slavery in Kansas Territory in the 1850s, groups seeking a free state as well as those committed to slavery formed claim clubs in their rush to pack the state with those who shared their beliefs. In other words, the conflict over slavery in Kansas, which is known popularly as "Bleeding Kansas," was a conflict between rival claim clubs. Despite obvious differences in terms of ideological motivation, both sides of the struggle for the soul of Kansas proved adept at establishing clubs.

Mining *camps* – small organizations with just a few people whose allocation rules were not typically based on private property – were important as systems of social order, and remarkable in their ability to allocate access to mineral land without much in the way of overarching systems of governance. Yet the true claim clubs on the mining frontier were the city-like mining *districts* that eventually emerged to impose order over loose collections of mining camps. The constitution of a district provided an overarching government for small-scale mining camps, the latter consisting of a few people, while a district often consisted of thousands of people and hundreds of mining camps.

The mining districts, unlike a camp, represented a basic system of government.[8] Some of these districts even set up systems of taxation despite the fact that they had no formal authority to do so (Smith 1973). They were the origin of governments that competed with the state, as well as a major source of private property institutions.

Like farmers' protective associations, mining districts provided mutual defense of members, who were in the miners' case gold and silver prospectors seeking to strike it rich. The preamble from the Gold Hill, Nevada, mining district in the late 1850s captures a general sentiment among club members regarding their role in establishing an independent system of government to defend themselves from their adversaries (Lord 1959 [1881]: 42):

> Whereas, the isolated position we occupy, far from all legal tribunals, and cut off from those fountains of justice which every American citizen should enjoy, renders it necessary that we organize in a body politic for our mutual protection against the lawless, and for meting out justice between man and man; therefore, we, citizens of Gold Hill, do hereby agree to adopt the following rules and laws for our government.

The constitution of this district – and many of the hundreds like it that sprang up all over Nevada in the 1850s and 1860s – went on to define rules that would govern land relations among miners, as well as a system for resolving disputes

[8] Economists interested in spontaneous emergence of property rights in U.S. economic history typically focus on developments on the mining sector, especially California. Umbeck (1981, 1977) suggested that they were the source of private property rights, though Clay and Wright (2010) and Clay (2006) have criticized the notion that the miners actually established excludable contracts. Rather, they argue miners were regulating access to a common property resource. These debates, while informative, the importance of emergence of frontier *governments* along with informal property institutions. It is instruction to consider the insights of Charles Shinn (1885), whose first-person account of California's mining boom is titled "Mining Camps: A Study in American Frontier *Government*" (emphasis added). Shinn recognized that the systems governing minerals were much more than property systems – that they were frontier governments, a point that has been somewhat obscured in economic studies seeking to understand the extent to which miners' contracts were excludable (or not, as the case may be). To an extent, these first-rate economic histories miss the forest for the trees, which is to say that these camps represented a remarkable process of government formation.

among competing claimants, that substituted for the state until the government formalized their norms over a decade later.

Ranchers also devised private-order governments to allocate land and land access, known as "cattlemen's associations," that operated over vast territory – even entire states. State-wide claim clubs convened in the key cattle-ranching states of Wyoming and Montana by the 1870s imposed order over local associations much like mining districts superseded mining camps. These associations regulated, usually with great success, hundreds of ranchers who collectively owned millions of head of cattle. Their deliberative features and vast geographic scale puts them at the forefront of examples of informal governance.

Finally, access to the nation's forests was regulated in large measure by organizations which I refer to generally as "loggers' unions." During much of the nineteenth century, the formal property regime governing forest land was state ownership, which the government imposed over forests shortly after ratification of the Constitution for reasons that included meeting the Navy's demand for timber for ships. The importance of timber for the machinery of warfare was one of the reasons why permits to cut timber on federal land were granted by an unusual source, the War Secretary, until the 1840s (Hurst 1964). However, the federal government's ambition to own vast forest lands outpaced the capacity of an overall weak land-administration bureaucracy. Despite the fact that there were formal regulations declaring state ownership, claim clubs disregarded them, utilizing frequent beatings and banishment of federal agents who sought to police the state-ownership regime to get their way.

The foregoing account suggests that claim clubs were institutional blueprints which people in other regions or sectors could copy, emerging first in agriculture and then spreading to other sectors. As such, Ostrom's (2005) insight into institutional diversity is relevant to the discussion at hand. From a design perspective, Ostrom argued that the concept of blueprints can be dangerous in light of the diversity of successful property regimes, showing that efforts to impose a one-size-fits-all property regime typically undermine incentives for effective resource governance. Yet it is a separate question as to whether or not groups themselves view property regimes as blueprints. Ostrom's insights can be recast as a question about institutional emergence: Do groups or societies use past institutional choices as blueprints, or do they take local conditions into account, when crafting institutions? Or, is the process of institutional change better characterized as a combination of blueprints and local adaptation?

On one hand, claim clubs were blueprints. Once settlers perfected their organizational "technology" for claiming land, others seeking to occupy land without legal title could freely use it. Members of clubs also seemed to have had constitutions adopted by other groups in their hands when they convened their own associations, as constitutions were typically published in local papers. One the other hand, clubs were also locally tailored in important ways. For example, clubs in different sectors differed in terms of regulations on size of claims, provision for trade, and occupancy requirements.

Despite the aforementioned diversity, the basic structure of clubs – selection of an individual (president) of a club, deliberative forums for members to decide matters of collective importance, and presence of informal judges to resolve disputes, as well as overwhelming reliance on private property institutions to manage access to resources – was quite similar regardless of time, place, or economic sector. The stories in the pages ahead will show that members of these clubs understood well differences between institutional function and form, as they typically borrowed functions while tailoring institutions to the demands of their sector or region. For this reason, it is perhaps most appropriate to characterize claim clubs as institutional blueprints in terms of their general features that were tailored to local conditions in terms of the details of their property regimes.

For reasons that will become clear in this book, the key features of claim clubs are perhaps better described in terms of institutional isomorphism rather than institutional diversity. Ostrom (2005) explained why it is often inappropriate to think of property regimes as "private property," "state ownership," and "common property," because within each of these general categories of regimes, there is tremendous variation in the structure of property institutions. Ostrom's argument is compelling because it is based on hundreds, if not thousands, of field studies of self-governance. Yet on the American frontier, across vast distances and time periods, there are remarkable similarities in the kind of property regimes people desired (nearly always private property), as well as the way they administered it (through an informal constitution that established a basic system of governance that looked much like governments in the places they left behind). In fact, coordination on a similar notion of private property was one of the reasons claim clubs so thoroughly and completely substituted for the state as a source of private property institutions. Despite the complexity of institutional origins and change, claim clubs demonstrate how basic notions of private property and deliberative governance were sufficient to permit individuals to fundamentally redefine the institutional landscape of the United States. Indeed, institutional similarity – as well as simplicity – helps understand why seemingly anyone who so desired could establish a club in each of the major frontier sectors, oftentimes with great success.

These examples provide a glimpse into the political economy of claim clubs, which is itself a remarkable story. Yet stories are not sufficient for a study of property institutions on the American frontier, or frontiers more generally. As North (1966) observed in one of his earliest works articulating a field now known as "new institutional economics," systematic theories and empirical evidence are necessary to understand American land laws. Accordingly, this book considers claim clubs analytically, approaching them through the lens of political science, law, and economics. At the same time, this book also suggests that existing analytical studies of property institutions are incomplete. One of the main contributions of this book is to bring claim clubs to the forefront of the new institutional economics and in the process offer a new perspective on institutional transformation in a critical period in the political economic history of the United States. In addition, this study complements historians' perspectives on property institutions by offering sufficient empirical evidence regarding claim clubs to illustrate a more general theoretical argument regarding where private property institutions come from and why they change. Substantively, none of the wonderfully rich stories of transformation of property institutions in North America provide a satisfactory account of how distributive-minded groups such as claim clubs specified and enforced property institutions on their own or how they subsequently ensured the state met their demands.[9] Finally, for political scientists and legal scholars, this book offers insight into the process of government formation and the various ways that organizations undermined, frustrated, and challenged attempts by the early American state to administer its land, as well as into the politics and political economy of the price of land.

THREE LEVELS OF SOCIAL CONTROL

Part I of this book considers the origins of private property institutions, which in the simplest sense are the rules governing individual ownership relations in society. The initial economic studies of private property institutions focused on excludability (Cheung 1970; Demsetz 1967). Subsequent studies improved the precision of the concept of private property institutions by specifying four dimensions of property systems, including clarity of allocation, security from trespass, alienability, and credibility of persistence (Riker and Weimer 1995). Successful property regimes are effective on each dimension. However, security is perhaps the most important dimension because without it, the other dimensions mean little. For example, if property can be allocated by force or the threat of it, then there are few reasons to trade for property; powerful individuals and groups would rather steal than purchase it, but weaker members of society have few reasons to buy land if others can simply take it away. Thus, security tends to be prioritized in terms of the dimensions of a property regime.

Property institutions are an important subject of inquiry because of their economic implications. Absence of property institutions, which is referred to as open access, is the main threat to economic development because it can lead a "tragedy of the commons." Although many economic studies emphasize the role of private property institutions in economic development (e.g., Acemoglu and Robinson 2012; North 1981; North and Thomas 1973), the most general implication of these studies is that appropriately designed property institutions, whether private property, state ownership, or common property, can improve

[9] Some of the best examples of historical studies of development of economic institutions include Weaver (2003), Karsten (2002, 1997), and Clarke (2001). In addition, Watson (2012, 2011) provides an exceptional account of settlement of the American frontier, in particular the relationship between soldiers and settlement of the nation's borderlands.

prospects for economic prosperity. Accordingly, a fundamental challenge of institutional design is getting property institutions "right" in the sense that the rules governing ownership are tailored appropriately to local context (Bromley 1991; Ostrom 1990; Libecap 1989).

Once we figure out the consequences of alternative property regimes, we are inextricably led back to their origins. If property institutions are important because of their economic, political, and social consequences, then we must be clear about where they come from. To gain traction on the issue of emergence of property institutions, it is helpful to consider them from the perspective of three levels of social control.

The first level of social control can be termed spontaneous order. The defining feature of spontaneous-order processes is their effectiveness despite absence of government, or even any hierarchy at all.

According to a spontaneous order perspective, property systems arising without conscious design may be self-enforcing in the sense that an external party is not necessary to enforce an agreement or social norm. Sugden's (2004, 1986) excellent example of a spontaneously arising property system is the centuries-old procedure for claiming driftwood along English coastal regions whereby claimants acquired a right to driftwood by placing two stones on it. People claiming driftwood on the English coast followed these rules even though the norms had no known designer and had no enforcers. At a more fundamental level, Hayek (1960, 1948) argued that market institutions arise without conscious design, attaining success that could not be rivaled by institutional design.[10] Perhaps more than anyone else, Hayek recognized the potential for individual interactions to provide social order that could not be achieved by design.[11]

Norms such as this are widespread. For example, in Pittsburgh, Pennsylvania, there is an informal system for claiming parking spots in the winter,

[10] As one suspects, this view of spontaneous emergence of markets has been challenged. This much was clear from an example that has always stuck with me from Daniel Bromley's doctoral seminar in institutional economics at the University of Wisconsin. During one of the first seminars, he asked us about the "farmers' market" near the state's capitol, which is quite famous in Madison and the surrounding area. The professor began by remarking about the farmer's market, "it seems like a wonderful example of markets arising spontaneously, without regulation?" Some took the bait and agreed. He then produced a fifty-page thick manual of regulations governing this little market that meets only for a few days for about four months each year. The implication was clear: if even a tiny market like this depends on regulation to work well, then how could we expect a much larger market to arise and function without conscious design? As the pages ahead will show, that example (and that particular course) shaped my thinking about the importance of governance in emergence of property institutions, although the account that follows will give more weight to informal governance as a substitute for the state than is typical of the "old" institutional economics of Commons, Bromley, and others.

[11] As Hayek (1945) explained, the fundamental challenge for the state is that it generally lacks information necessary for design.

whereby a person who shovels out a spot and places a piece of furniture at the spot, typically a lawn chair, acquires a "right" to that spot. The piece of furniture signifies that someone has done the oftentimes hard work of shoveling the snow. Based on my observations, the system is self-enforcing, much like Sugden's driftwood example, even though these norms governing access to parking spots have no apparent designer or much, if any, need for enforcement. One expects that spontaneously arising institutions specifying ownership will be present at least to some degree in all modern and pre-modern societies.

Reputations are one of the main mechanisms governing spontaneously arising social order. Economic studies of reputations generally fall within the spontaneous order framework because social order does not depend on presence of a hierarchy, formal or informal, to enforce contracts or property arrangements.[12] A great example of reputational contracting is Ellickson's (1991) study of ranchers in Shasta County, California. Ellickson's ethnographic interviews with ranchers (the fieldwork for the study took place in the early 1980s) showed clearly that individuals he talked to did not depend primarily on the government to enforce contracts. Rather, each rancher typically relied on norms, enforcing order through graduated punishments that were implemented by individuals themselves rather than third parties. More importantly, norms and reputations, because the contracting parties in Shasta County were well aware of them, helped prevent disputes among neighbors. Similarly, Anderson and Hill (2004) vividly recounted how American ranchers historically enforced their agreements through trust and a handshake rather than formal law.

One can see the intrigue of such arguments about spontaneous order. Even in a modern state in which the rule of law is strong and there is no doubt that there is a government in charge, informal norms held together by reputations are often a primary way people avoid conflict as well as resolve it when it occurs. Nobody designed them, yet they seem to work well – in some situations, they may even be economically efficient.[13] A critical implication of these studies is that *private property institutions will emerge without devising governments, formal or otherwise*.

Theories of spontaneous order, even though they have no real role for government (or, indeed, any role for hierarchy), provide insight into several features of property relations on the American frontier in the nineteenth century, in particular norms of first possession. Under a first-possession norm, whoever was

[12] One difference is that in classic spontaneous order arrangements, there may be less threat of coercion, which reflects the underlying assumption that the problem is coordination rather than cooperation. For now, it is sufficient to note that coordination games have less inherent conflict of interest than games of cooperation, although economic solutions to each situation involve no real role for hierarchy of any sort. These ideas are discussed more fully in Chapter 2.

[13] For example, Ellickson (1991) and Barzel (1989) each argue that locally devised norms are often efficient in an economic sense that they are wealth-maximizing. Although the efficiency criterion is often challenging to satisfy, it would perhaps be more useful to simply view these norms as expedient or appropriate.

first to claim land acquired a presumptive private property right to it. These norms were often effective even though they lacked conscious design or third parties to enforce them.

In the empirical studies in the pages ahead, I will use these remarkable norms of first possession as a testament to the explanatory power of theories of spontaneous order. Nonetheless, spontaneously arising norms of first possession proved to be fleeting. Theoretically, it is unlikely that such norms will last long as society develops in terms of population, heterogeneity, and complexity of economic activities. For example, unforeseen contingencies are likely to undermine spontaneously arising property arrangements. Reputational systems also make strong assumptions about the nature of information flows within and across communities. Indeed, much of the research on cooperation suggests that population growth and heterogeneity of the claimants will undermine simple property arrangements (e.g., Stewart 2009). In particular, transaction costs are likely to undermine simple property systems as frontiers develop, increasing demand for legal title (Alston et al. 2011; Alston et al. 1999). For this reason, it should be unsurprising that spontaneously arising property norms were fleeting.

The limits of spontaneous order require us to consider a second level of social control: the state. Sened (1997) and Riker and Sened (1991) emphasized the state above all as a source of private property institutions in explicitly deriving a political theory of property rights. The role of the state (as well as political conflict) is also quite prominent in Libecap's (1989) theory of emergence of private property institutions. Similarly, institutional economists such as Bromley (2006) and Commons (1924) view the state as the fundamental source of property institutions. These political theories of property institutions have a clear implication: *an all-powerful state is the fundamental source of property institutions when spontaneously arising property institutions break down*.

The political perspective of "no state, no property rights" contrasts with the finding of spontaneous order frameworks telling us that a state is not necessary for a system of ownership to emerge. However, proponents of each perspective tend to agree that complexity will lead people to petition the government to specify and enforce their property institutions. Yet theoretically and empirically, a state is not the only source of property institutions when decentralized contracting arrangements break down or are otherwise unavailable. Claim clubs were informal governments arising through a voluntary exchange whereby claim officials (namely, those who agreed to be leaders and judges) promised to resolve contracting problems in exchange for a fee. These associations were effective precisely because they had features of a state despite operating outside of the aegis of the state. Mafias, which Olson (2000, 1993) recognized, were stationary bandits capable of performing economic functions, were similar to claim clubs, although mafias had far less in common with governments than claim clubs and mafias have never, in any country or any time period, been nearly as successful as claim clubs in transforming de facto power into de jure legal recognition.[14] Nor did Olson explain how nonstate bandits emerge within the state or their role in the process of formal institutional change.[15] Thus, we require a theory of how bandits emerged within the state to enforce property institutions, which is exactly what this book provides.

My theory of private property institutions is inspired by Milgrom, North, and Weingast's (1990) law merchant framework, which considered how trading relations emerged in the absence of formal law during the medieval period. The "law merchant" was itself a body of mainly private commercial law development in the medieval period to facilitate trade, although economic studies of the law merchant focus on the role of private judges in facilitating trade. These judges, by collective past information about traders' behavior, permitted even strangers to trade even though they might not interact frequently. In this way, private judges solved an information problem and increased the ability of people to realize gains from long-distance trade prior to emergence of formal commercial law.

Drawing on the law merchant framework, I conceptualize of the origins of institutions through a voluntary contract. Like the law merchant model, my framework considers trade – although trade in the case at hand is trade in land, rather than long-distance trade among strangers. One can see the information problem between trade with strangers differs from trade of land (in the latter case, people are tied by the land to a specific region). However, there was often a great deal of incomplete information that could derail exchange in legal title. For example, it was not always clear if people seeking to sell claims had legitimate legal titles. Because relations were fairly haphazard on the frontier, clubs required institutions to provide information about potential trading partners.

More fundamentally, my conceptual framework extends the law merchant framework in two ways. First, it integrates the problems of trade with the additional challenges of collective defense and adjudication in the absence of a state. Second, I explicitly recognize that success requires that the contracting parties actually establish their own government. Although they did not make this point explicitly, Milgrom, North, and Weingast were describing a process of government formation. The law merchant, as a judge, represented the origins of part of a government, and so as a system of private order, it was closer to the state than to reputational contracting arrangements typically emphasized in economics.

[14] Gambetta (2009, 1993) is perhaps the best source on the economics of mafias.

[15] The consequences of claim clubs in terms of institutional change can be described in terms of the relationship between de facto (economic) power and de jure (legal) authority (Acemoglu and Robinson 2008, 2006; Knight and Sened 1995; Knight 1992). Knight (1992) was one of the first scholars to articulate clearly the importance of de facto or bargaining power as a generalized mechanism of institutional change.

The origins of property rights and governance are thus conceptualized as a social contract or social compact with the following general features: all the people who who join can claim some land for themselves; members pledge to respect the claims of others; and each agrees to participate in governance of a club. Officials promise to adjudicate disputes over land and to provide basic public goods, such as security, in exchange for a fee. In particular, leaders promise to act as judges to resolve disputes, to mobilize members to provide collective defense, and to screen all trading partners to ensure they are honest. Members who join a club promise to abide by the decisions of judges, to participate in collective defense, and to trade honestly. In this theoretical framework, informal property institutions and political institutions emerge simultaneously: a club's leadership structure is the essential machinery of government, and the rules the club specifies are a basic property arrangement.

The idea that governments and markets arise simultaneously is itself a fairly unique take on the interrelationship between contracting and coercive institutions. For example, Greif (2005) recognized that government and market institutions coevolve, which is an important corrective to theories suggesting that politics drives market processes. Yet Greif does not go far enough in recognizing this interrelationship. The theory of claim clubs shows that they do not simply coevolve, but they are oftentimes inextricably bound up, oftentimes arising at the same time.

The theory of clubs is also informed by Calvert's (1995) theory of social institutions, which clarified that the fundamental condition for emergence of institutions is that all relevant actors have incentives to abide by rules. Accordingly, one of the keys to emergence of private property institutions is that all relevant contracting parties (claimants, officials, and outsiders who may covet what members of a club possess) had incentives to abide by the rules embodied in a club's constitution. In particular, two conditions must be satisfied for private property institutions to be self-enforcing.

The first condition is that members join a club and play by its rules. This condition will generally be satisfied as economic development proceeds, because the complexity that accompanies economic, social, and political development all but ensures many of them will eventually break down. Indeed, it is the prospect of claiming land outside of a claim club under conditions of anarchy – in the sense that there are no institutions, formal or otherwise – that provides incentives for people who covet land to join a club and follow its rules.[16]

[16] Hobbes famously conceptualized of anarchy as absence of a common power, which he called a state of war. In such a state, "there is no place for Industry . . . and consequently no Culture . . . no Navigation . . . no Arts; no Letters; no Society; and which is worst of all, continual fear, and danger of violent death; And the life of man, solitary, nasty, brutish, and short." Perhaps more than any other work Ostrom's (1990) *Governing the Commons* has shown that Hobbes dramatically understates the capacity for individuals to overcome conflict even without relying on the state. Yet for reasons mentioned earlier, the experience of the early United States

The second condition for emergence of property institutions is that leaders/officials follow the rules they set forth. In general, there are two reasons leaders keep their promises. One is a desire for profit. By cheating members, leaders can appropriate fees in the short term but over time, fewer members will join a club and profits will decline. Leaders also have incentives to carry out their duties because they lack legal protection themselves (after all, they are leaders of a claim club, which was an illegal or extralegal entity) and therefore benefit from the public goods provided by the club. In other words, a club's leaders have stronger incentives to keep promises because they are themselves consumers of the public good of security they help to provide. Profit and security arising within claim clubs provide self-interested incentives for a club's leaders to carry out their duty.

As long as these two conditions are satisfied, I hypothesize that claim clubs will substitute for the state as a source of property institutions. The primary implication of my theory of the origins of property institutions is that *claim clubs will be effective in providing private property institutions when spontaneous order breaks down, yet the state is unwilling or unable to specify and enforce property rights.*

In contrast to existing theories of emergence of property institutions, property institutions and political institutions are conceptualized of as arising simultaneously through voluntary exchange. Claim clubs are not the state, nor are they spontaneously arising institutions that lack the coercion associated with governments. They are products of conscious design, but the formal state does not design them. Nor can we say that they are an example of spontaneous order simply because they did not come from the state. Theories of spontaneous order are powerful precisely because they can explain order without conscious design or enforcement.[17] However, they have trouble explaining governance organizations such as clubs. As such, claim clubs can be thought of as a third general level of social control between spontaneous order and the state. These three levels of social control, and their key features, are summarized in Table 1.3.

Claim clubs, as a level of social control, do not have a prominent place in any of the major theories of property institutions. As mentioned earlier, North suggested that firms continually put pressure on the economy to change institutions. A Northian perspective on the importance of firms is also present in Kuran's (2011) comparative economic history of the Islamic and Western world, which explains economic divergence in terms of private economic organization – specifically, presence or absence of firms that permit accumulation of capital on a grand scale.

will show that clubs were more closely related to a Hobbesian covenant – one backed by the sword – than Ostrom's findings suggest.

17 The meaning of "spontaneous order" is discussed at length in Chapter 2. For now, it is sufficient to note that I define spontaneous order primarily by absence of hierarchical organization.

TABLE 1.3. *Three Fundamental Levels of Social Control*

Level	Primary Features
State	The state issues legal title, enforces it, and provides a formal legal system to adjudicate disputes.
Claim club	Informal property institutions are specified, enforced, and adjudicated by informal organizations with features of a government that exists outside of the formal contours of the state.
Spontaneous order	Informal property institutions are self-enforcing without conscious design, hierarchy, and, in some situations, without enforcement.

In focusing on the importance of firms in shaping economic development, neither North nor Kuran considered organizations as a source of institutions, including property institutions. Indeed, in each of their studies, the state is a source of institutions, and organizations exert pressure on them to change, but they did not consider organizations themselves as a source of institutions.

As introduced earlier, political theories view the state as an essentially all-powerful organization in the sense it is the only source of private property institutions. Indeed, Sened's (1997) fundamental condition for emergence of private property institutions is that political officials have an incentive to grant and enforce them.

Despite the appeal of political theories, the state was not always the most important source of property institutions on the borderlands of the United States in the eighteenth and nineteenth centuries. Rather, claim clubs were often a source of property institutions. As such, it is necessary to consider more explicitly bandits within the state, in particular when the state was too weak, or lacked incentives, to sweep away clubs from the land it formally owned.

Ostrom (1990) articulated the role of organizations in the emergence of property institutions yet focused almost exclusively on common-property regimes. A common-property regime is defined by co-ownership of a resource, which is an important alternative between state ownership and private property institutions. Ostrom's fundamental contribution was to show that there are three alternatives (private, state, and common property) that can mitigate the tragedy of the commons, not simply private property or state ownership.

This study complements Ostrom's work by explaining the origin of informal private property institutions as well as their political consequences. As far as consequences are concerned, claim clubs lacked the benevolent role attributed by Ostrom to informal contracting associations. Ostrom's studies have not, generally speaking, illuminated the distributive consequences of informal property organizations. This is an important limitation in terms of understanding key developments in property institutions in the United States, because informal associations had profound distributive consequences throughout the nineteenth century across all major economic sectors. In addition, Ostrom was unable to consider in detail the origins of institutions governing the commons, admitting: "It is not possible to reconstruct how earlier users of Swiss alpine meadows, Japanese mountain commons, the Spanish *huertas*, or the Philippine *zanjeras* devised rules that have survived such long periods. We do not know who originated or opposed various proposals, or anything about the process of change itself" (1990: 103). In contrast, this book considers explicitly the process by which self-governing organizations formed, and the simpler contracting arrangements they replaced, which is a luxury that we do not have in considering most long-standing, traditional systems for managing common-pool resources.

Greif (2005) offers perhaps the closest account of the relationship between markets and coercive institutions to the framework introduced above. Greif considers the interrelationship between contract enforcement institutions and coercion–constraining institutions, recognizing that some private contract enforcement institutions can arise by design, with features similar to those of the state, and that there is not a one-to-one relationship between coercive-constraining institutions and the state. As noted earlier, Greif also clarifies that markets and governments coevolve.

My framework complements Greif's perspective by considering explicitly the transition between different types of private-order contracting arrangements (in Greif's framework, this is the transition between "organic contract enforcement institutions," which arise spontaneously, and private-order contract enforcement institutions, which are designed, but not by the state), as well as the idea that markets and government coevolve. Greif's typology, although it anticipated differences between spontaneous order and associations such as clubs, does not consider explicitly the transition from one system to the other. In addition, claim clubs are not only examples of co-evolution of market institutions and political institutions, but of the inseparability of the origins of private property institutions and political institutions. Thus, claim clubs are an excellent empirical example of the tight relationship between contracting and coercive institutions.

More generally, this book complements economic studies that have sifted through history to shed light on contracting behavior when formal economic institutions are weak or ineffective. One well-known example is the private judge of the medieval trade fairs made famous in economics through the law merchant model. Another example of an informal solution to contracting problems was the *podesta*, a local administrator that emerged in the twelfth century in Italy in order to prevent conflict between cities (Greif 2006). Credit bureaus, which emerged in the nineteenth century in the United States to increase viability of credit markets by serving as repositories of information about consumers, were an important private source of impersonal exchange (Klein 1992).

Finally, trading coalitions of Mexican California in the 1840s are exemplary private-order institutions that facilitated exchange prior to development and implementation of modern commercial law (Clay 1997).

Claim clubs join private-order judges, the *podesta*, credit bureaus, and trading coalitions as exemplary cases of private-order solutions to contracting problems. Claim clubs may even be more impressive arrangements than the aforementioned organizations because they were a source of private property institutions as well as trade relations, including trade among people who were not necessarily well known among members of the community. In contrast, each of the examples just mentioned emphasized trade alone. Claim clubs were also more sophisticated governing arrangements than those in the aforementioned examples because they had executive, legislative, and judicial functions that were divided among several individuals. The law merchant, for example, only performed the functions of a judge, while the trading coalitions in Mexican California had no real political functions; and the *podesta* was a single person who melded various functions. This study places claim clubs firmly in any conversation regarding large-scale, informal order in the shadow of the state. Perhaps more importantly, claim clubs had a much more direct role in the process of formal institutional change than the law merchant, *podesta*, credit bureaus, or trading coalitions.[18] As we will see, political influence was one of the defining features of claim clubs.

CLAIM CLUBS AND THE PROCESS OF INSTITUTIONAL CHANGE

The remarkable ability of claim clubs to self-govern was rivaled only by their political consequences. Part II of this book considers the problem of institutional change explicitly, articulating the various ways claim clubs influenced who received legal title, and at what price, throughout the nineteenth century.

A theoretical framework helps to sort through the complexity of institutional change. At a fundamental level, theories of institutional change can be divided into perspectives suggesting institutions change in response to opportunities for efficiency gains versus those emphasizing distributive conflict (Knight and North 1997). Distributive conflict has several main sources, such as economic groups, political interests, and bureaucratic preferences (Bromley 1989).

[18] Of course, the consequences of trading coalitions more generally included political change. For example, trading coalitions would eventually become extremely important organizations in the development of Western European institutions, mainly because they would ensure that the state's institutions reflected mercantile interests. By exerting pressure on the government to choose policies that encouraged productivity, the presence of trade associations helps explain why European countries diverged from other regions in the last 500 years (Kuran 2011). Claim clubs were interesting because their impact was much more immediate in terms of influencing political and economic development, frustrating the state, and securing advantages, not over decades, but often in a matter of years or months.

As a study of institutional change, one of the main contributions of this book is to assess efficiency and distributive perspectives as explanations for changes in property institutions during the nineteenth century, as well as to articulate more clearly the role of economic organization in the process of institutional change. In particular, it considers sustained conflict over the price of land from roughly 1780 to 1880. The reason for focusing on the price of land is that it was perhaps the fundamental dimension of institutional conflict during the nineteenth century.[19]

As the site of prolonged conflict over the price of land, the public lands of the United States during the nineteenth century are an excellent laboratory in which to assess alternative perspectives on institutional change. As a general matter, an efficiency perspective predicts that institutions will evolve in response to opportunities for Pareto improvements. Using the standard definition, a Pareto improving institutional change is one that can make some members of society better off without making others worse off. For example, Barzel (2002, 1989) suggests that institutions will seamlessly change in response to opportunities for Pareto improvements, subject to transaction costs. According to Barzel, "institutions emerge as a result of the action of wealth-maximizing individuals. Subject to the costs of transacting, these individuals will *always* create institutions that maximize wealth" (emphasis added) (2002: 9). There are no mistakes of institutional design in Barzel's framework; there are only transaction costs.[20] Barzel offers perhaps the clearest example of a wealth-maximizing perspective on institutional change, yet the perspective that relative prices will, in general, lead to superior institutions is also present in North (1981), who argued that competitive pressure drives societies to choose more efficient property regimes.[21]

[19] Ross (2001) also considers the relationship between prices and institutional conflict in the context of timber booms and busts. In Ross' framework, resource booms lead to "rent seizing," which refers to political conflict to redefine authority to allocate land. For example, in response to increasing timber prices, politicians may remove authority over land use decisions from government bureaucrats with expertise on conservation so that they can grant more timber concessions to loggers. In the United States, there were similar conflicts over land, although the driving force for change was not politicians, but rather economic organizations. Organized squatters engaged in rent-seeking as well as rent-seizing from the bottom up, using their capacity to undermine federal auctions. Whereas Ross offers a top-down explanation for institutional outcomes based on political conflict, the American frontier requires a bottom-up explanation that centers on economic organizations.

[20] There is also an important tradition in the literature that accords a stronger role to mistakes in the process of institutional change, suggesting that efficiency may motivate change although mistakes can lead to inefficient outcomes. In particular, economic studies of ideology and institutional change suggest that inefficient institutions are a consequence of flawed mental models rather than transaction costs. On the role of mistakes and ideology in institutional change, see especially North (2005), Acemoglu (2003), and Denzau and North (1994).

[21] Wittman (1995) argues that democratic institutions are sufficient to produce efficient policies.

There are certainly some situations in which institutions change in response to opportunities for Pareto improvement, and many societies have, over time, evolved to provide a framework for economic and political development (North, Wallis, and Weingast 2009). Yet there are two important weaknesses with the efficiency perspective as articulated above. One is that it cannot explain persistence of inefficient institutions, except with reference to "transaction costs." Such explanations leave much to be desired because transaction costs can be defined broadly enough so that essentially any institutional configuration becomes "efficient," once we take into account the costs of transacting. It is for this reason that transaction-cost economics is often deemed Panglossian in that it is excessively optimistic, rationalizing any institutional arrangement as efficient.[22] Dahlman states the issue quite well: "If we include transaction costs in the constraints, this appears to be the unavoidable conundrum we end up in: externalities are irrelevant, monopoly problems do not exist, public goods present no difficulties, and so on" (1979: 154). More fundamentally, an efficiency perspective does not have a realistic theory of political institutions: politicians respond to the demands of contracting parties without exerting any will of their own. For these reasons, an efficiency perspective has been described as a naive theory of property institutions (Eggertsson 1990).[23] Theoretical weaknesses aside, the efficiency hypothesis also suffers from important empirical weaknesses. For example, Karsten (1997) has shown that it is exceptionally difficult to find historical evidence in support of efficiency as a general explanation for legal change. More generally, there are many property regimes that seem quite clearly to undermine rather than encourage productivity, which is hard to explain in terms of the efficiency perspective outlined above.

In contrast to the naive theories described above, Knight and Sened (1995) and Knight (1992) devised a generalized distributive theory of institutional change, one that has been extended by Acemoglu and Robinson (2006, 2008). These distributive perspectives view institutional change as a consequence of the bargaining power of groups, with institutional transformation occurring in response to changing configurations of group strength.

A distributive perspective is also explicit or implicit in many important studies of change in property rights. For example, North and Thomas (1973) recognized the importance of distributive conflict in seeking to understand the economic and political decline of Spain and France relative to England and the Netherlands in long-run historical perspective in their foundational

22 This is a reference to Dr. Pangloss, a character in Voltaire's *Candide*, who proclaimed "all is for the best in this best of all possible worlds."

23 The naive theory most closely associated with Demsetz (1967). Although it has been criticized as naive, it is also the starting point for all subsequent theoretical and empirical studies of property rights.

work in what would become new institutional economics. Specifically, rent-seeking by powerful groups put pressure on governments to choose policies that undermined property rights in Spain and France, undermining prospects for long-run economic growth. Similarly, distributive conflict is one of the key parameters preventing emergence of private property rights in Libecap's (1989) empirical studies of development of property rights in American economic history. Theories of selective enforcement of property rights also accord a role for conflict over the gains associated with contracting for property rights in recognizing that property protection can be selectively provided to some but not others (Greif 2006; Haber et al. 2003). The possibility of selective enforcement arises because politicians can bargain with powerful groups in society, offering protection in exchange for political support. As Onoma (2009) explains in the context of land reform in Kenya, "State leaders often withheld protection from many land users. In the 1990s, the security forces refrained from protecting hundreds of thousands of people who were seen as supporters of opposition parties when they were evicted during land clashes across the country" (151). It is hard to come up with a clearer example of selective enforcement than withholding property protection from people because they happened to be members of a different political party than the one controlling the government. Despite differences within the family of distributive theories, they share a common implication: changes in property institutions will reflect the interests of powerful politicians or groups.

Efficiency and distributive perspectives provide a useful framework with which to consider conflict over the price of land. The reason for focusing on conflict over the price of land should be clear in light of the acquisition of nearly two million square miles of land between the end of the Revolutionary War and Civil War. This land provided the government with a potentially vast and unprecedented source of revenue, but its value also made these new lands a target. How would the government allocate land?

In the most basic sense, governments at various levels had a choice between allocating state-owned land through competitive auctions and allocation based on bureaucratic priorities. Throughout this book, land allocation through bureaucratic priorities will refer to allocation of land at a price that is (often substantially) below market price. Competitive land auctions, in contrast, are typically considered an efficient mechanism to allocate land (Libecap 2007b; Coase 1960). As such, the actual choices governments made involving the method of land allocation – either competitive auctions or allocation based on bureaucratic priorities – provide an opportunity to evaluate efficiency and distributive perspectives on institutional change. In particular, laws strengthening competitive land auctions are evidence in support of an efficiency perspective, while laws weakening competitive auctions support a distributive perspective. In addition, the extent to which land is allocated efficiently will be assessed by considering whether the price at land auctions is a competitive price, that is, whether prices reflected the market value of land or the bargaining power of individuals and groups participating in markets.

Some may scoff at the notion that the government would choose an efficient system to allocate land, especially those versed in public choice perspectives that have done so much to articulate the problem of government failure. Yet several prominent theories of institutional change predict competitive auctions will be chosen to allocate land. For example, Levi's (1988) theory of the state implies competitive auctions will be chosen. Levi's state maximizes revenue, and competitive auctions of land provide the state the most revenue it can get from land. Similarly, Olson (1993, 2000) argued that the state will often choose to provide private property rights to increase its long-run revenue prospects, which suggests that the state would also choose competitive auctions to increase its short-run revenue. Relatedly, Wittman (1995) posited that democratic institutions often are sufficiently competitive to produce outcomes that are for all practical purposes efficient.

These perspectives suggest the following hypothesis for the method of land allocation: rational leaders will seek to establish private property institutions, doing so through competitive auctions. The state has incentives to choose private property institutions because it is a residual claimant in production, while competitive auctions provide the state with revenue in the short run. As a corollary, land allocated at competitive auctions will reflect actual demand and supply conditions; that is, the price will be an actual market price of land.

There are two main sources of empirical evidence that are used to assess these hypotheses about institutional change. One is the state's institutional commitment to auctions: did governments (national and state) legislate to strengthen competitive land auctions, or did legislation undermine or otherwise weaken them? On this measure, an unmistakable theme on the frontier is the state's tendency to give away its land, a finding that holds across all relevant economic sectors and in nearly all time periods. The second source of evidence is the going price of land at auctions: did auctions produce prices of land that reflected market demand and supply, or where prices determined by bargaining power of strong groups? On this measure as well, we shall see that auctions almost never led to a price that could reasonably be called a "competitive" price of land.

Thus, the two fundamental features of institutional change on the frontier we must explain are the following: institutional decay of land auctions (through legislation giving land away, or de jure transfers) and institutional manipulation of land auctions (through coercion and corruption at government auctions, or de facto transfers). To explain this outcome, I turn to claim clubs, which emerge as the driving force behind observed institutional outcomes. Rather than a benevolent response to a slow-moving federal government, clubs are more appropriately conceptualized of as rent-seeking organizations in the sense that they used their bargaining power to secure benefits from governments that they could not secure in markets.[24] Most often, their rent-seeking was directed at securing land for a low price and, if possible, for free (although they would also engage in other sorts of rent seeking, for example, enlisting California's state government to tax foreign miners at an exorbitant rate so that they would have to work for domestic mining companies). Their rent-seeking activities, rather than political interests, ultimately explain why the state so rarely translated its landholding into government revenue.

Much of the evidence in this book emphasizes social conflict, in particular how organizations drive the process of institutional change. To the extent political interests come into play, they enter the equation through the lens of credibility of commitment, but not in the usual way credibility is considered in the political economy of property rights. Existing studies of credibility of commitment generally (if not exclusively) emphasize the problem of a government committing credibly to protecting *private* property institutions (Gehlbach and Keefer 2011; Stasavage 2003; Haber et al. 2003; Weimer 1997; North and Weingast 1989; Root 1994, 1989). My argument is that the state also has to commit credibly to *state* ownership.

Conflict and change in nineteenth-century land laws illustrate the fiscal implications of declining credibility of commitment to state-owned land. When squatters began to occupy land illegally, political majorities in Congress believed it was possible to provide them with one-time concessions (rewarding those who occupied land prospectively with a legal title) without setting a precedent. However, once federal legislators rewarded squatters with concessions, the government's commitment to state ownership was no longer credible, and in the process government choices made free land a self-fulfilling prophecy: concessions emboldened squatters, increased the government's cost of policing state-owned land, and in the process increased political incentives to forgo policies that would have increased the state's revenue.

The empirical studies of institutional change suggest that clubs were a source of social costs. At the same time, a case can be made that they were in some ways a solution to incomplete laws in some regions or time periods. In this respect, claim clubs are similar to merchant guilds, which have been studied extensively by Greif (2006, 1998, 1992). Merchant guilds established in Europe during the Late Middle Ages may have initially been an efficient response to incomplete trade and contract law but they introduced subsequent policy inefficiencies. The Hansa, for example, which was one of the more important early trading associations, initially increased opportunities for interregional trade, but once

[24] Krueger (1996, 1974) developed the theory of rent seeking as well as applied it to important cases, such as sugar quotas. Tullock (1980) clarified the theory of rent seeking in arguing that monopoly rents will be short lived. In particular, rent seeking refers to the expenditure of resources to secure nonmarket benefits. Because rent seekers will expend up to the amount of the rent to acquire monopoly privileges, the social cost is not simply the familiar deadweight loss, but also the dissipation of resources through lobbying, as the expenditure on lobbying enters no socially relevant utility function.

organized it was more concerned with crushing other traders' groups than preserving trade.

Much like the Hansa, claim clubs were in some regions and some time periods a socially desirable response to incomplete land laws, although over time, they became rent-seeking organizations whose *raison d'etre* was to extract land from various levels of government. In other words, both the Hansa and claim clubs were each private-order contracting arrangements that transformed into powerful rent-seeking organizations. In fact, in the case of claim clubs, there was often no transformation – they were rent-seeking organizations right from the start.

A distributive perspective also differs fundamentally from prevailing economic perspectives on claim clubs. One of North's (2005, 1990) major contributions to the study of economic development has been to articulate the importance of adaptive efficiency, which refers to the ability of institutions to respond to new problems and opportunities. Although the U.S. economic system generally fares well in terms of adaptive efficiency, North suggests government policy regarding land during the period with which I am concerned left much to be desired. As North explains, "after the Revolutionary War, squatters had traditionally settled on land and the states had granted them preemption rights [squatters' rights]. However, when the federal government took over land disposal in the 1790s, it did not follow suit but instead burned out squatters. An ongoing tug of war resulted and led to inconsistent policies, widespread evasion, and more than twenty acts by Congress between 1799 and 1830 that granted preemption rights to squatters in specific regions" (1990: 88). Claim clubs, in North's interpretation, were the dynamic aspect of the economy; eventually, the federal government recognized their virtues, formalizing their claims. De Soto (2000) offers a similar interpretation of claim clubs, defending them as a dynamic response to economic opportunities in the face of a slow-moving federal government.

The aforementioned perspectives tend to wholly ignore the distributive consequences of claim clubs. The idea that the federal government simply began burning out squatters is, to put it mildly, misleading. To the contrary, the federal government created a system to allocate land through competitive auctions, one that had the noble purpose of paying down an unprecedented debt while states relied on public lands to fund development of a system of education. Yet members of clubs cared less about the public good than securing their share of free land. Claim clubs, rather than an inefficient and slow-moving government, were oftentimes the source of social costs in the process of land allocation rather than a response to them. That is, in other words, these clubs were less a *response* to transaction costs than a *source* of them.

Understanding claim clubs is not simply a matter of clarifying the details of our political economic history. Important policy implications follow from our interpretation of analysis of land policy during this period. According to most economic studies, the American experience demonstrates the desirability of legal recognition of informal claims to land (e.g., North 1990; Libecap 1989). However, we should pay closer attention to ensuring that the state, especially a weak one, can profit from its land ownership. This study recognizes, without perpetually defending state ownership (indeed, quite the opposite), the importance of balancing the interests of land demanders with the state's interest in providing public goods, including national security. Indeed, this book defends both private property rights and markets, while criticizing land giveaways. It is concerned with the process of allocating land and the endgame, which is to establish an effective system of private property institutions. In the end, strengthening markets for state-owned land, rather than formalization of legal title, is perhaps the fundamental lesson we should draw from the American frontier.

Up to this point, my introductory comments have suggested the various ways claim clubs influenced origin and change in property institutions. The significance of these clubs extends beyond property rights, however, as their activities influence the trajectory and development of the American state itself. Existing studies of state-building in the United States emphasize expansion of bureaucratic capacity during or after the American Civil War (Bensel 2000, 1991; Skowronek 1982). Carpenter (2001), for example, emphasized how bureaucrats who developed a reputation for competence increased state capacity in the period after the Civil War.[25] Merit has also been emphasized as an explanation for expansion of state capacity (Horn 1995; Johnson and Libecap 1994). Centralization is viewed as important because of its consequences for provision of public goods (Dougherty 2001), economic development (Bensel 2000), and emergence of civil rights (Mickey 2012). Another line of inquiry focuses on the stability of the federal system itself, in particular the conditions when federal institutions are self-enforcing (Mittal et al. 2011; Bednar 2008; Weingast 1998).

There are at least two ways to strengthen the aforementioned perspectives on the state. One is by considering more carefully the relationship between land and state capacity. Land was not simply an important issue, but arguably among the most important, when it came to state building during this period. Second, none of these perspectives considered in any depth how claim clubs shaped and constrained development of the state. By considering the decentralized sources of state weakness, this study complements existing ones by articulating social conflict, as opposed to political interests and ideology, as a driving force in development of the American state.

To foreshadow the empirical findings, claim clubs undermined the state, varying their tactics between taking what they liked from it and coopting it to serve their purposes. In one of the key periods of development of property institutions in the United States, claim clubs replaced federal and state governments with their own governments before welcoming it back on their

[25] See also Bensel (1991) and Skowronek (1982).

terms. In particular, claim clubs help us understand one of the great puzzles of nineteenth-century American land laws, which is the failure of an allegedly revenue-maximizing state to realize revenue from its vast landholding.

THE FRONTIER OF THIS BOOK

Chapter 2 specifies theoretically claim clubs as a level of social control between decentralized and state-backed specification and enforcement of property institutions. One of the central contentions of this chapter is that economic studies of informal order, which have a limited role for informal political institutions, understate the ability of individuals to establish private property institutions in the state's shadow. Specifically, economic studies, because they emphasize spontaneously arising and reputational enforcement systems with no real role for hierarchy, do not have much, if any, role for organizations such as claim clubs that can often supersede or replace simpler, fully decentralized contracting norms. The other main contention is that political theories of property institutions, by focusing overwhelmingly on the state as a source of property institutions, are also incomplete because they do not anticipate the possibility of endogenously arising governments that challenge the state. The theoretical analysis produces the following hypothesis: claim clubs, rather than spontaneously arising norms or the state, will be an important source of property institutions in the major frontier sectors.

Chapter 3 articulates the constitutional features of claim clubs, as well as those of the simpler contracting systems they typically replaced. Much like a gold rush prospector's search for gold, constructing an account of these clubs involved a lot of time searching for a few nuggets of value, which for me were pieces of information about informal property regimes and land laws that could be used to evaluate alternative theories of the origins of property institutions. The empirical studies of claim clubs, which are drawn from archival evidence, first-hand accounts from settlers, and historical studies of American land laws, reveal a progression from norms arising more or less in ways predicted by theories of spontaneous order to overwhelming reliance on claim clubs. Besides providing evidence to assess alternative perspectives regarding where private property institutions come from, the empirical cases remind us of the importance of private-order contracting arrangements during the early stages of capitalist development, a finding that suggests studies focusing disproportionately on the state and formal law in American political and economic development miss an important part of the story.

Chapter 4 considers claim clubs on each of the relevant dimensions of a private property system, including clarity of allocation, security from trespass, alienability, and credibility of persistence. The primary contribution of this chapter is to expand upon existing assessments of informal private property regimes, which typically emphasize excludability. Although excludability is perhaps the most important feature of a property regime, it is only one dimension.

Existing studies of informal private property regimes thus provide an incomplete picture of the emergence of informal property institutions. Even when we take account of each relevant dimension of a property regime, the evidence reveals that private property institutions devised within the confines of claim clubs were in fact effective on each of these dimensions. This evidence suggests clubs indeed competed with the state as a source of property institutions. The chapter concludes by summing up the extent to which the theory presented in Chapter 2 fits key facts during the period in question for each of the frontier sectors.

Chapter 5 is the first of several chapters considering the political consequences of claim clubs. The first part of this chapter, which is mostly theoretical, articulates the implications of efficiency and distributive theories of institutional change in the context of nineteenth-century land laws. These alternative theoretical perspectives are used to derive two basic hypotheses regarding the government's choice of mechanism to allocate land: an efficiency perspective predicts that the state will choose competitive land auctions to allocate its land, and a contrasting distributive perspective that suggests that economic organizations will create incentives for the state to allocate land based on bureaucratic priorities. The second part of this chapter considers one of the most important types of legislation in nineteenth-century land laws: "squatters' rights," which were formally known as preemption laws. The empirical study of preemption laws reveals that policies weakening competitive markets for land were far more common than policies strengthening competitive land auctions, and that claim clubs were a fundamental mechanism governing changes in the price of land as well as the institutions to allocate land. Perhaps more importantly, it shows that where land was allocated through markets, the price of land reflected the bargaining power of claim clubs rather than actual market price of land – yet another piece of evidence that lends support to a distributive interpretation of claim clubs.

Chapter 6 considers homestead legislation, which went beyond preemption laws in allowing anyone – not just squatters – to claim a section of "free" land. The analysis of homestead legislation consists of a test of alternative theories of support for homestead laws, as well as a welfare assessment of the homestead principle. In terms of institutional change, the chapter econometrically analyzes roll-call votes in the House and Senate on four failed homestead bills to sort out competing hypotheses for sectional interests, political parties, and economic interests as mechanisms of policy change, finding that sectional interests were a driving force behind support for homestead legislation. The evidence indicates that support for homesteads was highest in states in which claim clubs were most common, lending additional support to the hypothesis that claim clubs were a source of distributive policies. The assessment of homesteads from a social welfare perspective focuses on President James Buchanan's veto of an 1860 homestead bill. Buchanan's veto provides a point of department to contemplate what can be termed the "economic case for free land," which is essentially an argument that free homesteads were efficiency-enhancing because they reduced the state's cost of policing the nation's borderlands. Buchanan's veto message reminds us that the economic defense of free land fails to account for negative fiscal consequences of free land. Nor do defenses of free land take account of the social costs of homesteads in terms of conservation. Once the full set of benefits and costs associated with homesteads is taken into account, there is a compelling case to be made that the homestead law was a source of social costs rather than benefits.

Chapter 7 traces development of land laws governing minerals, timber, and pasture – the key natural resources on public land – in the Far West after the Civil War. Amidst the complexity of transformation of land laws in the wake of the nation's bloodiest war was incredibly nuanced, we can also detect a general feature: the spread of rent-seeking west of the 98th meridian, the conventional dividing line between east as west in terms of geographic differences in rainfall, as squatters secured vast amounts of mineral, timber, and rangeland at a minimal price. Indeed, the low price paid for land seems to be a truly general feature of federal land laws in the Far West regardless of the economic sector under consideration. All told, this period witnessed a massive transfer of scarcity rent associated with minerals, forests, and pasture from the state to a bourgeoning capitalist class bent on getting what it wanted without paying for it.[26] In terms of explaining institutional change, powerful economic organizations provide insight into why politicians proved unwilling or unable to implement a land-allocation system in the Far West that meaningfully increased the state's revenue.

Chapter 8 provides several exemplary cases, constructed from congressional journals, state legislative journals, county histories, legal documents, and historical studies of land laws, of the political consequences of claim clubs in state and local politics. The case studies include an oftentimes bloody conflict over land that raged in Pennsylvania between "Wild Yankees" from Connecticut and settlers with ties to the Commonwealth government from the 1760s to 1810s, discriminatory taxation against Chinese miners in California in the 1850s, an effort by the federal government to sort out land claims in California during the gold rush, political dominance of the Montana Stockgrowers' Association in the 1870s, and political and legal conflict over value-added rights, which were laws forcing landowners to pay squatters for improvements they made to land while illegally occupying it. These examples, which are drawn from many different time periods and several states, share in common the finding that claim

[26] Natural resources tend to have rents above their costs of extraction. Property rights determine who controls these scarcity rents. Competitive auctions allow the state to reap the benefits associated with these rents, while free land transfers it to squatters. The theory of scarcity rent was initially discovered by von Thünen (1966 [1826]) in *The Isolated State*, a work that also provided the foundation for land economics as it is the foundation of bid-rent functions that provides the foundation for welfare analysis of land use. Essentially, these ideas laid the groundwork for the idea that land conversion should occur closer to market centers.

clubs were often quite successful in their rent-seeking efforts at the state level, affirming a theme uncovered at the federal level. One can quibble with the case selection, as any student of frontier development (especially historians!) knows that there are literally hundreds of interesting cases, perhaps more, that would be worthwhile subjects. Yet these cases each deal with important policy issues of the day, as well as are interesting stories. In terms of the main findings, claim clubs tended to prevail in their effort to secure benefits from the state. As such, the case study evidence affirms a more general theme uncovered in the politics of land during this period, which is the power of clubs to impose their will upon the state at all levels – federal, state, and local.

The concluding chapter draws three primary conclusions. First, claim clubs were an important source of property institutions when spontaneously arising norms were unavailable and the state was unwilling or unable to enforce property rights. Second, claim clubs were fundamentally rent-seeking organizations rather than an efficient response to incomplete land laws. Clubs swept aside the state when it served their purpose, capturing it when they wanted legal title. Third, claim clubs shaped the development of the state itself because of their important fiscal implications. The state's ability to provide public goods hung in the balance of a struggle between clubs and government officials. All told, claim clubs were transformational organizations, both in their ability to manage land relations informally and in their ability to influence the going price of land in each of the major economic sectors. As such, this book brings claim clubs to political economy, new institutional economics, and American political development, explaining precisely how they influenced the origins of and change in property institutions during a critical period in the United States.

PART I

THE ORIGINS OF PRIVATE PROPERTY INSTITUTIONS

2

A Theory of Claim Clubs

Where do private property institutions come from? According to economic studies, private property institutions may emerge spontaneously. Political theories, in contrast, posit the state as the main source of institutions establishing private ownership. This chapter contends that neither perspective anticipates claim clubs: private-order governments arising to protect private property when spontaneously arising norms were unavailable and the state was unable or unwilling to enforce property rights. The theory presented below articulates claim clubs as a level of social control between decentralized order and the state, explaining why and how they substituted for the state as a source of private property institutions.

The main theoretical contribution is refining existing economic and political perspectives on the origins of private property institutions, which typically contemplate either simple contracting norms (in economic versions) or formal (state-enforced) property rights (in political versions). For example, North (1991) suggested that wealth-maximizing individuals will cooperate when play is repeated, that these individuals possess complete information about past performance of other players, and that there is a small number of players. Simple exchange institutions such as this may permit low-cost transacting under these conditions. Yet when these conditions do not hold, North concluded that the state is necessary to provide institutions, such as private property institutions, in order to facilitate exchange and production. Although informal private property institutions could be effective provided a number of conditions are satisfied, such as that groups are small, homogeneous, or geographically proximate, or that shared norms exist, such informal contracting systems are expected to break down as development proceeds.

Similarly, Alston et al. (2011) and Alston et al. (1999) found that informal practices for land allocation and land use dominate when land values are too low to justify formal documentation of claims or costly conflict among claimants in frontier environments. Low resource values imply small populations and relatively homogenous claimants with respect to education, wealth, age, and expectations for land use. However, when land values rise over time in response to reductions in transportation and related transaction costs, informal private property institutions and conflict-resolution mechanisms will likely be insufficient to ensure orderly land relations. For these reasons, private property institutions arising early in the process of frontier development are hypothesized to be limited in scope and based on informal arrangements that will be difficult to maintain as migrants with different experiences and expectations arrive on a frontier.

In the most general sense, these studies hypothesize that simple property norms that arise spontaneously will break down in response to changes in "transaction costs," which North (2005, 1990, 1981) conceptualized of as the costs of identifying market trading partners and negotiating and enforcing agreements. Whereas Coase (1937) considered transaction costs as an explanation why organizations exist, North extended the transaction cost framework to assess adaptive efficiency, which is the extent the institutional matrix of society responds to new problems. The new problems, in the Northian framework, constitute the "transaction costs" confronting society. As frontier development proceeds, governments are necessary to reduce these transaction costs, although a government is not in itself sufficient to resolve them, as the political process is often slow to respond to changes in the transaction cost matrix of society. Nonetheless, the main implication is clear: as transaction costs increase, governments are necessary (though not sufficient) to specify and enforce property institutions.

The studies by North and Alston et al., which divide contracting arrangements into a world of simple, spontaneously arising norms early on in the process of economic development, and formal governments later on, are examples of economic theories of property rights. To the extent economic perspectives assume that the state is eventually needed to specify and enforce property institutions, they share a fundamental assumption with Sened's (1997) and Riker and Sened's (1991) political theory of property institutions: when simple contracting norms break down, the state is a primary, if not the only, source of private property institutions.

This chapter contends that existing economic and political perspectives do not provide a satisfactory framework to understand clubs that emerged within the state as contracting situations became more complex and simpler norms broke down.[1] Clubs bear closer resemblance to governments than

[1] An alternative critique of spontaneous order is that it does not take into account bargaining power. As Knight (1992) explained, bargaining power is one of the most important explanations for the evolution of institutions yet economic theories of spontaneous order have essentially no role for it. The critique of spontaneous order presented in this chapter is not only that it lacks a role for bargaining power, but that it has no real role for governance, which is complementary to Knight's theoretical framework.

spontaneously arising arrangements of the sort described above, placing more of a premium on violence or the threat of coercion than is typically afforded in economic studies of informal order. At the same time, they were not part of the state; indeed, they fought it at seemingly every turn when their interests conflicted with the intentions of formal governments. In other words, economic studies underestimate the importance of endogenously arising political organizations as a source of private property institutions, while political theories overemphasize the state's role. The proposed remedy to these drawbacks is a conceptual framework that rationalizes claim clubs as a third level of social control between spontaneously arising arrangements emphasized in economics and the all-powerful state of political theories of the private property institutions.

Besides articulating claim clubs as a general level of social control, the theoretical framework clarifies the relationship between governments and property institutions. John Locke famously observed in his *Second Treatise of Government* that "the reason why men enter into society is the preservation of their property." As is well known, Locke viewed the state as preserving private property rights that exist in a hypothetical state of nature. However, as the theory in this chapter explains, governments do not *preserve* preexisting property institutions but rather *create* them in the sense that private property institutions do not exist, hypothetically or otherwise, unless there is a system of governance to specify and enforce them. Indeed, if property rights come from god, then organizations such as police, armies, or even claim clubs would be unnecessary. The fact of the matter is that private property institutions come from human organizations. The remainder of this chapter sets forth a theory that will guide the inquiry in the rest of Part I of this book, which focuses mainly on the origins of private property institutions.

SPONTANEOUS ORDER AND ITS LIMITS

Spontaneous Emergence of Institutions

One of the fundamental insights of economic studies of the origins of institutions is recognition that a great deal of social order has little to do with government action. Ellickson, for example, accords tremendous weight to unwritten norms as an explanation for social order:

> The stuff of a civilization consists largely of its substantive norms. These norms identify the everyday behaviors that call for the informal administration of rewards and punishments. In a well-functioning civilization, these informal rules – which have no identifiable author, no apparent date of origin, no certainty of attention from historians – are among the most magnificent of cultural achievements. (1991: 184)

One of the goals of this chapter is to develop a framework to assess Ellickson's hypothesis regarding the sources of informal order, which is shared by many proponents of economic modes of thinking about human behavior and social norms. Ultimately, we will see that the most important norms on the frontier had identifiable authors and fairly clear origins. Yet before turning to the critique, as a first step, it is necessary to define more precisely what is meant by "spontaneous order."

Unlike many concepts in economics, there is no standard definition of spontaneous order. Here, I define "spontaneous order" by two main features: (1) nonstate origins of order and (2) absence of hierarchy. The essence of this definition is that norms arise through a decentralized, unplanned process. Some studies take a much broader perspective on what constitutes spontaneous order, defining it as essentially any nonstate order.[2] However, for reasons mentioned below, it is useful to define spontaneous order as a theory of nonhierarchical social control.

In addition, the definition above makes no mention of enforcement even though Ellickson's account tends to view absence of enforcement as a key feature of spontaneous order. Rather than include absence of enforcement as a defining feature, I choose to divide spontaneously arising property norms into two types depending on the extent of enforcement. The first type, which can be called "spontaneous order without enforcement," consists of spontaneously arising property institutions that emerge without conscious design or even enforcement. Sugden (2004, 1986) and Hayek (1960, 1948) articulated this sort of order, in which human societies coordinate economic activities in the absence of hierarchy, conscious design, or even enforcement. As Sugden focused on the process of spontaneous order itself, Hayek (1945, 1944) was also concerned with using the logic of spontaneous order to articulate the inability of governments to design effective institutions.

The second type, which can be deemed "spontaneous order with enforcement," emphasizes the role of reputations in the emergence of property institutions and contracts. In economics, a reputation is simply a summary of past behavior of an individual or a group that others may use in making choices about how to deal with that individual or group. Reputational approaches to social norms, which have a much more prominent role for enforcement, are nonetheless useful to think of as a type of spontaneous order since they typically lack hierarchy or conscious design. For example, most of these reputational studies are based on a repeated game, which typically assumes all players are on equal footing. In addition, applications of these models, more often than not, consider the economic function of norms that have "always existed" in the sense that it is not clear who designed them, if they had a designer at all. Examples of reputational arrangements include social norms of participation in provision of public goods or "contracts" struck even though

[2] A broad perspective on spontaneous order has provided many insights into phenomena. For excellent examples of theories of spontaneous order that adopt this broad definition, see Leeson (2008, 2007a,b, 2006, 2005) and Leeson and Coyne (2012).

formal law may not regulate these agreements.[3] In such situations, a reputation in a community or one's word substitutes for formal law, with the value of one's reputation driving people to abide by their agreements. Yet unlike the first type of spontaneous order, reputational studies of spontaneously arising norms are driven by enforcement or the threat of punishment, which is the essence of these reciprocal relationships.

For either type of order, the most important feature is that norms may emerge without hierarchy or conscious design. Ultimately, I will use the extent of hierarchy and conscious design to distinguish theories of spontaneous order from order arising from both claim clubs and the state. At the same time, it is worthwhile to consider separately the two types of spontaneous order since each provides insight into different aspects of emergence of private property institutions. In particular, spontaneous order without enforcement provides insight into clarity of allocation, whereas the spontaneous order with enforcement helps us understand security and alienability.

Fortunately, both types of spontaneous order can be illustrated using concepts from game theory. The first perspective on spontaneous order, which considers how order arises without hierarchy, conscious design, or even enforcement, is essentially a model of coordination. Indeed, it is the assumption that the underlying social problem is coordination that reduces demand for enforcement. Below, I review Myerson's (2004) model of coordination on ownership in order to illustrate spontaneous order without enforcement. In addition to illustrating the logic of spontaneous order without enforcement, Myerson's model has an important interpretation in terms of clarity of allocation, which is essentially a problem of coordination on ownership. Since my concern is with property rights on the frontier, the discussion below refers to "squatters" rather than "players."

To see the logic of spontaneous order, suppose two squatters, denoted i and j, each choose between claiming and forgoing land with value $B > 0$. Players can take turns claiming land, they can choose to fight over the land, or they can both forgo claiming it. When both squatters choose to claim land, fighting breaks out, which is an anarchic state characterized by dissipation of resources as individuals compete to control resources. In the property rights literature, this is a situation of open access, defined in Chapter 1 as the absence of institutions, either formal or informal. The early months of the gold rush in California conjure up an image of anarchy of this sort, as people ran roughshod over the land in an effort to get to those precious nuggets. Such conflicts to establish ownership are costly, which can be represented by a parameter $f > 0$

[3] The classic study of reputational contracting is Macaulay (1963), whose study of business relations showed that informal norms are often as important, if not more important, than formal rules in regulating behavior. Macaulay, as a legal scholar, did not rely on economic reasoning, although his remarkable study anticipated much of the findings in theoretical and later empirical studies in the economics of reputation.

TABLE 2.1. *Payoffs in the Coordination Game*

		Player Two	
		Claim	Forgo
Player One	Claim	$-f, -f$	B, 0
	Forgo	0, B	0, 0

Note: Assume $B > f > 0$.

where the object's value is assumed greater than fighting cost, $B > f$. When both squatters claim land, their payoffs are $-f$. When a squatter claims land and the other forgoes it, the one who claims it receives B and the other receives 0. The best outcome is for one of them to claim the land, which is better than fighting or the 0 payoff when neither claims it. Payoffs in the coordination stage game are summarized in Table 2.1.

There are three equilibria of this game, which is a standard two-player coordination game. In the first equilibrium, squatter i claims land, and squatter j forgoes it; in the second, squatter j claims land, and squatter i forgoes it. The payoffs in these equilibrium are (B,0) and (0,B), respectively. The reason why they are an equilibrium is that whenever one of the squatters expects the other to claim land, it makes more sense to accept the other's claim (with payoff 0) than fight (with payoff $-f$); and when one expects the other to defer, that individual will claim the land because the payoff for doing so is B, which is greater than the payoff for not claiming land (which is 0). These equilibria are self-enforcing that neither of the squatters has incentives to deviate once they expect the other to claim land.

Myerson showed that there is also a third equilibrium in which both players choose to play a randomized strategy independently of the actions of other players. It is this equilibrium that is the primary threat to emergence of property institutions. Myerson works out the details of this equilibrium, which are less relevant to my purposes than the conclusion: in the third equilibrium, both squatters have expected payoffs of 0. The reason why the payoffs are zero is that two squatters who cannot agree on a way to divide land will fight over ownership, dissipating the gains from contracting in the process.

This third equilibrium can be interpreted as a war of attrition in which property rights are established through conflict, although Myerson's conclusion that resources would be dissipated in the war of attrition is probably too strong. Several theoretical studies have shown that a war of attrition to establish ownership need not lead to complete resource dissipation. As a general matter, resources may be allocated even when fighting is one of the ways of establishing ownership (Hafer 2006; Muthoo 2004; Grossman 2001). Nonetheless, the process of allocating ownership is expected to be inefficient in the absence of coordination, mainly because fighting involves a socially costly externality (Hafer 2006).

There is no hierarchy, conscious design, or enforcement in the model above. As such, it is a useful model to understand the first type of spontaneous order. For example, markets, which are among the most important of human-devised institutions, are often invoked as an example of institutions that tend to arise without conscious design or enforcement. They are also examples of institutions that solve a coordination problem.

The model above also suggests that it would be possible to coordinate on an equilibrium without the help of the state. After all, there is a good equilibrium in the model the players can reach even though we have made no mention of the state to this point. In fact, "anarchy," which can be defined by the absence of a government striving to plan out human behavior, may be socially desirable because it allows institutions to arise as the by-product of numerous human interactions, producing rules that the state could not have anticipated, let alone designed (Leeson 2007a,b, 2006).

The compelling logic and intriguing examples require us to take seriously models of spontaneous order without enforcement. And as the empirical studies in Chapter 3 will show, the logic of spontaneous order without enforcement provides insight into some of the most fascinating institutional arrangements on the American frontier, including norms of first possession, which were common among farmers, miners, loggers, and ranchers when individuals initially migrated to parts unknown. Remarkably, these first-possession norms lacked conscious design or enforcement, yet they appear to have been self-enforcing under certain conditions (namely, that there was a manageable number of fairly homogenous claimants participating in the property system).

First-possession norms solved a coordination problem of the sort described above. Fear of a costly fight ensured that individuals had incentives to respect another's claim to land. The system of first-possession norms for claiming land was effective because claimants understood well the costs of fighting and basic features of private property institutions. These norms, which seem to have selected an equilibrium that was optimal for squatters, were notable precisely because they were effective even though they had no conscious design or enforcement.

A coordination model is quite useful for explaining certain features of emergence of property institutions. However, such models describe only one dimension of a property system: clarity of allocation, which is a problem of dividing land clearly so as to avoid conflict over boundaries. As the previously presented model illustrates, the underlying problem of attaining clarity of allocation is drawing lines around what one owns because without them, fighting blurs borders and boundaries. However, as discussed in Chapter 1, dimensions of a property system also include security from trespass, alienability, and credibility of persistence. Upon attaining clarity of allocation, people who divide their land must defend it from others, as well as figure out ways to transact informal deeds to land they believe they own.

In contrast to the problem of dividing land, public-good aspects of collective defense and trade involve cooperation rather than coordination. The difference is that these norms have to be enforced, which is possible through reputational arrangements in which people use past behavior to compel socially desirable behavior.

The challenge of providing collective defense can be illustrated with a simple prisoner's dilemma game. Collective defense is individually costly, which creates incentives to shirk when a group is defending land from outsiders. For example, a self-interested squatter would rather spend more time working his land or investing in structures that secure it, such as a fence, while others are out defending the property of members of their community from "outsiders," such as land speculators or agents of the state. Indeed, until squatters devised a system to defend their land from others who coveted it (including the formal owners), their land tenure could not reasonably be described as secure even if they were able to divide it through spontaneously arising first-possession norms.

To illustrate the social dilemma, suppose our squatters have divided their land, perhaps through a spontaneously arising norm, and now have a choice to participate in collective defense of their land claims from a group of outsiders seeking to remove them from their land. I assume that as long as all participate, they can collectively counter the threat, although each would rather shirk, improving his land or fortifying it while others are out defending their interests.

When each squatter participates, he receives payoffs (P, P), which are the payoffs associated with (informal) land ownership. The benefits of shirking on participation in collective defense are denoted by V, which can be thought of as the gain from extra time to invest in land or added security from fortifying one's land from threats while members of the group are out defending land from others. The payoff for unilateral defense is M, which is the cost people must bear when they mobilize against outsiders. When a squatter participates in defense and his partner shirks, his payoffs are (M,V), whereas his payoffs when he shirks and his opponent participates are (V, M). When both players shirk, payoffs are (S, S). If we assume the payoffs are such that $V > P > S > M$, then this game will have the structure of a prisoner's dilemma. To make sure this game makes sense in the current context, we can assume the payoffs to mutual shirking are 0 in the current period and all future periods of the game because undefended land is assumed to be reallocated. In addition, unilateral defense is assumed inefficient so that the aggregate payoffs are lower when a single squatter defends claims, $2P > M + V$. These payoffs are summarized in Table 2.2.

As is well known, the unique Nash equilibrium in the stage game is for both squatters to shirk. Incentives to shirk create the possibility neither of the

TABLE 2.2. *Payoffs in the Collective-Defense Game*

		Player Two	
		Participate	Shirk
Player One	Participate	P, P	M, V
	Shirk	V, M	S, S

Note: $V > P > S > M$ and $2P > M + V$.

members of this community will participate in common defense of their land despite it being in their collective interest.

Although dividing land and defending it are clearly important in a private property regime, effective self-governance also requires a framework for alienability of land, as well as trade in goods and services. Alienability, which is necessary to allocate property rights efficiently, was also an important feature of informal contracting on public lands during the nineteenth century. Squatters typically wrote up their own deeds, and when they secured legal title, they often had extralegal means to regulate trade in state-backed legal title that would have otherwise been prohibited by formal land laws.

Trades in both land and goods are essential for a property regime to be effective: although trading land is essential to attaining economies of scale as well dynamic efficiency, land will lack value beyond its subsistence value unless people figure out a way to regulate trade in the fruits of the land. At the same time, trade presents opportunities to cheat partners. For example, some people may try to sell land they do not actually own, or lie about the quality of land. Dishonesty of this sort can undermine incentives to trade, and in the process reduce the chances that a property system attains allocative efficiency, in either a static or dynamic sense.

Analytically, the structure of trade interactions is nearly identical to that of collective defense. When squatters comply with a norm of honest trade, payoffs are (C, C) where C is the benefit of the trade relationship. In terms of alienability of land, this could be the payoff when two squatters conduct a land transaction (buying and selling land) or when they simply trade honestly with a fellow squatter. When a squatter cheats a trading partner, he receives a payoff of W, while the cheated partner receives a payoff of L. Thus, the payoffs for cheating while a partner complies are (W, L), while the payoffs for complying when an opponent cheats are (L, W). When both cheat, their payoffs are (D, D), which are the payoffs associated with possession of land without trade. Payoff D can be thought of as the subsistence value of land. In such situations, $D > 0$ and players continue to receive a positive payoff even if they fail to cooperate in trade relations. These payoffs, which are summarized in Table 2.3, are assumed $W > C > D > L$.

TABLE 2.3. *Payoffs in the Trade Game*

		Player Two	
		Comply	Deviate
Player One	Comply	C, C	L, W
	Deviate	W, L	D, D

Note: Assume $W > C > D > M$.

Since the last two games have the same structure, the implications are identical. Trade also requires cooperation, but in the Nash equilibrium of the stage game, each squatter rationally chooses to engage in predation rather than trade.

Although the Nash equilibrium in these games is socially suboptimal, decades of research into repeated games show that people can cooperate when the game is repeated.[4] When the games just mentioned are repeated (i.e, people expect to confront the same decisions with their partners over and over again), individual squatters can use the threat of future punishment to elicit cooperation. To see how cooperation arises in a repeated game, suppose that squatters in a community have available a social norm of the form "Participate in collective defense provided my partner has participated in all past periods; otherwise, shirk." Patience is represented by a discount factor $\delta \in (0,1)$ that determines how much value players place on future payoffs from cooperation. In a repeated game, loss of future payoffs from cooperation may exceed the gain from shirking provided players are sufficiently patient. Specifically, the condition for cooperation is that the gain from future cooperation exceeds the one-time gain from shirking on defense, which is formally stated as $\frac{1}{1-\delta}P \geq V + 0 + 0 + \cdots$ or $\delta \geq \frac{V-P}{V}$. According to this condition, incentives to defend land increase with land value and decrease when shirking is relatively more attractive. Similarly, trade relations can be sustained through a social norm of the sort described above. In the trade game, the condition that must be satisfied for cooperation is $\frac{1}{1-\delta}C \geq W + \frac{\delta}{1-\delta}D$ or $\delta \geq \frac{W-C}{W-D}$. This condition implies incentives to trade honestly increase when gains from trade increase and decrease when subsistence value of land and the one-time gains from cheating a trading partner increase. More generally, these conditions suggest that cooperation is possible provided people are sufficiently patient.

[4] In fact, repetition creates its own problems. A standard conclusion in the literature on repeated games is that any feasible, individually rational outcome can be sustained as an equilibrium outcome in a repeated game provided the players are sufficiently patient, which suggests a need for a leadership system to resolve the consequent equilibrium-selection problem. The discussion that follows is deliberately simple to illustrate the possibility of cooperation while emphasizing that one of the general weaknesses with these games is that they have no real role for governance. On the theory of repeated games, see Mailath and Samuelson (2006), Osborne and Rubinstein (1994), and Myerson (1991).

Usually, the requirement for cooperation in these sorts of games is that individuals are engaged in tightly knit, repeated interactions. However, cooperation is possible even when individuals do not interact on a regular basis. In games of "community enforcement," cooperation can be attained provided players have a mechanism that provides them with information about past behavior, such as a system of gossip (Mailath and Samuelson 2006; Kandori 1992).[5] In the presence of such information-transmission devices, social norms may be enforceable even when relationships are not tightly knit. A network of this sort provides information about past play even if a player has never had interactions with or will never again interact with a cheating player – a remarkable finding that generalizes a two-player game to a community of people interacting with haphazard information flows. Of course, the ability to contract through community enforcement depends on the strength of social networks.

Several studies of property institutions in the United States assess reputational hypotheses for emergence of property institutions and contracts. Ellickson's (1991) study of extralegal contracting among ranchers in California is one of the best-known empirical studies of reputational contracting. Anderson and Hill's (2004, 2002) studies of ranchers in the American Far West are also exemplary in this regard, showing how contracts among ranchers were self-enforcing even though they usually made agreements based only on trust and a handshake. Anderson and Hill remind us that the West was often far from violent despite weak formal institutions. And as we will see in the chapters ahead, such reputational arrangements provide insight into certain aspects of economic and social relations among squatters, such as sharing rules among miners.

Anderson and Hill view agreements based on trust as evidence that social interactions among ranchers involved less coercion than game theory requires – in other words, they take these as examples of spontaneous order without enforcement. Yet they are not explaining coordination, but rather, cooperation. And when it comes to cooperation, there is always some enforcement, even if they are not using punishment in the relevant equilibrium. As the prior discussion illustrates, coercion sustains cooperation even if there is no actual enforcement. In particular, theories of reputation suggest ranchers cooperated because they understood well that violating trust of their neighbors would mean they would lose a valuable relationship in the future. Rather than eschew game theory, as Anderson and Hill do, my interpretation of these norms is that ranchers were long-run players in the game-theoretic sense that they were

[5] Kandori (1992) generalized the argument about community information flows set forth by Milgrom et al. (1990). That is, the law merchant is an empirical example of a community enforcement mechanism in a repeated game. Similarly, Stewart (2009) applied the theory of community enforcement to illuminate conflict and cooperation during the California gold rush, a period in which oftentimes large communities attempted to establish property institutions. However, Stewart (2009) did not clarify that what occurred during the gold rush was emergence of informal governments, an organizational transformation that requires moving beyond standard models of community enforcement to understand the emergence of property institutions.

cooperating because they feared retribution when they violated social norms. In other words, coercion undergirded these social norms among ranchers – norms that can be explained and understood quite well in terms of game theoretic models.

Breakdown of Spontaneously Arising Institutions

Despite many examples of order despite absence of hierarchy, there are also many examples in which social and economic development – such as a growing population, increasingly haphazard interactions, or broadening heterogeneity of claimants – undermine spontaneously arising norms. Over time, changes of this sort are generally expected to undermine highly decentralized property arrangements of the sort described above.

At least two threats to spontaneously arising coordination norms (spontaneous order without enforcement) are bound to arise as a frontier develops. The first is unforeseen contingencies. Norms that establish ownership without a conscious designer have to specify appropriate behavior in various situations. As societies develop, new contingencies are increasingly common, and the effectiveness of spontaneously arising social norms to clearly allocate land is likely to decline. In these situations, a "judge" – in the general sense of someone who adjudicates disputes – will improve prospects to resolve ongoing disputes over ownership. However, in spontaneous-order theories of coordination on ownership, there are no judges.

A second threat to spontaneously arising property arrangements is a change in the background expectations of contracting parties. For example, continued effectiveness of a decentralized norm of first possession depends on several factors, including a shared cultural understanding of how a private property system works, as well as a belief in the desirability of private ownership. A first-possession norm, for example, is unlikely to be effective unless claimants share an underlying belief in the fairness of first possession, or in the appropriateness of private ownership of land. The fact that these first-possession norms were sometimes effective on the American frontier undoubtedly reflected shared background expectations on the part of claimants, including a shared understanding of how a private property system works. In particular, squatters more or less understood the basic features of private property institutions prior to occupying land – a shared framework for understanding how the world works undoubtedly improved their ability to contract without conscious design or enforcement. Of course, sometimes their coordinated beliefs led them astray, such as when people believed (wrongly) that they could as easily establish farms in the Far West in the same way they did in the more fertile Midwest. This important example of "desert farmers" will be discussed at length later on in the book precisely because it reminds us of the importance of considering how ideology and mistakes enter into the rush to allocate land. That is, mistakes were made that had their origins in flawed beliefs about how the world works.

Yet overall, there was substantial cultural coordination on the nature of private property, how to establish institutions governing private ownership, as well as the appropriate type of property regime in a given circumstance.

Each of the problems described above are likely to put pressure on norms that arise without design or enforcement. Unforeseen contingencies are expected to arise on a regular basis, and background expectations are likely to become increasingly diverse. In addition, as a frontier develops, it is less likely that claimants will share similar background expectations regarding the details of a private property system; it is precisely these details that will ultimately determine whether a private property regime is effective.

Social and economic development is also likely to weaken reputational contracting arrangements. Increases in population will ordinarily reduce opportunities for groups to enforce social norms unless they develop a system of leadership and administration. In many frontier situations, incentives to cooperate in the absence of a larger system of governance may be weak or nonexistent.

To summarize the discussion to this point, several theoretical frameworks predict that property arrangements will be effective even if members of a community cannot call on the state to specify and enforce private property institutions. This general theoretical finding is indeed remarkable because it suggests that much of the observed order we see regarding property institutions is not a result of a state. In fact, as we will see in the empirical studies later on in the book, theories of spontaneous order provide insight into many features of the American frontier – affirming the prediction that people can attain order in the absence of a state or even hierarchy. Yet under reasonable assumptions about economic development, such as increasing population or heterogeneity or changing background expectations, these theories suggest that a state is necessary to enforce contracts and ownership norms. Based on the foregoing observations, the primary empirical implication of economic theories of informal order can be stated as follows: *Property institutions may arise without hierarchy or conscious design, but as transaction costs increase, the state is necessary to specify and enforce property institutions.*

POLITICAL THEORIES OF THE ORIGINS OF PROPERTY INSTITUTIONS

Political theories of property institutions were primarily a response to economic studies suggesting that efficiency motivated contracting parties to demand and politicians to supply property institutions.[6] The initial economic theories of the origins of property institutions were content to assume that changes in relative prices motivated people to demand a system of private property rights, viewing government officials as passively responding to societal demands by supplying property institutions. Such theories, which will be discussed more extensively

[6] Examples of an efficiency perspective include Barzel (1989), North (1981), and Demsetz (1967).

in Chapter 5, have been described as naive because they have no real role for political interests or institutions (Eggertsson 1990).

Political theories of property institutions make political interests and political institutions explicit and in the process provide insight not only into institutional change, but also into the origins of property rights. Sened (1997) and Riker and Sened (1991) stated several conditions that must be satisfied in order for private property rights to emerge, including politicians having an interest in recognizing property rights, individuals valuing the content of property rights, others respecting these property rights, and the content of property rights being valuable. In political theories, property institutions emerge when political actors have an interest in specifying and enforcing them. An implication is that change in property institutions is unlikely to reflect efficiency considerations because politicians have few incentives to choose efficient policies. Yet there is also another implication: the state is the main source of property institutions.

Whereas Sened's theory of property institutions focuses on political interests as an explanation for emergence and change in private property, a related political perspective considers credibility of commitment to protection of private property institutions. According to this complementary perspective, a fundamental problem for a government is committing credibly to respect for private property rights (Weimer 1997; Riker and Weimer 1995, 1993). Credibility, in turn, is influenced by political institutions. In particular, political institutions that constrain rulers from reneging on their promises, such as democracy, separation of powers, and political parties, are expected to improve ownership security (Gehlbach and Keefer 2011; Haber et al. 2003; Stasavage 2003; Diermeier et al. 1997; North and Weingast 1989; Root 1994, 1989).

Besides criticizing efficiency as an explanation for institutional change, political theories do not have much of a role for spontaneously arising property institutions. Since the state in political theories is all-powerful, the state is the main source of property institutions. Political theories, which accord far greater significance to political interests and institutions, have a clear implication for the origins of property institutions: *The state is necessary to specify and enforce property institutions, with the effectiveness of property institutions ultimately contingent upon features of political institutions.*

As mentioned above, in addition to offering a fundamental hypothesis regarding the origins of property rights, political theories also reject a generalized efficiency perspective regarding institutional change. Part II of this book provides a substantial amount of evidence that an efficiency rationale cannot explain many of the critical institutional developments in nineteenth-century land laws, a finding that is largely anticipated by political theories of property institutions with respect to the process of institutional *change*. Yet my finding regarding the *origins* of property institutions suggests political theories leave much to be desired. In particular, political theories of property institutions do not have a role for governance organizations such as claim clubs, or even spontaneously arising property norms, because of their preoccupation with the formal/legal state. Thus, political theories tend to perform better as explanations for institutional change (in particular, as a critique of efficiency perspectives on property rights) than they do regarding institutional origins.

PRIVATE-ORDER GOVERNMENTS: HOW CLAIM CLUBS SUBSTITUTE FOR THE STATE

Economic and political theories, for reasons outlined earlier, do not have much of a role for associations such as claim clubs. The framework to follow explains precisely how claim clubs specified and enforced property institutions. In it, property institutions and government arise simultaneously: there are no property institutions without governments and there is no reason for government except to protect property. As such, the theory of claim clubs differs with existing theories of the origins of property institutions in recognizing the role of governments in protecting property while also considering how basic political institutions may arise endogenously, through voluntary exchange.

My framework draws on insights from the law merchant model of Milgrom et al. (1990), which considered emergence of long-distance trade relations. As explained in the introductory chapter, the theory of claim clubs differs from the law merchant framework by considering the origins of property institutions as well as trade relations. More fundamentally, I stress the role of informal political institutions in the emergence of informal property institutions. Although the law merchant was, in fact, a simple political institution, Milgrom et al. did not explicitly interpret it as a basic feature of government.

In addition, the theory of claim clubs complements Olson's (2000, 1993) theory of stationary banditry by explaining the process of state formation explicitly. Olson articulated why a state, once established, could improve prospects for property protection. However, Olson did not consider explicitly how governments arise, but rather, compared property protection under a situation with no state to one in which a single, all-powerful Leviathan has defeated all adversaries vying for power and authority. The conceptual framework that follows considers explicitly the possibility that these governments arise within the state when the state of Olson's theory, as well as of Sened's political framework, declines to respect private property institutions.

A fable helps us understand how voluntary exchange produces private property institutions and governments. Suppose that a group of people seeks to establish private property institutions yet transaction costs prevent them from relying on spontaneously arising norms to establish ownership. Recognizing that they may not be able to reap the gains associated with private property institutions, one or more of the people decide to announce a club, agreeing to lead it and to serve as judges, provided people who join to pay a fee to leaders in exchange for services provided (if several people decide to announce a club, the leaders would share in the profits). Anyone can join a club provided one agrees to live under its rules. This club can be represented by a contract with the following form:

> **The Claim Club Contract.** For a fee, anyone can join this organization. We agree to provide judges to resolve disputes, to monitor participation in collective defense, and to collect information on all potential trading partners. Each member must agree to resolve disputes without fighting, participate in collective defense when called upon, and to trade honestly. Individuals who join agree to only deal with other members of the club. Anyone who ignores a judge's ruling, fails to participate in claim defense, cheats a member, or makes arrangements with any outsider is permanently excluded from this organization.

This simplified but general contract represents the key features of an informal property regime in the sense that all property regimes have to perform functions of adjudication, claim defense, and trade. That is, the club promises to solve the problems of coordination and cooperation confronting squatters seeking to establish property institutions.

This contract also captures the idea that political institutions and property institutions arise simultaneously in a claim club. Property institutions are embodied in a club's rules, while the system of leadership and judges represents the origins of basic political institutions. The questions then become: Will people join the club and abide by its rules? And will leaders and judges fulfill their promise to govern?

These questions can be recast as two conditions that must be satisfied in order for private property institutions to be self-enforcing. The first condition is that individuals have incentives to join a claim club and play by its rules, provided they elect to join it. The second condition is that leaders perform their duties. As long as these two conditions are satisfied, property contracts will be self-enforcing even though decentralized arrangements are unavailable and the state is unwilling to enforce property contracts.

The first condition requires that the payoff from joining a claim club exceeds the payoff from not joining. Satisfying this condition requires that we compare the future stream of payoffs from joining a claim club with the payoffs one expects to receive if they do not join a claim club. At most, the future payoffs from joining a claim club are the payoffs associated with coordination and cooperation in the games described above.

The payoffs for joining a claim club can be calculated explicitly, beginning with the payoffs to coordination described above. In each period, squatters continue to claim or forgo land with value $B > 0$. Based on the foregoing analysis and the assumption that players face substantial transaction costs as a frontier develops, anyone who decides against joining a club can expect a war of attrition to establish control of resources with an expected payoff of 0 because fighting dissipates gains from exchange.

In contrast, the per-period payoffs from coordination on ownership are positive when an individual joins a claim club and uses a judge to resolve disputes. The particular value of per-period payoffs depends on assumptions about the probability individuals are victorious in their property disputes when they petition a club's judges. Under the assumption that the probability winning before a judge is equal, these per-period payoffs are $\frac{1}{2}B$, which is the payoff for joining a club due to coordination on ownership. Clearly, the threat of the war-of-attrition equilibrium, as well as ability of judges to resolve a coordination problem, creates incentives for people to join a club. In particular, the threat of fighting makes the decisions of judges self-enforcing: people accept judicial decisions because the alternative, fighting, is worse than accepting an adverse decision.

The foregoing logic illustrates why a state is not necessary to provide judges. Rather, the only requirement for successful dispute resolution is that there is agreement that someone is in charge; it is irrelevant whether the source of authority is the state or a claim club. As Myerson (2004) observed, agreement on a judge, even an unfair one, is the main requirement for successful ownership.

The payoffs associated with successful collective defense and trade also influence incentives to join a claim club. Although it is possible to enforce a norm of cooperation in collective defense when a system of gossip exists (one in which the community shares information about past behavior, thereby allowing anyone in the community to enforce social norms even if they themselves did not experience violations of social norms), transaction costs will eventually undermine the ability of members of a community to monitor behavior unless people develop a more specialized system such as a club to monitor and enforce trade relations. For example, when membership in a community is fluid or people are separated by long distance or interact infrequently, a system of gossip may not be sufficient to sustain cooperation. Clubs, by providing information on past behavior as well as enforcing it, can overcome these problems. In particular, when individuals join a claim club, they expect to receive the payoffs associated with possession of land, P, which is the most that individuals can receive by joining in terms of collective defense. In contrast, their payoffs outside of a club under increasingly haphazard interactions will be zero in terms of collective defense.

Trade relations specified and enforced through decentralized norms are also expected to deteriorate as society develops in terms of number of people, heterogeneity of members, and the like. Specifically, as transaction costs increase, the payoffs in the trade game described above will move toward zero: cheating trading partners is the best action when people are interacting with strangers on a regular basis with no overarching system of leadership and administration. In contrast, joining a claim club promises members will reap gains from trade by virtue of the ability of leaders to monitor trade relations. In particular, the most that a claimant can expect to receive by joining in terms of trade relations is C, the payoff for honest trade. Individuals have incentives to join a claim club because they anticipate trade when they join it and predation outside of it.

The decision to join a claim club amounts to adding up the payoffs from joining a club and comparing them with the payoffs from not joining it: squatters add up the expected benefits from coordination on ownership and cooperation in the collective defense and trade games, minus the fee for joining, and compare it with their expected payoff outside of a claim organization. In terms of dimensions of a property system, potential members add up the benefits associated with clarity of allocation, security from trespass, and alienability, weighing them against the cost of joining a club.

This condition can also be interpreted with respect to specific variables and parameters. First, increases in the expected payoffs from coordination (B) and cooperation (P and C) increase incentives for individuals to join a claim club. Second, joining a club only makes sense if members expect it to exist in the future. Future payoffs are discounted when members believe that the club's days are limited; discounting, in turn, makes people less likely to join the club ex ante. Third, an increase in opportunities to contract outside a club reduces incentives to join. These payoffs outside a club, which are normalized to zero, could easily be represented by a parameter that measures opportunities to contract outside of a claim club such that incentives to join a club are greater when there are fewer opportunities to contract outside of it. Summarizing, on the members' side of the equation, the success of a club in providing property protection depends on the expected gains from establishing property institutions, beliefs about whether or not the club's days are numbered, and opportunities to contract outside of it.

The second basic condition for emergence of property institutions is that leaders abide by rules specified in a claim-club contract. A club's leaders promise to uphold these rules but their word cannot be taken for granted. Rather, leaders require self-interested incentives to uphold their end of the bargain. The following factors influence leaders' incentives to actually follow the rules they promise to uphold.

First, fees, as well as in-kind benefits, are important to ensuring leaders abide by their promise. From a rational choice perspective, leaders have incentives to uphold their end of the bargain is because it is profitable for them to do so. For example, exchanging fees for information was a central feature of the law merchant model: judges provided services because traders were willing to pay them to provide information they required in order to ensure their trading partners were honest. Fees of this sort also provide insight into the origins of property institutions. A club's leaders abide by their promises to specify and enforce property institutions to the extent that it is profitable for them to do so. In addition, even if they do not receive fees or payment, they may receive additional benefits as leaders of their organization (such as prestige in a community) that constitute "payment" for services in the sense that prestige and the like benefit them.

A second reason leaders carry through on their promises is that they benefit from the public good of security, which is a rationale that the law merchant model did not consider. Although the law merchant model focused on a single judge who was not himself a trader, leaders of claim clubs were political leaders as well as landholders. For this reason, when club leaders kept their promises to govern honestly (and in the process improved land tenure security for members), promise keeping benefited them as well because they were themselves landholders. Ex post shirking on their promises made less sense for a club's leaders because they were themselves beneficiaries of the land-tenure security they helped to provide.

Several additional factors besides fees and mutual dependence provide incentives for leaders to behave honestly. The third and fourth factors are presence of a local monopoly and constraints on leaders, each influencing the discount rate of a club's leader. Discount rates, which represent patience of leaders, provide insight into important outcomes in political economy such as emergence of property institutions (Haber et al. 2003; North and Weingast 1989), state failure (Bates 2008), and credibility in sovereign debt markets (Stasavage 2011, 2003). For example, Bates (2008) has shown that one of the most important reasons why some countries avoid civil war and conflict is that their leaders believe that they will be in power for a long time. In contrast, when leaders expect to be out of power shortly, violence typically results. A general implication of these studies is that leaders who are long-run players have stronger incentives to make choices that benefit society.

Discount rates also provide insight into the success of claim clubs as a source of property institutions. If a club's leaders have long time horizons, then it stands to reason that they will have fewer incentives to expropriate wealth from members or to otherwise shirk on promises. Discount rates of a club's leaders, in turn, are governed by two factors. The first is the extent to which a club must compete for members with other clubs. Competition among several claim clubs can undermine incentives for a club's leaders to do their work by reducing fees they can extract. For this reason, the extent to which a club enjoys a local monopoly will influence the overall stability of the club and its property institutions.

A second factor, constraints on leaders, has perhaps a more direct and profound effect on leaders' discount rates. A club's leaders will discount more heavily future benefits from playing by a club's rules as constraints deteriorate. One of the most important sources of constraints is the democracy, both generally speaking and within the confines of claim clubs. To the extent a club has elections or other methods of popular control, its constitution could build into its structure means of increasing leaders' time horizons because representative institutions reduce incentives to forgo predation to the extent leaders want to remain in a position of power.[7]

[7] Democracy, however, is not necessary for credibility. Indeed, as Gehlbach and Keefer (2011) have shown, the key to emergence of (formal) property institutions is that rulers expect to be in power for a long time. Specifically, they provided evidence, both theoretically and empirically, that

The first four factors – fees/profit motivation, mutual dependence, local monopolies, and constraints on leaders – share a common emphasis on incentives. In addition, capabilities also influence the ability of leaders to uphold their promises. Transaction costs, which as defined broadly include the costs of governance, also influence the ability of club leaders to carry through on their promises.[8] As governance costs rise, representatives may have *incentives* to govern honestly yet cannot govern effectively because they lack *capacity*. In such situations, society may have to appeal to a state to manage land relations even though representatives have the proper incentives.

The theoretical framework presented above suggests how bandits arise within the state through a voluntary transaction even a frontier's complexity undermines spontaneously arising property institutions. In an illuminating study of informal order, Dixit (2004) observed that economic problems often create economic opportunities for people to privately provide services for a profit that are ordinarily associated with a state. The logic of claim clubs draws on Dixit's insights, in particular how members of a club could take advantage of opportunities created by the breakdown of spontaneously arising norms. However, Dixit was not explicit that what was occurring was a process of government formation. The foregoing discussion suggests that the key to emergence of property institutions is government formation – even that of informal governments. In particular, political institutions embodied in claim clubs make property institutions self-enforcing. To paraphrase Ostrom (1990), self-governance was indeed possible, yet effective private property institutions require a bandit to arise within the state in order for private property institutions to be effective.

The theory presented above also complements the political perspectives of Olson (2000) and Sened (1997), which focused on the conditions when political leaders have incentives to provide the public good of property protection rather than explaining origins of organizations to specify and interpret property institutions. As a consequence, political theories understate the possibility of endogenous government formation.

To summarize the argument so far, frontier development typically undermines opportunities to contract through spontaneous order and reputations. However, the state is not the only source of property institutions when simpler arrangements break down. Accordingly, my central hypothesis is that *political*

ruling-party institutionalization can substitute for constraints such as democracy and separation of powers as a source of commitment to private property institutions. Gehlbach and Keefer's finding helps us understand why an autocratic government such as China can commit credibly to respecting private property.

8 Transaction costs also can be used to analyze incentive problems, such as Williamson's (1996) concept of "opportunism with guile," a concept in which an incentive problem is a source of transaction costs. Thus, we can think of transaction costs as encompassing any costs of governing, including those that arise because of incentives.

institutions are generally necessary to specify and enforce property institutions, yet the state is not the only source of political institutions or property institutions when spontaneously arising norms break down or are otherwise unavailable.

ARE CLAIM CLUBS "SPONTANEOUS ORDER?"

Some may argue that claim clubs arise spontaneously and so are an example of spontaneous order. After all, the defining feature of claim clubs is that they emerge in the state's shadow. Should we view all nonstate order "spontaneous order"?

On one hand, such a broad definition of spontaneous order seems to obfuscate one of the main contributions of theories of spontaneous order, which is to explain order that arises without hierarchy. Theories of spontaneous order provide a powerful and compelling explanation for norms that are widespread yet have no designer or enforcer, such as those allocating "property rights" to shoveled-out parking spots during Pittsburgh winters, discussed in Chapter 1. Spontaneously arising reputational norms also provide insight into a stunningly wide range of behavior, including codes of revenge or collective punishments that are often remarkably effective in policing group behavior. One of the most remarkable features of those norms is that they work without any hierarchy at all.

On the other hand, it seems like a stretch to view highly decentralized norms as arising from the same general process as organizations such as mafias, cartels, or claim clubs. Such organizations move substantially beyond the highly decentralized contracting norms of the sort just described in terms of division of authority, specialization, and coercive authority. Organizations such as the ones mentioned previously also tend to replace simpler systems of social order, which suggests that the emergence of hierarchy is something we should strive to explain. It is not clear that existing studies of spontaneous order actually explain why hierarchy arises.

In the current context of explaining institutional development in the American frontier, there is a clear transition from the spontaneous order perspective, as I have defined it, to claim clubs in each sector. By viewing all of this as "spontaneous order," we would miss the important transition from simple social norms to the well-defined hierarchies the frontiers developed in economic and social terms. More importantly to the case at hand, we would potentially gloss over the emergence of frontier governments.

In any event, even if one rejects my definition of spontaneous order, this book shares in common with studies of spontaneous order a deep appreciation for order that arises outside the aegis of the state, as well as a concern with the consequences of these nonstate sources of order. At the same time, it is my contention that existing perspectives on nonstate order tend to overstate the ability to manage relations without creating basic political institutions, even ones that are informal. Thus, much like Knight (1992), who expanded the range of theories of spontaneous order by considering explicitly bargaining power in the process of institutional change, this study refines existing studies of spontaneous order as well as Knight's insightful critique by considering more explicitly the spontaneous origins of *political* institutions.

CONCLUSION

With a theoretical framework in hand, the next two chapters describe key empirical developments in property institutions and governments in the economic history of the United States. To foreshadow the findings, governments and private property institutions emerged more or less simultaneously whenever interactions on the frontier were fairly haphazard. These private property institutions were effective because people devised bandits within the state with all the key features of a government despite standing in the state's oftentimes pale shadow. Ellickson's "remarkable cultural achievements" that have *no conscious designer or enforcer* were not a primary source of order. North's firms were nowhere to be found, nor was Sened's state a force to be reckoned with. Rather, claim clubs – consciously designed associations with a powerful enforcement mechanism – substituted for the state as a source of the constitutional and working rules necessary for capitalist development in each of the major economic sectors of the American frontier. The discussion now turns to the origins of property institutions on Western lands throughout the nineteenth century.

3

The Constitution of Claim Clubs

According to the theoretical framework presented in the previous chapter, economic studies consider spontaneous processes, but political theories prioritize the state, as sources of private property institutions. In contrast to prevailing perspectives, I posited bandits arising within the state as a third, important source of private property institutions. This chapter provides evidence of the origins of private property institutions on the American frontier that will ultimately be used to assess these contrasting theoretical perspectives.

The empirical studies of the origins of informal property institutions are organized by economic sector, beginning with agriculture before proceeding to consider property relations among miners, loggers, and ranchers. Agriculture is a logical starting point because it emerged prior to the other sectors, but also because farmers' associations were in many ways a blueprint for establishing property institutions that was copied in other sectors. As such, a thorough understanding of agricultural claim clubs reduces the need for as much empirical evidence of the features of claim clubs in subsequently emerging sectors. In terms of organization, the discussion proceeds by first describing essential features of decentralized contracting arrangements, such as first-possession norms, before considering constitutional aspects of claim clubs in some depth.

The findings presented in this chapter draw mainly on historical studies of the American frontier, as well as some primary sources (and many secondary sources that were written so long ago they constitute, for all practical purposes, primary source material). These histories of the frontier multiplied as it expanded westward, producing a marvelous tapestry of perspectives on the development of the land and land laws during the nineteenth century. The accounts that follow thus owe a great debt to historians of social, political, and economic development of the "western lands."

The narrative that follows also has an additional goal: to present a concrete representation of claim clubs, one that contrasts with the richness of dates, times, people, and places characteristic of histories of the frontier. Such abstraction is not only helpful to compare informal contracting arrangements in four sectors, but probably necessary. Indeed, the emergence of informal property institutions in each sector is sufficiently complex and interesting to warrant four separate books if one is mainly interested in producing a history of claim clubs. Thus, the pages ahead seek to provide enough empirical evidence to understand general features of clubs, as well as to evaluate theoretical hypotheses regarding the origins of private property institutions.

AGRICULTURAL LAND

Once settlers arrived in the New World, they began to establish political institutions, such as towns and governments, along with economic institutions. Yet settlers' formal governments were generally weak compared to the governments they left behind in Europe and would remain so for much of the nineteenth century, in particular in the regions that were most recently settled. Indeed, though there were a few pockets of administrative competence, the American state had very little in the way of formal bureaucratic capacity prior to the Civil War (Carpenter 2001; Bensel 1991).

In an environment of formal institutional weakness, people often had to provide their own institutions. Agriculture was the first economic occupation to emerge. The initial property norms allocating agricultural land were based on first possession.

First-Possession Norms: How Farmers Allocated Land without Conscious Design or Enforcement

First-possession norms are excellent examples of the decentralized emergence of property institutions discussed in Chapter 2. As anticipated by studies of spontaneous order, people were able to divide land for private use through social norms that had no designer or enforcer yet turned out to be effective.

The account of first-possession norms that follows is meant to illustrate their essential features rather than to provide a full-fledged account of these institutions, a task that would take me too far afield from the central objective of this chapter, which is comparing progression of informal political and property institutions across major frontier sectors. In addition, first-possessions norms were unwritten, unlike claim constitutions, which were often published in local papers, and so the herculean task of producing a truly systematic account of where and when they existed is better left to historians. Nonetheless, the descriptions that follow are more than sufficient to illustrate key features of first-possession norms, as well as to evaluate alternative theories of the origins of property institutions.

Before providing greater detail regarding these norms, it is helpful to summarize their key features. In general, first-possession norms established private ownership based on first-in-time occupation of land. Farmers referred to first-possession norms by various names. Erecting a structure was the basis for cabin rights, raising a corn field was the basis for corn rights, and deadening trees was the basis for tomahawk rights. During periods in which these first-possession norms held sway, individuals divided land and began to till it even though they lacked legal title and had yet to convene claim clubs. Despite their various names – "cabin rights," "corn rights," or "tomahawk rights" – these norms shared in common certain features, namely that they tended to emerge without hierarchy, conscious design, or, in the case of first possession norms, even enforcement, as anticipated by theories of spontaneous order. Nonetheless, these simple norms were sufficient for individuals to divide land, as well as to buy and sell claims.

Early land-claiming norms that arose in Ohio and Pennsylvania illustrate key features of first-possession norms. Again, because records of these norms are hard to come by, I selected these states for a few examples in part because there is a historical record available from which to construct an account of the initial norms for claiming land. In addition, because my focus is on claim clubs, it is only necessary to provide enough detail for the reader to judge whether claim clubs had fundamentally different structure than the first-possession norms described below.

The first wave of settlement in Ohio was facilitated by the Ohio Land Company, which was chartered in 1748 to deter French aggrandizement (ironically, the company's activities would ultimately contribute to the French and Indian War).[1] English traders established trading posts shortly thereafter, along with a stockade for defense. Traders provided for their own defense from Indian war parties, as well as defense from their colonial competitors.

Land companies were often the first organizations to locate in a region after a fort was established, and they would eventually compete with the state in the business of selling land to settlers. As early as the 1750s, land markets existed, both privately and publicly run. Land companies, as well as the success of the military in clearing the land of Indian tribes, created new options for those seeking legal title.

Private land companies typically had an advantage over the government because they could more easily respond to changes in the quantities of land demanded by individuals. Yet many people began occupying land without legal title even though there was a legal way to attain land. For example, in Montgomery County, Ohio, people would come, in groups varying in size from two or three people to collections of several families, to a region armed with rifles and hatchets to attain food from the forests. Settlers often took months to get to the land they eventually settled. Prior to surveys, settlers fully respected tomahawk rights made by deadening trees. "Settlement rights," which were

[1] On the property norms in Ohio, see *Ohio: History of Montgomery County* (1882). For an account of the Ohio Company, see especially Proctor (1959) and Bailey (1939).

rights backed by occupation, were an even stronger source of land-tenure security because someone was on hand to defend claims.

Tomahawk and settlement rights were both recognized as establishing a legitimate claim, and most accepted a claim rather than fought over it. These norms appear to have been common in Pennsylvania as well. A soldier described the norms governing land-claiming activities along the Monongahela River near Pittsburgh, as well as Fort Pitt, in late 1772 (Day 1843: 43):

> There was, at an early period of our settlements, an inferior kind of land title denominated a "tomahawk right," which was made by deadening a few trees near the head of a spring, and marking the bark of some one or more of them with the initials of the name of the person who made the improvement... These rights, however, were often bought and sold. Those who wished to make settlements on their favorite tracts of land, bought up the tomahawk improvements, rather than enter into quarrels with those who had made them.

These norms arose spontaneously, although they were enforced – just not by third parties. Rather, individuals were on hand to give force to their land-claiming convictions. Tomahawk rights were as strong as the occupants themselves; a claimant could lose his land if personally unable to defend it. The soldier went on to describe the need for enforcement (Day 1843: 44):

> Other improvers of the land, with a view to actual settlement, and who happened to be stout veteran fellows, took a very different course from that of purchasing the "tomahawk rights." When annoyed by the claimants under those rights, they deliberately cut a few good hickories, and gave them what was called in those days a "laced jacket," that is, a sound whipping.

These norms are interesting because they were effective in allocating land even though there were no governance institutions in place. Occupation was important, and if someone made a claim but was not there or was too weak to defend it, ownership could easily change hands. Nonetheless, this rudimentary property system appears to have been somewhat effective in allocating ownership.

Of course, norms of this sort raise the specter of justice, as well as economic efficiency. Fairness considerations are beyond the scope of this section. However, these property norms can be assessed from an economic perspective. On one hand, an occupation requirement reduced transaction costs of identifying who owns land. Land-claiming activities could take on elements of a free-for-all in borderlands, and colonial Pennsylvania certainly constituted a borderland. From a transaction-cost perspective, occupancy requirements may have been expedient.

However, there are at least three reasons why occupancy norms were a source of social costs. First, occupancy norms of the sort described were used to restrict trade in claims whenever a group believed a purchaser was a land speculator. Although speculation may have produced social costly externalities (such as instability in land prices), many of the "speculators" were simply legal purchasers of land that a club desired. Occupation norms were thus a way to restrict speculation, which often has an important economic function. Second, as Bromley (2006) reminds us, having a property right means not having to continually stand guard over what you own. A system of ownership based on occupation meant that people had to occupy land or they risked losing it, which is certainly not an ideal situation in terms of a property regime. Third, the property system just described fell short in terms of procedural democracy. Institutions that are perceived as legitimate or the outcome of deliberation are more likely to be followed (Calvert 2006). The absence of mechanisms of procedural justice, such as a way for a claimant to take his or her case to a collective body when confronted by "stout veteran fellows" in the example above, likely undermined the effectiveness of this property regime.

These observations suggest that a system of occupancy rights fell short of an economically efficient arrangement. These inefficiencies associated with occupation requirements, as well as diseconomies of scale with personal enforcement, would eventually give rise to demand for claim clubs. Nonetheless, first-possession norms were impressive sources of social order. First-possession norms were often effective in allocating ownership among people who lacked legal title despite having no designer or third-party enforcers (though as the soldier's account indicates, there was personal enforcement).

The fact that these claimants were also more or less equally matched probably had a lot to do with the effectiveness of these norms as well. Umbeck (1981) posited equality of fighting skill as a precondition for the emergence of property contracts among miners on the gold frontier in the 1850s. Equality of fighting skill also appears to have also influenced emergence of private property institutions governing agricultural land. To the extent settlers in Ohio and Western Pennsylvania were evenly matched in terms of fighting skill, moving on to claim new land makes more sense than fighting to establish ownership. In this regard, first-possession norms permitted frontier farmers to allocate land without fighting despite their inability or unwillingness to call on the state in the event of property disputes. More generally, these norms for claiming land for private use were effective because they solved a coordination problem of the sort described in Chapter 2.

The Fair Play System

First-possession norms are intriguing systems of social order. Although there were no leaders, judges, or secretaries to record claims during periods in which tomahawk rights governed land relations, the various accounts that have just been described indicate that such norms were fairly effective. Yet for all their interesting and remarkable features, these spontaneously arising norms were not the fundamental source of private property institutions on agricultural land prior to claimants acquiring legal title. Rather, property institutions were typically specified and enforced within the confine of claim clubs. "Farmers' protective associations," as farmers' claim clubs were typically called, imposed order over millions of acres of public land. These clubs, which were eventually most common in the Midwestern states, where some states may have had up to a hundred claim clubs, initially emerged in the Eastern states.[2]

Institutionally and organizationally speaking, agricultural claim clubs differed substantially from the systems of tomahawk and occupation rights: claim clubs represented the origins of governments and property institutions, while a defining feature of tomahawk and occupation systems was absence of hierarchy. As the empirical studies make clear, political institutions were the defining feature of clubs, and it was precisely these political features that made private property institutions self-enforcing in what was oftentimes an otherwise anarchic environment.

Claim clubs were typically convened in response to legal uncertainty and threats from "outsiders," the latter category variously including Indian tribes, other squatters, land speculators, and federal agents. Conflict between Indians and settlers was somewhat common during the various periods in which clubs convened, although these conflicts did not necessarily motivate people to convene a club or call it to arms. Rather, they motivated settlers to appeal to the military to clear land of Indians before settlement resumed. Upon resuming settlement, conflict often arose between various categories of settlers, in particular, between initial settlers and "latecomers," which were settlers who happened to arrive after others were already in a region. These conflicts of "Greek against Greek" – between rival bands of settlers – were usually the driving force behind claim clubs, rather than conflict with Indian tribes.

One of the first agricultural claim clubs, which its framers named the "Fair Play System," emerged in disputed territory in Pennsylvania in the late eighteenth century in the present-day country of Lycoming (at that time was called Northumberland County), in the northeast part of the state. In the borderlands of pre-Revolutionary Pennsylvania, legal uncertainty and competition between rival settlers were the two most important reasons why bandits emerged within the state. The particular source of legal uncertainty surrounding the Fair Play System was a dispute over the boundaries of a large land purchase that commenced in 1768, which had as its western boundary Tiadaghton Creek. Indians had the lands to the west of the boundary, and so settlers were supposed to stay on the eastern side. The problem was that the two sides could not agree which of several creeks was "Tiadaghton Creek." The settlers believed it was the present Pine Creek, fourteen miles west of the present Lycoming Creek, while the Indians believed it was the latter. This was a high-stakes boundary dispute because the land in question was some of the most fertile land in the country (Lloyd 1929).

[2] Even though club constitutions were published in local papers, the historical record is incomplete, and so estimates of the number of clubs must be considered to be just that: estimates.

The legal thing to do was to wait until treaties were resolved diplomatically and politically, and then to purchase land from the government or landholding companies. In a sign of things to come on the frontier more generally, settlers declined to wait for treaties, electing instead to occupy disputed Pennsylvania land without legal title. These men, women, and children seeking were some of the first squatters and also were among the first groups to form a claim club to give force to their convictions.

The remarkable feature of this club, which had no legal sanction, was its unmistakable political structure. Members of the Fair Play System called themselves "Fair Play Settlers" and their leaders were known as "Fair Play Men." Fair Play Men comprised a tribunal of three with executive, legislative, and judicial authority over the residents.[3] Democratically elected Fair Play Men were responsible for settling boundary disputes among members and defending claims from competing claimants, including other squatters and Indian tribes. It was the first local government in the disputed lands, as it also remained for a while, lasting from 1773 to 1785 (Wolfe 1969; Lloyd 1929; Meginness 1892).

Individuals who elected to occupy disputed land recognized that failure to develop political institutions would lead to instability. In the absence of government, these settlers believed their community "would become a lawless aggregation, in which the weak would be oppressed by the strong and every semblance of a well-regulated society destroyed" (Meginness 1892: 193). To avoid chaos, settlers quickly developed a "constitution," which defined legitimate behavior and penalties for noncompliance. This was a constitution in the sense it represented the rules at the highest level of their society, as well as a code of conduct, even though it had no formal sanction. All newcomers were invited to join and to submit in all respects to the club's rules (Smith 1810). Many joined freely because the organization provided benefits to members in exchange for their agreement to participate in collective action, although the club expected all to join its ranks. Fair Play Men also had the authority to levy taxes, "but as the community had not gone crazy over public improvements, the advancement of civilization and the development of its mighty resources were kept at a minimum" (Lloyd 1929: 84).

The core functions of the Fair Play System were adjudication and collective defense. A club court, which had jurisdiction over the entire region occupied by members of the club, could be convened at any time in response to conflicts. Anyone who violated its substantive norms was banished, usually by being put into a canoe without a paddle, towed to the middle of the river, and set adrift (Lloyd 1929; Meginness 1892). "Legal" decisions handed down by a club's judges were generally considered just. In fact, as formal law became

[3] It goes without saying that indigenous groups probably viewed these clubs as anything but fair. "Fairness" and "fair play" should be interpreted as fair with respect to other members of the group.

institutionalized, formal judges often accepted the rules of claim clubs as law (Smith 1810).

Although the political consequences of claim clubs are the subject of Part II of this book, it is helpful here to foreshadow how these associations influenced the process of formal institutional change. In 1784, after more or less securing de facto private property rights, members of the Fair Play System had to figure out a way to secure legal title. To push things forward, they petitioned the Commonwealth government for legal recognition of their land claims (they called upon the state government because the Confederation Congress had no authority over land disposition in the Commonwealth). Their self-described enemies were land speculators, or as they described them, "some evil disposed persons" who "have lately sold the rights of other improvers in their absence" and also made private surveys. This conflict arose because during this time, the Commonwealth government was going about the business of legally resolving land conflicts, and with resolution came land sales to legal purchasers – thus thrusting the first settlers into conflict with the (new) formal owners. The "improvers" in this case were the squatters who had improved the land. Their petition, directed to the "Honorable Representatives of the Freemen of the Commonwealth of Pennsylvania," does an excellent job of illustrating moral appeals settlers made in defense of "squatters' rights" (Meginness 1892: 197–8):

> Your petitioners . . . have made very considerable improvements without having procured any officers' rights under the former government, and were at the beginning of the war obliged to abandon our farms and fly to the interior parts of the State for refuge, where we were under the necessity of selling our stock for the support of our families.
>
> We have lately understood that application has been made for the lands we have improved, and which we have defended at the risk of our lives. We humbly conceive that your honorable House will rather give the preference to those whose lives have been spent in endeavoring to procure an honest livelihood on lands which were unappropriated, and we do conceive that the merits of defending the frontiers and being the most active against the savages will have its due weight with your honorable House. All that your petitioners desire is to have your sanction for retaining our improvements, and that those only who have been tillers of the ground and livers on the land – their rights alone shall be deemed valid.

Their petition went on to ask for a committee to hear the claims of the "real improvers," and that "disinterested men" serve on the committee. The state legislature responded with an act granting these settlers preemption rights (Meginness 1892).

Successful collective action by squatters in Pennsylvania foreshadowed dozens of major preemption laws the federal government enacted in the nineteenth-century benefitting squatters on government-owned land in the public-land states. As Chapter 5 will argue, preemption laws, which allow squatters to acquire a legal title by virtue of prior occupation of land, are best understood through the lens of distributive conflict. At the same time, the state legislature's decision to reward squatters with land in Pennsylvania in the 1780s is a rather compelling example of what we can call the "economic case for free land," which is in its simplest sense an argument that the government can reduce its costs of policing borderlands by packing the land with settlers. Allen (1991) and Barzel (1989) used the Homestead Act of 1862 as an example, hypothesizing that free land reduced the costs to the federal government of policing borderlands by increasing population density in the Great Plains and beyond. Because the economic case for free land is an important thesis, I will make reference to it in this and several other chapters when the discussion warrants it.

Although Allen and Barzel confined attention to the Homestead Act, a public-policy rationale for awarding property rights to low-cost enforcers of borderlands actually emerged nearly one hundred years before homestead legislation. In their petition seeking legal title, squatters on disputed Indian lands in pre-Revolutionary Pennsylvania intimated that they were able to defend the borderlands from outside threats to established towns. In particular, members of this club produced one of the first policy arguments that free land could reduce the state's cost of policing borderlands as they were, in their words, "defending the frontiers and being the most active against the savages." What is interesting in this case is that the settlers packed the borderlands themselves, rather than waiting for the government to encourage them, so in this case a positive grant of legal title was more like a reward. As we will see later on in the book, homestead legislation was a prospective policy that gave land to those not yet on the land, while squatters' rights rewarded those who were on the land.

The issue of whether the government is rewarding those who settle land or prospectively attempting to encourage settlement is an important one. In terms of defending borderlands, the retrospective aspect of squatters' rights makes for a stronger case for free land than we have with homesteads, mainly because these settlers had proven their ability to defend the borderlands, while homesteaders had not.[4] That is to say, the economic case for free land makes more sense when free land is conceptualized of as a payment for *proven* ability to defend borderlands (which it would be with squatters' rights), as opposed to

[4] Although Barzel's and Allen's conjecture is intriguing, it suffers from several limitations. First, they likely overstate the security benefits created by homesteaders. It is not clear that most homesteaders could actually defend their land from Indian tribes because they oftentimes lacked organizations comparable to those of squatters. Thus, homesteads may have forced the government into defending borderlands in areas where there were a few homesteaders who were incapable of providing for their own defense. Second, economic defenses of homesteads pay little attention to important social costs of homesteads, two of which are particularly noteworthy. One is declining ability to provide public goods. By transferring scarcity rent to claimants at zero price, the state forgoes revenue from public land, which undermines revenue available to provide public goods, including security. Second, free land encouraged settlement of marginal frontier lands that ultimately dissipated asset value of land. These points are discussed more fully in Chapters 5 and 6.

hypothetical ability to defend land (as is the case with homestead legislation). In addition, to the extent squatters have proven themselves capable of doing the hard work of defending borderlands, rewarding them with legal title is also something of a payment, and so there is an equity rationale for it.

At the same time, although we might argue that squatters' rights (which are retrospective) are more defensible than homesteads (which are prospective), it is important to see that each is a land giveaway that need not reflect security considerations. Settlers would often jump the gun as far as legal settlement is concerned simply because it increased the chances that they could later secure a concession from the state. This tension between efficiency and rent-seeking is a recurrent theme in this book, one that seemingly emerged from the earliest moments of American economic history.

The Fair Play System is significant because it illustrates how governments emerged within the state to specify and enforce private property institutions. In contrast to decentralized norms, such as tomahawk and occupation rights, private property institutions arising within the Fair Play System required a stationary bandit for them to be effective. Yet the significance of this organization lies in its generalization. As settlers pushed west, they set their eyes on the fertile Midwestern lands. As we will see, squatters seeking new fields to till would perfect the organization features of the Fair Play System.

The Proliferation of Agricultural Claim Clubs

As interesting as the Fair Play System was, the truly astonishing feature of institutional and organizational transformation on agricultural land was how claim clubs spread like wildfire. The challenge in considering these changes is to characterize the key features of these clubs, as well as to understand why they arose. Before considering in greater detail their features, it is helpful to consider some of the reasons that led people to convene them.

In the most general sense, claim clubs were born in conflict of one sort or another: between competing claimants, between the state and squatters, and between squatters and various Indian tribes. Westerns and Hollywood accounts of the frontier devised an entire genre of conflict between settlers and Indians. In reality, the conflict of interests over land was often between competing settlers. Indeed, fear of land pirates bidding on land that a collection of squatters had already scoped out, or even improved, was perhaps the most important rationale why a club was convened. The preamble from one of these clubs from Wisconsin in the 1830s illustrates the extent to which members were concerned with land speculators[5]:

[5] Constitution of Pike's River Union, a claim club formed in 1837 in Wisconsin Territory. The complete constitution is produced in the *Wisconsin Legislative Assembly Journal*, 1856. The full preamble is included in the appendix to this chapter.

> And knowing, that in some instances our neighbors have been dealt with in an unfeeling manner, driven from their homes, their property destroyed, their persons attacked, and their lives jeopardized, to satisfy the malignant disposition of unprincipled and avaricious men; and looking upon such proceedings as unjust, calculated to produce anarchy, confusion and the like among us, destroy our fair prospects, subvert the good order of society, and render our homes the habitations of terror and distrust, agree to abide by and support the following constitution.

As we will see, what constitutes a "speculator" was often up for debate. As Bogue (1958) explained in his brilliant revisionist account of claim associations – revisionist in that it laid to rest earlier, romantic notions of the clubs as benevolent experiments in frontier democracy – members of claim clubs were often themselves speculators.[6] Thus, when a club spoke out against speculation, they often meant simply speculators who got there second. Nonetheless, it was typically the case that a speculator motivated development of a club, although what constituted a speculator was up for interpretation.

These conflicts between farmers and speculators, and between early-arriving and late-coming speculators, were some of the most pervasive dynamics on the frontier. For example, claim clubs near Chicago, Illinois, came together in response to increasing speculation after the conclusion of the Black Hawk War, which was itself a conflict over land. In May of 1832, Black Hawk led an army of Sauk Indians from Iowa in an effort to reclaim territory that the tribe had ceded to the federal government on behalf of white settlers in 1804 and 1830. By the time warring Indians returned to reclaim their ancestral land, squatters had already occupied it. In response, Illinois's governor called out the militia to defend against Black Hawk and his fellow warriors, and many squatters sent their families to Fort Dearborn in Chicago for protection (Richmond and Vallette 1857). Even though most of the men remained to defend claims, the population in Chicago declined from 450 to 370 from 1831 to 1832 in response to the threat from Indian tribes (Davis 1998).

Ultimately, the U.S. army won a decisive victory, in part because of alliances the government made with Indian tribes quarreling with the Sauk. Military historians remind us of the role of the armed forces in paving a path for emergence of claim clubs, for it was not the clubs that defeated their Indian adversaries, but rather the army (Hall 2009). Although it is easy to view settlers as taming the wilderness – the image of Daniel Boone crossing the Cumberland Gap of the Appalachians to get to Kentucky in the 1770s comes to

[6] One of the great debates in the economic history of frontier land concerns the profitability of land speculation, or whether it was even profitable at all. These debates are covered in remarkable detail by Swierenga (1977, 1966) and Bogue and Bogue (1957). My argument is not about the actual long-run profitability of speculation but, rather, the relationship between expected profit and emergence of claim clubs. For my argument to work, all that is required is a belief that land speculation would be profitable, which would be sufficient to establish clubs even if it turned out that the members of associations did not strike it rich. In other words, the expected increase in the price of land, rather than the actual price of land, drove formation of clubs.

mind – the Black Hawk War tells us they often had help. Rather, it was the government that cleared the Indian tribes from Illinois and the surrounding territory (Bogue 1963). Indeed, soldiers often helped the federal government provide security on the frontier (Prucha 1969).

The military puts claim clubs in perspective. The state may have been weak but it was strong enough to exclude some groups, notably Indians, from the land. The strength of the army vis-à-vis its competitors reduced an important constraint on settlement, not only legal settlement, but illegal and extralegal settlement as well. These accounts remind us that squatters had a lot of help that freed up space for them to mobilize.

All of this tells us that conflict with Indian tribes did not generate sufficient demand for clubs. As a more general matter, prior to the Black Hawk conflict, several factors reduced the demand for claim clubs: homogeneity among the initial settlers, coordination on the desirability of private ownership of land, military presence, and abundance of land. Each of these conditions changed with the conclusion of the Black Hawk War. Settlers were less homogenous in terms of their origins and occupations. There was also a fundamental conflict over the property regime between new groups of loggers, who viewed forests as private property, and farmers who viewed forests as common property the community could use to fit its needs. Demand for clubs also increased because the military had to move from Illinois to help defend ever-expanding borderlands.

Despite the importance of these changes, the most important one may have been an increase in scarcity in response to speculation. To get an idea about just how much it increased, we need only look to the data on land sales in Illinois. There were 266,448 acres sold by the land office in 1830, over two million in 1835, and a peak of over three million in 1836. Many of these acres were purchased by speculators, who came from all classes, from poor squatters to wealthy nonresidents (Hibbard 1924).

These increases in speculative activity led people to convene clubs, although for reasons already introduced, speculation itself was not a problem. Rather, farmers near Chicago looked down upon *nonresident* speculation. In fact, their clubs were an in-kind response to speculation, as nonresident speculators were actually the first group to establish claim clubs once the region was secured by the military.[7] In particular, a company referred to by local farmers in the region as the Land Pirate Company, which was nothing but a claim club formed by speculators to allocate and defend land they coveted, claimed four sections of the best timber land in what was known as Big Woods between 1832 and 1835.[8] Despite the fact that neither group had legal title, farmers demonized

[7] The details of claim club activities in the Chicago area are drawn from Richmond and Vallette (1857).

[8] As discussed in Chapter 1, a section of land is 640 acres (one square mile). Farmers usually claimed a quarter or a half section.

their competitors, establishing claim clubs to give force to their belief it was their land. In 1836, farmers at Big Woods responded with a club of their own, one that they hoped would protect their claims from speculators and settle disputes between squatters. A similar society called the Du Page Society for Mutual Protection sprang up in 1839.

Like clubs in other sectors, the Illinois claim clubs were covenants backed by the sword. Delegates of these associations brandished clubs to deter "anti-social" behavior at auctions, which for club members was a bid in excess of the minimum legal price of $1.25 (Davis 1998). Clubs viewed collusion as the best outcome for the group, and so anything that threatened the group's interests was punishable (and oftentimes punished).

Similar dynamics of competition between claim clubs influenced organizational transformation in Iowa, where claim clubs were convened by speculators and farmers alike. Indeed, it was inspection of all available records of the Iowa claim clubs that led Bogue (1958) to conclude "If we are to understand the role of the claim club, therefore, we must not confuse the symbols of agrarian democracy with its substance." For Bogue, the substance of Iowa's claim clubs was, more often than not, speculation.

Regardless of the long-term goals of members (speculation or agricultural pursuits), claim clubs in Iowa, like those elsewhere, required provisions for collective defense. To this end, anyone who was not in the club was declared an enemy, and whenever outsiders bid against a member of the club they were outlawed, if not beaten up or forced from a region. Claimants pledged never to borrow from speculators, lend to them, or associate with them.[9]

Moving west, claim clubs in Dane County, Wisconsin, were called "squatters' protective associations."[10] Much like their counterparts elsewhere, members were unforgiving when dealing with outsiders. According to one of these constitutions (included in the appendix to this chapter), violators would be rebuked "with such severity as has been common in the settlement of Western country." Members pledged to be ready to carry out the group's will, and there was a common set of procedures for dealing with outsiders. Whenever a land pirate occupied or bid on land claimed by a member of a claim club, a collection of squatters would bring a justice of the peace (appointed by the club) armed with a deed ready for the offender's signature. Squatters usually showed up carrying guns and ropes to convince the claim jumpers to settle quickly. Claim jumpers – which were defined broadly to include even those legally purchasing

[9] Several studies consider the Iowa claim clubs in depth, including Bogue (1958), Hibbard (1924), Paxson (1924), and Shambaugh (1894). The details in this paragraph draw on these sources.

[10] Clubs appear to have been common throughout the state. For example, there were also clubs that formed at Pike's River and in Milwaukee County. The constitution of the Milwaukee Claim Club is included in the appendix to this chapter, as is the preamble to the Pike's River Union.

land at auction – sometimes resisted. However, they did so with considerable risk, as the following account indicates (Hibbard 1905: 98):

> The committee exhausted verbal arguments...then putting a rope around the waist of the culprit, led him to a pond, cut a hole in the ice, and immersed him. He was soon drawn out, but being still in a combative and profane frame of mind, was treated to another dunking and on his second coming out was unable to continue his side of the debate.

The "culprit" in this case was someone who naively thought he could purchase a legal title to land that happened to be occupied by a club's member. Most interlopers relented to members of a club once they showed up to "discuss" matters (i.e., to enforce a club's self-proclaimed rules) because the alternative was oftentimes quite severe punishment (Hibbard 1905).

In Nebraska, penalties for crossing a claim club's members were similarly severe.[11] Claim jumping was a frontier crime of the highest order, and the club's courts were self-authorized to hear any case involving claim jumping. Offenders were required to relinquish all contested claims and no system for assessing fines – or even jails – existed. When a claim jumper failed to abide by a tribunal's decision, he or she was forcibly removed from the territory. More generally, when anyone attempted to acquire a legal title through a land office to territory that was already staked out by a club's member, the organization would respond swiftly and decisively, as the following account of the tactics used against someone who *legally* purchased land illustrates (Dick 1954: 27):

> The certified claimant was knocked down, tied, thrown into a wagon, and taken to a big cotton-wood tree. Here a rope was placed around his neck and he was told to say his last prayers. He was to be hanged at once unless he signed over the certificate. Inasmuch as he declined either to pray or to sign away his land, he was instantly suspended and allowed to hang for a time. He was then chopped down and as he still remained obstinate after regaining consciousness, the performance was repeated. He was still obdurate so that after a consultation the committee decided to lock him up, place a sentinel over him, and secure submission by starvation. After enduring extreme torment, the claimant sent for the captain of the club and signified his readiness to sign over the certificate which he had received from the land office and to sign a quit-claim deed.

Legal purchasers faced the prospect of signing a quit-claim deed – which is what club members often used to transact land – or risking death by holding out against the will of the assembly. In essence, they were given a choice between dealing in the bogus-yet-enforceable property deeds of a club and standing behind their government-issued legal title. Because the state was either

[11] See, for example, Sorenson's (1889) account of the constitutions of the Omaha Claim Club, which comprised most settlers in Omaha and Douglas Counties, and the Bellevue Claim Association.

nowhere to be seen or far in the background, many abandoned their legal claim to land.

Protecting property against speculators was a primary rationale for clubs, but it was not the only one. Claim clubs in Kansas, in contrast to the ones discussed so far, had two motivations. One is the standard rationale we have seen so far, which was making it possible for people to jump the gun as far as legal settlement was concerned. Pressure to open up Kansas Territory for settlement emerged almost as soon as the government allocated the same land for Indian settlement in 1830. In response to demands by white settlers to open the territory up to settlement, the federal government began renegotiating Indian treaties in hope of making new states that would quench would-be settlers' thirst for land, and in July of 1854, Congress responded to pressure by extending the Preemption Act of 1841, which granted squatters' rights to claimants on government-owned land, to Kansas and Nebraska.[12] Squatters, however, began to arrive in the region in February of 1854, before the government formally began assigning property rights to land (Gates 1954). As men, women, and children arrived, they often established claim clubs.[13]

That squatters violated the law should not be surprising. Settlers anticipated an extension of preemption to Kansas because Congress had already adopted dozens of "temporary" and small-scale preemption laws by 1854. That is, by the 1850s, Congress's commitment to competitive land auctions was no longer credible, with widespread and complete occupation of land in Kansas Territory a rather direct consequence of declining credibility of commitment to state ownership.

Yet there was also a second rationale for clubs popping up all over Kansas, one that was explicitly political: increasing support for the members' preferred constitution, either for or against slavery. Besides a desire to acquire land, people moving to Kansas from Missouri formed claim clubs in the hope of securing a pro-slavery constitution in the state. In 1854, for example, Missourians convened the Platte County Self-Defensive Association and other claim clubs inside the Kansas border in an attempt to influence support for slavery rather than to permanently relocate (Gladstone 1857). As in other states, competition for land increased demand for claim clubs to organize members for collective defense of their claims, yet in this case, one of the primary dimensions of conflict between squatters was a group's preference on the slavery issue, not simply land speculation. "Jayhawkers," a guerilla force who gave Border Ruffians a hard time at every turn, are perhaps the best known organizational weapons wielded in support of a free-state constitution.[14] However, claim clubs were perhaps the primary ones utilized in the struggle over slavery.

[12] These and other preemption laws are discussed in greater detail in Chapter 5.

[13] For an account of these clubs, which appear to have systematically covered the state prior to formally opening for settlement, see Cutler (1883).

[14] On the activities and tactics of the Jayhawkers, see especially Starr (1974).

Once it was clear that slavery would be determined by war rather than democracy, speculation took its usual place as the primary issue dividing competing claimants in Kansas. Claim clubs reemerged in the mid-1860s to combat speculation by railroad companies, which was perceived by settlers as illegitimate. Railroads were able to acquire over a hundred million acres of cheap land from the federal and state governments, often becoming powerful landholding companies because the land near their tracks was some of the best land.[15] Conflict was bound to occur not only because railroad land grants opened a fertile ground for speculation but also because railroads companies could not monitor all of the land they were granted, providing yet another opportunity for organized squatters to secure additional land.

For example, the Settlers' Protective Association of the State of Kansas (which was informally referred to as "The League") came into being in 1866 to defend squatters occupying railroad lands from outsiders who purchased title from railroad landholding companies. Eventually, land was sold by railroad companies to settlers in the East who arrived in Kansas unaware of the legal dispute. Easterners formed a new organization, called the Anti-Leaguers, with bloody conflict resulting (Dick 1970). Who won in these struggles is less important to the goal of this chapter than to simply observe that both parties to the conflict leaned on claim clubs to defend their land interests.

Although these clubs were capable of specifying and enforcing property institutions, it is important to keep in mind their ultimate purpose: securing legal title on terms favorable to members. In this regard, clubs were remarkably effective. For example, when land auctions were held at Burlington, Iowa, in 1840, there were at least eighteen local claim clubs representing 20,000 local farmers present for the auction. As each farmer secured at least 160 acres, sometimes more, claim clubs extracted at least three million acres of government land at the minimum legal price of $1.25 an acre – only $200 in total – even though it was some of the most fertile land in the country (Gates 1968; Tuttle 1876). In terms of today's dollars, the going price for a farmstead was only $5,200 – not a trivial price, but a small sum for 160 acres of excellent farmland.[16] Outcomes such as this lend support to the central argument of this book, which is that claim clubs provide insight into the origins of private property institutions, as well as why they change.

[15] Engerman (1972) considers the economics of the railroad land grants, while Fishlow (1965) and Fogel (1964) famously debated the economic consequences of railroads for economic development, each suggesting that railroads were not as important for economic development as previously thought. More recently, White (2011) argues that the transcontinental railroad would never have been built so early without a tremendous amount of pressure from railroad interests. Each of these perspectives recognizes how rent-seeking drove development of railroads, and so it should not be surprising that the impact of railroads for development was not as great as is often assumed in popular accounts of railroads as the fundamental engines of development during the nineteenth century.

[16] This calculation uses real price data and a base year of 1840. The desired year is 2010.

The Constitution of Agricultural Clubs

Agricultural claim clubs cropped up over a tremendously large geographic area. Nonetheless, these associations had common functions. Based on my inspection of constitutions of these clubs from various states as well as all major historical studies that have included examples of claim club constitutions, there were eight main features of these clubs:

1) Regulation of claim size.
2) Occupancy requirements.
3) Provisions for trade in claims.
4) Provisions for participation in collective defense.
5) Political institutions.
6) Judicial institutions.
7) Procedures to change rules.
8) Democratic procedures.

Together, these eight characteristics represent the constitution of agricultural claim clubs. As explained below, it was difficult to find associations that did not have provision on each of these dimensions. These features are explained more fully below.

1. *Regulation of claim size*: One of the defining features of agricultural claim clubs was regulation of claim size. Clubs typically imposed a ceiling on landholding to deter large-scale speculation. However, clubs also allowed people to attain economies of scale relative to federal land programs by typically permitting members to claim between 160 and 480 acres. In contrast, federal programs only allowed people to enter a claim of 160 acres. The fact that claim club members often took claims in excess of 160 acres suggests that federal land laws imposed inexpedient size constraints.

In addition, many clubs adapted regulations to local conditions. For example, claim clubs in Dane County, Wisconsin, allowed each person to claim 160 acres of farmland as well as 40 acres of timberland. As another example, the Canon City claim clubs in Colorado allowed a mill operator to claim 640 acres of timberland, while a town company seeking to organize land for a town could claim 1,280 acres provided the claim did not infringe on any member of the club.[17] Each of these features illustrates a general function of claim clubs, which was regulating claim size.

2. *Occupancy requirements*: Agricultural claim clubs typically had provisions requiring occupancy. One of the reasons why occupancy was

[17] Anderson (1939, 1936) provides an account of several of Colorado's clubs, as well as their actual constitutions.

required was to deter speculation by those deemed by a club to be "outsiders." As we have seen, clubs generally looked on absentee ownership negatively. Under a claim club's constitution, claim size was larger than federal rules required, yet smaller than acreages that speculators dealt in, and an owner had to occupy it. People could speculate, but those who decided to partake had to keep it to a fairly small scale.

To the extent occupancy requirements were enforced, they had social costs. An occupation requirement forces people to stand guard over their property. Indeed, several clubs seem to have anticipated the costs of occupancy requirements. For example, farmers at Cherry Creek Valley in Colorado permitted anyone over the age of fifteen to claim land and required improvement of $50 within 50 days with $25 of improvements to be added during each succeeding quarter – each a typical feature of a club – yet this particular club also allowed claimants to be absent for six months for a fee of $100. In today's dollars, this amounted to a fairly sizable deposit of about $2,700.[18] This was overall a use-it-or-lose-it property regime, with the associated costs of such a regime. However, the last provision, one that allowed people to be absent from their land for a fee, reduced the need for people to continuously watch over their possessions. Requiring a fee to leave land was also socially beneficial because it allowed people to commit credibly to their desire to stay in a region. Nonetheless, agricultural claim clubs generally required occupancy for one to remain a member in good standing.

3. *Provisions for trade in claims*: Agricultural claim clubs generally had provisions for trade, which is one of the main dimensions of a property regime. Settlers could buy and sell claims, provided other members of the organization approved a purchaser. Quit-claim deeds mentioned above were an informal fee-simple legal title sufficient to allow buying and selling of claims. For example, Iowa's claim clubs allowed nearly anything to be traded, provided trading parties were approved by the club.[19]

The main economic reason why trade provisions are important is to attain allocational efficiency. For a property regime to be effective in terms of allocative efficiency, claimants whose marginal benefit of ownership is highest acquire land. Thus, trade is desirable from this perspective.

The aforementioned rationale is, of course, subject to certain assumptions about the nature of the transactions. If there are externalities in trade markets, then restrictions on trade are desirable. These restraints on trade may have been reasonable regulations to the extent speculation is a "public bad."

[18] This calculation uses 1860 as the base year. The desired year is 2010.

[19] The various sources on Iowa claim clubs cited above provide insight into norms governing trade.

To the extent they represented a basic system of zoning, such provisions remind us that clubs presided over emergence of managed trade rather than free trade.

4. *Provisions for participation in collective defense*: Agricultural claim clubs had to defend the interests of members from outsiders. This was a challenge for the group, as it sometimes involved over a hundred men showing up to deter outsiders from bidding on land claimed by club members. For example, members of Nebraska's Omaha Claim Club, which formed in July of 1854, reaffirmed their pact to defend claims in response to an increasing number of individuals claiming land under the aegis of Congressional approval in 1857. To carry their will, armed groups of men, numbering 100 to 150, showed up whenever anyone challenged their intentions (Sorenson 1889). As we have seen, these were legal claims, yet might made right, and legal claimants usually elected to move elsewhere rather than fight with a club.

There were various ways clubs ensured compliance with rules. Claim jumping was even used as a penalty by clubs to enforce compliance with a club's rules. For example, it was common in some of the claim clubs in Illinois to encourage claim jumping when a member violated a club's norms (Davis 1998). A supply of potential claim jumpers increased incentives to abide by a club's rules because noncompliance opened one up to jumpers. More generally, presence of a club was a source of a reputation that meant its anticipated response often allowed members to get what they wanted without a fight.

5. *Political institutions*: One of most important features of a club was presence of clearly defined political institutions. Club constitutions typically established a president, vice president, secretary, and a board of directors of the club. Although names sometimes differed between clubs, functions were essentially the same. The Pike's River Union of Wisconsin, for example, divided authority between a chairman, a clerk, and twelve censors (see the appendix to this chapter). The chairman was the leader of the organization, elected by common consent, and the clerk recorded the organization's business as well as claim locations. Censors were the club's judges, and they were endowed with authority to make fines after trials. People who did not attend as witnesses were debarred from a club's protection as well as its benefits. To use another example, the Bellevue Claim Association in Nebraska consisted of a president, two vice presidents, a register, and a marshal, and a committee of five authorized to decide all disputed claims subject to an appeal from the association (Dick 1954). Clubs paid a marshal three dollars a day for service, paid by the party obtaining redress.

These provisions represented the origins of basic political institutions. These features of clubs are the reason why they are best described as governments within a state. However, clubs also required judicial institutions to truly rival the state.

6. *Judicial institutions*: One of the most important features of claim clubs was an informal legal apparatus that typically included judges as well as juries. Members agreed to abide by decisions of an organization, including those by their "courts." The constitution of the Milwaukee Claim Club, which is included in the appendix to this chapter along with several other claim club constitutions, specified an elected Board of Arbitrators consisting of five members that was authorized to hear cases arising under the club's auspices. In the event of disputes over land, a jury would oversee deliberations. In order to give force to the law, members agreed to fund any enforcement activities of the Board of Arbitrators.

As with political institutions, judicial institutions had similar functions despite different names. In Kansas, many of these organizations referred to their lawmen as "vigilance committees," which were typically organizations consisting of at least ten members of the association who could decide all disputed claims.[20] Importantly, a vigilance committee generally had the power to call together an entire squatters' association. Such powers were important in enforcing an association's rules.

There were nonetheless undesirable elements as far as legal reckoning was concerned in some regions and time periods. In Kansas Territory, for example, it was not uncommon for vigilance committees to engage in frontier "justice" through mobs. Such examples could certainly call into question claim clubs as organizations of social control.

It would be a mistake to infer that there was no law within a club, or that law was ad hoc, simply because a club also relied upon the machinery of vigilantism. There was also a highly regularized system for resolving disputes *within* a club. When assessing clubs from the perspective of rule of law, it is important to keep two things in mind. First, it is clear from constitutions of claim clubs that ad hoc mobs were not the only source of justice, in particular in dealing with relations among club members. Rather, judges and juries from the club dealt with many property issues arising between members as well as non-members. This distinction will come up again in the discussion of the mining frontier, where claimants typically had two types of judicial institutions in many regions: the miners' court, which was highly regularized, and the people's court, which was not so regularized, and closer to what we think of as a mob.

Second, it is uncontroversial to assert that formal law left much to be desired in this period. In order to assess claim clubs, it is necessary to compare clubs not to an ideal system of procedural justice but to the formal legal institutions

[20] There are several excellent accounts of vigilance committees, in particular Langford (1957), Dimsdale (1949), Gard (1949), McConnell (1926), and Gladstone (1857).

on the frontier that people would have to work through if not for the clubs. Komesar (2001, 1997) stresses the importance of comparing actual institutions (what he calls "imperfect alternatives") rather than existing institutions with some hypothetical, "optimal," or idealized ones. Komesar's insights ring especially true when assessing claim clubs as political and legal institutions, as well as when we assess clubs as frontier democracies. By comparing imperfect alternatives – clubs versus highly imperfect local governments of the day – clubs do quite well as a stand-in for the state.

Of course, there is also a case to be made that even the vigilance committees were expedient. Dimsdale's (1949) account of these committees in Montana is relevant to understanding the logic of vigilance committees more generally, as the associations were similar in each state. Dimsdale (1949) opens his account with following thought experiment:

> Let the reader suppose that the police of New York were withdrawn for twelve months, and then let them picture the wild saturnalia which would take the place of the order that reigns their now. If, then, it is so hard to restrain the dangerous classes of old and settled communities, what must be the difficulty of the task, when, tenfold in number, fearless in character, generally well armed, and supplied with money to an extent unknown among their equals in the east, such men find themselves removed from the restraints of civilized society, and beyond the control of the authority which there enforced obedience to the law?

The task of justice, in other words, is much more challenging in frontier situations than it is in established communities. Dimsdale went on to explain that vigilance committees, which were highly secretive and informal, were actually quite effective in preventing violence:

> In a few short weeks it was known that the voice had just spoken, in tones that might not be disregarded. The face of society was changed, as if by magic; for the Vigilantes, holding in one hand the invisible yet effective shield of protection, and in the other, the swift descending and inevitable sword of retribution, struck from his nerveless grasp the weapon of the assassin; commanded the brawler to cease from strife; warned the thief to steal no more; bade the good citizen to take courage, and compelled the ruffians and marauders who had so long maintained the "reign of terror" in Montana, to fly the Territory, or meet the just rewards of their crimes. Need we say that they were at once obeyed? Yet not before more than one hundred valuable lives had been pitilessly sacrificed and twenty-four miscreants had met a dog's doom as the reward of their crimes.

Dimsdale's account of vigilance committees is unrivaled, and so it must be taken seriously. Yet even if one accepts that vigilance associations were expedient, it is also possible to conclude club courts were also expedient, as well as different from vigilance committees. Taken together, the club courts and vigilance committees provide insight into the diversity of modes of legal reckoning during a period in which the state clearly lacked a monopoly on coercion, as well as the various ways nonstate legal institutions provided a forum for justice.

7. *Procedures to change rules*: Claim clubs defined political and legal institutions, each of which are important in terms of constitutional procedures. Organizations must also have built-in procedures to respond to new problems to be effective (North 2005; Ostrom 2005). Provisions for changes in the rules are particularly important in frontier environments because they are some of the most dynamic regions of a country as far as institutions are concerned (Alston et al. 1999).

Clubs generally had provisions for modifying the rules. For example, the Canon City Claim Club in Colorado set up a procedure to amend rules by two-thirds vote.[21] Clubs in Wisconsin and Iowa had similar rules, allowing members to change the rules when they showed up to vote on procedures as a collective body. Indeed, such procedures to change the rules of a club appear to have been one of the defining features of these organizations.

8. *Democratic procedures*: Procedural democracy was the final general feature of agricultural claim clubs. In essentially all constitutions I came across, members of "official" positions were often elected by common consent, as were judges. There were also juries, which are generally considered democratic committees. In addition, the procedures for calling together members of a club were democratic. For example, each of the claim clubs surveyed in Wisconsin allowed meetings to be called at any time by any members with proper notice. The Canon City Claim Club in Colorado allowed for a meeting to be called by the president or by any five members. The claim clubs of Iowa, Nebraska, and Illinois also had these features. Decentralized participation in meetings helped ensure that clubs were responsive to changing conditions.

Of course, a large literature from economics and political science tells us that the mere presence of democracy need not produce socially desirable public policies.[22] However, if Calvert (2006) is correct that democracies reduce arbitrariness of decisions or increase incentives to follow rules once they are agreed on, then participatory procedures within claim clubs may have been socially desirable in the sense that they made it more likely that members would abide by the rules that members agreed upon. In other words, democratic procedures may not have produced efficient institutional choices, but likely increased the enforceability of their rules. Enforceability, in turn, is desirable in its own right, and should be considered along with efficiency as a desirable goal of a social system.

These eight functions characterizing agricultural claim clubs can be further divided into two categories. The first three functions involve regulation of

[21] Many of the constitutions that were published in the *Rocky Mountain News* in the late 1850s and early 1860s had these types of procedures.

[22] For an excellent review of alternative perspectives on democratic institutions, see Caplan (2007).

property institutions. Getting the details of property institutions was certainly important during this period, and these three functions went a long way in improving property relations. However, the last five functions were political features of clubs. Clubs, in other words, were both property systems and a political systems. In contrast with economic studies of informal order, which generally consider features of economic institutions without considering explicitly their informal political origins, it seems clear that political development is perhaps the defining feature of property relations on the agricultural frontier.

It is also useful here to pause to consider how claim clubs also contrast with Ostrom's (2005, 1990) common-property regimes. One difference is that claim clubs were a source of private property institutions rather than co-ownership. Second, claim clubs emerged rapidly in response to changing conditions and were consciously designed, which contrasts with long-standing, evolutionary processes emphasized in Ostrom's studies of the commons. Third, self-governing organizations on the agricultural frontier shared much more in common with a modern government than Ostrom's traditional systems for managing resources. The political economy of agricultural claim clubs thus complements the political economy of common-property regimes while also reminding us of the importance of considering self-governing *private* property regimes.

The Demise of Agricultural Claim Clubs

Agricultural claim clubs were pervasive, permitting people to claim land in the state's shadow wherever land was valuable. These clubs knew no geographic boundaries. Yet we also know that the clubs at some point ceased to exist. What happened to them?

For the most part, farmers' protective associations faded away once members secured legal title, which was the primary objective of a club's members. They secured legal title in two ways: either by colluding during land auctions or through government policies recognizing squatters' rights; they were remarkably successful in this regard, as Part II of this book will show. Acquiring a legal title from the state usually meant that these settlers no longer had to worry about their chief rivals on the frontier – new waves of squatters or land speculators. For this reason, a club was usually a moribund institution once members secured a legal title.

Some might view clubs as insignificant because, in the grand scheme of history, they were arguably fleeting, typically governing economic activities for less than a decade – sometimes just for a couple years. Claim clubs in Colorado, for example, first sprang up in 1859. In 1861, Colorado Territory was formally recognized, the first legislature made provisions for county organization, and Indian titles and claims to land were extinguished. Surveys were made in 1862 and an act of Congress extended preemption to Colorado as well as established a system to regulate preemption on unsurveyed lands. Clubs were successful in getting what members desired yet they were no longer necessary after 1862–3.

Of course, if we step back far enough in terms of historical time frame, then nearly all substantive organizations and institutions appear fleeting. A more appropriate standard to evaluate the significance of organizations and institutions lies in their consequences. Judged in this way, the temporary existence of claim clubs in no way undermines their significance and in fact affirms their importance. Private-order systems existed for a short time because they were remarkably successful in achieving their political and economic objectives. In Kansas, for example, claim clubs were so pervasive and effective that most of the desirable land in the state was allocated informally within months. This process of informally allocating land also had tremendous distributional implications. In particular, the state lost out on revenue opportunities as tens of thousands of squatters colonized the state, ensuring that Congress had little choice but to give them a title to land they occupied.

All told, the fact that they existed for only a short time should be interpreted as a sign of their strength because it meant they were overwhelmingly successful. A more accurate assessment is that farmers' protective associations, and claim clubs more generally, were so remarkably effective in sweeping away the American state that they were only necessary for a relatively short period. As we will see, this logic applies equally to the other sectors under consideration – sectors in which members got what they wanted through clubs before disbanding them after they served their purpose.

MINERAL LAND

In every way, the claim clubs devised by miners rivaled agricultural claim clubs. Like claim clubs, mining districts were defined by a combination of informal political institutions and private property institutions. As the following accounts show, the mining frontiers of California and Nevada provide additional insight into the origins of property institutions as well as governments. Similar to the empirical study of agricultural claim clubs, the account that follows seeks to provide manageable detail sufficient to test alternative hypotheses. Interested readers are directed to historical studies of the gold frontier that inform the discussion that follows.[23]

Claim Clubs and the California Gold Rush

Before considering development of property institutions on mineral land, it is useful to clarify how my interpretation of claim clubs on mineral land differs from Umbeck's (1981, 1977) insightful studies of property institutions on California's gold fields. One of Umbeck's contributions was to recognize

[23] Some of the most thorough accounts include Gates (1991) and Paul (2001).

that the California gold rush is as close as we come to an experiment in the origins of property institutions because, he argues, there were essentially no property institutions prior to those established by miners.[24] This clever observation regarding the experimental characteristics of California's political and legal environment provided a nice research design to study the origins of private property institutions.

Umbeck's otherwise pathbreaking account can be clarified in two ways. First, claim clubs were not the only source of property institutions in California in the 1840s and 1850s. Indeed, many people in California had legal title to land and the state formally owned mineral land during this period. Claim clubs ignored formal law in specifying and enforcing property institutions, suggesting the mining frontier is most appropriately characterized by emergence of a different, or parallel, system of private property institutions rather than an example of private property institutions arising in a "state of nature." To be sure, the state was weak, but California was by no means a situation devoid of institutions.

Accurately describing the institutional status quo is important to understanding the consequences of claim clubs in terms of efficiency or distributive perspectives on institutional change. If clubs were a response to poorly designed, weak, or predatory formal institutions, then a case could be made that clubs were socially desirable source of change in property institutions. In contrast, if clubs essentially ignored property institutions when the formal rules did not fit their interests, then a distributive interpretation of claim clubs may be more appropriate. For reasons presented below, I argue that squatters on mineral land are more appropriately viewed as distributive coalitions because they disregarded existing law for self-interested purposes. This rationale, introduced in this chapter, will be considered in much greater depth in the discussion of institutional change in Part II of the book.

Second, and more importantly to the task of this chapter and the next one, Umbeck's study underemphasizes the role of informal political institutions in the origins of property institutions on the gold fields. Part of the reason is that Umbeck did not clearly distinguish between mining camps and mining districts – a transition that involved the origins of basic political institutions. Our understanding of emergence of private property institutions during the gold rush can be improved by explicitly considering how informal political institutions made possible the emergence of private property institutions.

Returning to the first point above, the institutional status quo during the gold rush was primarily state and private ownership of mineral land. In particular, state ownership was the defining feature of the property regime. During the

[24] Umbeck's perspective has been challenged elsewhere for different reasons, most notably by Clay and Wright (2010, 2005), who argue that property institutions on the gold fields left much to be desired, even suggesting that the gold rush did not even produce a private property regime. I contrast my findings with Clay and Wright's perspective later on in this chapter.

period in which the mining sector emerged in California, the government formally owned all mineral land discovered and yet to be discovered – a provision that would only be repealed with the Mining Act of 1866, nearly two decades after the discovery of gold.

During a period in which the state had few means to attain revenue, minerals provided an important resource. Indeed, state officials attempted to create a system to ensure it profited from its mineral wealth. After the Mexican War from 1846 to 1848, the formal property regime in California was initially a system of lease rights to mineral land that provided the state with a potential source of revenue from land. However, the leasing policy was repealed in 1846 and 1847, when a system of competitive allocation of property rights to mineral land was substituted, with a minimum lot size of 40 acres at an auction. In addition, in 1851, Congress authorized all land to be classified as "mineral" and "nonmineral" to facilitate allocation through competitive auctions (Paul 1966, 1947; Clawson 1951).

Consistent with Levi's (1988) perspective that the state's fundamental objective is raising revenue, the state established a framework to profit from its mineral lands. In this case, creating private property institutions was the means to profiting from land. Even though the Mining Act would not emerge until 1866, decentralization of ownership occurred much earlier than 1866, in particular when the government established a framework for people to lease and (later) to purchase land for private use.

It is easy to see that there were potentially important fiscal consequences hanging in the balance of how the government decided to allocate mineral land. In terms of the overall context, revenue from mineral land was important because the federal government had few other options during much of the nineteenth century besides tariffs or land sales. In an environment of highly imperfect mechanisms to collect taxes, competitive land auctions promised to increase government revenue to provide public goods.

As one might anticipate given the developments recounted on agricultural land, the government proved incapable or unwilling to rebuff squatters seeking access to mineral lands. By 1850, informal property regimes emerged within the confines of claim clubs throughout California. Squatters occupied land without legal title in order to extract land rents without paying for the privilege to mine gold.

From an analytical perspective, the problem with the formal property regime was that it was not self-enforcing. Because the logic of self-enforcing institutions was discussed in Chapter 2, it is sufficient here to remind ourselves that the defining feature of self-enforcing institutions is that all relevant individuals have incentives to abide by the rules, including enforcers (police, the state, and so on) as well as duty bearers (individuals whose behavior is regulated by rules). The formal mining regime was anything but self-enforcing in the sense that none of the relevant actors had incentives to abide by formal rules: government officials neglected to fund enforcement activities, enforcers had few incentives to abide by rules that were on the books, and squatters had few incentives to respect anyone's property rights except those that arose within the confines of their clubs.

One of the most powerful forces working against the formal property regime (state and private ownership) was the belief common among squatters that they had a right to use land formally owned by others, not only state-owned land but also land that was owned by private claimants. Miners declared war on those who opposed what they called "free mining," rejecting not only state ownership but also legal title held by nonminers. In their eyes, mining was the highest-value economic activity, and therefore the only legitimate economic activity. Their deeply held beliefs emboldened and coordinated them in their effort to capture the land for themselves.

The struggle over John A. Sutter's lands, which is a focal point in the many conflicts between owners and squatters in California, illustrates how squatters undermined legal title. Sacramento's squatter war was tied to Sutter, who had established an estate he called "New Helvetia" in the years preceding discovery of gold.[25] Sutter's estate had feudal characteristics, with his workers on hand to defend his lands against outsiders in exchange for payment and protection. One of the features of feudal arrangements is participation in defense of a lord, and Sutter was the New World version of a lord if there was one. Yet even a powerful landholder such as Sutter was overmatched by the "barbarians at the gates," as he certainly would have viewed squatters. By 1849, Sutter was besieged by squatters, but had to wait for a formal government to meet before he could seek protection from the state, as the first state legislature did not convene until December 1849. As soon as it convened, Sutter petitioned the military government for protection from squatters. His demands were at first ignored, although the city council later prohibited squatters from defending themselves in court and required all lots to be marked by the city surveyor. In response, squatters made a pact to disregard all adverse political and legal decisions, and vowed to only respect land claims of those who never took up arms against squatters.

Umbeck, in devising his theory of the origins of property institutions, claimed that the mining frontier had no formal law. However, squatters in Sacramento did not face a condition of lawlessness. There were local governments in place, and even a basic system of zoning by 1849. The federal government may not have had a strong presence, but there was clearly a local/state government. Squatters were not forced to devise their own institutions in a "state of nature." After all, property institutions, both private and state-owned, already existed in California! Rather, squatters devised competing institutions because it permitted them to extract scarcity rent associated with mineral land without paying it.

Although the institutional status quo may have been more crowded than economic studies of the origin of property rights to mineral land allow, it is undeniable that squatters were remarkably effective in establishing their own

[25] The details of Sutter's predicament are drawn from Pisani (1996, 1994) and Paul (1966).

system of governance. They were able to push the state aside, and in the process replace it with something that looked a lot like a state. This leads us back to the second point introduced earlier: what made informal private property institutions self-enforcing? Umbeck, who understood quite well the property institutions arising during the gold rush, did not explicitly consider emergence of basic political institutions. To understand the importance of political institutions in emergence of property institutions, it is necessary to conceptually clarify differences between mining camps and districts.

Mining Camps: The First Organizations on the Gold Fields

As introduced earlier, there were two organizational systems for claiming land on various mining frontiers in the mid-nineteenth century: mining camps and mining districts. Mining camps were collective organizations that consisted of a small group of men who agreed to share in the value of their claims. The mining camps, in the early period of the gold rush, had no overarching structure beyond the camp. Mining districts, in contrast, imposed order over hundreds of mining camps and thousands of people. The fundamental difference between camps and districts was presence of political institutions in districts: mining districts were frontier quasi-governments; in contrast, mining camps lacked any real political features.

Mining camps were nonetheless important because they were the first organizations convened to manage access to California's gold fields. Umbeck (1981) recounted a soldier's description of the process of forming a mining camp during the early days of the gold rush, which began when a small group of men wrote down a set of rules that they agreed to live under. Camps usually consisted of groups of three, five, or ten men. Generally speaking, a group drew up rules and agreed to bear an equal share of all expenses incurred, to proceed together to the gold mines together (none was allowed to separate from the group), that if separation became necessary the person leaving would take out an amount of goods equal to the original investment, and to purchase tools in common. Members agreed to stand by each other in all circumstances, never to abandon sick members, and to share in the provision of small-scale public goods, such as chopping wood, cooking, and fetching water. Finally, they agreed that anyone guilty of thievery would be banished and lose his investment.

Substantively, property norms during the early months of the gold rush involved sharing rules as well as first possession. Sharing norms involved equal division of the gains from high-value lodes among a small collection of miners. Oftentimes, members of mining camps agreed to work a lode and share in the fruits of their collective labor. Substantively, sharing norms governed behavior within a camp, while relations between camps were regulated by first-possession norms. When seeking out a new spot in which to set up camp, a group would move to alternative locations when another small group of miners physically occupied land. Individuals were content to move to another region when territory was occupied even though there was no forum for agreement on rules beyond the confines of a camp (Zerbe and Anderson 2001; Umbeck 1981, 1977).

The early mining camps, despite providing a basic way to allocate access to minerals, were at best a weak system of private property. Umbeck concluded the mining camps during the early months of the gold rush fell short on the dimension of excludability:

> In the first 6 months after the initial discovery [of gold], the size of the known gold fields increased from a small area around Sutter's mill to an area covering over 10,000 square miles. For the early miners, it was apparently less costly to move to a new discovery than to use violence to acquire someone else's mining rights. As long as gold land remained relatively abundant, small groups of miners found the sharing arrangement to be the most economical. I can find no contracts, in 1848, in which it was agreed to assign and enforce an individual's exclusive rights to a given parcel of gold land (1977: 213).

The system of sharing rules seems to have prevented violence and facilitated production during the first year after gold was discovered. There were nearly 10,000 people who entered California in 1848 with hopes of striking it rich but several authoritative accounts suggest there was almost no crime in areas where gold was discovered. Shinn's (1885) first-hand account published after the conclusion of the gold rush in California claimed that crime was unknown in the first months of the gold rush. Nor did Umbeck uncover evidence that there was a great deal of either crime or property insecurity in that period. Simple organizations and first-possession norms appear to have been effective in allocating access to minerals.

If these accounts are to be believed (and I have no reason to doubt them), then the next question to ask is why political institutions were unnecessary during the first months of the gold rush. There are several plausible answers to this question. One was a relatively small number of miners in a region. In addition, mineral may have had characteristics of a free good during this period, one in which there is positive supply even when there are no property institutions.[26] Small numbers meant that the first property arrangements required no real division of authority and so they did not represent emergence of bandits within the state. Rather, small-scale mining camps arising during the initial months of the gold rush are perhaps most accurately described as what Alston et al. (2011) call "commons associations," which they defined as informal associations that manage access to a common-pool resource.[27] Indeed, mining camps were simple property systems that arose to manage access to a common-pool resource.

[26] On characteristics of free goods, see Weimer and Vining (2010).

[27] Clay and Wright (2005) and Grossman (2001) also view institutions arising during the gold rush as essentially a system for managing access to a commons.

Mining Districts: The Political Origins of Property Institutions on the Gold Fields

Sharing rules were important institutions but they did not last long. Umbeck concludes "This particular contractual arrangement [sharing rules] did not last very long, probably because it failed to assign exclusive rights to a scarce resource. As I have already discussed, in the absence of exclusive rights the income generated by the resource tends to dissipate" (1977: 212). Umbeck, whose study clearly recognizes the importance of exclusive contracting institutions, did not clarify *why* excludable contracts were effective requires us to take into account presence or absence of political institutions. The defining organizational feature of the system of sharing rules was lack of excludability as well as absence of political institutions comparable to agricultural claim clubs. As economic development commenced, political institutions were necessary to impose order on miners as they colonized the gold fields. In this regard, the key feature of the mining district was presence of political institutions that would ultimately make property institutions self-enforcing.

Mining districts were substantially more complex political entities than sharing systems consisting of five to ten miners. The constitution from the mining district that formed in Kelsey district in 1856, which is reproduced in Umbeck's study of property rights, captures the critical features of a mining district. The rules of the Kelsey district specified size of claims, granted ownership to discoverers, appointed a recorder to write down all mining claims, required all to make claims within five days with the recorder, imposed a work requirement, required that only miners would arbitrate disputes, and created a fee for recording claims.

The organization arising at Kelsey was a claim club because it had political institutions that rivaled formal city governments on the frontier. In my framework, the defining features of a claim club are property institutions *and* political institutions. The rise of claim clubs, as well as a system of political institutions, suggests that mining camps were ill equipped to manage land relations effectively after the initial months of the gold rush. Governments were necessary to manage land relations effectively once miners' societies began to mature in terms of heterogeneity of claimants and expectations. These governments, however, were not formally part of the state but rather emerged within the state.

Mining districts had a similar structure. Umbeck listed key features of these organizations based on his inspection of 200 constitutions: definite boundaries of a district, assignment of exclusive rights to individuals, rules regulating maximum claim size, conditions required to keep a right, regulation on maximum claim size, and some means of enforcement.[28] Because Umbeck has done the

[28] Clay and Wright (2010) argue that there were provisions allowing claim jumping that undermined the exclusivity of this system. Their argument certainly seems plausible, although its

service of collecting constitutions from California, it is not necessary to provide additional evidence regarding the features of mining districts that arose in that state during the gold rush. Rather, it is sufficient to observe what Umbeck left out of his list of key features of mining districts, namely, their political features. To the list above, several additional features must be added, in particular a system of leadership and administration, an informal judicial system, a system of trade, and democracy (or what could reasonably be described as democracy as it was popularly understood in the mid-nineteenth century). Each of these features represented the origins of government, and it is precisely government formation that made property arrangement on the gold fields self-enforcing.

Sened (1997) anticipated the argument made in this book in suggesting Umbeck was describing government formation rather than emergence of property rights. However, Sened did not explicitly consider the possibility of people creating their own governments in order to specify and enforce property institutions that would compete with the state. Indeed, Sened's observation is a footnote; rather than a footnote, it is perhaps the key to understanding the origins of property institutions on the California gold frontier. Rather, Sened's state is all powerful, and it exists prior to the origins of property institutions. A more precise statement of the situation in California is that private property rights and political institutions emerged at the same time and that the development of informal political institutions made property arrangements self-enforcing in the state's shadow.

Claim Clubs, Property Institutions, and Nevada's Mining Boom

In Nevada, the first property regimes arising with the discovery of silver were poorly defined, falling far short on dimensions of excludability.[29] Increases in mineral value led to ownership uncertainty and widespread claim jumping. Nonetheless, a show of force was usually sufficient for an owner to reclaim his property.

Eventually, population growth led to transaction costs that increased the demand for governments. Discovery of valuable minerals led to a substantial increase in the number of people in Nevada, as well as increasing diversity – groups included miners, merchants, gamblers, and prostitutes. As more miners showed up hoping to strike it rich, regulations appeared for laying out streets and collecting taxes by consent of the miners. Recognizing their mutual interest in forming associations, people agreed on rules that would govern members of

resolution is irrelevant to my central point, which is that neither Umbeck nor Clay and Wright appreciate political development on the gold fields.

29 The details of mining in Nevada are drawn primarily from Eliot Lord's (1959 [1881]) participant observation account as well Smith's (1973) excellent account of the development of the Rocky Mountain mining industry.

a mining district. As a constitutional system, mining districts standardized the more haphazard rules of mining camps by creating a system that rivaled a local government.

A claim club that emerged at Gold Hill, one of the districts associated with the discovery of the Comstock Lode, illustrates key features of mining organizations in Nevada. When ore was first discovered, mining camps had a simple structure. Miners did not acknowledge any arbiter, and claims to a valuable mineral deposit (known as "placer claims") were apportioned based on prior occupation or a sharing rule. During this period, occupying land was more important than a mining district's rules. A constitution was often agreed upon by common consent on arrival to a new region but miners did not pay much attention to these rules, as it was acceptable for a majority to decide to ignore rules. Shifting populations undermined legitimacy of any prior agreements. Informal institutions were not self-enforcing, and there was not much in the way of formal authority. Lord (1959 [1881]), in his first-hand account of the boom years in Nevada, traced the deficit of formal authority to the exodus of Mormon settlers who had provided political and legal order, but when they left the region in 1857 in response to the unruly conditions of Western Utah, their departure left miners without governments or judges.

As miners continued to arrive in large numbers, they recognized a need for organizations with a well-defined structure to regulate access to valuable mineral deposits. In 1859, for example, miners at Gold Hill agreed to rules defining criminal behavior, a property system, and a basic system of governance. Their constitution, which is included in this chapter's appendix, was a pact to limit lawlessness in their "isolated position far from legal tribunals." Their club included a justice of the peace, a constable, and a recorder of deeds. The framers of this club's constitution set out procedures to claim land, along with an occupation requirement. Similar to California's clubs, the district's rules established basic political institutions.

Clubs also wielded their power to exclude certain groups. Although all citizens were expected to join, Chinese miners were prohibited from the district (Smith 1973). It is worthwhile to consider briefly the nature and significance of the exclusion of Chinese miners from these districts.

These anti-Chinese regulations were frontier forerunners to "exclusionary zoning." Zoning regulations, which are part of the state's police powers, can be socially desirable to the extent they are a response to economic externalities. These powers, however, were often used as a pretext for discrimination.[30] An infamous example of the debasement of police powers is an 1880 ordinance in San Francisco that prohibited operating a laundry in a wooden building. On its face the law seems like a valid safety regulation, although it looks much different when we consider that the vast majority of laundry operators were

[30] On the arbitrariness of zoning more generally, see especially Nelson (1980). I consider the problem of excluding Chinese from mines more fully in Chapter 8.

Chinese immigrants who could not afford to house their businesses in brick buildings.[31] There are also many examples of efforts of predominantly white neighborhoods to keep blacks out as the government attempted to desegregate neighborhoods – such as restrictions on new apartment buildings that happened to have the side effect of essentially eliminating opportunities for minorities to live in certain neighborhoods.[32]

There is a large literature on exclusionary zoning, as one might expect. At the same time, there is no study that recognizes explicitly that such tactics were first tested within the confines of claim clubs, not only among miners (who often believed Chinese immigration was a source of social costs), but even earlier among farmers, who as we have seen viewed speculation as a negative externality. Clubs, besides providing insight into emergence of private property institutions, also made the first attempts at exclusionary zoning, wielding collective property rights to restrict access to land by those deemed by the club to be undesirable.

Besides providing a framework for informal regulation, Nevada's mining districts provided the essential machinery for adjudication. Indeed, judicial institutions were some of the most important features of a mining district. There were, however, different types of judicial institutions available to miners as well as others who began to show up in their territory. In particular, legal tribunals included two basic types: miners' courts, as well as collective bodies, which were known as "people's courts." As noted in the discussion of frontier justice in Kansas Territory and elsewhere in the Plains and Midwestern states, vigilantism was common. There was also a parallel divide between club courts and vigilantism in the mining sector. Miners called their system of popular justice the people's court, which was a temporary solution arising in response to mass meetings or meetings of a vigilance committee; yet the miners' courts dealt with their more pressing business involving land ownership.[33]

Nonetheless, the people's courts, which seem to have shared more in common with mob rule than formal legal tribunals of the nineteenth century, existed parallel to the order provided by miners' courts. In contrast to ad hoc people's courts, miners' courts were permanent. Popular courts had no procedures for appeal, although such procedures certainly existed in the miners' courts. Miners' laws were based on procedural rules of the *alcalde*, which was a judge in Spanish-speaking North America that facilitated a wide range of economic behavior in the absence of formal legal institutions. In this respect, there are important parallels between the private judges of medieval Europe

[31] The Supreme Court considered these issues in *Yick Wo* v. *Hopkins*, 118 U.S. 356 (1886). In that case, the court recognized that Chinese immigrants are protected under the Fourteenth Amendment, and found that the statute was discriminatory as applied. Nonetheless, exclusionary zoning would continue with constitutional sanction well into the 1960s.

[32] Early decisions upheld such powers of the state to exclude. See, for example, *Euclid* v. *Ambler*, 272 U.S. 356 (1926).

[33] On the functions of the people's courts, see Rogers (1949).

and the alcalde, which could be described as the law merchant of the American West. The informal judicial institutions that were weaved into the tapestry of mining districts generalized the alcalde, and the resulting legal tribunals were an important feature of these claim clubs.

There were no lawyers in the proceedings. Nonetheless, individuals had their day in a miners' court. Indeed, not having lawyers was arguably expedient because individuals had to resolve disputes quickly. Judicial institutions arising within mining districts on the frontier created order, balancing the demands of "popular justice" with more regularized legal rules necessary for capitalist development.[34] A regularized system of resolving disputes, along with legitimacy-conferring institutions such as juries and democratic procedures for selecting judges, enhanced ownership security among miners.

Nevada's mining districts were governments convened in the hope of enhancing land-tenure security. Mining districts defined boundaries, described claims (number, size, and procedures for filing), and created district officers with a set of duties. The number of officers was minimal, usually limited to a president, recorder, sheriff, and judge. The miners' court was a tribunal of justice, administered by majority vote or jury trial. It was precisely these political features that distinguished them from earlier, simpler organizations, as well as the major change that made self-governance possible amidst increasing political, economic, and social complexity.

Did Miners Establish Private Property Institutions?

One contentious issue in economic studies of the gold frontier is whether or not miners actually created a system of private property institutions during the gold rush in California. Although I address this issue more fully in the next chapter, it is useful here to introduce briefly the parameters of the debate. Clay and Wright (2010, 2005) argue that the mining frontier left much to be desired as far as property relations are concerned, in particular that property institutions during the gold rush were less private property systems than rules governing access to a common pool. Similarly, Clay (2006) provides evidence that incomplete property institutions continued to undermine productivity in California after the gold rush. In addition, Grossman (2001) and Grossman and Kim (1995) interpret land relations during the gold rush as an open-access situation characterized by weak property institutions. Each of these studies suggests that property institutions arising within claim clubs were inferior to state-backed legal title but even more fundamentally, that the property norms arising under mining districts were not even a private property system at all.

The aforementioned arguments are compelling. Indeed, if claim clubs were efficient organizations as far as provision of property institutions is concerned,

34 On the effectiveness of institutions devised among miners, including judicial institutions, see Perrigo (1941), Marshall (1920), and Lord (1959 [1881]).

then there would be few reasons for squatters to petition the state for legal titles. There are, however, at least four features of the mining frontier that suggest a system of informal private property institutions was in place, the first of which is positive prices of land. A widespread norm of acceptability of claim jumping implies lack of excludability and low land prices. Deeds to mineral lands, however, were valuable prior to federal reform of property institutions in Western lands (Libecap 2007b). Prices of land deeds should be low in an institutional regime in which claim jumping was an acceptable means of establishing ownership.

Second, mining became more capital intensive as the gold rush proceeded. Scale of mining operations quickly increased, and the industry was highly capitalized in a short time.[35] Increasing capital intensity is difficult to explain in the absence of effective private property institutions.

Third, constitutions of mining districts typically prohibited claim jumping unless land was unoccupied. In this sense, the property regime was a beneficial use regime, which has well-known drawbacks: when people have to use land or lose it, they have incentives to inefficiently use resources. Such beneficial use regimes are inefficient compared with situations in which owners have more autonomy over investment and extraction decisions. Nonetheless, a beneficial use system is still considered a private property system. Indeed, claim club constitutions explicitly outlawed claim jumping except in certain conditions, which is a characteristic of a regulated private property regime.

Fourth, mining districts included informal judicial institutions in order to resolve disputes over land, the primary purpose of which was to interpret ownership. Judges would have been unnecessary if there were no private property institutions. More generally, when a club's judges made a decision, they were creating private property institutions that would ultimately be backed by the will of the collective. And even if one argues that these were access rights, such rights were typically allocated privately, which is a feature of a private property regime.

These four factors – positive land prices, increasing investment, regulations on claim jumping, and emergence of judges and juries – suggest that mining districts created a basic system of private property institutions. Nevertheless, it is also clear that claim jumping had a role in mining districts, as well as agricultural claim clubs: rather than an acceptable method to claim land, it was used to punish people who violated club norms. Because these norms included respect for private property, when squatters encouraged claim jumping in response to a violation of their social and economic norms, it is more appropriately interpreted as an enforcement mechanism within a private property system, as opposed to evidence that this was not even a private property regime.

[35] Wyman (1979) provides insight into the relatively rapid increase in capital intensity, as well as technological progress in the mining sector, in Nevada.

TIMBERLAND

Forest land and mineral land were a state-owned resource during much of the nineteenth century. Ongoing state ownership of timberland in the United States was a legacy of feudal and manorial institutions of Europe, which involved perpetual state ownership of land with permission rights to use land and forests exchanged for goods (North and Thomas 1973). The colonial system in North America also had feudal elements, with use rights exchanged for an in-kind payment or a discount in price (Hibbard 1924). Although markets began to develop during the colonial period, there was not much progress toward a system of fee-simple (private) ownership of forests in North America during this period. Indeed, from the moment the new Constitution was agreed upon, timberland was mainly state-owned.

Pervasive state ownership of forests should not be surprising for both an economic and a security reason. The economic reason, which parallels the logic of state ownership of mineral land, was to provide federal and state governments with a revenue resource that could be used to provide public goods. The security rationale for state ownership of timberland was even more obvious: state ownership of forests benefited the Navy, which required a supply of timber to build ships. Maintaining state ownership of forests increased the nation's ability to conduct warfare.

As we have seen in other sectors, claimants generally ignored the formal property regime. Farmers were among the first groups to begin taking forest land in violation of the law, many of them believing that they had a right to use the nation's forests as they, rather than the government, saw fit. Nor were they particularly concerned with investment in forests as an asset, as farmers typically cleared land of timber to set up farms (Dick 1970). In the minds of many settlers, the nation's policy toward the West should have been the Jeffersonian ideal of encouraging smallholder agriculture, although the formal policy was anything but free land.

Of course, law on the books often differed substantially from reality, and forest land would prove no different than agriculture or mining in this regard. The discussion that follows focuses on developments in Wisconsin, both because it would become the leading timber-producing state by the late 1800s and also because Hurst's (1964) *Law and Economic Growth* – the classic study of the legal foundations of markets – was a case study of the development of the timber industry in Wisconsin. Thus, many insights can be gleaned from developments in this particular state.

Squatters would eventually attain much of the land they coveted for free during the timber booms. However, the federal government initially attempted to reinforce state ownership of timberland while simultaneously creating a framework to competitively allocate land. In 1820, for example, the government warned individuals to cease cutting trees on lands owned by the United States government. Yet the government also provided people with opportunities to acquire access rights to land. For example, it was common practice for the war secretary to issue logging permits on Wisconsin Indian lands though he had no formal power to do so. A land law of 1820, which remained in force until 1889, permitted direct sale of eighty acres or more for a minimum price of $1.25 an acre after lands were initially presented at public auction. There were also various grants of forest land to the states as a revenue resource. Indeed, land sales increased during the 1830s in states endowed with forest resources, in particular the fertile Midwestern states. In Wisconsin Territory, a sense of security, spurred by the military's successful campaigns to secure borderlands and negotiate treaties, encouraged land speculation, with settlers purchasing nearly 900,000 acres of land in the state by the end of 1836.[36] Although the panic of 1837 led to a decline in speculation, it was again on the rise shortly thereafter (Hurst 1964).

Despite legal options to secure title to forest land, formal laws were not self-executing. As Hurst (1964) explains, the war secretary did not actually assign private property rights to forest land. Rather, a permit only meant that the war department would not interfere with logging. Anyone who petitioned the state and received an approval was more or less on his or her own as far as establishing economic institutions. Consequently, anyone who possessed a permit assumed considerable risk in extracting resources for profit. In addition, following the rule of law did not make economic sense, because those who did so were at a competitive disadvantage as extralegal or illegal methods were more expedient.

In this political and economic environment, much of dynamism in the economy was a consequence of private rather than public organizations. As early as the 1830s, entrepreneurs were staking out the best land. As the logging industry expanded, entrepreneurs began to find investors to back their excursions. In Wisconsin, some ten to fifteen companies were established almost immediately after the cession treaties were signed, most employing about fifteen to twenty-five men. Initially, camp bosses had to function as storekeeper, diplomat, banker, and law enforcement officer. Loggers' unions were small prior to 1860, with a logging crew ordinarily consisting of no more than twelve or fifteen men. After the 1860s, camps routinely had more than fifty people, and by the 1880s, a loggers' union commonly numbered at least sixty, sometimes a hundred or more (Rohe 1986; Rosholt 1980; Hurst 1964).

The formal legal situation was also haphazard. In some situations, citizens in the logging camps would call together ad hoc associations known as "Vigilance

[36] It should be noted that the large number of land sales does not imply land markets were *competitive*. As Hurst (1964) and Fries (1951) explain, these land auctions were generally dominated by organized loggers seeking to extract land rents from the state. In comparison to farmers, loggers may even have been more effective rent-seeking coalitions at government auctions because their consortiums were backed by capitalists and also because the stakes of successful collusion were higher due to the price increases during the timber boom.

Committees" or "Committees of Safety." These committees were, however, less institutionalized and accepted than in other frontier occupations. Local authorities in lumber towns rarely used the vigilante alternative, and they did not generally usurp local police functions, or act as law enforcement agents, for a prolonged time (Kilar 1987). Thus, the vigilante system on the timber frontier contrasts to Dimsdale's (1949) account of the highly institutionalized, quasi-legitimate vigilantism that emerged in the American west.

One of the reasons there was less demand for a full-fledged alternative system of legal institutions comparable to those of other sectors was because company towns were quickly erected once logging operations began to boom, reducing the need for informal legal institutions. Nonetheless, formal law left much to be desired during this period, and the timber frontier was in many ways as prone to violence and conflict as other sectors (Kilar 1987). Uncertainty made logger unions an important organizational alternative to the state as a source of land governance as well as security. These private-order associations on the timber frontier were smaller, more tightly knit claim clubs than those that existed among farmers and miners. Nonetheless, loggers' unions were likewise bandits within the state providing a parallel system of governance as well as enforced norms of access to valuable resources.

One of the defining features of claim clubs is willingness to use violence to attain social order. They were, invoking the language of Hobbes's *Leviathan*, covenants backed by the sword. Much like in other economic sectors, claim clubs on the forest frontier imposed their will against anyone who dared to challenge their use of forest land. In particular, many of these nonstate bandits waged open conflict with the formal state. "Wars" between loggers and state officials seemed to break out on each of the timber frontiers, and there was also ongoing conflict between loggers and their competitors, which variously included farmers and Indian tribes. However, the federal government was perhaps their greatest adversary, as loggers had more and more encounters with federal agents as timber prices increased. States were also active in regulating forests. For example, as early as the 1830s, the federal attorney for the Territory of Wisconsin was aware of timber stripping and attempted to suppress trespass. In 1845, a preemption law was passed in Wisconsin in order to provide land to squatters but it did not provide for free cutting of timber, and so it did not do much to prevent unauthorized cutting on government land because settlers continued to view land as free, a conflict of ideology that often led to actual fighting. When federal marshals began seizing logs cut illegally in 1850, the response was violent, with timber wars being fought throughout the public-land states of the Midwest.[37]

The defining feature of the timber wars, besides an overwhelming victory for logging interests in attaining land access essentially for free, was relentlessness in dealing with government agents. Of the many stories of the tactics loggers

[37] Excellent sources on the timber wars include Dick (1970), Hurst (1964), and Fries (1951).

used when dealing with federal bureaucrats, one account is particularly vivid. In 1853, after a U.S. marshal shut down an illegal logging operation in Michigan, he was

> greatly lionized. The hands from the mills on the other side of the river resolved to give him a special display of fireworks. So they prepared large balls of wicking saturated in spirit of turpentine, and after His Excellency had retired for the night, the night being warm and the windows being open, they threw their lighted fireballs into the marshal's windows, and so gave him a grand illumination. To add to the taxation, the marshal's boat was sunk in the lake. (Powers 1912: 193)

Although fireballs would probably have been sufficient to get their message across, sinking his boat was a surefire way for these loggers to show they meant business. That the marshal was doing his job was irrelevant in the face of men convinced they – not the government – had the moral authority to use forest land, and that their actions giving force to their convictions were justified.

To use another example, when federal marshals attempted to prevent timber cutting on public land in Missouri, a group of loggers, numbering one hundred and fifty men, compelled him to leave the county and the state. Evidently, seeing him out the state's door was not enough for them. Seventeen of them gave chase, following the marshal to his place of retreat in Arkansas, eventually surrounding his hotel and demanding he surrender himself (Dick 1970).

As these stories indicate, in the war for the nation's forests, organized loggers were often on the winning side against overmatched agents of a weak federal government. Federal agents were harassed, chased down, and otherwise hassled by members of loggers' unions. When federal marshals disregarded informal property norms, a club often set its fury on transgressors. Because the conflicts were often one or a few against many loggers, the balance typically tilted toward the loggers' unions when push came to shove.

Just as we have seen in the case of California, the formal state ownership regime governing natural resources was largely ignored, even though the government provided people with opportunities to acquire private property rights. Yet the mere fact that these rules were not followed does not mean there was disorder. Rather, property institutions originated outside of the formal apparatus of the state, within the confines of organizations men forged in their effort to establish reliable routes of access to the nation's forests necessary for capitalist development.

The timber wars were an important aspect of frontier development. However, punishing federal agents was not the most important economic function of loggers' unions. Rather, the main function of these clubs was enhancing members' bargaining strength at auctions. These associations regulated bidding behavior at auctions in ways that that translated de facto (economic) influence more or less directly into legal representation. The timber wars were part of a more general strategy to appropriate the scarcity rent associated with timber – rents formally owned by the state – through collusion at government land auctions.

As one expects given their capacity for violence, clubs were quite successful at collusion, and the government knew about it. For example, it is clear from reports in the 1870s that the commissioners of the General Land Office recognized that land sales were far lower than market value, and that purchasers were colluding to keep the price of land down. Timber dealers would bid a high price, forfeit after sale, and then allow a partner to purchase land at the minimum legal price.[38] Technically competitive, these "auctions" were nothing more than a de facto transfer of scarcity rent from the government to organized claimants.

It should be noted that collusion may have been a solution to poorly designed federal land laws. Indeed, if it was socially desirable to simply give land away rather than try to profit from it, then collusion may have been "optimal" because it informally reduced land prices. Such a rationale, which suggests the federal government should simply have given land to those who could use it, has obvious merits – economics and moral philosophy each have traditions justifying the conditions under which violating rulers' laws can enhance social welfare. At the same time, it is also important to recognize the opportunity cost of giving land away. During the nineteenth century, the federal government transferred a substantial amount of timberland to the states for education and infrastructure purposes. For example, the state of Wisconsin acquired five million acres of timberland from 1838 to 1866 to be auctioned off with proceeds used to fund public goods, in particular education. Competitive auctions of this sort are often an efficient way to allocate resources because in a fair auction, bidders bid their value, and social surplus is maximized.[39] However, realizing this objective required the state to set up as well as strengthen existing land markets, and there were some efforts to do so, such as an 1849 act that entrusted a special commission to sell land to the highest bidder and required that no land be sold for less than its appraised value. Nonetheless, the state generally failed to realize much if any profit from land sales. From 1855 to 1870, the average price of timberland on markets ranged from $2.50 to $20 an acre, yet the state received less than $1 an acre (Hurst 1964; Fries 1951). The difference between the price paid and market price is the value of the transfer in scarcity rent, which was substantial because loggers were receiving up to twenty times the purchase price of land on competitive secondary markets.

38 *Report of the Commissioner of the General Land Office* (Washington, DC: Government Printing Office, 1874).

39 Libecap (2007a) provides an excellent comparative institutional analysis of alternative systems for allocating land. The foundational study of allocation of property rights through auctions is Coase (1966, 1960).

Nor were the state governments alone in their inability to regulate markets effectively. The federal government also faced challenges implementing land auctions.[40] For example, when federal officials opened bids on 31 million feet of timber confiscated in Minnesota in 1856, only one man bid, acquiring the whole lot for less than $320 (or $8,600 in today's dollars).[41] He turned out to be bidding on behalf of those whose logs were confiscated. According to first-hand accounts, there was good attendance at the auction but nobody dared to bid against members of the cartel. Collusion was a substantial transfer in land rent, as a simple calculation shows. The going price of a thousand feet of lumber was highly variable in this period, peaking at $30 before the panic of 1857, falling to between $4 and $5 in 1860, while the prices during the Civil War held at about $20 in the Chicago market (Nesbit 1973). A reasonable estimate is the Chicago rate of $20 per thousand feet which suggests loggers appropriated nearly $620,000 in scarcity rent – a sizable $16.8 million in today's dollars – from the state to private claimants (including loggers, mill owners, and capitalists).[42] Because collusion was illegal, it is not documented precisely. However, anecdotal evidence of the sort just mentioned suggests that competitive auctions of federal land were few and far between.

Even after the federal government passed the Homestead Act, which was a massive free land program, it withheld some forest land to be allocated through public auction. Unfortunately for those members of the federal administration who supported auctions, the American state remained relatively feeble, and collusion continued to undermine competitive markets for land. For example, in 1873, bidders formed a collusive machine but it broke down, with bidding reaching $19.75 an acre. In response, the winning bidder forfeited the claim. The next morning the tracts were offered again, and purchased for $3 an acre. At a sale of state school lands in 1883, parties bid $3 an acre (school lands were so called because they were to be sold with profits used to build schools in new territories). At private sale of these same lands, colluding parties received up to $50 an acre, with an average price of $8 to $10. As these examples show, collusion was good for businessmen, but bad for the state.

Claim clubs, as we have seen in other sectors, were a thorn in the state's side. However, these associations appealed to the state as the industry began to mature. Returning again to the example of Wisconsin, people who purchased legal titles in the 1840s petitioned the government to help them limit theft. The state legislature responded with several bills seeking to strengthen private property rights. An act of 1844 prohibited willful theft of timber from another's

[40] These examples of collusion are drawn from Nesbit (1973), Hurst (1964), and Fries (1951).

[41] Calculation made using real price data with a base year of 1860 and desired year of 2010 using the "Measuring Worth" service of the Economic History Association: http://www.measuringworth.com/.

[42] Calculation made using 1860 as base year and 2010 as desired year.

private lands. Penalties were increased in 1849 and 1855 (Hurst 1964). The state was thus active as far as legislation is concerned, even if its capacity was underwhelming.

Loggers also began to increasingly rely on the state as their industry became more capital intensive. Organizations that mobilize capital on a grand scale are fundamental to economic growth and development because they permit realization of economies of scale. Yet as Commons (1924) observed, accumulation of capital depends on legal institutions. Commons, like Hurst, recognized that markets require legal institutions to flourish. These legal institutions provided a framework for what Cronon (1991, 1983) described as a capitalist transformation of nature. The fundamental changes to ecology during this period in American economic history masterfully documented by Cronon depended on a state that was responsive to the demands of capitalists. As timber prices increased, the state increasingly reinforced market developments and limited costly competition over natural resources, thus providing an ideal legal foundation for attainment of economies of scale, as well as transformation of natural assets demanded by modern capitalism.

Although the state's role must be acknowledged in the massive expansion and capitalization of the logging industry, the government was never alone as an engine of institutional transformation. Loggers' unions were perhaps the initial source of order on the forest frontier, imposing their own rules before eventually working in tandem with the state to perfect their influence. They banished the state before welcoming it back on their terms when they needed it to realize their aspirations.

RANGELAND

Claim clubs devised by ranchers in the American West would eventually cover even more territory under the aegis of single clubs than any of their counterparts. Like claimants in other sectors, ranchers had to establish their own institutions because many of their activities occurred without legal sanction. However, unlike agriculture and mining, and even logging, the property regime governing rangeland combined aspects of private and common property institutions. In particular, ranches were private property (the largest ones even had characteristics of a company town), yet the open range – the vast lands where ranchers in the Far West drove their cattle – was shared by authorized ranchers. Thus, the range was not "open" in the sense of open access because ranchers allocated rights to use it. Open access means that there are no property institutions, formal or informal (Ciriacy-Wantrup and Bishop 1975; see also the discussion of alternative property regimes in Chapter 1). As such, the open range was more like a regulated common-property regime, an aspect of property relations that differed from the other major sectors under consideration. Despite variation in institutional form, the institutional problem on rangeland was the same as in other sectors: people seeking to transform the frontier for their purposes had to devise property institutions without the state's benediction, and as we have seen in the previous examples, they too were effective in their endeavor.

Much like in other sectors, cattlemen's associations were forged in conflict. In the ranchers' case, the main wellspring of conflict was not so much speculation as political ideology that supported agricultural development regardless of geography. To say the formal land system in the Far West was "incongruous," to use Gates's (1936) remarkably apt characterization of land laws in this period, would be an understatement. The federal government actively and continually promoted agriculture through a series of free land programs to encourage migration for the purpose of tilling the earth despite the overwhelming economic importance of open-range ranching in the region. Most importantly, agriculture and open-range ranching were in many ways incompatible, or at least perceived to be incompatible by many on the range: the defining feature of the open-range system was using vast stretches of land, which came into conflict with the fixed boundaries required for agriculture.

The origins of this conflict were in many ways political. Federal legislators believed that smallholder plots would encourage development of the Far West, conventionally defined as the region west of the 98th or 100th meridian (see Map 3.1). In essence, federal politicians simply extended the concept of preemption and homestead rights, which were designed to reward Midwestern farmers (preemption) or to encourage farming in the Western states (homesteads), to lands further west. Yet these policies, when applied to the Far West without modification, were economically inappropriate as far as conservation incentives are concerned (Hansen and Libecap 2004a,b; and Libecap and Hansen 2002). Encouraging desert farmers would be troubling enough even if there were no competing uses of the land. However, there were additional costs, as these policies also contributed to substantial conflict between competing claimants because they threw farmers and ranchers into conflict. As we can see, the Far West consists of various plains, many of which were particularly well suited to cattle ranching. Federal policies thus created and perpetuated conflict among various users of land in the Far West, in addition to undermining incentives for conservation.

In this legal environment, property institutions initially emerged through a more or less spontaneous process. Ranchers contracted through simple first-possession norms that had no real designer or enforcer when their sector first began to develop. Under the first-possession system, claims were established by grazing a certain area. Newcomers understood that they should move on whenever others were there first to graze their cattle (Anderson and Hill 2004). These "grazing rights" were ranchers' version of tomahawk and occupation rights.

First-possession norms were simple but they allowed ranchers to allocate access privileges to the range. Line camps formed with cowboys riding boundaries to prevent cattle rustling and to drive cattle back to their customary

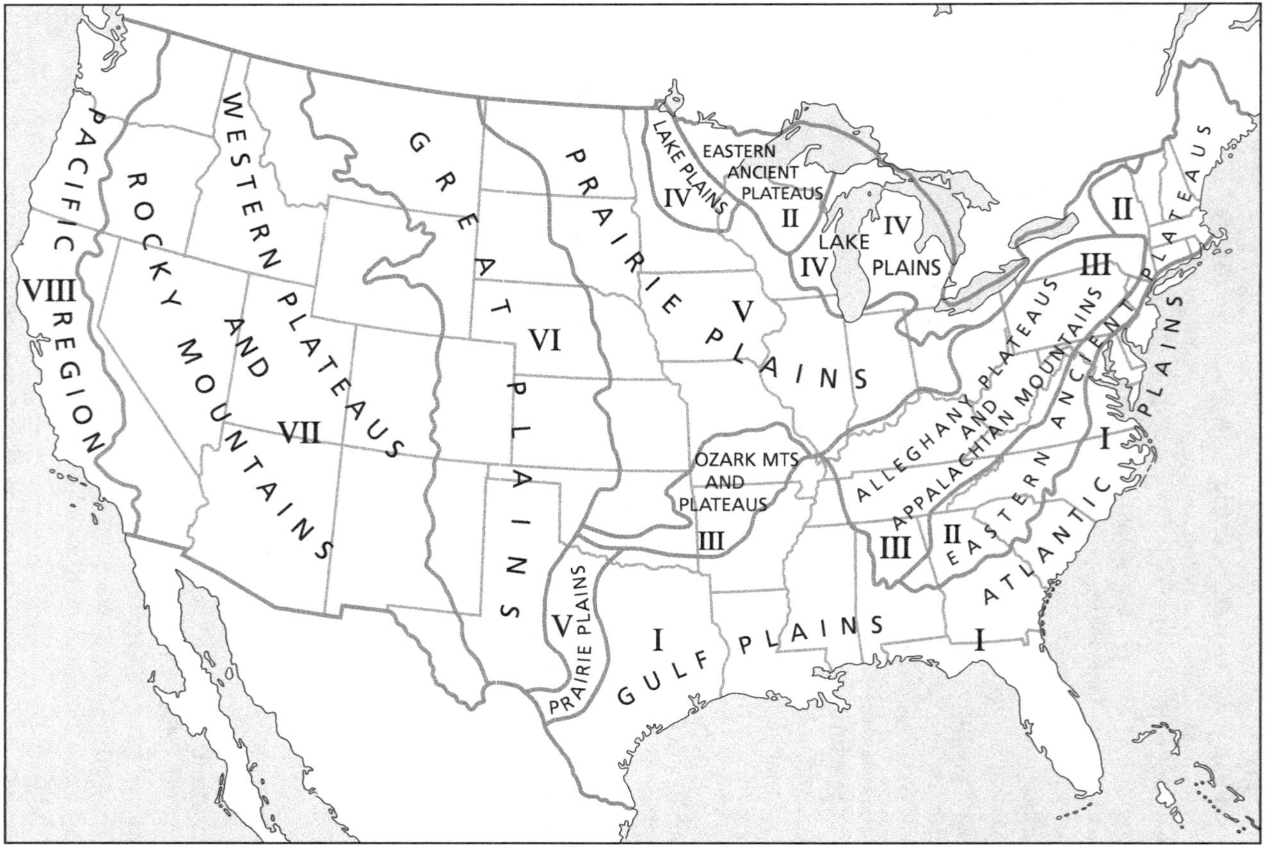

MAP 3.1. The plains regions of the Far West. *Source*: Redrawn from Libecap (2007b).

ranges. Anderson and Hill (2004, 2002) use these norms as evidence in favor of what we can call a "trust thesis," introduced in Chapter 2: trust, not conflict, characterized economic and social relations among ranchers. Anderson and Hill provide a great deal of evidence that small collections of ranchers protected their capital investment and that members of their communities routinely cooperated because they trusted one another. Lack of conflict is perhaps the central theme in their various studies of economic relations on the range.

There is certainly something to be said for theories of spontaneous order as applied to norms governing behavior among ranchers. However, institutions were also present that extended well beyond highly decentralized systems in which reputations alone sustain cooperation and compliance with social norms. As the presence of claim clubs reveals, ranchers relied on far more than a handshake to enforce norms governing rangeland use as operations expanded. Indeed, it is useful to divide rangeland contracting arrangements into three types. To be clear, these systems did not linearly replace one another; rather, they tended to coexist. Yet accounts that focus on highly decentralized systems of social control underplay other forms that were as important, if not more important, during these formative decades of the range cattle industry.

The first type of arrangement had no real organizational structure. These were also the earliest contracting systems among ranchers, such as norms of trust system. Their defining feature was that they were highly decentralized, arising with limited conscious design or enforcement. Such norms can be understood quite well in terms of standard theories of spontaneous order, as noted above. They also never go away, as nearly all business relations will have some behavior regulated by social norms rather than formal rules, such as reputational arrangements whereby businessmen honor their word because it is the "right thing to do." Whenever partners expect to interact long into the future, such relationships can oftentimes be quite effective.

A second system was based on local cattlemen's associations. These local associations were necessary for reasons we have seen in other sectors – namely, collective security. Outsiders, including rustlers and farmers, were an important reason why private protection organizations were desirable (Dennen 1976). Rustlers, for example, often led ranchers to band together to protect their cattle. Besides outsiders, there were many other activities requiring cooperation, including use of common corrals and group participation in roundups. Farmers represented a different sort of threat because they potentially cut off access to the open range. Competing uses of land were exacerbated by the creation of barbed wire, which allowed farmers to challenge the rule of ranchers on the plains. Barbed wire technology reduced the transaction costs of enclosure while at the same time creating new transaction costs between groups.[43]

[43] For an economic analysis of fencing and property rights from a transaction cost perspective, see especially Kantor (1998). The foundational study of the economic significance of enclosure movements from the perspective of new institutional economics is North and Thomas (1973).

These conflicts required associations as well as appropriately designed working rules. In this regard, rules of local stock associations coexisted with a body of precedent, custom, and principles known as "cow custom" throughout the entire Western region.[44] The men Gates (1948) would refer to as the "cattle kings of the prairies" had their origins in the local associations that operated based on cow customs. Some cow customs would have inevitably been enforced through "trust and a handshake." However, economic organizations were also present to give force to them. To be sure, trust reduced the costs of enforcing norms. Yet if trust were sufficient, then it is hard to explain why organizations were necessary.

Local associations may have been effective but the open range certainly extended beyond the boundaries of any local club as the scale of ranching operations increased substantially between 1850 and 1890 in terms of the area covered. As early as the mid-1860s, ranching began to dominate the open range as an economic activity.[45] Herd sizes controlled by an individual rancher increased to thousands. In 1880, six million cattle were driven north. In the period between 1870 and 1890, availability of public forage land led to an economic boom in Western livestock production (Dale 1960, 1942).

Like miners, ranchers faced a situation in which they risked substantial losses unless they devised a system to impose order upon smaller, competing organizations. In particular, changes in the scale of the industry as well as competition from rustlers and farmers required centralized claim clubs capable of imposing order upon various organizations and individuals. State-wide peak associations were a third system of social control on Western rangelands, one that was even more impressive than local stock associations. These state-wide associations were unprecedented compared to mining districts and farmers' protective associations in terms of their scale because they spanned entire states. If the cattlemen's associations were "little claim clubs," the peak associations were "big claim clubs" that presided over local cattlemen's associations in the same way a mining district presided over mining camps.

Improvements in organizational capacity were particularly important during winter months in which ranchers had to drive their animals to remote grazing lands. Despite the seemingly obvious importance of ranching in the Western states, the federal government was generally unresponsive to changes in economic activities. Although ranching took its place as the predominant economic activity, no laws were passed reforming the open range system for decades. To be specific, the open range was not fundamentally reformed until the Taylor Grazing Act of 1934.

A dearth of formal law is cause for concern, in particular if one subscribes to political theories of property institutions. The state was largely an absentee landlord, a finding that may lead us to hypothesize ownership insecurity and

44 On extralegal norms among ranchers, see especially Dale (1960, 1942).
45 Gates (1948).

perhaps even a "tragedy of the commons" because rangeland/grassland is the classic example of a common-pool resource. After all, in political theories of property institutions the state is the fundamental source of institutions governing ownership relations in society. Without the state, one expects chaos, in terms of both violence and resource overuse.

Despite these forebodings, clubs mitigated conflict and overuse of resources even as ranchers began to drive their cattle across entire states and into adjacent ones. Indeed, state-wide cattlemen's associations defended investments (primarily their cattle) as well as access to the range in the state's stead. State-wide cattlemen's associations, by coordinating activities of local ranchers, permitted expansion of the cattle industry on a grand scale. As the following accounts indicate, a majority of cattlemen operated under a single claim association in several of the key ranching states by the late 1870s. Ranchers established corporations, but it was their claim club that provided a system of political and economic governance that made possible the ranching boom. The discussion that follows considers claim clubs in Wyoming and Montana, mainly because they were the main ranching states in the Far West.

The first state-wide claim club in Wyoming was called the Stock Graziers' Association. It was organized in Cheyenne in 1871 and reorganized in 1879, along with a change in its name to the Wyoming Stock Growers' Association (WSGA). Large-scale private-order associations were necessary as the number of cattle in Wyoming territory increased from 90,000 in 1874 to 530,000 in 1880. In Montana, cattlemen tried but failed to convene an association in 1874. They were more successful in 1879, establishing an association called the Montana Stock Growers' Association. As Montana geography included hills and mountain valleys, ranchers kept their cattle within comparatively small areas. The Black Hills Livestock Association was organized in the spring of 1880 with sixty ranchers and 264,200 head of stock (Briggs 1934).

These claim clubs presided over a fairly complete property regime, both in terms of regulation of access to the range (a common property regime) and in protection of private property (ranches and cattle). Indeed, one of the main functions of these clubs was protecting cattle, the primary capital asset on the range. Besides regulating access to the open range, these associations standardized a branding system essential to orderly roundups, handled disposition of stray cattle, secured protection from cattle thieves, and secured beneficial legislation from territorial legislatures (Briggs 1934).

Like other claim clubs, these state-wide associations wielded political clout. The ranchers' association in Montana, for example, was a formidable force in both business and politics in the 1880s (Stuart and Phillips 1925). Similarly, the state legislature in Wyoming, which included many of the most powerful ranchers in the state, often formalized rules voted on by the voluntary WSGA (Jackson 1947).

It is also worth noting that these associations allocated access rights to water, a particularly important function because Eastern water laws were inappropriate for the conditions of the Far West. Even more troubling was a federal prohibition against private ownership of water in the western United States, a policy that was out of step with the requirements of economic activities in the region. In particular, private ownership was desirable for the industry to thrive because water was scarce and investment depended on securing reliable access to water, as well as because it was viewed with as a fair and equitable alternative to corporate monopolies (Schorr 2012; Libecap 2011; Kanazawa 1998). Ranchers responded by developing a system to trade water along with claims to land, viewing title to land as including any water that had been appropriated for use on that land (Dunham 1941; Webb 1931). This was an informal "prior appropriation" system, which is an allocation system that assigns ownership based on prior use and diversion of water. Informal norms encouraged production by reducing risk associated with uncertain water supply.[46]

There are several reasons why a more political interpretation of contracting among ranchers is appropriate than is found in the story Anderson and Hill told. First, there was enforcement within these organizations. For example, the practice of "hating out" newcomers was institutionalized within claim clubs. Hating out a newcomer referred to removing anyone from a region who failed to abide by local customs.[47] Such norms were quite different from norms of trust, and they were put into action by clubs rather than individuals. Second, cattlemen's associations were political organizations. They had leaders, collective choice procedures, and a forum for resolving conflicts over ownership. More generally, they were hierarchical. However, there is no real consideration of political organization in Anderson and Hill's account, only trust. Political features of large-scale cattlemen's associations provide additional evidence of the importance of political institutions in the origins of property institutions. This does not in any way undermine their first-rate account. Rather, it suggests that they leave some important developments out in their desire to show the importance of reputational arrangements.

In a remarkably similar fashion to earlier-developing economic sectors, ranchers convened political organizations that were capable of regulating economic relations in an increasingly complex frontier environment. The economic, political, and social problems facing ranchers were that they had to

[46] Some have argued that the law evolved efficiently in the West and that it needed to because Eastern water law was wholly inappropriate for the geography of the Western United States. See, for example, Kanazawa (1998) and Colby (1990). A more general statement of the efficiency view is provided by Barzel (2002) and North (1981), each hypothesizing that institutional change seeks efficiency subject to transaction costs. Posner (2002), in his *Economic Analysis of Law*, and Rubin (1977) applied similar reasoning to the development of common law. Although the logic of the efficiency perspective is compelling, Karsten (2008) finds little, if any, evidence that the common law seeks efficiency based on his inspection of hundreds of common-law decisions by Anglo-American judges, thus refuting the Posnerian hypothesis that common law seeks efficiency.

[47] Dale (1960, 1942) describes procedures for hating out newcomers as well as other extralegal practices common during the years in which the range cattle industry began to take off. Osgood (1929) also provides an excellent account of norms governing use of the range.

defend cattle from outsiders, allocate land for grazing, effectively allocate access to water, and mobilize resources for political collective action. Substantive rules in cattlemen's associations included restrictions on the number of animals that could be placed in common herds, restrictions on who could participate (membership was limited to local ranchers with patented homesteads or locally recognized rangeland claims), allocation of land to individuals for their ranches, registration of cattle brands, and specification of the labor each rancher was to contribute for managing the herd. Ranchers maintained common herds to limit drift of their collective livestock, to control breeding within the herd, and to cooperate in branding young animals. They also blocked entry by outsiders and cooperated in annual roundups. Yet to understand these norms, and the extent to which they were effective, we must keep in mind that they were specified and enforced within the confines of large-scale *political* organizations that moved substantially beyond the local cattlemen's associations and certainly beyond decentralized norms of trust.

Without downplaying the seriousness of these breakdowns, it is also important to remember that in any system of social control, there are going to be periods that challenge order, and the cattlemen's associations on the Western frontier were no different in this regard. In some years, the open range succumbed to a de facto open-access situation characterized by too many cattle on the range. For example, WSGA membership increased from 267 individual members in 1883 to 363 in 1885, with members owning collectively over two million head of stock by 1885. By 1886, the ranges of both Montana and Wyoming were saturated. Increasing scale of operations contributed to boom and bust dynamics. Many pioneer ranchers sold their interests in the range in exchange for capital stock in new companies. Capitalization increased speculation and absentee ownership of rangeland. In part because of overcapitalization, the industry suffered a severe downturn in the following years (Briggs 1934).

This downturn, which is referred to by historians as the Great Starvation of 1886–7, should not be surprising in light of developments just mentioned. Part of the problem was that the capitalists who were fueling expansion of the ranching industry were pushing for too many cattle on an already overstocked pasture, leading drovers to graze low-quality pastures. Use of marginal lands is usually a sign of poor conservation practices. Only a few companies had purchased lands to serve as grazing grounds, the rest relying on the open range. Poor conservation, in turn, means thinner cattle and greater risk of starvation in hard times. Better management was necessary to improve the productivity of the cattle industry but these lessons would only be learned after the Great Starvation.[48]

[48] I return to the example of the Great Starvation in Chapter 4, explaining why it is not necessarily an indictment of cattlemen's associations as organizations for managing rangeland resource use. To foreshadow my argument, there are few reasons to believe that the federal government had superior information or stronger incentives than cattlemen's associations to appropriately ensure against risks of overstocking the open range. In fact, the ranchers' associations, not governments, were the groups with the best information and appropriate incentives.

The economic and political organizations of the mid- to late-century ranchers of the American West, including their claim clubs, declined as legal corporations modernized the industry. Peak organizations remained relevant as a source of political capacity but they were increasingly controlled by corporations. Eventually, they were moribund institutions, like agricultural claim clubs and mining districts of a different time and place. However, it would be a mistake to sweep cattlemen's associations into the dustbin of history because they faded away. Claim clubs provided a system of ownership during the takeoff phase of the ranching industry. Before the demands of large ranching companies led to replacement of customary norms by formal law, claim clubs presided over an informal property regime that may have been unprecedented in American economic history as far as geographic scale is concerned.

CONCLUSION: DOES THE THEORY FIT THE FACTS?

These empirical studies produce several interwoven themes, each of which is consistent with the conceptual framework outlined in Chapter 2. The main theoretical predictions were that hierarchy would be necessary to enforce property institutions as the frontiers became more complex, that the state was not the only hiearchical organization capable of specifying and enforcing property instituitons, and that governments and private property institutions arise more or less simultaneously. On each count, the theory fits the facts that have been presented.

First, farmers, miners, loggers, and ranchers each established private property institutions even though the state was unwilling to enforce them. In the loggers' and ranchers' cases, property institutions included, in addition to private property institutions, self-governing common property regimes. Emergence of informal private property institutions was a general feature of frontier development in each of the major frontier economic sectors.

Second, highly decentralized enforcement systems gave way to claim clubs as economic and social complexity inevitably increased. Governments appear to have been necessary for property institutions to be self enforcing as the number of claimants on the frontier increased, yet these governments arose in the state's pale shadow rather than as a part of the formal state. As the empirical studies have shown, clubs were bandits within the state, oftentimes competing with it.

Third, claim clubs and private property institutions emerged more or less simultaneously. Governments were necessary because of a desire to specify and enforce property institutions, and government formation gave force to ownership norms. John Locke, in his *Second Treatise of Government*, proclaimed that people enter into society to preserve their property. Implicit in Locke's argument is a belief that property rights exist in a state of nature and that the only real enforcer of property rights is the formal state. Yet claim clubs were not *preserving* private property institutions but rather *creating* them. Nor was the state, as Locke assumed, the only enforcer of private property institutions.

Rather, claim clubs provided the property protection we normally associate with a state.

This finding regarding the relationship between market institutions and government complements Greif's criticism of political economy perspectives that view the state as a source of property institutions. As Greif explains, although markets are often assumed to follow creation of public order institutions, it is more likely that "limited government, representative bodies, and modern markets co-evolved in a process reflecting deeper institutional variables" (2005: 778). Claim clubs are an important empirical example of this presumed coevolution of markets and governments. In fact, they represent the simultaneous emergence of contract institutions and coercion-constraining institutions within the state – a situation that Greif did not fully consider, but nonetheless anticipated.

Despite some clear themes that have emerged in this chapter, more is necessary before we conclude that these associations competed with the state as a source of private property institutions. In particular, to rival the state, private property institutions must be effective on each of the dimensions of a property regime. The evidence in this chapter, in focusing on the constitutional features of claim clubs, is merely suggestive in terms of emergence of private property institutions. The next chapter considers explicitly the extent to which a club's property regime was successful on the dimensions of clarity of allocation, alienability, security from trespass, and credibility of persistence. Only after considering carefully these four central dimensions of a property regime can we reasonably conclude that claim clubs truly rivaled the state.

APPENDIX TO CHAPTER 3: EXAMPLES OF CLAIM CLUB CONSTITUTIONS

A3.1 Claim Club of Milwaukee County

PREAMBLE

That we the undersigned, as settlers of public land within the County of Milwaukee, deem it of vital importance, that there should be, for the interest of the settlers, cordiality of feeling among them. That should Congress refuse to extend the preemption law, our whole dependence is upon union, and our respect for each others' rights: if we go on contending and striving one against another until the day arrives when it shall be decided whether we are to leave a home upon the spot that we have selected, there will be no hope of success. And now let us come forward determined to protect one another, and our success will be complete; let not the imprudence of any one destroy the fair prospects of the whole. What must be the condition of those who have expended [all their money] in reaching the spot they claim, if they are to be driven from their temporary refuge by a mob of the unfeeling speculator? To the instigator of the mob we would say, beware! To the speculator, remember the mourning feeling of the emigrant, sobbing adieu to the tombs and temples of his fathers, his toils and sufferings in building up a new habitation, and gathering manna of heaven, like the Israelites, from the bosom of the wilderness.

And now, as American citizens (and there is a charm and magic in the word), we pledge ourselves to support and protect each other in holding our just and lawful claims, also to support and abide by the following resolution: for support of this, we solemnly avow to each other, and call upon God to witness their truth and sincerity, and invoke disgrace upon our heads, should we prove guilty of duplicity:

Art. 1. That the County be divided into two districts.

Art. 2. That each district shall be entitled to a Register, who shall be a surveyor, legally appointed by the county surveyor, by the recommendation of the district in which he may reside.

Art. 3. To constitute a claim, there shall be a house erected of at least 12 feet square, to be performed within forty days of adoption of this constitution.

Art. 4. That all male citizens, over the age of eighteen, and females over the age of sixteen, shall be entitled to a claim by complying with the forgoing resolutions.

Art. 5. That every person wishing to make or hold a claim within this county, shall make such claim in person, and comply with the 2d and 3d resolutions, except females, who shall reside within the county.

Art. 6. A Treasurer shall be appointed in each district by their own delegates in the Convention, who shall receive all money paid into the Treasury.

Art. 7. That a Board of Arbitrators, consisting of five, shall be elected by the people of their district. The duty of said Arbitrators shall be to attend to all summons legally served, coming from a Judge or Justice of the Peace, to sit at the Board of Arbitrators, to hear and try any case brought before them, within the meaning of this Constitution. In all cases the decision of the Board shall be final. All the proceedings of said board shall be made a rule of the court, and the Judge or Justice shall proceed accordingly; and each member summoned and appearing to sit upon any such case, shall be entitled to two dollars.

Art. 8. That each member and clerk of this Convention shall be entitled to two dollars per day while attending, including the time going to and returning, to be paid equally, out of the funds of each Treasury of the district.

Art. 9. That all decisions of the Board of Arbitrators, in conformity with any of the following resolutions, shall be put in force and complied with, peacefully if *can be*, and forcibly if *must be*. In case forcible means should be resorted to, all reasonable expenses shall be paid out of the treasury.

Art. 10. That in case any difficulty should arise, in regard to claims, not comprehended by the foregoing resolutions, the Board of Arbitrators shall have universal jurisdiction over the same, and their decision shall be final.

Source: Wisconsin Legislative Assembly Journal (1856)

A3.2 Claim Club of Sun Prairie

At a large and respectable meeting of the inhabitants of Sun Prairie, convened at the house of A.W. Dickenson, March 5, 1845, for the purpose of deliberating upon and making arrangements with regard to their situation as squatters:

Resolved, That in case any person or persons shall purchase land in this vicinity at the time occupied by claimants; that they shall be disregarded as neighbors, and that no dealings of any kind be had with them. That we will neither lend to them, nor visit them, not act with them in any capacity whatsoever, nor upon any occasion.

Resolved, That we will protect each other in the claim of a quarter section, admitting that it should embrace no more than forty acres of grove timber.

Resolved, That in case any person or persons should violate the sense of this meeting and deprive claimants of their just expectations, that we will not fail to rebuke his conduct with such severity as has been common in the settlement of Western country.

Resolved, That opportunity be given to persons who have entered claims to settle with the claimants, previous to the institution of any other measures.

Resolved, That we pledge ourselves to be in readiness at the call of each other for the purpose of carrying the above resolution into full effect.

Resolved, That two registers be appointed to keep a record of all lands claimed in the vicinity, who shall receive twelve and a half cents for every record made. Whereupon, Volney Moore and Russel T. Bentley were appointed registers.

Resolved, That it be incumbent on every claimant, to enter his claim with one of the above registers, and that all such persons be recognized as members of this association.

Resolved, That all persons desirous of this association shall enter their names on the book of the register.

Resolved, That the registers be authorized to call a meeting of the people when they shall deem it expedient.

Resolved, That the proceeding of this meeting be signed by the Chairman and Secretary and published in the *Madison Express*.

Source: Benjamin H. Hibbard (1905)

A3.3 Claim Club of Canon City

Art. 1. There shall be elected annually hereafter one president, one vice president, one secretary, and six directors who shall constitute a board of directors or managers.

Art. 2. It shall be the duty of the President to preside at all meetings of the managers or club and perform all duties generally devolving on presidents of such meetings and in case of a vacancy the vice president shall act in his stead and in case of the absence of the vice president the managers shall constitute a quorum to transact business.

Art. 3. Any person taking a claim for farming purposes shall be entitled to one hundred and sixty acres in one body, provided the same shall be in a square.

Art. 4. All persons now taking claims shall within sixty days have the following improvement to wit: one log cabin, twelve foot square, covered with dirt roof.

Art. 5. All claims taken within the boundaries of this claim club shall not be permitted to run across the Arkansas River but said River shall be the boundary of claims contiguous to it.

Art. 6. Two or more persons may hold a claim in common provided the claim does not exceed the number of acres they would be entitled to hold individually.

Art. 7. Nothing in this constitution shall be so construed as to prevent parties from selling or alienating their claims when the parties have complied with the constitution in making the improvements or holding the occupation or occupancy.

Art. 8. Owners of saw mills shall be entitled to the use of the timber on six hundred and forty acres of land anywhere they may select the same in one body so as to not interfere with any other claim.

Art. 9. Any town company that has or may hereafter be organized shall be entitled to all lands they may take for the purpose of town sites provided they do not infringe on the rights of any claimant but in no case to exceed twelve hundred and eighty acres.

Art. 10. Any difficulty that may occur concerning claims or their ownership shall be referred to the managers whose decision shall be final in all cases brought under this constitution.

Art. 11. All claims made prior to this date shall be respected provided the claimant make by himself or an agent satisfactory evidence that he or they have complied with the laws.

Art. 12. The president shall and it is hereby declared to be a part of his duties to call a meeting of the managers whenever notified that it is necessary by any members of the club. Also a meeting of the whole club can be called at the request of five members of the club.

Art. 13. The Board of managers shall make such rules for their government as they think proper provided they do not conflict with this constitution.

Art. 14. All persons whose names are hereto attached are hereby declared members of this club and all persons desiring the protection of this club shall sign the same and cause a description of their claims to be filed with the recorder.

Art. 15. This constitution may be revised or amended at any meeting of the claim by a two-thirds vote of the members present.

Source: George L. Anderson (1936)

A3.4 The Claim Club of Gold Hill Mining District

PREAMBLE

Whereas, the isolated position we occupy, far from all legal tribunals, and cut off from those fountains of justice which every American citizen should enjoy, renders it necessary that we organize in a body politic for our mutual protection against the lawless, and for meting out justice between man and man; therefore, we, citizens of Gold Hill, do hereby agree to adopt the following rules and laws for our government:

ARTICLE 1. There shall be elected one Justice of the Peace, one Constable, and one Recorder of this district for the term of six months...

ARTICLE 4. The duty of the Recorder shall be to keep in a well-bound book a record of all claims which may be presented for the record, with the names of the parties locating or purchasing, the number of feet, where situated, and the date of location or purchase; also to return a certificate for such claim or claims...

SEC. 7. Evidence of record of claims shall be considered title in preference to claims that are not recorded; nor shall the recorder record more than one hill, dry gulch, or ravine claim in the name of an individual unless the same has been purchased.

SEC. 8. All claims shall be properly defined by a stake at each end of the claim, with the number of members forming said company and the number of feet owned.

SEC. 9. All claims shall be worked or the notice renewed in sixty days from the date of record, and no claim shall exceed 200 feet square, hill claims excepted, which may be reduced to 50 feet front.

SEC. 10. The Recorder shall be allowed the sum of twenty-five cents for recording the claim of each individual or members of a company.

SEC. 11. No Chinaman shall be allowed to hold a claim in this district.

SEC. 12. The district shall include all the territory from the meridian of Johntown to Steamboat Valley.

SEC. 13. All quartz claims shall not exceed 300 feet in length, including the depths and spurs.

SEC. 14. Any person or persons discovering a quartz vein shall be entitled to an extra claim on all veins he or they may discover.

SEC. 15. All persons holding quartz claims shall actually work the amount of $15 to the share within ninety days from the time of locating.

SEC. 16. All persons holding quartz claims and complying with section 15 shall hold the same for the term of eighteen months of actual property.

SEC. 17. All quartz claims shall be duly recorded within thirty days from the time of locating.

SEC. 18. No person shall locate more than one claim on a vein discovered.

SEC. 19. Any and all persons locating for mining purposes shall have the same duly recorded within ten days from the time of locating.

SEC. 20. Resolved, that the above rules and regulations shall be signed by the citizens of this district and all who may locate hereafter.

Source: Eliot Lord (1881)

4

Rivals to the State

The previous chapter articulated the constitutional and political features of claim clubs in each of the major frontier sectors. In this chapter, I consider explicitly the extent to which private property institutions arising within claim clubs were effective on each of the dimensions of a property regime. In order to justify my argument that these private-order associations competed with – and even substituted for – the state as a source of private property institutions, it is necessary to assess these informal property institutions on the dimensions of clarity of allocation, security from trespass, alienability, and credibility of persistence.

The analysis of property regimes presented in this chapter contrasts with existing studies of the emergence of private property institutions, which typically focus on security from trespass (or what can interchangeably be called "excludability"). As Cheung (1970) has shown, income from nonexcludable resources generally diminishes in the absence of excludability. Excludability is also central in Barzel's (1989) foundational analysis of private property institutions. In addition, North and Thomas (1973) prioritized the "enclosure movement," which was largely defined by emergence of excludable private property institutions, as perhaps the key explanation for economic prosperity in Western European economic history. Several other studies, such as Umbeck's (1981) articulation of the development of property institutions on California's gold fields (discussed at length in the previous chapter), as well as Libecap's (1989) comparative analysis of the evolution of property rights to manage common-pool resources rights, take for granted that excludable contracts are the most important dimension of a property regime. These studies prioritize excludability/security from trespass over other dimensions of a property regime.

A narrow focus on excludability in studies of informal private property institutions contrasts with Ostrom's (2005, 1990) studies of common property regimes, the latter providing many insights into variation in these types of property regimes. Rather, studies of informal private property institutions tend to define private property narrowly, in terms of excludability alone. As such, the analysis presented in this chapter brings the concern with institutional diversity characteristic of studies of common property regimes to bear on analysis of informal private property institutions. More generally, this chapter provides a framework for assessing informal private property institutions that moves beyond excludability.

CLARITY OF ALLOCATION

Clarity of allocation refers to how completely ownership is allocated over valuable objects. Attaining success in this dimension requires effective systems for drawing boundaries and resolving disputes. When boundaries are imprecise and there are few clear procedures to resolve disputes, fighting to establish ownership is more likely. The problems of drawing boundaries and resolving disputes are also interrelated: The ease and effectiveness of adjudication of disputes depends to an extent on the effectiveness of a system for drawing boundaries, and vice versa.

One way to measure clarity of allocation is presence of bureaucratic procedures to specify land ownership and judicial procedures available to resolve disputes over boundaries. For reasons mentioned above, procedures for drawing boundaries are an important aspect of clarity of allocation. In addition, clarity of allocation requires institutions that allow people to resolve disputes without fighting. However, a system in which force determines ownership is unlikely to be efficient, as resources are dissipated during conflict to establish property institutions (Hafer 2006). Disputes over land are going to arise even with when boundaries are precise, and when they do, judicial institutions – formal or informal – are necessary to resolve these disputes without fighting.

Drawing on the theoretical framework of Chapter 2, there are three general ways to resolve disputes over land: spontaneously arising norms, claim clubs, or formal courts. In some situations, spontaneously arising norms may be sufficient to limit conflict over land. First-possession norms, which were common in each economic sector under consideration, are examples. Yet unforeseen contingency is likely to put pressure on spontaneously arising norms. In such situations, judges are necessary to resolve disputes over land. Presence of judges is particularly important as economic interactions become more complicated, for in such situations unforeseen contingencies are increasingly common.

For these reasons, the way I gauge clarity of allocation is presence of procedures to draw boundaries as well as presence of judges to resolve disputes over land within a claim club. In the absence of more precise data on clarity of allocation of ownership, an assessment of bureaucratic and judicial institutions is perhaps the best way to measure informal property arrangements in terms of clarity of allocation. Thus, the effectiveness of clubs in terms of clarity of allocation will be judged by the extent to which these organizations provided a framework for drawing boundaries as well as mechanisms to adjudicate disputes.

The evidence presented in the previous chapter suggests that claim clubs in each sector typically had clear rules for drawing boundaries as well as informal judicial institutions where they were needed.[1] Agricultural claim clubs had perhaps the most precise rules compared with clubs in other sectors. The constitutions of these clubs generally allowed people to enter a claim provided they marked their territories, recorded their claims, and (typically) occupied land. In addition, agricultural associations typically had judges, and in many situations they also had juries, authorized to hear disputes between members as well as between members and nonmembers. These informal judicial institutions had an important role in permitting members to resolve disputes without fighting, enhancing clarity of allocation in the process. Without judges, farmers would have been more likely to resort to force to resolve disputes, and in doing so their property regime would have been less effective in terms of clarity of allocation.

The judges and juries arising within claim clubs are quite interesting – indeed, they constitute an important part of the informal origins of judicial and legal institutions in the United States. However, it is also clear that there were two sources of clarity of allocation: a system of drawing boundaries and recording claims as well as judges/juries to resolve disputes. In studying agricultural claim clubs, I could not find any examples in which claim clubs lacked procedures for drawing boundaries *and* constitutional specification of informal judicial institutions to resolve disputes. The fact that these clubs seem to always include provisions for both drawing boundaries and for judges and juries suggests that they were general features of claim clubs.

These findings are also instructive for proponents of legal titling who suggest that writing down legal titles is key to improving a property regime (e.g., de Soto 1989, 2000). Legal titling is mainly an exercise in writing down boundaries. Clubs certainly drew boundaries, but to conclude that the boundaries themselves were the source of effective ownership would be naive. Rather, presence of informal judicial institutions had a great deal to do with the extent to which property institutions were effective. An implication is that legal titling, in the absence of a formalization of dispute resolution mechanisms or presence of an effective judicial system, will be unlikely to strengthen investment incentives.

Miners also developed a relatively complete set of procedural rules to claim land and resolve disputes. Mining districts had strict occupancy requirements and rules for recording claims. Miners forfeited claims by failing to occupy them, with forfeiture conditions defined in a mining district's rules. Although occupancy requirements are inefficient to the extent that they force people to lord over their possessions, these regulations were perhaps expedient during the gold rush because they limited confusion over claims, while also providing

[1] Chapter 3 includes relevant sources on the empirical features of claim clubs. The discussion in this chapter draws on those sources.

disincentives to jump claims (for fear of a fight). In addition, procedures for claiming land were transparent, as they were codified in the miners' constitutions that were typically published in local papers. Constitutions of mining districts, at least on paper, made it clear that claim jumping was unacceptable unless land was unoccupied.

As with farmers, miners also recognized that drawing boundaries could only take their society so far with respect to establishing ownership. Like agricultural claim clubs, mining districts had a clear set of procedures to adjudicate disputes, enshrined in the institution of the miners' court. Miners in conflict could call on judges and juries to resolve their disputes. Presence of boundary-drawing procedures complemented a system of informal judges, together enhancing the miners' property regimes on the dimension of clarity of allocation.

Of course, such systems of social control were imperfect, and they sometimes succumbed to conflict and violence. A general conclusion drawn from the experiences of California and Nevada is that mining districts *generally* suppressed conflict among diverse groups seeking to establish control of resources, and that ownership was clearly allocated. There were, however, important periods of disorder. As Stewart (2009) has shown, inflows of prospectors with different backgrounds and divergent expectations put pressure on social norms of cooperation within mining districts. Findings that inflows of people destabilized mining districts should not be surprising when we consider North's (1990) definition of institutions as shared expectations. For North, the key feature of institutions is that they stabilize expectations about behavior of others. Increases in heterogeneity exert pressure on any institutions, including informal ones, because of their effect on the extent to which expectations are shared.

The finding that mining districts often failed to provide sufficient social control raises some serious questions about the extent to which property regimes were effective in terms of clarity of allocation. However, my characterization of the districts as attaining success in the dimension of clarity of allocation only requires that the property institutions arising within their confines were generally effective, as well as comparable to what one might have expected from the state – not that they were perfect. If we compare private property rights arising within miners' clubs with what the state had to offer, then it seems reasonable to conclude that informal property institutions were a fairly effective alternative to formal ones, at least in the dimension of clarity of allocation. After all, during this time, the state's private property rights were largely disregarded by miners seeking to strike it rich, and so from that perspective, informal property institutions were presumably more effective than legal titles supposedly backed by the state.

Mining districts also enhanced clarity of ownership over water by incorporating appropriative norms into mining codes and into ditch companies or irrigation districts that brought water to local properties (Libecap 2007b). For example, norms of beneficial use, which provided for continued ownership as long as individuals were using water for productive activities, were common in mining camps. Even with the qualification that beneficial use may undermine incentives to conserve water (under such property regimes, it is better to use it up rather than to lose the right, which implies resource overuse), it seems clear that procedures to allocate ownership of water were more or less appropriate for the demands of the mining industry of the 1850s and 1860s. In particular, rules governing water use that emerged in the American Far West were superior compared with the Eastern system they replaced given vast differences in the geographic conditions between the regions.

Loggers and ranchers also required provisions for clarity of allocation, yet differed from other sectors in the sense that their institutions were not exclusively based on private property. Unlike farmers and miners, loggers and ranchers generally established access rights to a common-pool resource. However, as decades of research into the commons has shown us, the fact that loggers and ranchers secured primarily access rights for a group of claimants does not deny that this was a property regime (Bromley 1991, 1989; Ostrom 1990). Access rights perform the same essential functions as private property rights in that either system of property institutions encourages incentives to engage in productive activities. Their regulated common property regimes were effective, mainly because users could exclude others from the resource.

Features of a common property regime notwithstanding, loggers and ranchers also established private property institutions. In particular, claimants in these sectors each had to find a system to demarcate ownership of their capital assets – timber and cattle, respectively, each of which was regulated through a system of branding. These provisions requiring and standardizing branding systems were particularly important to attain clarity of allocation.

Informal property regimes governing timberland generally had a somewhat different constitutional structure than did other sectors. They did not write down constitution or have a clearly defined system for claiming land, most likely because it was larger-scale organizations seeking access to forests rather than individuals, a feature that reflected economies of scale in logging. A single person could become a farmer, but a logging operation required a company of men. Loggers' unions suppressed individual competition, transforming conflict from one in which many individuals were claiming land to one in which organizations were interacting. Consequently, one of the central functions of loggers' unions was establishing orderly access to forests, not in adjudication of disputes between individuals or even between logging camps in conflict. However, loggers nonetheless developed private-property norms that enhanced clarity of allocation, in particular log-marking norms. Without a log-marking system, the procedure of driving logs to markets using natural waterways over great distances would have been even more chaotic.

Ranchers had their own system of justice parallel to the state that enhanced their ability to delimit access rights to land as well as to establish a system to provide information regarding ownership of their primary capital asset. The system providing such information, of course, was branding cattle. These norms for branding assets, as well as provisions governing access to the open range, enhanced clarity of allocation.

Unlike loggers, ranchers devised an overarching organization that members could use to resolve disputes over land use. In particular, loggers did not have a structure analogous to cattlemen's peak associations until the logging industry was formalized. Informal judicial systems were not as precisely defined as in other sectors but cattlemen's associations themselves provided a forum to sort out competing "legal" claims. Even though they did not have dedicated legal institutions such as the miners' courts or the juries farmers used to resolve disputes, cattlemen's associations provided a forum for adjudication.

Of course, the question of how well ranchers regulated access to the range remains. It is easy to find fault in the informal property system as a method of conserving resources, especially by focusing on events such as the mass starvation of cattle during the harsh winter in 1886–7. This catastrophe, known as the Great Starvation, resulted because cattle were not fat enough to withstand the winter. It stands to reason that they would have been fatter – and less vulnerable to harsh environmental conditions – had there been better regulation of rangeland use. In terms of the discussion at hand, the Great Starvation is an issue of clarity of allocation, that is, of clearly defining who has access to the open range.

The crisis on the range during the late 1880s calls into question the effectiveness of informal mechanisms to manage access to rangeland. However, the fact that claim clubs rather than the state had the primary responsibility for regulating access to the range does not mean that the state would have prevented mass starvation, or that the state's rules would have been more expedient than those promulgated by claim clubs. Rather, the relevant question is the following one: Would government bureaucrats, at either the state or federal level, and most likely with very limited resources given the overall lack of state capacity in this period, have been better able to determine the carrying capacity of the range in the event of a harsh winter? In other words, why should we infer that the government would have set limits on use that would have been effective in fending off starvation during an extremely harsh winter?

It goes without saying that calculations regarding the carrying capacity of a range were difficult to make in the 1880s, not only for a claim club, but also for government officials. For example, it was only with the Morrill Act of 1862 that the federal government began setting aside lands for universities with the requirement that they establish "colleges for the benefit of agriculture and the mechanic arts." These land-grant universities, as they would come to be called, would ultimately supply training that would permit more effective management of the open range, but such schools were relatively new during this period, and it was far from clear that people would be rushing to the government with their newfound skills. In light of the unusual problems posed by that winter, mass starvation may not have been a result of ineffective claim-club property regimes, but rather an unforeseen contingency (weather) that ranchers or the government was unaware they had to ensure against. Government regulators would likely have been caught off guard by such a shock as well, especially because far less was known about scientific management of the range in the 1880s. An unpredictable act of nature, and not an inherent weakness in organizations regulating access to land, may be a more compelling explanation for the Great Starvation.

The problem just described is fundamentally one of information. Hayek's (1945) observation that governments lack knowledge of the "man on the spot" – the knowledge of local problems, namely what to produce and how to produce it – is relevant here. One of the implications of Hayek's insights regarding knowledge utilization is that political decentralization increases the ability of the government to utilize local knowledge. Accordingly, the question with respect to information is one of degree, in particular the extent to which political institutions facilitate utilization of knowledge. Cattlemen's associations were local political institutions with representatives much closer to the open range, in both geographic proximity and experience, than politicians from the nation's capital. For this reason, they would be more likely to utilize any knowledge available about rangeland management compared to the federal government (which would have had jurisdiction over the open range because it spanned public-land states).

Besides better knowledge, it also stands to reason that members of cattlemen's associations had much stronger incentives to acquire information regarding carrying capacity of the range, mainly because it was their livelihood on the line. It is not clear why government bureaucrats would have been better motivated to acquire such information. From a purely informational perspective, cattlemen's associations may have been the best bet as far as loss prevention from overgrazing is concerned. Yet once we take into account incentives, there are even fewer reasons to believe that the formal government would have been more motivated than cattlemen's associations to acquire relevant information.

Cattlemen's associations also had desirable features in terms of their capacity to govern effectively the behavior of key economic agents. Federal regulation, to be effective, required a government agency strong enough to enforce the law. In the dimension of likelihood of enforcement, it is highly unlikely that the federal government would have done much regarding rangeland management in the 1880s. As Carpenter (2001) explains, the bureaucracy in the Far West remained quite weak even as the American state expanded in the period after the Civil War. In this bureaucratic milieu, a more likely outcome of expansion of state authority over the range would have been a de facto open access situation. This problem is a more general one that continually confronts weak states seeking to manage access to natural resources. Indeed, inability of the state to manage natural resources is what motivated Ostrom (1990) to consider alternative ways to govern the commons besides state ownership or privatization.

Applying the insights of Hayek, Carpenter, and Ostrom to the events on the Western range in the 1880s, one could reasonably conclude that more effort by the federal government to regulate the open range would have created a free-for-all rather than stave off the Great Starvation. In terms of information, incentives, and capacity constraints, there are few reasons to believe that the federal government would have managed ranchers' affairs better than they did themselves, even though they sometimes failed in their efforts to regulate access to the open range. A more reasonable conclusion garnered from the experience of the range cattle industry during its takeoff phase is that cattlemen's associations did an effective job attaining clarity of allocation, and that the bust of the late 1880s was not due to inherent limitations with claim clubs as property regimes, but rather an unanticipated event that the federal government would in all likelihood have failed to ensure against effectively.

A final feature of claim clubs relevant to understanding clarity of allocation is procedural democracy. Calvert (2006) theorized that procedural democracy enhances legitimacy of a group's decisions, mainly because it increases incentives for individuals to abide by the rules collectively decided upon. In a sense, Calvert formalized von Mises's (1944) observation that "A lasting order cannot be established by bayonets." Like von Mises, Calvert recognized the interrelationship between political institutions, legitimacy, and political order. In the absence of institutions that confer legitimacy upon decisions, establishing a lasting order is difficult, and certainly more costly.

Calvert and von Mises provide a hint as to why property regimes on the American frontier were effective. Claim clubs typically included democratic procedures, such as common consent, to determine leadership positions within a club, and they also included jury trials. As the Condorcet jury theorem instructs, increasing the size of a jury increases the likelihood a decision reached is the "correct" one.[2] Yet a larger jury is also desirable because it increases the *enforceability* of decisions independent of whether or not the decisions are *correct*. Democratic procedures within claim clubs increased incentives for members to abide by rules and accept judicial decisions by lending legitimacy to decisions. Enhancing legitimacy meant that a judge's or jury's decisions and those of a club more generally were more likely to be followed, and these improvements in legitimacy likely increased clarity of allocation of property rights.

Of course, some might challenge the idea that claim clubs were democratic. My response is that claim clubs were not ideal democracies. Rather, they were "frontier democracies" comparable to formal democracy of the nineteenth century. Komesar's (2001, 1997) framework for comparative institutional analysis, which counsels us to compare actual institutional alternatives rather than to compare real-world institutions to some hypothetical "optimal" situation,

[2] For an excellent account of the implications of the jury theorem for democratic theory, see Elster and Landemore (2012).

TABLE 4.1. *Provisions for Clarity of Allocation*

Sector	Provisions
Agriculture	• Provisions for drawing boundaries and recording them. • Judges or juries hearing cases involving claim jumping and other disputes over ownership.
Mining	• Procedures for drawing boundaries and recording them. • Regularly meeting miners' courts with jury trials heard cases involving oftentimes complicated conflicts over claims.
Logging	• Regulation of access to forests for authorized logging companies. • Log-marking systems required of all loggers using a particular waterway.
Ranching	• Regulation of access to the open range. • Branding systems were required of all members using an area of the open range. • Cattlemen's associations provided a forum for resolving conflicts over land-use rights, trespass, and rustling.

helps us interpret claim club democracy. Clearly, claim clubs should not be compared to modern democratic institutions but rather to the actual alternative, which was formal democracy as it existed in newly chartered towns. In terms of a comparison with actual democratic institutions at the formal level, claim clubs were arguably as democratic as formal democracies that were available nearby in that they allowed most of the men to participate in their deliberations, and many also took a stand against slavery.

Even if one hesitates to view clubs as comparable with frontier democracies, it stands to reason that even a flawed democracy can enhance legitimacy of rules. This is not to say democracy produces efficient results. Indeed, there are many reasons why we should not expect democracies to produce efficient results. However, the main consequence of democratic procedures may lie in their contribution to legitimacy and hence enforceability of rules – regardless of whether they are efficient or not. It stands to reason that even imperfect democratic procedures increased clarity of allocation by lending legitimacy to decisions affecting members' land claims. Provisions for attaining clarity of allocation are summarized in Table 4.1.

ALIENABILITY

Alienability refers to the extent individuals can transfer property ownership. Institutions facilitating alienability are important because they determine the extent to which a property regime permits members to attain economies of scale in landholding. In addition, because it is unlikely that an initial allocation will allocate land rights to those who value them most, trade is essential to ensure those who value land most end up with it.

Alienability in terms of trade in deeds to land alone is important, although it is also important to consider whether or not people have sufficient opportunities to trade in the fruits of the land. As the following account indicates, clubs were generally effective in facilitating both types of trade.

Before discussing alienability in the case at hand, a few examples help motivate the importance of considering alienability. McChesney's (1981) analysis of Bureau of Indian Affairs (BIA) policies governing Indian lands in the 1870s and 1880s is exemplary in this regard. McChesney showed that government-imposed limits on alienability were perhaps the most important reason why Indians on BIA land typically failed as farmers, thus rejecting a commonly held belief that Indians made poor farmers. The BIA allocated to individual Indians a small amount of land, one that was far too small to achieve economies of scale. Specifically, Indian farmers were allocated fewer than 50 acres, whereas white farmers typically had several hundred acres of land. Vast differences in the amount of land allocated to Indians relative to whites made it exceptionally difficult for Indian farmers to attain economies of scale. McChesney provided compelling evidence that size constraints, rather than an inherent inability to succeed as farmers, were the primary reason why Indian farmers failed.

McChesney's insights are twofold. First, he explained how small claim size can doom productivity. Although economic studies tend to emphasize large landholding as a source of inefficiency (Bardhan and Mookherjee 2010; Sen 1981; Bardhan 1973), McChesney showed that government-imposed maximums can do just as much harm. Second, McChesney showed that trade in property rights can remedy a faulty initial allocation of resources. Although the government made a mistake by distributing land in sections that were too small for productive agriculture, the faulty initial allocation did not doom the landholding system as far as scale is concerned. If there had been opportunities to trade claims to BIA land, then Indian farmers who were the best at farming could attain economies of scale. Over time, Indians who recognized that they were not cut out to be farmers could trade land to better farmers, allowing the best farmers to accumulate enough land for them to compete with white farmers. However, because federal laws prohibited trade in claims, Indian farmers could not overcome initial allocational inefficiency. In this regard, the government created path dependence in the property system. The defining feature of theories of path dependence is that long-run evolution of institutions is often influenced by early choices (Pierson 2004, 2000; North 1990). As we can see, the BIA's no-trade provisions made overcoming initial policy mistakes difficult by design.

The experience of former slaves in the United States shortly after emancipation also illustrates the importance of alienability. Although the initial economic studies of emancipation of slaves and agricultural productivity emphasized credit constraints, such as Engerman's (1982) finding that ex-slaves were more likely to fail as farmers because they lacked access to credit, Miller (2007) explained why credit constraints were not the only problem facing former slaves. According to Miller's evidence, black farmers failed primarily because they were given only forty acres of land under the program popularly known as "forty acres and a mule" and prohibited from trading these claims. General Sherman's field orders – the source of forty acres program – reflected a belief that forty acres was enough to start a family farm in areas formerly controlled by the Confederacy.[3] Miller tests Sherman's implicit hypothesis that forty acres was sufficient to establish an occupation by comparing productivity of black farmers who took up forty acres (the federal government's program) and those who claimed land on Indian Territory (specifically, on Cherokee lands). The key difference (or what could be called a natural experiment) was that former slaves could claim as much land as was available on Indian land. Without the size constraint imposed by the forty acres program, black farmers on Indian land were essentially as productive as white farmers, holding constant other relevant factors. Taken together, these studies suggest economies of scale, as well as access to credit, drive improvements in agricultural productivity.[4]

The federal government also limited the ability of white farmers to obtain economies of scale under various federal "free land" programs. From the 1830s onward, the government allocated land in sections of 160 acres. Claims of this size were much larger than those granted to former slaves and Indians. They were nonetheless insufficient for many farmers. Size constraints, along with no-trade provisions of preemption and homestead laws, posed a substantial problem for farmers because 160 acres was often smaller than the size they believed was required for profitable agriculture.

When it comes to economies of scale, claim clubs injected efficiency into the preemption system by allowing members to evade the size constraints imposed by federal legislation. Indeed, one of the most important substantive features of agricultural claim clubs was allowing members to claim more than 160 acres of land. By denying trade in preemption claims, the federal government reduced the efficiency of the formal property regime. In terms of alienability, property regimes arising within claim clubs not only competed with the state but were superior to them because clubs allowed members to attain economies of scale. This does not mean that giving land away makes economic sense. Indeed, preemption was a massive transfer program. However, if the government was going to give land away, then it should have given it away in a size that makes the most economic sense, or at least allow trades in claims. Thus, claim clubs

[3] The forty acres policy was issued by William Tecumseh Sherman, Special Order 15, January 16, 1865. After Lincoln's assassination, Andrew Johnson rescinded the orders.

[4] Bromley (2008b) makes a similar point in arguing that legal titling is unlikely to improve economic fortunes unless people have jobs and access to credit. Bromley's point echoes Engerman's (1982) finding regarding the fate of emancipated slaves in the American South: legal title, without access to credit, is unlikely to help individuals attain economic development.

enhanced the efficiency of property regime by permitting those who acquired legal title to obtain economies of scale.

Of course, we have seen that trading systems arising within agricultural claim clubs had undesirable features. For example, farmers' associations engaged in a simple but pervasive form of protectionism. Claim constitutions specified that claims could be sold to any person provided an organization approved a buyer who was then bound by the rules of the organization and the privileges and obligations of the original claimants (Shambaugh 1894). An organizational veto over trade may have restrained beneficial speculation activities or artificially increased social and ethnic homogeneity.

Nevertheless, farmers' club-backed prescriptions governing trade appear to have been effective overall in terms of improving allocational efficiency. In general, farmers had opportunities to take up claims in excess of federally mandated minimums. In some regions of the Midwest, claim clubs allowed members to secure up to 640 acres of land. For example, most farmers in Nebraska claim clubs held 320 acres or more (Dick 1970, 1954).

Allowing individuals to double claim size relative to federal laws was a substantial innovation, especially in light of federal inaction. Congress eventually relaxed size constraints, but policy change occurred quite slowly, with formal changes occurring only with the 1909 Enlarged Homestead Act, which authorized claims of 320 acres in several Western states. However, these changes were clearly economically insufficient for the Far West (where scale was far larger than in the Midwest) and there was no legal reform to claim size in the Midwest even though a norm of 320- or 640-acre plots emerged by the 1840s – over a half century before the federal government adjusted claim size! In this inhospitable institutional environment, settlers had to devise their own methods to attain economies of scale, which they did by devising informal procedures to trade preemption claims.[5]

There is not a tremendous amount of evidence regarding conservation when claim clubs ruled the land. However, there is an analogy from the Dust Bowl that suggests the importance of provisions regarding scale. Using evidence from farm failure in the 1930s, Hansen and Libecap (2004a,b) showed that farmers with smaller claims were less willing to invest in conservation practices, making their farms more susceptible to busts because of drought. In contrast, larger farms were better able to withstand harsh economic conditions because they were able to practice superior crop rotation techniques. Indeed, they attribute

[5] One might counter this argument by suggesting that the larger claim sizes within claim clubs were evidence of speculation. This was likely the case, as many clubs included speculators who might have desired larger sections simply to increase their wealth rather than to obtain economies of scale in agricultural production. Yet speculation is not itself a "public bad," but rather, serves an important economic function in terms of allocating resources in an economy. Clubs were a source of economic efficiency even if they were allowing speculators to obtain economies of scale, because constraints on speculation could lead to allocational inefficiency even if none of the claimants themselves intended to till the land.

the Dust Bowl itself to the structure of property rights, in particular the constraints on landholding size. Applying Hansen and Libecap's insight to claim clubs, trade in preemption claims likely increased the ability of farmers who initially claimed land under the aegis of a club to weather the storm, literally and figuratively.

Besides permitting accumulation of preemption claims, clubs regulated trade in informal deeds more generally. In Colorado, for example, trades in informal deeds to land were common, with prices ranging from $1 to $750 an acre (Anderson 1939, 1936). To get an idea just how high land prices could climb, $750 an acre is around $20,000 in today's dollars. Despite regulations regarding speculation, there does not seem to be any evidence that clubs spent a lot of their resources seeking to prevent trade. Rather, provisions permitting trade, subject to certain restrictions, were built into the general constitutional matrix of agricultural claim clubs.

Like farmers' protective associations, mining districts included rules regulating trade in claims and goods. Codes of conduct rivaled state criminal codes, and they included regulations designed to facilitate economic transactions. Popular justice is more likely to make its way into Hollywood accounts of the gold rush. However, economic regulations – such as those regulating trade – provided the institutional foundation of emergence and expansion of a mineral sector in Western lands.

Trade appears to have been vibrant within the mining districts. During the heyday of mining districts, there were almost no restrictions on private sale of mineral claims despite lack of formal law to regulate trade. Although there may not have been many trades during the early years of the mining boom because of the costs of marketing, enforcing, and exchanging deeds in periods of great uncertainty, sale became routine as conditions settled down. As scale of operations increased, land prices increased dramatically and some of the mining companies were incorporated, with shares sold on the San Francisco Stock Exchange and other western financial markets to raise capital (Libecap 2007b).

Ranchers also developed innovative systems to trade informal deeds to land (Libecap 2007b; Anderson and Hill 2004; Dennen 1976). The underlying problem facing ranchers, which was first articulated in John Wesley Powell's *Report on the Lands of the Arid Region of the United States* in 1878, was inability to obtain land in sections large enough for activities in the Far West. In the Far West, 25 acres or more were required to sustain a single cow for a year, with upward of 10,000 acres necessary to achieve economies of scale in grazing for a single rancher. For this reason, many informal transactions involved vast sums of land even though the only source of "ownership" was only a claim club. One sale involved a deal where the seller had a legal title to 527 acres but the amount actually sold was 220,000 acres, for a price of $900,000 (Dick 1970). A price of $15 million (in today's dollars) seems like a paltry sum when we consider it included over two hundred thousand acres of land (or, to put it differently,

TABLE 4.2. *Provisions for Alienability*

Sector	Provisions
Agriculture	• Deeds to land (formal and informal) were tradable, subject to organizational approval. • Regulation of illegal trade in preemption claims to facilitate accumulation of legal title in excess of federal limits.
Mining	• Commercial codes of the mining districts facilitated trade in claims. • Criminal codes outlawed dishonest trading in goods. • Regulations governing trade in water rights.
Ranching	• Trade in access rights to the range was permitted, as membership in organizations was traded along with land rights. • Regulation governing trade in water rights.

$15 million for around 350 square miles of land).[6] Claim clubs facilitated the development of these informal yet effective markets in land formally owned by the government.

Another interesting aspect of economic institutions on the range was the practice of trading membership in a club along with deeds to land. Bundling claims with membership in a club affirms Bromley's (2008b, 2006) observation that a legal title means little unless there is someone willing to enforce it. Although Bromley emphasized the state as a source of enforcement, the more general point is that property institutions are collectively enforced, whether the enforcer is the state or some other organization. A deed to land, formal or otherwise, meant little unless a rancher could call on a cattlemen's association to give force to these ownership claims, which is why property deeds came with a club's membership.

Finally, ranchers and miners also developed rules to trade water claims. In the Far West, water claims were critical to reduce the risk associated with the ranching occupation. Nonetheless, federal law constrained ability of individuals to trade water claims even when they had legitimate claims to land. Cattlemen's associations, by including provisions granting authority to trade water along with deeds to land, improved informal property regimes in the dimension of alienability.

These findings suggest that each sector had provisions to facilitate trade when such regulations were expedient. I left out the logging business because loggers were more interested in clear-cutting forests than trading property rights to forest land (Carstensen 1958). Thus, alienability was not a relevant provision during the takeoff phase of the logging industry. Provisions for alienability for the remaining sectors are summarized in Table 4.2.

[6] Calculation made using a base year of 1870.

SECURITY FROM TRESPASS

Security from trespass, which refers to ability to defend claims from those who may covet what a person or group possesses, is perhaps the most important feature of a property system. As explained in Chapter 1, clarity of allocation and trade may be irrelevant if a property system lacks excludability. The reason is obvious: property insecurity means that someone will simply take, rather than trade, to obtain one's clearly demarcated land.

The importance of collective defense in the constitutional fabric of claim clubs affirms economic studies emphasizing the importance of excludability/security from trespass. Claim clubs in each sector defended members' land from outsiders as well as ensured that anyone within a club respected the "rights" of other members. Collective defense was particularly important in claim clubs because the state also had an interest in land, which created a potentially powerful adversary for a club's members – not to mention the threat posed by various competing groups, such as other squatters or Indian tribes. As such, it was essential for a club to defend members' interests, whether the threat originated from the state or other groups.

The names of agricultural claim clubs provide an important clue regarding the importance of collective defense in their mission. Farmers usually called their claim clubs "protective associations," a label that conjures up an image of exclusion. Nearly everywhere they existed, agricultural claim clubs included provisions stating that members owned land and that the club stood ready to give force to these convictions. At the heart of every claim club was a commitment to exclusivity as well as a collective defense pact to bring their vision closer to reality.

Agricultural associations were impressive in their ability to defend members' interests against outsiders, the latter category variously including claim jumpers, speculators, and Indian tribes. Indian tribes were sometimes a force to be reckoned with, in particular when settlers first began arriving in new territories in the late eighteenth and early nineteenth centuries. However, claim jumpers and speculators generally weighed heavier on the minds of the framers of the constitutions of these clubs than Indian tribes. The military, not claim clubs, typically swept Indian tribes from the land, with migration generally increasing on the heels of military success (Prucha 1969). More generally, the state was a driving force behind development of lands occupied by Indians.[7] Once the proverbial dust settled between the Army and Indians, wagon wheels began to kick up more dust. Claim jumpers were an important threat, and most claim constitutions explicitly prohibited claim jumping as a method of acquiring land. Anyone who jumped a claim faced the prospect that the compatriots

[7] On the state's role in conquest of Indian lands, see especially Rockwell (2010). As Rockwell explains, administration of Indian lands was one of the most important early demonstrations of the administrative capacity of the American state. On the role of the army in frontier development, see especially Watson (2012, 2011).

of the "victim" who would show up to enforce a club's rules. However, for reasons mentioned in the previous chapter, a club's primary adversaries were speculators, including anyone with aspirations to legally purchase land occupied by a club member. Because legal title was their ultimate goal, squatters had to organize collectively to ensure speculators did not bid on land they coveted. These changes in the contracting environment created a demand for excludable contracts, which, as it turned out, clubs could supply.

Miners faced a similar challenge, as they had to defend land from formal owners or collections of squatters from other regions or states. At a fundamental level, mining codes were agreements to defend claims from all challengers. During California's squatter wars, formation of a mining district was meant to be a warning shot to anyone who challenged the rule of squatters, including formal owners as well as the state (Pisani 1994). However, exclusion from mining districts was not limited to formal owners and the state. Claim clubs in California sometimes prohibited Chinese immigrants from owning mines (Kanazawa 2005). As mentioned in Chapter 3, claim clubs in Nevada were also known to include restrictions on Chinese ownership of mines in their constitutions (Lord 1959 [1881]). Discrimination of this sort is of course socially costly but it illustrates the power of clubs to exclude unauthorized users from land they coveted. All told, miners were effective in excluding formal owners and unauthorized miners from land they coveted, establishing access to valuable minerals regardless of the formal legal rules on the books. Yet as efforts to exclude Chinese miners illustrate clearly, establishing security from trespass inherently involves distributive conflict: the power to exclude is the power to distribute and redistribute the gains from establishing property institutions.[8]

Mineral rights, oftentimes sufficient to encourage production, were not always effective on the dimension of excludability. Local rules were slow to change, leading to widespread claim jumping and inundation in courts with ejectment claims (David and Wright 1997; McCurdy 1976). In addition, Clay and Wright (2010, 2005) and Clay (2006) suggest that there was widespread evidence of outright dispossession and disputes arising from ambiguities of mining district rules. Nonetheless, mining districts were often – though not always – effective in attaining security from trespass, at least as well as could be expected given the uncertain conditions on the mining frontier.

Loggers and ranchers also had to secure their claims from outsiders. Weak federal and state laws, as well as unwillingness to pay for access rights to forests, were some of the basic rationales for loggers' unions. Loggers' unions defended claims from Indian tribes and competing squatters, although as we saw in the previous chapter, their primary antagonist was often the federal government. The property regime governing timberland was closer to regulated common property than private property. Nonetheless, property regimes

8 Indeed, most processes of institutional change involve distributive conflict rather than Pareto improvements, a point made clear by Knight and Sened (1995) and Knight (1992).

governing timberland attained excludability, as loggers ensured that unauthorized users, such as the government, stayed off the land they desired. One of the most obvious examples was excluding federal agents from timberland formally owned by the state. In terms of explaining excludability, loggers' unions are the obvious mechanism translating individual interests into collective security: loggers were able to exclude outsiders from their territory was because they were collectively organized.

Finally, collective security was a chief concern among ranchers, who faced several threats to their access to the range as well as their cattle. Farmers were among their chief antagonists, with cattlemen's associations often mobilizing to secure access to the range when farmers occupied it, leading to what are popularly referred to as the "range wars." For example, farmers commonly confronted ranchers over the latter's "ticky cows" (for farmers, range cattle were varmints) and oftentimes unrestricted use of rangeland (Kantor 1991). In an environment of formal institutional ambiguity, claim clubs increased ranchers' ability to defend their interests against farmers. Rustlers were also a threat to ranchers, and the stock associations stood ready to defend their cattle from collections of bandits (Stuart and Phillips 1925).

All told, stock associations secured access to the range and provided security for their capital investments on long drives. Through their claim clubs, ranchers increased their ability to collectively defend their property from threats they faced collectively. Their ability to convene "small armies" in response to rustling, to use Granville Stuart's phrase, undoubtedly helped them provide for collective security.

As a more general matter, one of the reasons clubs were successful in their conflicts without outsiders was their ability to acquire reputations, a phenomenon that appears to have been common across sectors. As game theorists instruct, reputations are like assets.[9] Because a reputation is like an asset, an investment is required to acquire one. Clubs acquired a reputation by challenging the first people who ventured to bid on their land or jumped a member's claim. Because collective punishment is costly and risky, it signaled to future transgressors that a club meant business. Indeed, the tactics of claim clubs in each sector appear to have been well known, with their reputations ultimately improving their property regime in the dimension of excludability. Provisions of the dimension of security from trespass are summarized in Table 4.3 for claim clubs in each sector.

CREDIBILITY OF PERSISTENCE

The foregoing dimensions of a property system are static measures of effectiveness of ownership norms. A property system also varies on the dimension of credibility of persistence, which is a dynamic aspect of property relations

[9] On the role of reputations in economics, see Mailath and Samuelson (2006).

TABLE 4.3. *Provisions for Security from Trespass*

Sector	Provisions
Agriculture	• Exclusive ownership for members. • Collective shows of force when dealing with "outsiders." • Rules prohibiting claim jumping, provided members abided by a club's rules.
Mining	• Exclusive ownership for individual miners. • Collective enforcement mechanisms, including the people's court. • Pacts to defend those who supported free mining against authorities bent on other uses of land.
Logging	• Exclusion of outsiders (Indian tribes and the government) from timberland. • Enforcing bidding cartels to defend land interests against outsiders.
Ranching	• Collective defense of the open range territory. • Sometimes forming ad hoc "armies" to defend their access rights from other users of the land as well as from cattle rustlers.

that refers to the likelihood that property institutions will exist in the future. For claim clubs to be effective as private property regimes, they also required provisions in the dimension of credibility of persistence. Because credibility is fundamentally a political and constitutional problem, we can look to constitutional features of claim clubs in order to better understand their performance in this dimension of a property regime.

The problem of credibility of commitment was articulated primarily by political scientists and political economists interested in the relationship between constitutions and emergence of private property rights. Scholars working in this tradition conceptualized of the credibility problem in terms of incentives of the government to renege on its agreement to protect private property rights once investments are made (Haber et al. 2003; Weimer 1997; Riker and Weimer 1993; North and Weingast 1989). The logic can be stated simply, as follows. Prior to investment decisions, the government has incentives to promise to protect property rights because the state is a residual claimant in production through its taxation authority. However, once investments are made, the government now wants to extract as much wealth as possible. In the absence of constraints on rulers, a government's promise is likely to be time inconsistent in the sense that an optimal decision for the government differs between time periods: before investments are made, the government's optimal decision is to respect property, though the optimal decision ex post is to extract as much as possible (Diermeier et al. 1997).[10] Individuals

10 The theory of credibility set forth by Diermeier et al. (1997) is a wonderful application of the time-inconsistency problem famously articulated by Kydland and Prescott (1977).

recognize that the government's incentive is to take everything once investments are made, and so they rationally choose not to invest anything in the first place.

The main implication of these studies is that the government can do better by "tying its own hands," that is, by limiting its discretion. We might assume more choice is always better. However, this is not always the case. Indeed, economic historians have shown the importance of political institutions and political reform that limit the choices available to government as an explanation for long-run improvements in investment and economic growth (Rosenthal 1992; North and Weingast 1989; Root 1994, 1989).

Although existing studies of credibility stress the extent to which *formal* organizations, namely governments, can commit credibly to respect for private property institutions, credibility is also relevant in *informal* organizations such as claim clubs because they represented the origins of political power as well as property institutions. Thus, it is important to consider whether or not the constitutional features of claim clubs include provisions to enhance credibility of persistence in our effort to understand the nonstate origins of private property institutions.

The specter of reallocation of property from weaker to stronger members arose with establishment of a club's hierarchy. However, several factors enhanced credibility of commitment to respecting property institutions within a club. One of the most important was constraints on leaders. Generally speaking, a club's leaders, as well as its judges and juries, were appointed through popular consent or other democratic procedures, constraints that reduced the incentives of leaders to expropriate land from members. Because these political constraints were documented in the previous chapter, it is sufficient here to note that they had an important role in facilitating credibility of persistence.

Economic interdependence also enhances credibility of persistence. In each sector under consideration, enforcers were themselves vulnerable to outsiders. Because a club's leaders were themselves vulnerable, it reduced their incentives to redistribute wealth or land of weaker members because they ultimately depended on the club for their own property protection as well.

Mutual dependence of this sort was common in each sector. Officials in agricultural claim clubs were themselves farmers dependent on other farmers for their security. Similarly, mutual dependence among miners in the face of formal property owners (both the state and citizens) reduced incentives of more powerful miners to reallocate access from weaker ones. In addition, as individual miners were also themselves relatively strong and prone to building "garrisons" when they had disputes, it was less likely that a club's leaders would be able to take from them (Lord 1959 [1881]). Strength of individual miners, or at least their ability to impose costs on others seeking to dislodge them, suggests a relative balance of power between the "lawmen" and the regular miners. Finally, ranchers who were in leadership positions were themselves dependent on cattlemen's associations to provide order on the range, thus

TABLE 4.4. *Provisions for Credibility of Persistence*

Sector	Provisions
Agriculture	• Democratic procedures for selecting leaders. • Mutual dependence between a club's leaders and members for collective defense.
Mining	• Democratic procedures for selecting leaders. • A balance of power between district leaders and regular miners.
Ranching	• Democratic procedures for selecting leaders.

reducing the chances that the associations wielded their power against weaker members of the club.

Thus, in each sector, mutual dependence reduced incentives of leaders of clubs to renege on their promise because it would ultimately harm their own interests. Because providers of public goods were also consumers of the security they helped to provide, leaders of these associations had fewer incentives to shirk on their duties. More generally, mutual dependence is a source of credibility that has not received much attention in the literature on credibility of commitment. The discussion of its role within claim clubs suggests its importance as well as an avenue for future research.

Provisions associated with credibility are summarized in Table 4.4. Because loggers' unions did not provide property protection to individual claimants, credibility of persistence was not as relevant in that sector. However, their organizations certainly imposed costs on the state for reneging on any private property rights promised to loggers.

Property systems arising within claim clubs thus had provision on all four dimensions of a property system, with few exceptions. Clubs were capable of drawing borders and boundaries, regulating trade, and defending claims from outsiders. In addition, political features of claim clubs, such as democracy and division of authority, as well as what appears to be mutual vulnerability among leaders and ordinary members of a club, increased the credibility of private property institutions arising within claim clubs. Based on these findings, it is reasonable to conclude that clubs were worthy competitors to the state in the provision of property institutions.

CONCLUSION TO PART I

Part I of this book is now complete. The theoretical and empirical study of claim clubs complements economic studies of informal order, which use history to illustrate how individuals can contract effectively without relying on the state, by showing how claim clubs fit into the framework of "order without law." Claim clubs can be added to the list of important private-order solutions to contracting problems in the shadow of the state, such as private-order judges during medieval times and the trading coalitions of Mexican California. Claim clubs were the primary source of property institutions among individuals who occupied government land without legal title. They were also more sophisticated organizations than trading coalitions and related organizations in terms of their political features, and the economic activities they regulated were more diverse than trade alone.

The account of private-order contracting arrangements is interesting from a theoretical and empirical perspective. At the same time, the role of the state must be acknowledged in the origins of private property institutions. Despite sweeping away the allegedly all-powerful state of political theories of property rights, claim clubs also relied on it in many ways. For example, the state often cleared the land of Indians and, more generally, it was the state that policed the nation's borders, as well as acquired land from foreign adversaries. For these reasons, we cannot ignore the state. At the same time, the evidence presented in Part I demonstrates that something fundamental is missing from political theories of property institutions. As the theory of claim clubs predicts and the empirical evidence validates, the state was not the only source of private property institutions on the American frontier. This finding is consistent with the central claim of my theory: claim clubs rivaled the state as a source of private property institutions.

These accounts of informal order, while intriguing, provide an incomplete account of the political economy of claim clubs. The fact that claim clubs were a remarkable achievement in terms of self-governance does not necessarily imply that they were a socially beneficial response to poorly designed land laws. Land laws, if anything, were ineffective *because of* claim clubs. The remainder of the book explores the political consequences of claim clubs. As it turns out, these organizations, which were remarkable in their capacity for self-governance, were also exceptionally effective as rent-seeking organizations.

PART II

CHANGE IN PRIVATE PROPERTY INSTITUTIONS

5

The Distributive Politics of Squatters' Rights

Why do property institutions change? Claim clubs often pushed the state aside in the rush to specify private property institutions on their own. However, their members eventually had to harness the state's power to receive legal title. This chapter presents the first of several empirical studies of change in property institutions, focusing on one of the fundamental policies governing property rights to agricultural land in the nineteenth century: preemption laws, which were popularly known as "squatters' rights" because they awarded legal titles – typically in the amount of 160 acres – to individuals who prospectively occupied government land. To help sort through the process of institutional change, the first part of the chapter provides a theoretical framework that will guide the empirical inquiry in the rest of the book.

The goal of this chapter (and Part II of this book more generally) is to understand the extent to which change in major land laws affecting participants in each of the sectors under consideration reflected efficiency or distributive considerations, as well as to better understand the consequences of claim clubs in the process of institutional change. Economic studies of institutional development during this period provide a preliminary answer to these questions, outlined in Chapter 1: federal land laws were poorly designed, with claim clubs pushing for more effective land laws. Eventually, the federal government realized that the clubs were the source of innovation in the economy, reversing course and recognizing their property rights. Overall, economic accounts tend to look favorably on squatters' rights as well as the role of claim clubs in the process of institutional change, saving their criticism for what they viewed as a slow-moving federal government.

This findings presented in this chapter (as well as the ones that follow) call into question economic perspectives of the sort outlined above. My argument is that economic studies praising claim clubs overlook distributive features of claim clubs. To assess this economic hypothesis as well as my alternative perspective on claim clubs, it is necessary to first step back and identify the outcomes of interest.

As a general matter, my concern is with the alternative mechanisms of allocating state-owned land, namely the extent to which the government allocated land through competitive land auctions, as well as the extent to which auctions produced a price that reflected demand and supply conditions, as opposed to bargaining power of key groups. For reasons explained later, the efficiency perspective will be represented by the extent the federal government and state governments allocated land competitively through auctions. Competitive land auctions were socially desirable because they put land into the hands of those who valued it most while at the same time providing the state with revenue to provide public goods.

Consistent with an efficiency rationale for institutional change, the government created markets for public land as early as 1785, while the Articles of Confederation still remained in effect. Competitive auctions allowed individuals to acquire private property rights while also providing the state with an important potential source of nontax revenue it could use to provide public goods, including national defense.

Once we understand the status quo of competitive land auctions, the political economy of claim clubs comes into clearer focus. Claim clubs, rather than a socially desirable response to poorly designed land laws, were a source of social costs precisely because of their effort to dismantle, evade, or otherwise undermine competitive land auctions. Besides providing a source of nontax revenue to fund an army and infrastructure necessary for capitalist development, revenue from public land was to be used for education expenditures. Despite these desirable uses of revenue from land, clubs worked to undermine auctions at every turn. These remarkable self-governing organizations also undermined institutional innovations seeking to balance the state's interest in revenue with individual thirst for land. They were rent-seeking organizations by design.

At a more fundamental level, claim clubs undermined the fabric of the young American federal system during a time in which the power of the federal government was by no means institutionalized. As Bednar (2008) explains, federations must satisfy several conditions in order to be considered "robust," in particular that there are overlapping constraints on leaders. The political economy of early land policy complements Bednar's framework by illustrating the importance of overlapping sources of *revenue* as an additional explanation for federal stability.[1] Securing a fraction of the scarcity rent associated with state-owned land took on greater significance because collecting taxes presented logistical

[1] Specifically, Bednar's design problems that destabilize federations include incomplete coverage of opportunism, ineffective safeguards, unreliable safeguard response, overly frequent sanctions, adapting the distribution of authority, and identification of socially beneficial adjustments. To this list, we could add lack of reliable revenue sources, with overlapping sources of revenue as an additional design principle for robust federations.

and bureaucratic challenges throughout the early nineteenth century (Grubb 2010; Pollack 2009). Each mechanism for generating revenue was imperfect, and overreliance on any single source of revenue threatened the robustness of the American federal system. For example, Shay's Rebellion and others like it demonstrated the costs of implementing direct taxes, and indirect taxes, such as a tax on imported goods, threatened an outbreak of protectionism. In an environment of institutional weakness, nontax revenue from the nation's vast stock of land had special significance. By systematically undermining nontax revenue opportunities in a context with little slack as far as revenue is concerned, claim clubs undercut an important leg of a weak federal state.

Besides providing insight into the political economy of federalism, a distributive perspective on claim clubs complements existing perspectives on property institutions utilizing the framework of "new institutional economics" by considering explicitly conflict over the *price* of land.[2] For example, North and Rutten (1987), in analyzing the Northwest Ordinance of 1787, were more concerned with emergence of private property institutions during this period than distributive conflict over the price of legal title that followed. Sened (1997) also used the Northwest Ordinance as an example of emergence of private property institutions, yet did not consider the prolonged conflict over the price for the next century. Likewise, Libecap (1989), in his remarkably insightful study of emergence of property institutions in American economic history, clearly articulated how distributive fights could prevent emergence of private property institutions without giving much attention to the price at which land changed hands. Accordingly, each of the aforementioned perspectives, which are among the most compelling studies of origin and change in property institutions, are nevertheless incomplete, mainly because they underestimate distributive conflict over the price of land.

There are, however, a few important studies that consider land auctions from a political economy perspective. For example, Grubb (2010, 2007) offers many insights into the distributive dimensions of land policy from 1781 to 1802, as well as precise data regarding the relationship between public land and government debt. In addition, Dougherty (2001) articulates precisely the revenue challenges confronting the Articles of Confederation from 1781 to 1787. The main problem in terms of revenue was that the Articles funded the federal government almost entirely by voluntary contributions from the states, and so the constitutional structure institutionalized a collective action problem.

2 The main difference between the "old" and "new" institutional economics is mainly a concern with rational choice and institutions as the product of strategic interactions between rational individuals in the latter. The old institutionalists, such as Thorsten Veblen and John Commons, were more concerned with providing the reasons for institutional emergence and change rather than using history to assess different mechanisms of institutional change. My approach tends to draw on insights from each perspective. An excellent explanation of the differences between alternative perspectives in institutional economics is Bromley (2006).

The analysis in this chapter complements these earlier studies of revenue generation in the early republic by considering protracted conflict over auctions after their initial creation, one that would continue long into the nineteenth century. The aforementioned studies focus mainly on the period shortly before, during, and shortly after the Articles of Confederation. However, distributive conflict over land was a much more general feature of American land laws. In addition, neither of these earlier studies considers explicitly land auctions from the process of institutional change, focusing instead on a static economic assessment of different institutions during the late eighteenth century.

This chapter, as well as subsequent ones, also provides insight into the organizational foundation of political advantages of first possession. Economists interested in evolution of property rights have shown that those who first claim land often have advantages keeping it (Alston et al. 2011; Libecap 2007a, 2007b, 1989; Alston et al. 1999). Claim clubs are an excellent example of how first-in-time possessors can translate a first-mover advantage into formal representation. These first-move advantages also validate Knight's (1992) theory of bargaining power in the process of institutional change, which stressed how de facto influence generally translates into de jure representation.[3] It is hard to imagine a group that was more successful in translating informal norms into formal representation and legal rights than American squatters, an outcome anticipated by Knight's theory of institutional change. At the same time, my empirical studies alert us to organizational strength, not simply first possession, in the struggle for legal title. Economic studies tend to emphasize that those who first acquire land have advantages without considering the extent to which those possessors are organized. First possession was not a source of political advantage in and of itself but rather it was advantageous because those who were first in time to claim land had the strongest groups.

One of the central lessons of the empirical studies of land laws in Part II of this book is that changes in institutions governing agricultural land were full of contradictions. On one hand, a formal system of private property institutions emerged seemingly wherever land was valuable, a finding that lends evidence to an efficiency perspective on institutional change: the fact that private property institutions emerged in response to substantial opportunities for Pareto improvement can certainly be interpreted as socially desirable institutional change. Yet we do not necessarily want to cast aside institutional conflict simply because private property rights eventually emerged. This period witnessed one of the most thorough subversions of competitive markets in American economic history. From the moment land markets were created, illegal occupation undermined federal institutions designed to *facilitate* decentralization of ownership. To be sure, the government did not stand idly by as squatters disregarded formal law – for example, Congress responded to illegal occupation

[3] Acemoglu and Robinson (2008, 2006) also emphasize the relationship between de facto and de jure authority, although many of their conclusions are anticipated by Knight.

with an intrusion bill in 1807 that sought to protect legal owners from squatters. However, the federal government repeatedly chose, or was coerced into making, concessions to illegal occupants. Formal private property institutions emerged during this period, but the underlying mechanism governing institutional development was distributive conflict.

This chapter is organized into two parts. The first part considers implications of alternative theories of institutional change. The thrust of the discussion is that an efficiency perspective suggests land will be allocated competitively through markets, while a distributive perspective, which introduces claim clubs as mechanisms of institutional change, predicts that the state will allocate land based on bureaucratic priorities. The second part of the chapter is a case study of the origins of preemption laws. To foreshadow the conclusions, proliferation of agricultural preemption laws is a remarkable example of successful rent seeking, one that has been overlooked in existing studies of change in private property institutions. Throughout the period under consideration, public policies rewarding frontier farmers and speculators with cheap land were far more common than laws strengthening markets for public land, affirming implications of distributive theories of institutional change. As such, the findings of this chapter are a prelude to a more general theme uncovered in Part II of this book: claim clubs were distributive-minded organizations that were typically successful in their efforts to extract scarcity rent from the state.

EFFICIENCY AND DISTRIBUTIVE PERSPECTIVES ON INSTITUTIONAL CHANGE

Before considering alternative perspectives on institutional change, it is necessary to consider briefly the efficiency properties of alternative land-allocation mechanisms. Libecap (2007a,b), drawing upon and extending Coase's (1966, 1959) insights regarding the virtues of markets as a mechanism to allocate property rights, explained why competitive auctions of state-owned land are generally considered an efficient land-allocation mechanism. The reason is straightforward: when property is allocated through competitive markets, individuals whose marginal benefit is highest receive land and the state receives, at a minimum, its reservation price. Although economic perspectives tend to focus on the efficiency of allocation from the perspective of individuals who themselves secure the property rights, it is also important to remember that competitive auctions provide the state with revenue to provide public goods.

Alternatively, land may be allocated based on "bureaucratic priorities," which can be defined generally to include any nonmarket pricing system. In contrast to competitive allocation of land, allocation based on bureaucratic priorities is unlikely to produce an efficient allocation of resources because doing so would require the government to acquire information regarding people whose marginal value of land ownership is highest even though they are allocating land through nonmarket institutions. Because markets provide important information regarding marginal valuation through the price mechanism – information that governments cannot generally obtain regarding marginal benefits – an allocation based on bureaucratic priorities is unlikely to be economically efficient. Of course, though it may not be efficient, bureaucratic allocation may be politically expedient.

For these reasons, competitive land auctions – both institutions creating them and their successful implementation – are a reasonable choice as an efficient land-allocation mechanism, while institutions that allocate land based on bureaucratic priorities, or successful efforts to collude at auctions, will generally reflect distributional concerns. Yet my primary interest is not in a static assessment of the welfare properties of alternative land-allocation mechanisms. Rather, it is in the process of institutional change. As Riker and Weimer (1995) observed, once efficient institutional outcomes are identified, a theory of institutional change helps to limit the range of possible choices. In order to facilitate such narrowing of choices, two hypotheses are proposed: the first is that political actors will choose competitive markets to allocate land (an efficiency hypothesis); the second predicts that the state will allocate land based on bureaucratic priorities (a distributive hypothesis). Each of these hypotheses will be empirically evaluated using key developments in nineteenth-century land laws, beginning with preemption laws in this chapter before assessing these theories more broadly in subsequent chapters.

An Efficiency Hypothesis

In the most general sense, an efficiency perspective on institutional change suggests that institutions will change in response to opportunities for Pareto improvement (see, e.g., Barzel 2002, 1989; North 1981; as well as the discussion of efficiency perspectives in Chapter 1). Despite the fairly clear implications of a generalized efficiency perspective, it is still necessary to fill in some details in order to understand why governments are hypothesized to choose competitive auctions to allocate their land. To do this, I make use of the theoretical perspectives of Levi (1988) and Olson (2000, 1993), which help sort out the hypothesized interrelationship between political interests, revenue, and private property institutions. In addition, the discussion below draws on insights from evolutionary perspectives on property institutions. Taken together, these various perspectives can be used to construct an efficiency hypothesis for change in nineteenth-century land laws.

Levi's fundamental contribution to understanding of the "state" – defined conventionally as the organization that enjoys a monopoly on coercion in society – was to articulate clearly that the state's main goal is to maximize its revenue. Olson's theory of the origins of property institutions complements Levi's generalized theory of the state in arguing that property protection is a source of long-run revenue for the state, in particular that private property institutions encourage production, which in turn increases the state's revenue basis.

A virtuous outcome in which the state provides private property protection and individuals invest in land contrasts to the situation under roving banditry, the latter involving unrestrained expropriation of wealth, mainly because nobody is powerful enough to establish property rights, and so the optimal action is to extract as much as possible before someone else does the same.[4] Olson recognized that establishing private property institutions is perhaps the fundamental means by which the state increases its long-run revenue prospects. Whereas Levi understood the *ends* the state seeks, Olson clearly articulated the *means* to attain that end.

In contrast to Olson's static theory, evolutionary perspectives on institutions also provide a rationale for emergence of private property. Evolutionary theories specify competitive pressure as a mechanism of change in institutions, including property institutions.[5]

The logic of evolutionary change in property rights can be stated simply. First, private property institutions are assumed to be a source of productivity. Second, the state is viewed as a residual claimant in production. However, to make this an evolutionary account, we require a few additional assumptions about political and economic competition. For example, suppose we assume that as revenue declines, a state that fails to provide for property protection will weaken relative to its competitors, and its security declines along with revenue. The hypothesized relationship between revenue and war creates competitive pressure for leaders to create or adopt private property institutions. In particular, a state that fails to provide property protection can expect less revenue to provide public goods, including security, and in the face of declining capacity vis-à-vis its adversaries, a state will be compelled to adopt private property institutions (I say "adopt" rather than "choose" private property because the notion of "compelled choice" is conceptually incoherent). In the long run – perhaps over centuries – revenue incentives may force states to adopt private property institutions in order to survive because it is private property protection that ultimately provides the revenue base that fuels the state's military might and hence its security.

The perspectives offered by Levi and Olson can be interpreted as an efficiency rationale for institutional change. The Olsonian state maximizes revenue, as Levi suggested, with private property institutions posited as a fundamental

[4] Olson is perhaps most closely associated with the argument that the state provides property protection in exchange for tax revenue. However, North and Thomas also recognized that a state is more likely to be successful in the long run if it provides private property rights. Olson's contribution was to more explicitly relate property protection, revenue, and state formation. North and Thomas's neoclassical theory of the state also anticipates much of Levi's theory of the state and Sened's theory of the origins of property institutions.

[5] North (1981), North and Thomas (1973), and Alchian and Demsetz (1973) provide insight into competitive pressure as a source of emergence of private property institutions. One of the foundational theoretical studies of evolution and economics is Alchian (1950), who explained that firms survive not if they maximize profit, but if they realize positive profit.

means to increase revenue. An implication, one that is echoed by the evolutionary rationale outlined above, is that the process of institutional change will culminate with emergence of private property institutions, which are generally considered efficiency-enhancing institutions. Each of these perspectives also has implications for the choice of land-allocation mechanisms. Because competitive land auctions maximize a state's short-run revenue prospects, these theories suggest that a state will choose competitive auctions as a means of decentralizing property ownership. More generally, these theoretical perspectives suggest the following efficiency hypothesis: *a revenue-maximizing state will privatize state-owned land through competitive auctions.*

Of course, the introduction to this chapter hinted that the defining feature of conflict over land in U.S. economic history was a weakening of land auctions. To understand these dynamics, it is useful to consider the implications of generalized distributive theories of institutional change, which are tailored in the following to the context of early American land policies.

A Distributive Hypothesis

The primary hypothesis of generalized distributive theories of institutional change is that institutional change reflects conflict over division of wealth rather than creation of wealth (Acemoglu and Robinson 2008, 2006; Knight and Sened 1995; Knight 1992). Organizations are perhaps the primary source of distributive policies. For example, North (1990) viewed "organizational maximization" as the main obstacle to efficiency-enhancing institutional change. North (2005) and Denzau and North (1994) also articulated how cognitive constraints could contribute to inefficient policies, in particular how ideology can lead to socially costly mistakes in choosing institutions.[6]

One might conclude from these studies that things would be better as far as efficiency is concerned if there were no organizations or if the subjective models of decision makers were more precise. However, fundamental features of political institutions suggest that we cannot escape distributive conflict. Most notably, Arrow (1951) proved the inherent inability of democracy to coherently represents society's preferences. Strategic manipulation of voting agendas and majoritarian instability call into question the possibility of democracies ever producing efficient public policies. Caplan (2007) comes to a similar conclusion, albeit for different reasons, arguing that democracies produce inefficient policies, not because voters are rationally ignorant in the sense that they do not want to expend resources acquiring costly information, but because democratic procedures discourage rationality on the part of voters. In particular, democracies create few incentives for people to abandon their irrational

[6] Acemoglu (2003) also considers how ideology influences the process of institutional change, explaining how ideological mistakes all but ensure political bargaining will produce inefficient public policies.

beliefs. By recognizing that voters derive utility from their irrational beliefs, Caplan provides a rational route to irrationality in democratic policymaking. Organizational conflict and ideology, along with inherent features of political institutions, provide a powerful rational for distributive conflict as a general feature of institutional change.

Weimer (1997) and Riker and Weimer (1995) specified several sources of distributive policies, including political interests, bureaucratic interests, and interest groups.[7] Among these mechanisms, group conflict is perhaps most relevant to understanding the course of land laws during the nineteenth century, in particular claim clubs, which as we shall see were among the most important organizations in many regions during various periods throughout the late eighteenth and nineteenth centuries. Before specifying a distributive hypothesis, it is useful to consider the various ways claim clubs exerted pressure on formal land institutions, mainly because clubs were not "lobbying" in the modern sense of the term. Rather, their lobbying consisted of tactics appropriate and feasible for the period in question, which did not involve vote buying in the conventional sense, but were effective nonetheless.

Is This Land Worth the Trouble?

The first way claim clubs contributed to distributive outcomes was by increasing the cost of policing state-owned land. A state, if it hopes to profit from the land it formally owns, has to make capacity investments necessary to keep unauthorized users off the land. In terms of the dimensions of a property regime, the state's problem is attaining security from trespass because both private property and state ownership regimes vary in terms of security. Security from trespass on state-owned land, in turn, requires a bureaucracy capable of demarcating and policing state-owned land – monitoring land use, removing unauthorized users, creating disincentives to occupy land illegally, and so on.

Claim clubs contributed to distributive policies by increasing the state's costs of policing the state ownership regime, and in the process increased the return to bureaucratic allocation of land. Over time, increases in illegal occupation can alter the benefit–cost matrix such that the state no longer finds competitive auctions – or state ownership more generally – worth the trouble. As clubs fanned across the country, the return to allocation through bureaucratic priorities became more politically attractive.

[7] Bromley (1989) provides a similar framework, identifying various mechanisms of institutional change including rent-seeking by concentrated interest groups and changes in the "full social consumption set," which is essentially society's preference over social welfare. It should be noted that Bromley (2006) argues that his earlier characterization was too restrictive, proposing instead that only way to actually explain why institutions change is to understand the process by which people fix beliefs on the meaning of economic institutions. Although the later work by Bromley is compelling, the earlier version seems to be more useful to understanding change in property institutions on the American frontier.

Are You Sure You Want to Throw Your Hat In?

A second way claim clubs facilitated distributive outcomes was by creating disincentives for people who disagreed with them to enter elections. In nineteenth-century American democracies at the local level, anyone could enter elections provided they met basic constitutional requirements. Of course, reality dictated that practical considerations came into play when deciding whether or not to enter politics. These practical considerations include anticipated costs of political participation. More generally, economic and political theories suggest that reputations will come into play in politics (Wiseman 2005; Dharmapala 2002). These perspectives suggest that the decision to enter politics will depend on the ability of groups to credibly signal punishment for entry, which in turn depends on the ability of a group to make investments in capacity necessary to deter entry.

More formally, political entry can be conceptualized of as a game with two stages. In the first stage, associations such as claim clubs choose a level of investment in political capacity. In the second stage, candidates decide to enter an election or stay out. One expects that, in a subgame Nash equilibrium of such a game, incentives to enter elections will depend on investments in the first stage. Specifically, these models suggest that political entry by candidates who oppose interests of a club's members will be less likely when an organization is perceived as "strong." In other words, political entry can be analyzed in essentially the same way that Kreps et al. (1982) analyzed entry deterrence in markets: a firm's initial investments in capacity can increase its long-run profit by deterring incentives for competitors to enter markets.[8]

A full-fledged analysis of a game of this sort is beyond the scope of this section. However, the logic is straightforward, and it appears to fit well one of the aspects of the political economy of institutional choice on the American frontier. In particular, findings from studies of reputations suggest that claim clubs, because they were large and transparent investments in organizational capacity, contributed to electoral monopolies.

For example, stockmen's associations convened by ranchers throughout the Far West were capacity investments that increased ranchers' ability to secure political monopolies. Candidates seeking to run against incumbents who were sympathetic to ranchers were in effect running against a claim club and the resources it commanded. A club's resources included political ones, in particular a typically intimate relationship between local politicians and businessmen. Indeed, historical studies have shown how cattle ranching interests dominated

[8] As one expects, scholars have spilled a lot of ink trying to work out the details of applying the reputational model to politics, although in the end, the implications are similar: capacity investments can have beneficial effects for those who make them, under certain conditions. For an excellent example of how such models and systematic evidence enlighten our understanding of politics, see especially Dal Bo, Dal Bo, and Snyder (2009), whose cases include political dynasties in Congress.

the Montana and Wyoming state legislatures in the 1880s (Jackson 1947). Reputational effects of cattlemen's associations help explain this outcome, in particular why few would venture to challenge them politically.

You're Not Welcome Here

Third, clubs contributed to distributive outcomes by ensuring only like-minded settlers located in a region. It stands to reason that members of claim clubs preferred that others in the club shared their political preferences. Rather than influencing the decision of candidates to enter a race, they could influence who settled in their region. The logic is similar to deterrence in elections, except in this case, the primary objective is to deter settlement rather than political entry in order to increase long-run political interests. In essence, this is a much stronger sort of entry deterrence because it involves altering patterns of settlement rather than political entry.

An extreme example of an effort to cleanse the population of competing ideologies was "Bleeding Kansas," which is perhaps the best-known conflict over slavery in the history of the United States, besides the Civil War.[9] The trigger for violence in Kansas was the Kansas-Nebraska Act, which in 1854 declared "squatter sovereignty" in Kansas. Squatter sovereignty was essentially the idea that slavery would be determined by popular vote in new states without restriction, so called because these struggles were waged by those who often had no title to the land they occupied. The conflict in Kansas broke out when "Border Ruffians" from Missouri entered Kansas in large numbers with the hope of increasing support for a pro-slavery constitution. One of the most infamous of the many instances of violence occurred in 1856 when pro-slavery men tarred, feathered, and kidnapped a number of "Free State Men." In response, John Brown and his sons murdered five pro-slavery men, to which the Border Ruffians responded by killing five Free State Men in response. Conflict continued until Kansas became a state in 1861 by a vote of the wartime Congress.

Although the basic facts of Bleeding Kansas are well known, the role of claim clubs is not at the forefront of popular discourse about the struggle for Kansas. Slavery was a new dimension added to the already contentious political economy of claim clubs. Bleeding Kansas, in other words, was a political struggle between rival claim clubs in which these private-order associations served a dual purpose of establishing property institutions along with coordinating members on their political preferences regarding slavery. Indeed, the organizational "technology" utilized in the conflict over slavery in Kansas Territory – claim clubs – had existed for over eight decades before it was wielded by free- and slave-state men alike.

[9] Excellent historical studies of conflict over slavery in Kansas territory include Oates (1970), Monaghan (1955), Nichols (1954), and Gates (1954).

The conflict in Kansas also illustrates the importance of organizations in the emergence of segregated territory. Economic studies of geographic segregation have shown how small differences in preferences can lead to large differences in outcomes, such as a weak preference for living next to someone with similar racial characteristics can lead to segregated neighborhoods.[10] These models are remarkable in their ability to explain important outcomes through a highly decentralized, largely unconscious process. However, the strength of these models – their ability to explain aggregate behavior without organizations – is also a drawback for situations such as Bleeding Kansas, where segregation dynamics depended not only on beliefs and preferences, but on emergence of organizations that harnessed coercive authority.

This Land Is My Land

A fourth way clubs contributed to distributive outcomes was by colluding at government auctions. Squatters, either because they tried and failed to influence formal policy or because they believed collusion was a less costly way to acquire legal title, often focused their activities on manipulating government auctions. Indeed, collusion was one of the most important dimensions of the political economy of land relations in the nineteenth century, one that was common across each of the major economic sectors.

Clubs mattered in terms of collusion because they helped members overcome collective-action problems inherent in a bidding cartel. Successful collusion required members not to bid against one another, but more importantly, to deter any outsiders from bidding. To succeed, a club had to make clear that those who dared to bid against a club were risking physical harm, if not death. Indeed, it was precisely a club's capacity to visit pain upon those who crossed them that made them effective.

Of course, participating in a bidding cartel is itself collective action and subject to the usual problem, namely, free riding on "contributions" of other members. Contributions, in this case, meant showing up ready to administer punishment against anyone who elected to bid against the interests of the cartel. When a group of men proceeded to remove someone from land claimed by a club's members or to convince someone not to bid on land occupied by members of an association, those who ventured to participate took on substantial risk – they may not have known if outsiders were armed, or if the interlopers had confederates nearby. These costs created incentives to free ride in the sense that squatters would rather have their neighbors go out and have words with their enemies or, if need arose, to fight them. Clubs were important because they could, by virtue of their powerful organizational structure, overcome these free rider problems.

10 For a review of economic models of segregation, see Young (2001) and Schelling (1969). Schelling's study is the classic one; Young provides a modern game-theoretic treatment of dynamics of segregation.

Collective action also involves coordination, and by writing down rules, clubs may have also enhanced the ability of members to collude. As Weingast (1997) has shown, writing down rights is one of the reasons why constitutions limit transgressions of property rights. Although Weingast was primarily concerned with formal constitutions, it seems clear that informal constitutions also perform an important coordination function. Claim club constitutions coordinated members in opposition to any outsiders who threatened their claims, including speculators, thus providing a focal point in what can be thought of as a prisoner's dilemma game with coordination. The demand for coordination arises because collective action typically involves a large number of individuals, all of whom must participate for success.[11] Because there was a potentially large number of squatters in a region, the act of writing down rights in a constitution likely increased the ability of members to police bidding cartels by overcoming the coordination problem inherent in collective action situations with a large number of people. All told, clubs were the glue holding collusive agreements together, not simply by facilitating cooperation, but also by serving as a focal point for coordination.

Give Them an Inch and They Take a Mile

Yet a fifth way clubs weakened land auctions was by undermining credibility of commitment to state-owned land. Unlike the mechanisms just described, declining credibility of commitment reflected claim clubs as well as political mistakes. In particular, political decisions to reward squatters' entrepreneurship with a legal title undermined the government's credibility of commitment to state ownership, encouraged new waves of settlers to convene their own clubs, and ultimately increased incentives for the government to forgo competitive auctions of state-owned land.

One of the lessons to take from nineteenth-century land laws is that the government, besides committing credibly to *private* property, also has to commit credibly to *state* ownership.[12] Drawing on the insights from the credibility approach, we must conceptualize of the relationship between squatters and the government as a dynamic one in which squatters take into account the state's previous responses to trespass in calculating the benefits and costs of illegal occupation of land. If the state has removed squatters in the past, then potential migrants are less likely to break the law. Conversely, concessions to squatters, by undermining credibility of commitment to state ownership, can make additional land transfers a foregone conclusion as more groups occupy land in anticipation of a government handout.

11 Calvert and Johnson (1999) explain precisely why constitutional politics generally can be modeled as a prisoner's dilemma game with coordination.

12 Representative works in the credibility approach are cited earlier. The implications of my perspective on credibility, as well as the key features of the credibility approach, are discussed more fully later on in this chapter and the following one.

As the empirical studies will show, the government appeared to make mistakes in terms of its credibility of commitment to state ownership throughout the nineteenth century. Political considerations, which included ideological rationales such as fairness, often led to what were viewed at the time as one-time or temporary policies awarding squatters a legal title. The recurring theme of temporary preemption bills suggests that many in the government believed it was possible to reward squatters without setting a precedent. If the government truly believed they could make one-time concessions, then they were surely mistaken. Indeed, these concessions – which increased the cost of policing state-owned land by encouraging new waves of squatters – made free land on a grand scale a self-fulfilling prophecy.

Despite a fairly clear case to be made that political mistakes undermined the state's commitment to its landholding, it is important to remember that clubs put the government in a position to make these mistakes. Organized squatters set a trap, one that the federal government repeatedly walked into. More generally, existing studies of credibility of commitment focus on constitutional and political features governing commitment to private property rights without considering explicitly that organizational demands are often the underlying source of conflict over property institutions. As major developments in nineteenth-century land laws illustrate, even problems in the dimension of credibility of commitment can be traced to bottom-up processes of organizational conflict rather than top-down features of political struggle.

The foregoing discussion suggests several ways in which claim clubs influenced policy choice: by increasing the cost of policing state-owned land, intimidating candidates and settlers, and enforcing bidding cartel. Clubs also played a part in the emergence of a credibility problem for the government. These theoretical observations suggest the following distributive hypothesis: *Claim clubs, while sharing a common interest in private property rights with a revenue-maximizing state, create incentives to substitute from competitive allocation of land to allocation based on bureaucratic priorities*. Did the state create competitive auctions for land, consistent with an efficiency hypothesis? Or, did the state choose to forgo revenue, as hypothesized by distributive perspectives? The remainder of this chapter considers these questions in the context of squatters' rights, the first of several empirical studies of institutional change.

SQUATTERS' RIGHTS AND THE PROCESS OF INSTITUTIONAL CHANGE

Squatters' rights did not emerge with a single law but rather unfolded over a half-century. To facilitate analysis, I divided the complicated process of change in land laws into three fundamental stages. The first stage was expansion of state ownership of land. Although economists sometimes characterize development of private property rights on western lands as arising from a status quo of open access, or no property institutions at all (e.g., Libecap 1989; Umbeck 1981), the status quo was actually widespread state ownership of land. The second stage was creation and adjustment of institutions to competitively allocate public land. An efficiency perspective seems to best explain key institutional developments during this second stage. The third stage, which unfolded over decades, was a shift away from competitive auctions to nearly uniform support of squatters' rights.

Distributive conflict comes into clear focus during this third stage of the development of land laws. The first major example of this conflict concerned squatters' rights, which would award a legal title to people who occupied land prospectively for a nominal price. In terms of our understanding of why property institutions change, this case study illustrates a fairly complete reversal from efficiency to distributive considerations as the driving force of institutional change, as well as the role of claim clubs in the process of institutional transformation.

The Status Quo: State Ownership

Before assessing squatters' rights from the perspective of institutional change, it is useful to first consider the rather stunning expansion of state-owned land during the late eighteenth and nineteenth centuries. The federal government acquired around 1.4 billion acres of land for an average price of less than six cents an acre through cession from the states (1781 to 1802), the Louisiana Purchase (1803), the purchase of Florida (1819), annexation of Texas and the Texas Purchase (1845 and 1850), acquisition of Oregon Territory (1846), acquisition of territory from Mexico (1848), and the Gadsden Purchase (1853) (Hibbard 1924; see also Table 1.1 in Chapter 1). As Map 5.1 shows, these purchases represented huge sections of territory. Much of the federal government's land came through cession, which referred to the decision of states to transfer their land to the federal government to avoid confusion over ownership of public land. In this way, the federal government dramatically increased its potential wealth through expansion of land ownership (Grubb 2010, 2007).

The low price the federal government paid to acquire land, which is perhaps as stunning as the extent of state ownership, reflected bargaining power rather than the workings of a market. The U.S. government had the upper hand in negotiations with many of its competitors, most notably Indian tribes and vanquished foreign adversaries, an advantage that translated into a remarkably low price of land. As noted in Chapter 1, the government paid a mere $77 million for what would ultimately account for 65 percent of the entire land mass of the United States.

Through these activities of the federal government, state ownership of land expanded dramatically. Such expansive state ownership, as well as plans to maintain it until it can be allocated competitively, raises questions about the desirability of centralized ownership. Economic historians have shown that

MAP 5.1. Territorial expansion of the United States. *Source*: Redrawn from Fiske (1904).

private property institutions are the key to understanding economic growth and development (North 1990, 1981; North and Rutten 1987; North and Thomas 1973). Why not simply give land away? Although land privatization typically enhances efficiency, there are at least four reasons why ongoing centralization of landholding was desirable from a political economy perspective, in particular during early stages of political and economic development of the United States.

First, cession from the states to the federal government addressed a coordination problem. When the colonies broke from Great Britain, there were numerous, overlapping claims to land (see Map 5.2). This "giant jigsaw puzzle" of land ownership was a perfect example of a coordination problem for a property regime.[13] New York, Virginia, North Carolina, South Carolina, Georgia, Massachusetts, and Connecticut each laid claim to vaguely defined western areas. Convinced that competing claims to large areas of the frontier could be more easily settled by turning disputed lands over to a new government that promised to represent all of the states, the states ceded millions of various "western" lands from 1781 to 1802, including Georgia's transfer of nearly 57 million acres, in exchange for a payment of $1.2 million, to the federal government.

Second, economic development depended to an extent on maintaining federal landholding for the purposes of later development of railroads. As economic historians have shown, railroads facilitated impersonal market exchange while permitting attainment of economies of scale in business (Fogel 1964). Although there is some debate about whether or not the transcontinental railroad actually contributed a great deal in terms of development – White (2011), for example, argues that it was built mainly because of pressure from railroad interests rather than actual demand – it is clear that state-owned land was an important aspect of the railroad subsidies. As Engerman (1972) explained, development of railroads benefited from the state's ability to acquire large amounts of land as well as to secure it from various threats. For example, the Gadsden Purchase secured 19 million acres of Mexican territory to build railroads.[14] Although we can debate whether railroads were an important engine of national integration, it is undeniable that territorial expansion and land subsidies liberated and encouraged railroad companies in their effort to bridge the nation.[15] A land free for all may have reduced the government's ability to contribute to this process.

[13] Credit for this phrase goes to Shepsle (1978), who famously described Congressional committee assignments as a "giant jigsaw puzzle." The metaphor is perhaps an even better fit for the situation involving competing land claims in the early republic, which literally looked like a giant jigsaw puzzle.

[14] On territorial expansion, including the Gadsen Purchase, see Kluger (2007).

[15] Economic development also required a favorable legal environment. On the legal political economy of early expansion, in particular with respect to railroad development, see Schweber (2004).

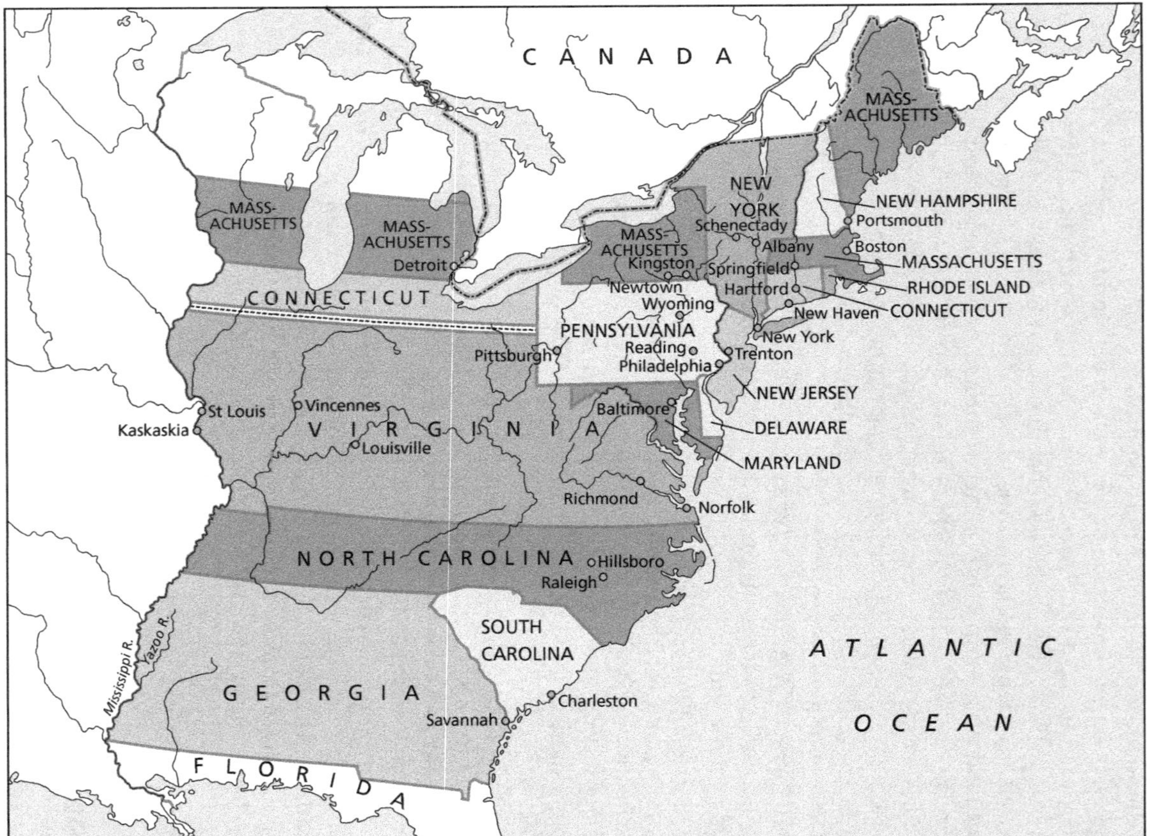

MAP 5.2. Land claims of the original thirteen states, 1783. *Source*: Redrawn from Adams and Trent (1913).

Third, federal acquisition of land had direct consequences for security. Control of land was intimately tied to geopolitical considerations. For example, prior to the United States acquiring land surrounding the mouth of the Mississippi, it was in the hands of foreign powers, first Spain and then France. In 1803, Thomas Jefferson negotiated with France to surrender 500 million acres of unsettled land for a total price of $27 million. Spain relinquished Florida to the United States in 1819 for a price of $6 million for nearly 43 million acres of land. In 1848, Mexico transferred the Pacific Southwest (California, Nevada, Utah, and parts of New Mexico, Arizona, Colorado, and Wyoming) to the federal government for $16 million. In 1850, Texas ceded 79 million acres to the United States for $15 million, reducing the potential for conflict between Texas and the federal government. France, Spain, and Mexico were serious adversaries, and Texas had to be a full partner in the new American federation. Each acquisition was relevant for economic development but each also had fairly obvious consequences for national security, for at least two reasons: the government was acquiring land previously controlled by adversaries, reducing an international threat, and centralization removed an important potential dimension of conflict between American states and the national government, thereby enhancing stability of the new American federation. Had the government simply given land for taking, many isolated settlers would have no doubt drawn on the government's military resources to help them defend themselves.

Finally, and most importantly for the account of land laws in this book, federal landholding was a potentially vast source of nontax revenue for the federal government. Nontax revenue was particularly important because it reduced reliance on direct and indirect taxes to fund public goods during a period in which tax revenue was highly uncertain. Provision of public goods, in turn, has obvious consequences for economic development because markets depend to an extent on infrastructure.[16] Some economists may raise an objection here, suggesting that markets often provide "public" goods privately. Toll roads are a well-known example of private provision of goods that are traditionally considered public goods (Klein 1992), and private armies suggest that even security – the provision of which is perhaps the main rationale for a nation-state – can be provided privately (Avant 2005; Singer 2003). Toll roads and private armies notwithstanding, markets generally depend for their effectiveness on provision of public goods, such as roads and security. Government defense of borderlands is an example: claim clubs benefited from the activities of the army in securing borderlands from various threats. The ability to provide public goods such as defense of a nation's borderlands, in turn, depended in part on the state's ability to profit from its landholding.

[16] Grubb (2010) is an excellent source on the value of land during the Articles and founding of the Constitution.

Nothing in the foregoing account suggests that the federal government would maintain state ownership perpetually. If anything, my argument suggests the virtue of strengthening markets; indeed, claim clubs are viewed as a source of social costs because they undermined land markets. Yet a defense of private property institutions that excludes from consideration the opportunity costs of land giveaways is incomplete, to say the least. Land acquisition and consequent state ownership were an expedient stage in the tapestry of American land laws, and American political development more generally.

Of course, realizing revenue from land required the government to create markets for public land. The initial efforts to establish land markets occurred under the Articles of Confederation (1781–9). Although the government created competitive markets shortly after the Revolutionary War, a reversal of fortune was on the horizon as far as the government's revenue aspirations were concerned.

Before considering creation of land markets in greater depth, a few observations regarding the price quoted above are in order. Obviously, $77 million – or $2 billion in today's dollars – is a small price to pay for the nation's lands. The federal government's acquisition of land could be described as first-order rent-seeking (federal government versus its international competitors, including Indian tribes), while the effort to undermine competitive auctions as second-order rent-seeking (claim clubs vs. the state). Through coercion, conquest, and purchase, the federal government was able to acquire formal authority over a vast empire of land. However, formal *authority* did not always translate into ability to *control* the land. Despite the success of the federal government in acquiring massive amounts of land vis-à-vis its adversaries, the state eventually became a victim of rent-seeking, in particular as claim clubs began cutting off opportunities for the state to profit from its landholding. My emphasis is on the second sort of rent-seeking, namely, clubs versus the state. As we shall see, rent seeking of the second sort emerged almost immediately after land markets were created.

The Creation of Land Markets in the Post-Revolutionary Period

As the colonial and later federal and state governments systematically acquired land, politicians were continually confronted with a choice between competitive and bureaucratic allocation of land. The colonial governments rejected competitive markets for land, electing instead to give land away in hope of erecting a barrier of settlers between established towns and Indians. Many of the colonial government followed a "headright system," one in which free land was made available to all eligible citizens, in order to encourage settlement. Under the headright system, settlers were expected to claim borderlands that surrounded established towns, with the expectation that such settlement would improve security in the more established towns (Hibbard 1924).

From an economic perspective, free land promised to reduce the cost of policing the borderlands by increasing density of settlement in regions surrounding towns. As such, the colonial policy supports the economic justification for free land introduced in Chapter 3. Using the Homestead Act of 1862 as an illustrative case, economic proponents of free land argue that packing less-settled regions of the frontier with settlers reduced the army's cost of clearing Indian tribes from the land. There was, however, a much earlier example that supports the economic logic of free land as a security source. Colonial governments viewed settlers as a buffer between unregulated territory and established towns. Giving land away in these chaotic times may have been expedient, perhaps even efficient. At the very least, the colonial government subscribed to a theory that border packing through free land would enhance security.

A cost-saving rationale for free land is compelling for the aforementioned cases. However, it is less appropriate for other cases. As a general matter, it is more challenging to justify free land as the opportunity costs of revenue forgone increase, or as threats from outsiders, such as Indian tribes, wane. For example, free land arguably made less sense under the Articles of Confederation, as opposed to the colonial period, because of increasing revenue demands.

Consistent with my hypothesis that there was a stronger case to be made for free land during the colonial period compared to subsequent periods, free land was rejected as a policy under the Articles of Confederation, and there was vocal opposition to free land throughout the 1850s even amid a growing chorus supporting it. Persistent opposition to free land suggests a cost-saving rationale was not particularly persuasive, at least in terms of winning support of large majorities in government.

Nor should rejecting free land be surprising from a political economy perspective, mainly because revenue shortfalls under the Articles of Confederation created a strong incentive to allocate land competitively. Under the Articles' system of voluntary contributions from the states to fund public projects, compliance rates with the states' levied contributions were generally low, a situation that called into question the effectiveness of the Articles as a fiscal mechanism.[17] Spending projects also required unanimous approval, which implies each state had a de facto veto over federal spending. Routine funding shortfalls raised the specter of defaults on foreign loans. Declining access to international credit markets is important for various reasons, for example, because of its implications for national security: weakness in debt markets, by reducing a state's

[17] Dougherty (2001), Dougherty and Cain (1997), and Cain and Dougherty (1999) consider the fiscal consequences of the Articles' contribution mechanism, arguing that the voluntary system ensured the demise of the Articles as a fiscal instrument. In contrast, Sobel (2002, 1999) explains why voluntary contributions promised to impose fiscal discipline on the states. Sobel makes the case by observing that the nascent government more or less provided all the public goods it needed to, while keeping expenditures down.

ability to finance war, can reduce a nation's ability to wage a war, in the process undermining its security.[18]

For these reasons, land began to take on greater importance as a source of stability for the new American state, mainly because it provided an additional revenue resource in a time when revenue was tight. Evidently, members of the Confederate Congress recognized that a robust federation also depended on overlapping, redundant revenue resources in order to improve prospects for the survival of America's first constitutional system.

Translating land into revenue required organizing the vast lands that the government won from various colonial competitors. One of the first challenges confronting the government under the Articles of Confederation was to organize the territory of northwest of the Ohio River, known as the Northwest Territory, which had no formal constitution in place after the Revolutionary War. To get an idea of the importance of this region, it would eventually become the present states of Ohio, Indiana, Illinois, Michigan, and Wisconsin (see Map 5.3).

In 1784, Jefferson made one of the first attempts to organize the territory with a bill, which would have eliminated slavery in the region as well as provided an institutional framework for economic development had it been successful.[19] Members of the Continental Congress eventually agreed on the Land Ordinance of 1785, which enacted many of the features of Jefferson's bill.[20] However, the Northwest Ordinances of 1787 and 1789 would become the best known of these bills (the 1789 bill carried over, in more or less direct fashion, the earlier bill from the Articles of the Confederation, which disbanded in 1787). The importance of these bills is hard to overstate because they arguably provided the institutional matrix that permitted economic and political development of the United States. Hughes (1987) eloquently captures the profound, though underappreciated, significance of these land laws:

> The land ordinances became the great American colonizing machine: they left the intellectual mark of the Americans on the nation's geography as indelibly as did the Roman roads on physical England, cutting straight across the undulating English countryside. The Northwest Ordinances were the colonial American's institutional thumbprint on the American continent all the way from the Ohio River to the Pacific... Uncelebrated in history books, unknown to the average citizen, the land ordinances of the "old Congress" achieved an almost ubiquitous domination beyond the Appalachians. The objects of those acts were achieved in a century of unparalleled economic development.

One of the defining features of these ordinances, in addition to the profoundly important prohibition on slavery in the new territories, was creating the basis

[18] On the relationship between credibility in debt markets and security, see Schultz and Weingast (2003), who argue that credibility in debt markets is a driving force behind success in war.

[19] *Journals of the Continental Congress* (JCC), 24 and 25.

[20] *JCC* 29.

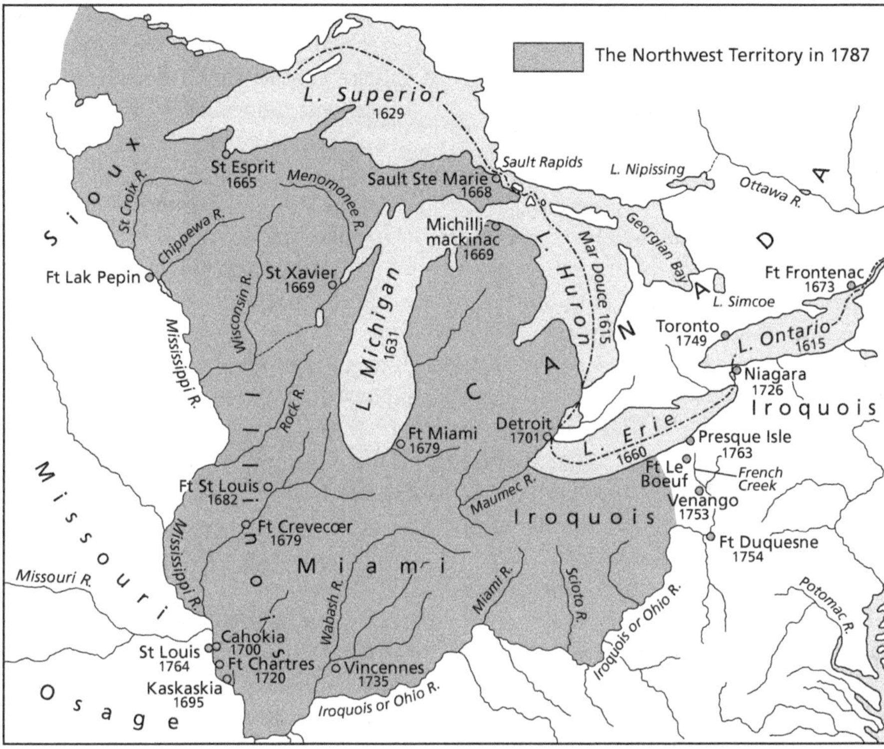

MAP 5.3. The Northwest Territory, 1787. *Source*: Redrawn from Adams and Trent (1913).

for the Public Land Survey System (PLSS), which created square townships of 36 square miles each, six miles across. Each township was divided into 36 rectangular sections of 640 acres each, with 16 sections reserved to support public schools, with the remaining 20 sections available at public auction (Hibbard 1924; see also Table 1.2 in Chapter 1). The PLSS contrasted with the older "metes and bounds" configuration used in England and much of colonial and postrevolutionary America, in which land boundaries followed natural contours and breaks such as creeks and ridge lines. The rectangular patterns characteristic of the PLSS reduced survey costs, reduced boundary disputes, and reduced odd lot sizes that were harder to sell (Grubb 2010).

As mentioned earlier, scholars have upheld these ordinances as fundamental to understanding emergence of private property institutions (Sened 1997; North 1990; North and Rutten 1987). These studies also recognize that the effectiveness of private property institutions depends on the structure of political institutions. In this regard, changes in political institutions increased the chances that these private property institutions would be effective by providing what was essentially a bill of rights for the Northwest Territory.

The method of allocating land receives less attention than the private property and political features of the Northwest Ordinance. However, the Confederation government also established a market-based method of allocating land. The Northwest Ordinance of 1789, which was agreed on during the first Congress, established rules for allocating land that were similar to the Land Ordinance, except that the minimum price increased to $2.00 an acre with a minimum tract size was 640 acres.[21] Although the government's preferred landholding size was far above the average landholding during this period – as Grubb (2010) notes, most farms were around a hundred acres – the government appeared committed to using land as a revenue resource.

The decision to use land for the public good was one of the most important "founding choices" for the early United States, to use Irwin and Sylla's (2011) characterization of American economic policies during the 1790s. States differed substantially in their preferences for how the government lands would be allocated. States with larger landholding, for example, preferred an orderly process of land distribution that kept land prices high; in contrast, states with less land were more inclined to support a more rapid system of allocating land (Grubb 2010). Despite these conflicts, the states agreed that land revenue should be used for the common good.

Implementing this vision, however, proved problematic. The government was inexperienced with land sales, and the fiscal provisions of the Northwest Ordinance required modification almost immediately. For example, Congress did not initially include a credit system to finance land purchases. Lack of markets for credit implies some farmers who valued land would be unable to acquire it. Indeed, Coase's (1960) well-known theorem that property rights will be efficiently allocated subject to the cost of transacting says nothing about credit market imperfections, which typically undermine the ability of competitive auctions to allocate land efficiently because high-value users of land would not be able to acquire a legal title in the presence of credit constraints.

Despite these challenges in terms of design of the auction system, institutional adaptation occurred fairly quickly through a series of changes aimed at increasing revenue prospects. An act of 1796 increased land available for competitive allocation, but only about 49,000 acres, primarily in Pittsburgh and Philadelphia, were sold under it. In 1800 and again in 1804, minimum lot size was reduced, from 640 to 320 acres and then from 320 to 160 acres. The Harrison Land Act of 1800 increased the period of repayment and reduced the price of land to $1.64 an acre (Hibbard 1924).

Despite modifying the credit system, defaults on government loans were common. According to a report compiled in 1806 by Albert Gallatin, for example, delinquent payments for land sold in the state of Ohio increased from nearly $1.1 million in 1803 to over $2 million in 1805. Gallatin, a Democratic-Republican from Pennsylvania who helped organize the House

21 *Statutes at Large*, 1st Congress, Session I, 1789: 50–51.

Finance Committee (the predecessor to the Ways and Means Committee) and also served as Thomas Jefferson's Secretary of the Treasury (an appointment that reflected his belief in limiting national debt and opposition to direct taxes), urged replacement of the credit system with exclusive cash sales because of high default rates under the credit system (Hibbard 1924).

Gallatin's recommendation, and incremental changes to competitive auctions that followed, indicate institutional learning, although these marginal adjustments did not resolve the fundamental conflict of interest between settlers and the federal government over the price of land. Under competitive auctions, the federal government secured the scarcity rent associated with land, while settlers received these rents under free-land programs. Distributive conflict over the price of land was one of the defining features of land laws in this period, a conflict that emerged as soon as the government established a framework to allocate land competitively.

Recognizing the problems posed by squatting, Congress early on attempted to stem the rising tide of squatting. By 1800, private claimants who had purchased legal title with cash petitioned the federal government to enforce their claims after squatters began to occupy their land, forcing Congress to choose between enforcing legal ownership and policies rewarding squatters. With the Intrusion Act of 1807, which authorized the president to use force to prevent settlement of state-owned land unless individuals had a legal title, as well as imposing fines on violators of $100 for illegal occupation, Congress sided with formal owners. Unfortunately for owners, the Intrusion Act, which was designed to give force to the state-ownership regime, as well as to ensure the state profited from its landholding, proved difficult to enforce. There were also appeals to go easy on squatters, with opponents of intrusion legislation arguing that squatters did not have much money, as well as pragmatic appeals that there were not even enough prisons to incarcerate the illegal occupants. Despite a few efforts to enforce these provisions, including the use of troops to remove squatters in Alabama in 1827, in Missouri in 1834, and in Iowa in the 1830s and 1840s, evictions appear to have been the exception rather than the norm (Dick 1970).

Lack of enforcement reflected a more general challenge, which was little investment in the land-administration bureaucracy in this period. Local land offices were established in 1800, yet the General Land Office was not created until 1812. Even when the offices were established, they had few resources. Consequently, there was almost no revenue collected from government lands prior to 1800, and defaults on loans from those who agreed to pay were common (Rohrbough 1968).

Investment in bureaucratic capacity was perhaps the key to policing state ownership. However, few resources were devoted to enforcing the state ownership regime. Consequently, the state's commitment to holding onto its own land was somewhat shaky. More fundamentally, concessions to squatters undermined Congress' commitment to competitive land auctions. Congress continually rewarded squatters in each sector with bills that reduced the price of land with preemption bills over the next sixty years, thereby inviting a credibility problem. Squatters' rights, considered in the following section, were the first major policies giving away the state's land, yet as subsequent chapters show, laws recognizing squatters' rights on agricultural land were only the beginning of a great land giveaway, one in which the free land would be extended in one form or another to squatters occupying mineral land, rangeland, and timberland.

The Decline of Competitive Markets for Agricultural Land

The idea behind preemption was simple: squatters could acquire a legal title to government-owned land, provided the land was not owned by another citizen. The usual amount was 160 acres of land at the federal level, although state-land states often recognized squatters' rights as well, allocating land in different amounts (such as 100- or 200-acre sections). The discussion below focuses on squatters' rights on land in public-land states, which are the ones where land policy is controlled by Congress.

Of the many preepmtion bills enacted by Congress, the one that receives perhaps the most attention is a temporary preemption bill enacted in 1830. For example, Kanazawa (1996) suggested the 1830 bill was a watershed moment because it allowed anyone on government land by the time the bill took effect to acquire a legal title to 160 acres of land. Even though it was temporary, Kanazawa characterized subsequent legislation as a *fait accompli*.

Despite Kanazawa's compelling insights into the political economy of preemption is compelling, the notion of a watershed moment presents a somewhat misleading picture of squatters' rights. As Table 5.1 shows, agricultural preemption laws represented an institutional transformation that unfolded from 1799 (the first preemption bill) to 1863 (the year the homestead bill took effect). Emphasis on the 1830 bill detracts from distributive conflict over land throughout the first half of the nineteenth century, as Congress continually responded to demands posed by claim clubs with preemption bills. Distributive bills rewarding squatters on agricultural land were the norm rather than the exception, and the steady flow of bills rewarding squatters suggests that there may not have been a "watershed moment." Rather, preemption was a steady flow throughout this period.

The pattern of preemption bills is revealing. On one hand, public policies weakening land auctions were common prior to 1830. For example, in 1808, Congress allowed all settlers who had prospectively occupied state-owned land in Michigan Territory to register their claims. On the other hand, many important preemption bills were enacted after the preemption act of 1830. An 1832 law allowed squatters to make claims in amounts of forty acres. In 1834, Congress allowed anyone occupying land (subject to minimal qualifications) in 1833 to make preemption claims. In 1838 and 1840, the preemption bill

TABLE 5.1. *Major Preemption Acts, 1799–1862*

Year	Applicability
1799	Squatters on government land illegally sold to them by a land speculator.
1808	Squatters located in Michigan as of March 1804.
1813	All squatters located in Illinois.
1814	French or Spanish grantees in Louisiana and Missouri.
1826	All squatters in Florida and Mississippi.
1828	Squatters in Louisiana as of March 1819.
1830	Anyone on surveyed government land in 1829 who filed claims within one year.
1832	Squatters on public land could claim forty acres.
1834	Anyone occupying a tract of land in 1833 who filed a claim within two years.
1838	Extension of the 1830 act to settlers on public land not owned by other citizens.
1840	Extension of the 1830 act to settlers on public land not owned by other citizens.
1841	Squatters on surveyed public land could enter a claim for 160 acres for $1.25 an acre prior to public sale, including prospective settlement in the regions covered by the act.
1853	Temporary preemption privileges for squatters on unsurveyed lands in California.
1854	Squatters in Kansas, Nebraska, Washington, and Oregon.
1854	Squatters in Minnesota and Wisconsin.
1862	Squatters on former Indian lands and unsurveyed lands in Colorado.

Source: United States Congress, *Annals of Congress*, various sessions, 1799–1862.

was again renewed, but by this time, preemption had been used for decades. The government also recognized squatters' rights with separate bills that covered territory in Kansas, Nebraska, and Colorado in the 1850s in response to widespread squatting on government land (Robbins 1942, 1931).

The design of the 1830 bill also suggests that Congress had not given up on the idea of competitive land auctions. By making the 1830 bill retrospective and available for only a single year, members of Congress seem to have believed that it was truly a temporary bill. A more plausible interpretation of the temporary bill is that members of Congress believed they could have their cake and eat it too, rewarding squatters without giving up on competitive land auctions. In reality, temporary and small-scale preemption laws ensured more squatters would occupy land, increasing the cost of policing state-owned land and ultimately forcing Congress' hand to enact new preemption laws.

Leaving aside issues of credibility of commitment for now, it is clear that substantial amounts of land changed hands as a result of these preemption laws. To understand just how much land was changing hands, it is useful to consider land entries made around the time of the 1830 preemption bill. Rohrbough's (1968) unrivaled study of land offices during this period provides data on land

TABLE 5.2. *Preemption Claims Entered, 1828–1836*

	Acres
1828	5,507
1829	2,623
1830	242,979
1831	557,840
1832	49,917
1833	31,756
1834	637,597
1835	574,936
1836	112,842

Source: Rohrbough (1968). These and additional data on public land sales are found in the U.S. Congress, *Senate Public Documents*, various years.

sales for the period from 1828 to 1837, which are reproduced in Table 5.2. Fueled by the preemption acts of 1830, 1832, 1834, and 1836, the government transferred over two million acres of land to squatters in the ten-year period from 1828 to 1838. To get an idea how much land was given away, consider that the township under the PLSS consisted of 23,040 acres (thirty-six square miles). By this measure, squatters claimed land equivalent to nearly 90 towns, a fairly large amount of land during an early stage of economic development.

How do we interpret these developments? Because the status quo was competitive allocation of land, which is perhaps as close as we come to an efficient mechanism to allocate state-owned land, the flood of preemption laws during the first half of the nineteenth century supports a distributive perspective on institutional change. After all, each of these land laws represented a substantial transfer in scarcity rent from the state to squatters. However, it is important to keep in mind that there were two ways in which squatters undermined markets for public land. One way, discussed up to this point, was agitating for legislation formally weakening auctions. In terms of formal legislation, preemption laws are some of the most important examples of successful rent-seeking in the nineteenth century.

Despite their seeming importance, as well as the long struggle to secure them, preemption laws never fulfilled their promise. For many of the preemption laws, few patents to land were actually entered.[22] Does this mean that rent seeking to attain agricultural land bore little fruit?

[22] The definitive study of the political economy of preemption is Gates' (1960) *The Farmers' Age: Agriculture, 1815–1860*. Gates provides remarkable insight into institutional foundations of agricultural development as well as the promise and limitations of preemption.

TABLE 5.3. *Land Office Revenue, 1828–1837*

	Acres Sold	Revenue
1828	965,000	$1,221,357
1829	1,244,860	$1,572,863
1830	1,929,733	$2,433,432
1831	2,777,856	$3,557,023
1832	2,462,343	$3,115,376
1833	3,856,227	$4,972,284
1834	4,658,218	$6,099,981
1835	12,564,478	$15,999,804
1836	20,074,870	$25,167,833
1837	5,601,103	$7,007,523

Source: U.S. Congress, *Senate Public Documents*, 27th Congress, 3rd Session; Hibbard (1924); Gates (1960).

In short, the answer is no. To understand the consequences of rent-seeking, it is essential to take account of the second, arguably much more pervasive, method for acquiring land: collusion at federal land auctions. Any study of nineteenth-century land laws that focuses exclusively on squatters' rights – legislation *formally* awarding title to illegal occupants – dramatically understates the political consequences of agricultural claim clubs. Successful collusion reduced the need for formal legislation because members of clubs received a legal title for a minimum price without changing laws regulating land distribution. In order to assess the full social cost of claim clubs, it is necessary to take into account their activities at land auctions, in particular collusion during auctions.

Once we account for collusion, the consequences of claim clubs come into clearer focus. Profit from land sales was far less than its potential because much of the land, if not most of it, changed hands under the watchful eyes of a claim club, which typically ensured that the price paid for agricultural land was a minimal one, if not the federally mandated legal minimum. The federal minimum price of preemption was, in most cases, $1.25 an acre. Despite formally conducting auctions, land purchased on "competitive" markets was almost never exchanged at market price, but rather at prices preordained by a club. The price the club chose was often the federal minimum, which happened to be the preemption price. In this regard, most land auctions were de facto preemption programs.

An important piece of evidence of the distributive consequence of collusion comes from Rohrbough's data on land sales from the 1830s, which are presented in Table 5.3. The most remarkable feature of these data on land is the average price of land. Of 50 million acres sold from 1828 to 1838, land was sold, on average, at the federally mandated minimum price of $1.25 an acre. In other words, the going price of land on "competitive" markets was the nominal price of land the squatters paid for preemption claims, a price that reflected the bargaining power of claim clubs.

For example, 20 million acres in land sales brought $25 million in revenue in 1836, which translates into an average price of $1.25 an acre. The difference between the average market price and the average price squatters paid at a "competitive" auction is the value of the transfer of scarcity rent. To illustrate the potential transfer in rent, if we assume the market value of land was $5 an acre, then squatters extracted over $300 million in scarcity rent through "competitive" land auctions in the ten-year period from 1828 to 1838. In today's dollars, that sum translates into about $7 billion in scarcity rent.[23] Although the government was bringing in some revenue through land sales, it seems clear that squatters and speculators, each group adept at collusion, secured most of the scarcity rent associated with the state's vast land resources.

Collusion was a good option for clubs because it required less work to get what they desired than did political change. Manipulating an auction only required a club's members to intimidate outsiders, and as we have seen, clubs were good at putting a scare into their foes. Even federal agents were generally too weak to challenge seriously a club's will.

Once we take into account de jure transfers through preemption legislation and de facto transfers through collusion, the social costs of claim clubs seem obvious. For example, suppose we assume that most of these acres changing hands through "competitive" auctions from 1828 to 1838 were influenced by clubs. The amount of land that changed hands through potentially rigged auctions is up to 50 million acres, which is over 25 *times* the amount of land patented through preemption. A precise quantitative estimate of the value of the de facto transfers is elusive (after all, these were illegal activities, and so they are challenging to measure precisely). However, it is reasonable to conclude based on the evidence that has been presented that the agricultural land grab was one of the most important examples of distributive politics in American political economic history.

Squatters' Rights as a Test of Competing Theories

What do squatters' rights tell us about efficiency and distributive perspectives on institutional change? On one hand, there is some support for an efficiency perspective in the first decades after the Revolutionary War. The great ordinances of the 1780s created a framework for private property rights as well as competitive land auctions. One of the most important contributions of the land ordinances was to establish private property institutions and a political framework to lend credibility to private property rights. Yet these ordinances also had important implications for the fiscal strength of the nation by creating

[23] Calculation made using a 1835 as base year and 2010 as desired year.

competitive markets for land. That these ordinances considered carefully the fiscal consequences of land laws speaks to their profound importance, beyond surveying the land and provisions for self-government. Besides these fiscal provisions of the ordinances, there were also a few attempts to enforce as well as to improve the design of federal auctions, as well as marginal changes to the auction system in response to challenges to it, such as credit provisions.

Several bills during this period were arguably a response to opportunities for Pareto improvement, which is the definition of efficiency in the process of institutional change. Nonetheless, the vast majority of legislation was distributive, transferring scarcity rent from the state to organized claimants. For example, a few laws strengthened the state's capacity to remove squatters, and others adjusted credit provisions and the size of land. Overall, however, policies removing land from competitive markets were much more common; laws strengthening markets were far and few between. All told, distributive conflict seems to be the overwhelming dynamic governing agricultural land laws in the first half of the nineteenth century.

If one accepts that preemption was a source of social costs and competitive markets a source of social benefits, then the next question to ask is why the federal government ended up giving away much of its vast landholding. One reason is formation of powerful economic organizations on the nation's agricultural land. As Chapter 3 showed, these claim clubs were common in each of the Midwestern states as well as public-domain states more generally. These economic organizations increased the cost of policing state ownership and the government responded with laws rewarding members of these organizations. In the absence of claim clubs, legislators would have had few reasons to give away the scarcity rent associated with public land.

There is, of course, the all-important question of whether claim clubs actually caused these changes in the prices of land. There are several reasons why a causal account stressing the role of claim clubs makes sense. First, the theory of distributive conflict linked claim clubs to policy choice. Second, clubs preceded changes in preemption laws. Third, there are few examples of the government providing land to unorganized squatters, and so it seems it was their organizations, not simply first possession, driving the process of institutional change. Finally, because preemption undermined government revenue, we can rule out revenue maximization as an explanation for changes in land laws. Because they satisfy most of the criteria for a causal relationship (theoretical relationship, temporal antecedence, correlation, ruling out alternative explanations), clubs are certainly plausible as a mechanism of change in land laws.

Although clubs are an important explanation for land giveaways, political mistakes also played a role. Some of the blame lies with Congress, which is clear when squatters' rights are considered dynamically, in terms of credibility of commitment. Although studies of credibility of commitment typically emphasize effectiveness of private property institutions, maintaining state ownership also involves a credibility problem. The initial preemption grants to squatters in Michigan and Illinois in the 1810s and 1820s – legislation that could very well have reduced the state's costs of policing borderlands by strengthening the property rights of those who might defend the nation's borderlands – also had a collateral consequence of increasing incentives to occupy state-owned land prospectively, as did the temporary preemption law of 1830. Each of these laws undermined credibility of commitment to state ownership, encouraged squatting, and ultimately undermined the ability of future governments to profit from state-owned land. Even after the permanent preemption act of 1841, claim clubs continued to divide land informally prior to government authorization in order to compel the government to extend to new territories yet another preemption bill. The mechanism that made preemption a self-fulfilling prophecy is declining credibility of commitment to state ownership.

During this time period, various political majorities seemed unaware of the consequences of their actions for credibility of commitment to state ownership. Nonetheless, there were some members of the federal bureaucracy who recognized that Congress was falling prey to a credibility problem (even if they did not describe it as such). For example, in 1829, Samuel Foot, a member of Andrew Jackson's administration, proposed inquiring into the possibility of limiting public-land sales in response to widespread corruption, as well as the possibility of eliminating the office of Surveyor General of the General Land Office (Robbins 1942). In addition, several of the key administrators in the General Land Office (GLO) were kindred spirits as far as support of competitive allocation of land was concerned. In 1830, the Senate Committee on Public Lands approved a preemption bill, and the House Committee on Public Lands asked the Commissioner of the GLO to review the Senate bill. Commissioner George Graham responded that the bill would threaten orderly sale of public land and encourage squatting. Jackson's appointment to head the GLO, Elijah Hayward, recommended rapidly surveying and selling public lands, leaving intruders and trespassers to local tribunals of justice (Rohrbough 1968).

These federal administrators recognized the importance of committing credibly to state ownership of land. Unfortunately, their wisdom met little political support. Despite these admonitions, Jackson's belief in smallholder farming as a development strategy led him to reject proposals to reform the preemption system (Feller 1984; Stephenson 1917). More generally, various majorities in Congress believed in the possibility of temporary preemption bills – bills that were meant to apply only to a particular group of squatters, and not to others. Taking the lessons of the credibility perspective seriously, there is no such thing as a *temporary* preemption bill when we take into account the consequences of such laws on incentives to occupy land. Beginning in 1799, the federal government, by repeatedly adopting temporary bills that were meant to be limited in scope, sowed the seeds of destruction of competitive markets to allocate land.

Thus, in seeking to understand policy choices during this period, policy mistakes and unanticipated consequences should take each factor into our account. Members of Congress seem to have underestimated problems of how piecemeal bills rewarding squatters would constrain their future choices. After all, legislators repeatedly adopted preemption bills that were limited in scope even though each bill undermined the government's credibility of commitment to state ownership.

The twin logics of rent seeking by claim clubs and declining credibility of commitment resolve a puzzle of the efficiency perspective on state-owned land articulated earlier in this chapter. Although Levi's and Olson's perspectives suggest that the government will allocate land through competitive auctions to increase revenue, the federal government did nothing of the sort. The structure of economic organizations – the proliferation of claim clubs – helps us understand why the government elected to forgo a substantial revenue opportunity. Yet it is also necessary to conceptualize of institutional change from a dynamic perspective in which past decisions involving land laws shape and constrain subsequent institutional choices. Claim clubs, by increasing costs of maintaining state ownership of land, created incentives for legislators to forgo land auctions, an effect that was amplified by declining credibility of commitment to state ownership. Ultimately, explaining institutional change thus requires us to consider insights from bottom-up mechanisms, such as claim clubs, and top-down mechanisms, such as declining credibility of commitment. Once we do this, it seems clear that economic organizations and political mistakes explain why the state realized so little revenue from its vast agrarian landholding.

Were Squatters' Rights "Efficient?"

The evidence just presented supports a distributive perspective on institutional change, provided one accepts the proposition that competitive auctions are economically efficient mechanisms to allocate land. There are, however, several counterarguments that can be raised in defense of squatters' rights, each suggesting that laws reducing substantially the price of land may have been expedient, if not efficiency enhancing. There are at least five arguments that suggest squatters' rights may have been socially desirable.

First, squatters rights may be justified as social welfare policies because they benefitted poor squatters with few opportunities elsewhere. Indeed, what we can call a public-good perspective on state ownership suggests that the state may often have incentives to give land away to vulnerable groups, and that such giveaways are socially desirable. According to a public-good perspective, which has its roots in the work of Commons (1924) and has been articulated more recently by Bromley (2006, 1991, 1989), the state has an interest in maintaining state-owned land as a resource to benefit its citizens. Indeed, in many societies, state-owned land continues to substitute for a system of social insurance (see, e.g., Cai 2012; Ho 2005a, 2005b; Liu et al. 1998). Maintaining state-owned land promises to limit vulnerability by providing people with land for subsistence agriculture.

Applied to the American frontier, a public-good perspective on state-owned land suggests that land transfers to squatters may have enhanced social welfare to the extent that these policies alleviated risks facing vulnerable groups. After all, if squatters were a vulnerable group that would have been dependent upon the state without the land they occupied, then it might enhance efficiency to provide them with land to the extent that such expenditures reduce the burden of the government to provide social welfare.

Although a public-good perspective on state-owned land is compelling in the abstract, it is important to keep in mind an important fact: much of the land on the frontier went to speculators and other people of means (see, e.g., Gates 1979, 1942; Bogue 1958). Realistically, there are few reasons to believe the land typically benefitted "poor squatters" on the agricultural frontier. And as Chapter 8 shows, the idea that land giveaways benefited poor people on the frontier makes even less sense in light of land grants to miners, ranchers, and loggers – the booming sectors of the America's western lands. In later-developing sectors, preemption laws are best described as corporate rather than social welfare, casting doubt upon any argument that land giveaways were socially desirable pro-poor policies.

A second line of argument suggests that preemption laws were desirable because land was idle or because it had limited value. De Soto (2000), for example, assumes that squatters did the federal and state governments a service by improving land that had little value.

There is much to be said for giving land away when the state overreaches in terms of land ownership. However, the idea that land was idle, or that the government was unwilling to assign legal title, flies in the face of increasing land office business in this period. Using the 1820s and 1830s as an example, it is clear that there was substantial demand for land in this period (see Table 5.3). The thirty months from the fall of 1834 to the spring of 1837 brought some of the largest land-office business in the history of the United States. According to these data on land sales, citizens purchased lands for the sum of $52 million between 1833 and 1836. Although land auctions brought in far less than its potential revenue (most of these sales were far from competitive because of collusion by clubs), it is clear that land was neither idle nor lacking in value.

Because land was increasing in value and often benefited speculators (or small-scale businessmen) as clubs proliferated, it stands to reason that preemption laws reflected distributive rather than efficiency considerations. In particular, these laws rewarded *enterprising* settlers rather than *poor* settlers. Preemption laws were like "manna from heaven" (to use a phrase squatters often used in their constitutions) to men who realized they could profit by occupying the government's land rather than playing by the legal rules. In fact, it was manna from Congress, and it was like manna precisely because it was valuable, not idle. An even more precise conclusion to draw is that these laws benefited *organized* squatters. Club members did quite well in this period, though it is not as clear they were doing good, in particular from a social-welfare perspective.

A third argument that can be raised in defense of squatters' rights is the economic case for free land, outlined earlier. One of the keys to the argument is assuming packing the borderlands would reduce the government's cost of policing them. If we assume that policing the borderlands is costly and that settlers can provide security at lower cost than armies, then it may be efficient to "rush" settlers into areas where the federal government faced a substantial threat from Indian tribes. It is useful to consider whether their argument also applies to preemption, which is a plausible additional case for the theory to explain (Allen 1991; Barzel 1989).

How does the economic case for free land stack up? As discussed earlier, the efficiency criteria set forth in the economic case for free land is a plausible rationalization for policies benefiting squatters in some periods. For example, in the 1810s, the American government was fearful of Spanish aggression (Adelman and Aron 1999). Frustrating foreign adversaries provides a compelling rationale for recognizing legal titles of settlers who initially had titles issued by the French or Spanish. In such situations, improvements on the security dimension – by forging common interests with settlers who may have in the past had loyalties to France or Spain – may have outweighed any social costs of giving land away to squatters in terms of revenue forgone.

For reasons mentioned earlier, the case for free land has a persuasive logic. However, it is essential to remember that clubs generally formed after the government cleared the land of Indian tribes. An efficiency rationale for preemption based on cost saving has some merit, but it does not explain why legislators would provide settlers with land *after* the government had already done the hard work of clearing the land of Indian tribes. Clubs were typically convened in the wake of the army's activities, which implies they were not saving the government much in terms of defending the borderlands after the early 1800s, contrary to the implications of the economic case for free land.

Fourth, occupation of land may have altered the transaction cost matrix in such a way that preemption is an efficient institutional choice. Once land was illegally occupied, the costs of removing people from it may have been so substantial as to make squatters' rights an efficient policy given transaction costs. This line of reasoning follows from Barzel's (2002, 1989) perspective on institutional change, which I introduced in Chapter 1: all institutional change is efficient, subject to transaction costs. As transaction costs of changing public policies increase, a seemingly inefficient policy can become an efficient one because the transaction costs of institutional change are prohibitive.

One of the weaknesses of transaction cost analysis is that it can rationalize any policy as efficient. For example, consider sugar quotas, which have rather large and obvious social costs to the extent that they raise substantially the domestic price of sugar. Despite their social costs, dismantling systems of quotas is difficult because beneficiaries have incentives to invest substantial resources to keep price supports in place (Krueger 1996). Applying transaction costs analysis to this example, because the costs of removing sugar subsidies to sugar producers are substantial, should we conclude that protectionist policies are somehow efficient policies because the transaction costs of institutional change are substantial? This is exactly what transaction cost economics asks us to do. Transaction costs analysis, used this way, rationalizes even policies that have obvious social costs, and so it is not particularly useful.[24]

Finally, productivity gains from rapid privatization and associated gains in tax revenue may have exceeded the loss in nontax revenue from free land programs and collusion. Because the state is a residual claimant from improvements in productivity through its taxation authority, it is possible that land giveaways may have increased tax revenue to the extent that rapid privatization increased production more quickly than it would have increased otherwise.

There seems to be little debate that private property institutions are likely to increase productivity as well as government revenue in the long run. However, in the political and bureaucratic environment of the nineteenth-century United States, it is a stretch to assume that politicians believed that legal title would translate into increased revenue for the state. For one reason, the state lacked capacity to tax its citizens in any meaningful way during this period. More importantly, I did not find evidence of politicians who argued that land should be given away because it would increase government revenue as a residual claimant as productivity increased. Rather, supporters of free land typically emphasized fairness over the state's interests in revenue. For these reasons, it is more plausible that the state was simply losing out on revenue by forgoing competitive land auctions rather than decentralizing land as quickly as possible to increase its long-run revenue.

We can conjure up various ways in which squatters' rights may have been efficiency enhancing. However, each of the arguments presented earlier has important flaws. Ultimately, my interpretation of land laws in the first half of the nineteenth century suggests that there are few compelling reasons to believe claim clubs contributed to efficient institutional change. Rather, they are more accurately described as rent-seeking organizations, perhaps the quintessential ones of the nineteenth century.

[24] For a compelling argument why transaction costs analysis is appropriate, see Zerbe (2000) and Zerbe and McCurdy (1999), who argue that the concept of market failure is more appropriately considered failure of economic models to adequately account for transaction costs. As they explain, many market failures do not justify government intervention once we account for transaction costs, which is an exceptionally important point that reminds us that we have to know something about the context of institutional choice in order to make policy recommendations. Their argument, although compelling and important, still has the undesirable effect of rationalizing even policies with obvious social costs as "efficient" whenever the costs of institutional change are prohibitively costly. Yet as a critique of government intervention based on assumptions about the existence of market failure for a general class of economic situations, their argument is a quite convincing and useful corrective to the standard economic theory of market failure.

CONCLUSION: THE DISTRIBUTIVE POLITCS OF SQUATTERS' RIGHTS

The main contributions of this chapter have been to show the tradeoffs inherent in early land policy, as well as to remind us of the importance of early land laws in economic development. As the quote from Hughes earlier in this chapter reminds us, these laws are often forgotten, yet they laid the framework for a prosperous nation. At the same time, Hughes understates the distributive politics of squatters' rights. In reflecting on the ordinances, Hughes remarks

> The distribution of the public land seemed to offer temptation beyond the capacity of common humanity to resist, decade after decade. The corruption and fraud, however, "made a market," and the lands went quickly enough into private hands, which was, after all, the object of it all. That the federal government hoped for a profit was a secondary consideration. What was important in the long run was that the land be distributed into private hands in the standard American land tenure, and that the titles be perfectly secure, and that the American political democracy be expanded in its pure form from east to west as the continental nation was formed, piece by piece, township by township. The people and wagons moved ever westward and a stable institutional framework of settlement went with them until the nation extended from ocean to ocean ... It is true that the machinery of the land distribution was oiled by fraudulence. But no amount of wisdom and virtue could have distributed without sin a legacy taken "from others of the Sons of Adam" by military force, or the threat of it, from the beginning. From the Ohio River to the Pacific Ocean, the American thumbprint covered it all. (1987: 13–15)

Hughes understands these ordinances as well as anyone and rightly acknowledges an important aspect of distributive conflict inherent in land acquisition – the great theft of land from native inhabitants. Yet to consider the ordinances without reflecting more carefully on their opportunity costs all but ensures historians and economic historians will look back on them as efficient. Glossing over the profound conflict over the price of land neglects one of the most important aspects of the ordinances, which was the effort to dismantle, weaken, or otherwise evade the provisions governing land allocation.

Squatters' rights were nevertheless only a beginning rather than an end to the run on state-owned land. The remaining empirical studies of formal institutional change consider homesteads (Chapter 6); the struggle over mineral land, pasture, and timberland (Chapter 7); and state-level contestation over land in each of the major frontier sectors (Chapter 8). These empirical studies demonstrate the pervasiveness of distributive conflict as a mechanism of institutional change in economic sectors besides agriculture.

6

The Political Economy of Free Land

If preemption was a crack in the dam holding back settlers seeking cheap agricultural land, then homestead legislation was the dam breaking. Unlike preemption laws, which retrospectively allowed those already on the land acquire a legal title, homestead laws prospectively encouraged settlement while also reducing the nominal fee under preemption to zero price. As such, homesteads were the first true "free land" policies. Of course, economics instructs us that nothing is free in the sense that opportunity costs are inescapable. This chapter considers free land from a political economy perspective, analyzing its origins and consequences, as well as the economic tradeoffs with free land.

The first two sections of this chapter analyze roll-call votes on four failed homestead bills, using econometric methods to estimate which factors influenced probability of supporting free land. These votes, which occurred between 1852 and 1860, were selected because they were hotly contested, and so they present a good opportunity to assess competing hypotheses for institutional change. Because the successful Homestead Act of 1862 was overwhelmingly supported by the wartime Congress, there is not much to learn from it using econometric techniques. In addition, I selected the unsuccessful bills for the simple fact that scholars tend to focus on the successful bill rather than its various failures, and so the analysis contributes something new. In terms of method, the main benefit of an econometric approach is that it nicely sorts out the influence of political party, economic interests, and sectionalism on support and opposition to free land.

To foreshadow the empirical findings, legislators from public-land states – states where the federal government controlled land allocation, including the Midwestern and Western states – were the strongest source of support for homesteads across various bills, holding constant economic interests and political party. The significance of sectional variables provides additional evidence of the distributive consequences of claim clubs because they were most active in precisely those states. At the same time, quantitative assessment of homestead votes illuminates our understanding of the relationship between group conflict and free land more generally, including the influence of political parties and agricultural, manufacturing, and slavery interests, in the struggle for free land.

The findings regarding these other variables of interest are surprising. For example, the evidence reveals that political party did strongly influence votes on homestead legislation. Although Foner's (1970) definitive study of this period articulated the importance of free land in Republican ideology, these ideological differences did not translate into statistical differences in voting behavior.

In contrast to partisanship, slavery interests fare much better as an explanation for voting behavior. The hypothesized link between slavery and homesteads arises because of the relationship between free land and the balance of free and slave states. As Weingast (1998) explains, the balance between free and slave states ensured that the Southern states could veto any legislation that seriously undermined slavery institutions. Homestead legislation threatened the balance of free and slave states by removing a constraint on migration. For this reason, legislators from districts or states in which slavery interests were stronger are expected to be more likely to oppose free land. Indeed, legislators from cotton-producing regions and the South were more likely, statistically speaking, to oppose free land, which lends support to my hypothesis that free land threatened the political bargain holding slavery together.

Econometric analysis of roll-call votes is supplemented by an exegesis of President James Buchanan's message accompanying his veto of the 1860 homestead bill. The veto message offers a compelling analysis of the social costs of free land, including reducing the government's ability to provide public goods, such as revenue to fund an army or to pay down debt. Besides providing insight into the more general argument against class-based legislation that was common during the nineteenth century, the veto message stands out for its recognition of the opportunity costs of free land, as well as a compelling counterargument to modern economic defenses of free land.

The veto message also provides an opportunity to evaluate distributive theories of lawmaking. According to distributive perspectives, when districts are small and legislators have opportunities to bargain over policies, elected officials are hypothesized to have stronger incentives to support policies providing particularistic benefits to their district, as opposed to legislation benefiting society more generally.[1] In contrast, incentives to engage in distributive politics are hypothesized to decline as the size of the constituency increases relative to the national electorate.

[1] There is a large literature on the political economy of legislative decision making, in particular from a distributive perspective. Some of the most important early contributions to distributive theories of legislative politics are Weingast et al. (1981) and Shepsle and Weingast (1981).

In the context of American political institutions and nineteenth-century land laws, these theories suggest that presidents will have stronger incentives to internalize social costs of free land by virtue of having a national constituency. Buchanan's careful consideration of the full set of benefits and costs of free land was arguably a consequence of institutional incentives, in particular the structural incentives for presidents to support policies promising revenue for the government – revenue that, by its very nature, benefits the United States rather than a particular section. Similarly, overwhelming support of homesteads in the House, alongside more vocal opposition in the Senate, reflects stronger incentives of members of the Senate to internalize the social costs of free land.

This chapter is organized as follows. The first part derives hypotheses from relevant theories regarding support and opposition to homestead legislation. Second, each of these hypotheses is evaluated econometrically to better understand various sources of support and opposition to homestead legislation. Third, the veto message accompanying the 1860 homestead bill is assessed from a political economy perspective to gain additional insight into distributive dimensions of free land. The fourth section considers explicitly homesteads from a static welfare perspective, in particular the economic argument for free land, introduced in earlier chapters, that suggests homesteads were socially desirable because they reduced the federal government's costs of policing the nation's borderlands. Finally, the chapter concludes by considering whether homesteads are better thought of as a component of social policy, or as a corporate welfare policy.

To foreshadow my findings, the fiscal consequences of homestead legislation during a period of mushrooming government debt make them less an efficient response to security considerations (as the economic defense of free land would have us believe) than a socially costly land giveaway. In terms of institutional change, claim clubs were a driving force behind free land, although the more generalized force for change was sectional interests, which included, but was not limited to, the influence of clubs. Overall, then, homestead laws are most accurately described as the fruits of rent seeking, with claim clubs and sectional interests as the most important mechanisms behind emergence of free land.

WHO WANTS FREE LAND? HYPOTHESES FOR INSTITUTIONAL CHANGE

The basic features of homestead laws, and the significance of homesteaders in settling the Western frontier, are well known in popular culture. Nor is there any shortage of attention to homesteads among historians. However, less is known about homesteads from the perspective of alternative theories of institutional change. To facilitate such understanding, this section derives alternative hypotheses for support for free land from various political and economic theories that will subsequently be evaluated by analyzing votes on four failed homestead bills.

The first hypothesis is that legislators from public-land states will support homesteads.[2] There were several reasons why legislators from public-land states had incentives to support homesteads. First, claim clubs remained in several of the public-land states in the 1850s and 1860s. Squatters continued to occupy public land because Congress had yet to formally extend preemption legislation to new territories that would eventually be covered by homesteads. Although homesteads were designed to encourage settlement, any homestead law would certainly have been used by anyone who had occupied land prospectively, even though such use would have violated the letter as well as the spirit of the law. Thus, a club's members would have been content with preemption laws or homestead legislation because the government would have had a hard time figuring out who was making a homestead entry as a squatter and who settled land after homestead legislation.

Second, legislators from public-land states had incentives to support homesteads as part of a strategy for economic development. Homesteads would certainly have increased the number of people in less populous Western states. Economic theory suggests that at low levels of development, increasing the population will increase economic growth.[3] To the extent that legislators from public-land states believed population growth would lead to economic development, they had incentives to support free land.

Third, homesteads may have been appealing to legislators from public-land states because of the perceived relationship between free land and security from Indian tribes. According to the economic defense of free land alluded to earlier, packing the borderlands with settlers may have increased security in Western states. To the extent legislators from the public-land states were convinced that homesteads would increase security, they had stronger incentives to support a homestead bill. A security rationale also suggests homesteads may have been efficient, a possibility I consider explicitly toward the end of this chapter.

These three factors suggest that legislators from public-land states had stronger incentives to support homesteads than legislators from state-land states in the Eastern states. In contrast to their counterparts from the public-land states, legislators from state-land states would only realize benefits from homesteads indirectly, at best – for example, packing the land with settlers benefited Easterners to the extent that such policies reduced the cost of providing security in the nation as a whole, assuming such costs are financed from a national pool of revenue. However, any security benefits for those in the

[2] See Chapter 1 for the distinction between public-land and state-land states as well as Map 1.1 for their location.

[3] Technically, population growth leads to extensive growth, which is growth that occurs by increasing land, labor, capital, and entrepreneur skill, holding constant technology. Intensive growth refers to growth attained holding constant inputs. At early stages of development, it is often desirable to increase the overall size of an economy by increasing population, although at later stages, intensive growth is critical to understanding long-run economic development. Larger populations may also contribute to technology by increasing diversity of ideas.

East were quite indirect. In addition, Easterners would have benefited from revenue-generating use of public land to pay down debt, which would have created incentives for legislators from state-land states to oppose homesteads. For these reasons, legislators from state-land states are hypothesized to have opposed homesteads.

A drawback to a public-land hypothesis conceptualized along these lines is that it includes several complementary rationales as to why legislators from public-land states would be more likely to support homesteads. Claim clubs are a plausible reason why legislators from public-land states supported homesteads, but so too are the goals of economic development or a belief that homesteads would improve security in Western states. Consequently, a public-land variable does not permit a precise test of my hypothesis that claim clubs were the fundamental mechanism of institutional change in the nineteenth century. Isolating the impact of claim clubs would require district-level data on presence of a claim club. Unfortunately, such a data set does not exist, and its collection is beyond the scope of this book. Nonetheless, a public-land hypothesis is a reasonable way to evaluate my theoretical argument that claim clubs increased incentives for legislators to support distributive policies, with the caveat that statistical significance of this variable reflects political interests as well as organizational influence.

Political party provides additional hypotheses regarding support and opposition to homesteads. There were four major parties during this period: Republicans, Free Soil Republicans, Democrats, and Whigs, each with preferences over land (there were a few other minor parties that will also be discussed). Republicans and Free Soil Republicans tended to argue that land should be used to encourage Western migration. Republican support of free land was based on the theory that a flood of settlers would undermine political support for slavery. Democrats, in contrast, generally had a stronger preference to use public land as a revenue resource.[4] Democrats also had reasons to oppose institutional changes that undermined slavery (see my hypothesis, explained later, relating free land to slavery institutions). Members of the Whig party, which convened in opposition to Andrew Jackson's Democratic Party, were less concerned with using public land as a revenue resource than Democrats. A few members were part of the Opposition Party, which had as one of its defining features opposition to the spread of slavery in Kansas, along with a dislike of the Democratic Party. Because the Opposition Party opposed slavery and democrats, its members had incentives to support free land.

For reasons outlined earlier, Democrats are hypothesized to have opposed homesteads, not only because free land reduced revenue but also because migration to the western states threatened slavery institutions. Whigs, Free Soil

[4] These hypotheses for partisan preferences over land are derived from Feller (1984), Stewart (1976), and Foner (1970). Feller provides the most thorough discussion regarding partisan preferences over land, as well as insight into roll call votes on various land bills.

Republicans, Republicans, and members of the Opposition Party are hypothesized to have supported homesteads for various reasons. Although these parties had their differences, each of them had at least one of the following ideological reasons to oppose homestead legislation: a desire to increase the number of free states, growing belief among party members that all people who so desired were entitled to a small section of land, and a conviction that free land would alleviate economic duress in the East. For this reason, members of these four parties are all expected to have opposed free land.

Economic interests are also expected to translate into legislative influence. There are at least four groups that had preferences over homestead legislation: farmers with legal title, ranchers, manufacturers, and slaveholders. Because homestead legislation was designed to benefit farmers prospectively, it may have been viewed by farmers with legal title as a subsidy to new entrants into agricultural markets. Of course, measuring presence of legal title in the 1850s presents a challenge. However, Clay's (2006) finding that farmers with legal title were more productive than squatters without formal documentation suggests a reasonable solution to this problem: agricultural productivity in a state (in analysis of Senate votes) or district (for House votes) as a proxy for the number of farmers with legal title. This is an acceptable measure under the assumption that greater productivity reflected more extensive formalization of land claims.

Similarly, legislators in districts with higher levels of livestock production are hypothesized to oppose homesteads. As the "range wars" would later demonstrate, farmers and ranchers often had serious conflicts of interest. In essence, both sides often viewed the other as a nuisance (Kantor 1998, 1994, 1991). For this reason, legislators from districts and states with greater livestock production are hypothesized to be less likely to support free land.

In contrast to the reasonable clear reasons for farmers with legal title and ranchers to oppose free land, the relationship between manufacturing interests and free land is somewhat more complicated. On one hand, economic theory suggests manufacturers had reason to oppose free land because it encouraged labor outmigration. As the supply of labor decreases, manufacturers have to pay higher wages, creating economic incentives to oppose homesteads. Manufacturers had incentives to oppose homesteads because free land increased wages in the relevant labor-market equilibrium. On the other hand, alliance politics during the 1850s may have led manufacturers to support homesteads for strategic purposes. According to Feller (1984), who authored the authoritative account of partisan politics of land from the 1830s through the 1850s, manufacturers and Westerners formed an alliance in hope of securing tariffs desired by manufacturers and free land benefiting Western interests. Benefits from tariffs may have exceeded costs of free land to manufacturers, leading them to support homesteads.

Because of these competing possibilities, I do not offer a hypothesis one way or the other how manufacturing interests will influence support for free land.

Certainly, the variable for manufacturing interests should be included in the model, although without a clear sign on the hypothesized direction. Rather, the statistical test can be used to sort out competing theoretical and historical perspectives on the relationship between manufacturing interests and support for free land.

Finally, legislators in cotton-producing districts or states are hypothesized to oppose homesteads. Fogel and Engerman (1974), in their unrivaled economic history of slavery in the United States, showed that abolition would devastate cotton-producing districts given their central finding that slaves were as valuable on the eve of the Civil War as they had ever been. Weingast's (1998) analysis of slavery complements the earlier study by Fogel and Engerman by offering a political theory of the American Civil War, one in which the balance rule of admitting free states with slave states – an informal norm – was one of the factors that held the Union together.[5] Weingast hypothesized that the balance rule was a source of federal stability because Southern interests could veto any legislation that weakened slavery institutions, a finding that makes sense only to the extent that slaves were valuable, which Fogel and Engerman demonstrated conclusively.

The analysis that follows complements these studies by considering explicitly the relationship between free land and the political institution of slavery. Fogel and Engerman's evidence that slaves were valuable, Weingast's theoretical and empirical take on the causes of the American Civil War, and the perceived relationship between free land and free states can be combined into the following hypothesis: legislators from cotton-producing districts will oppose homestead legislation because it threatened the political institution of slavery.

ECONOMETRIC ANALYSIS OF HOMESTEAD VOTES, 1852–60

An econometric approach to homesteads provides a convenient way to estimate the influence of variables of interest on legislative votes holding constant other relevant variables. At the same time, the econometric analysis presented in this section should be viewed as complementing historical and archival studies of homestead legislation because many of the hypotheses considered are derived from historians' studies of the politics of free land. To say that econometric analysis provides precise estimates of relationships between variables does suggest the work of historians is imprecise. Indeed, anyone who has read the wonderful histories of American land laws will recognize and appreciate

[5] Weingast's (1998) study of the American Civil War is an "analytic narrative," which uses game theory to better understand pivotal historical decisions and conflict. Analytic narratives provide insight into history by clarifying the underlying strategic situations giving rise to important outcomes, as well as by specifying precisely the important players, their preferences, and their choices, as well as providing insight into the institutional foundations of economic growth and development (Katznelson and Weingast 2005; Rodrik 2003; Bates et al. 1998).

the remarkable precision of their craft. As such, we can think of econometric estimation as offering a different, complementary kind of clarity.

In the quantitative models, outcomes are House votes on homestead bills of 1852, 1854, 1859, and 1860, as well as the Senate vote on the 1852 bill.[6] The smaller number of votes in the Senate, my reliance on several dichotomous independent variables, and a high degree of uniformity in partisan and sectional voting prevented econometrically analyzing all but the 1852 vote. Nonetheless, each Senate vote is considered descriptively even though not all could be assessed econometrically, as the votes are often informative and relevant to assessing the hypotheses that have been presented. A logit specification is used to estimate the relationship between variables on each bill because votes are dichotomous.

Legislators from public-land states are hypothesized to support homesteads. A variable for public-land state is included in all models (1 if a legislator is from Ohio, Louisiana, Indiana, Mississippi, Illinois, Alabama, Missouri, Arkansas, Michigan, Florida, Iowa, Wisconsin, California, Minnesota, or Oregon and 0 otherwise). Support for homesteads among public-land legislators can be interpreted as evidence that claim clubs influenced support for free land for reasons mentioned earlier.

All models of House votes include a variable for political party (1 if a legislator is a member of the Whig, Free Soil, Republican, or Opposition Party and 0 if a legislator is a member of the Democratic Party or a faction of the Democratic Party). Members of the Whigs, Free Soil Republicans, Republicans, and Opposition Party are hypothesized to support homesteads, while Democrats are hypothesized to oppose them.[7]

Four measures of economic interests are included in various models of House votes. District agriculture is measured by the number of bushels of corn and wheat (measured in thousands of bushels) produced in a district divided by total free population. The livestock variable is the value of livestock (in thousands of dollars) produced in a district divided by total free population. The variable district manufacturing is manufacturing product (in thousands of dollars) in a district divided by total free population. Data on agricultural production, manufacturing value, and livestock value for the House are district-level measures that are taken from the 1843 to 1883 data on Congressional districts (Parsons et al. 1986). Ultimately, these data are constructed from census data, which provide a great deal of information regarding economic activities during this period. Data for each variable used in the analysis of House votes are taken from the year closest to the particular vote in which data are available.

[6] Information on roll-call votes is found in the *Congressional Globe*, various years.

[7] Measures of ideology were not used in the econometric models because free land does not have a clear theoretical interpretation on the conventional spectrum of spatial models of politics, which is size of government. Political party has a much stronger theoretical and substantive rationale regarding support and opposition to homestead legislation.

Finally, in each econometric specification used to model House votes, cotton production is used as a proxy for slavery interests. Cotton production is a district-level measure taken from Parsons et al. (1986). A variable for cotton production is included in each model (1 if a district produced at least 100,000 bales of cotton in a year during the period 1843–55 and 0 otherwise).

The variables in the model of Senate votes on the 1852 bill are similar to those of the House votes. Partisan and sectional variables are defined identically. State-level measures of agricultural and manufacturing share are taken from the 1860 census.[8] Unfortunately, measures of livestock value and cotton production could not be included in the model of Senate votes because those variables were highly correlated with other variables in the model, and so they had to be dropped from the analysis.

House and Senate Votes, 1852

It may come as a surprise that the House approved four times a homestead bill prior to the successful bill, first in 1852. However, the fact that several bills were successful, although interesting, does not tell us much about why a particular legislator was more or less likely to vote for free land. Indeed, there was nontrivial dissent on each of the homestead votes. Econometric analysis of House votes on the 1852 bill, the results of which are presented in Table 6.1, provides additional insight into the political economy of homesteads by considering quantitatively the micro-level sources of support and opposition to free land.

As the statistical results for the 1852 roll-call vote reveals, legislators from public-land states were more likely to support land transfers to smallholder farmers, holding constant other theoretically relevant factors. Indeed, the public-land variable was the only statistically significant variable, as well as the only factor that would remain statistically significant across each of the bills considered. Sectional interests appear to have been a driving force behind free land, consistent with my theoretical argument outlined earlier.

Other hypotheses did not fare as well, at least on this particular vote. Contrary to expectations, political party, economic composition, and cotton production did not influence votes on homesteads in the House in 1852. The nonsignificance of political party is perhaps most surprising because all of the major political parties had preferences over land. As importantly, partisan preferences over land have had no shortage of attention from historians, in particular in Foner's (1970) work on Republican ideology. Although Foner's history is first rate by any standard, the ideological convictions of Republicans did not translate into observed differences in voting behavior on the first bill that successfully made it out of the House.

The 1852 version of the bill, failed in the Senate by a margin of 38 to 16 after it was approved in the House. More generally, the Senate typically opposed,

[8] Secretary of State, 8th Census, 1861.

TABLE 6.1. *Roll-Call Analysis of House Votes on the 1852 Homestead Bill*

	Coefficient (Standard Error)
Party (1 Whig, Free Soil Republican, Republican, or Opposition, 0 otherwise)	−0.19
	(0.38)
Public-Land State (1 Public-Land State, 0 otherwise)	1.97*
	(0.50)
District Agricultural Share	−0.00
	(0.00)
District Manufacturing Share	0.00
	(0.00)
District Livestock Production	−0.02
	(0.01)
Cotton Production (1 if a district is cotton-producing, 0 otherwise)	−0.29
	(0.54)
Observations	162
Likelihood Ratio Test (Chi-Square)	27.58*
Correct predictions	0.70

* Statistically significant at the 5 percent level
Logit Model: 1 for yea; 0 for nay
Dependent variable is House vote on the 1852 homestead bill

voting free land down 1852, 1854, and 1859, in contrast with the House, which typically supported these bills. As Table 6.2 indicates, Senators from public-land states were more likely to support homestead legislation, as expected. Similar to the finding in the House, political party did not influence votes in the Senate, which is again informative because there were clear theoretical expectations relating political party to votes on the major land law of the 1850s. Agricultural share and manufacturing share also had no effect, statistically speaking, in the Senate.

In this model, I could not include a variable for state-level cotton production because all Senators from cotton-producing states supported the bill. An alternative is to include a measure for the South, which also captures proslavery interests (coded 1 if a Senator was from a state in the South, 0 otherwise). Although cotton production is the preferred measure, one expects legislators in the South to also oppose free land because it potentially undermined the balance of power that made slavery a self-enforcing political equilibrium. This regional variable turned out to be statistically significant, lending additional evidence to the hypothesis that free land threatened slavery. If free land posed a threat to slavery institutions, then we would expect legislators in the South to be more likely to oppose it, which is what the evidence tells us on this particular vote in the Senate.

Additional insights into dynamics of support and opposition to homestead legislation can be gleaned by considering how senators from the Midwestern

TABLE 6.2. *Roll-Call Analysis of Senate Votes on the 1852 Homestead Bill*

	Coefficient (Standard Error)
Party (1 Whig, Free Soil Republican, Republican, or Opposition, 0 otherwise)	1.16
	(1.05)
Public-Land State (1 Public-Land State, 0 otherwise)	3.98*
	(1.61)
State Agricultural Share	0.00
	(0.00)
State Manufacturing Share	0.28
	(0.19)
South (1 South, 0 otherwise)	−5.31*
	(2.02)
Observations	54
Likelihood Ratio Test (Chi-Square)	37.02*
Correct predictions	0.76

* Statistically significant at the 5 percent level
Logit Model: 1 for yea; 0 for nay
Dependent variable is Senate vote on the 1852 homestead bill

states voted. Nine of eleven senators from Midwestern states supported this bill. Overall, nine of sixteen senators supporting this version of a homestead law were from Midwestern public-land states. Strong support among Midwestern senators reflects the influence of claim clubs, which were particularly active in those states.

House and Senate Votes, 1854

The defeat of the homestead bill failed in 1852 was only the beginning of the story of free land rather than its end. By 1854, another homestead bill was ready for consideration. Legislators in the House again approved the bill, this time by a margin of 107 to 72 after a motion to table it was defeated. Similar to the 1852 bill, House members from public-land states were more likely to support the bill (see Table 6.3). Once again, slavery interests appear to have influenced voting on homesteads, with legislators from cotton-producing districts less likely to support homesteads. The cotton variable also turns out to be statistically significant on the 1859 and 1860 votes on homestead bills. Political party and economic interests did not have much of an effect on this bill, either. Political party did not have a statistically significant impact on votes in 1854, while economic composition – measured by agricultural, manufacturing, and livestock values – did not influence House votes.

As mentioned, lack of influence of political parties on the 1852 and 1854 votes is somewhat surprising. However, modern theories of party competition provide some insight into these outcomes. According to the parties-as-cartels

TABLE 6.3. *Roll-Call Analysis of House Votes on the 1854 Homestead Bill*

	Coefficient (Standard Error)
Party (1 Whig, Free Soil Republican, Republican, or Opposition, 0 otherwise)	0.19
	(0.37)
Public-Land State (1 Public-Land State, 0 otherwise)	1.99*
	(0.46)
District Agricultural Share	0.00
	(0.00)
District Manufacturing Share	−0.00
	(0.00)
District Livestock Production	0.00
	(0.00)
Cotton Production (1 if a district is cotton-producing, 0 otherwise)	−2.07*
	(0.53)
Observations	179
Likelihood Ratio Test (Chi-Square)	45.12*
Correct predictions	0.65

* Statistically significant at the 5 percent level
Logit Model: 1 for yea; 0 for nay
Dependent variable is House vote on the 1854 homestead bill

theory devised by Cox and McCubbins (2005, 1993), political parties have the potential to influence public policies because they are organizations capable of providing selective incentives to members to choose a party's preferred policies.

One of the conditions for the cartel theory to work is that parties are sufficiently strong. On this measure, political parties were fairly weak during this period. Party switching and creation of new political parties, each common during the 1850s, undermined the ability of political parties to act as cartels by increasing competition between parties, dissipating partisan differences, and contributing to fragmentation; each of these features reduces political parties' ability to provide selective incentive necessary to compel compliance with partisan platforms. For example, the Opposition Party, Whigs, and Republicans, although sharing certain ideological perspectives, had not yet coordinated their interests. For this reason, it should not be especially surprising that political parties did not translate ideological interests into voting behavior.

More generally, there are few reasons to expect political parties to influence policy choice in a separated system in which the electoral connection between voters and candidates is strong. Krehbiel (1998), one of the architects of a separation-of-powers approach to the modern study of Congress, argued that veto players, not majority party control, govern the process of institutional change. From a separation of powers perspective, it should not be surprising that political party exerted little impact on House and Senate votes in the early

1850s despite the importance of land in party platforms. The reason is simple: candidates in a system in which districts select candidates without relying on things such as party lists have stronger incentives to respond to the demands of their constituents rather than their parties.

Returning to the votes, the Senate approved this bill by a margin of 36 to 11. Although unified support Democratic senators and senators from public-land states prevented me from analyzing the bill econometrically, the voting patterns are revealing. As expected, there was strong support among senators from public-land states, with each of the 22 senators from public-land states who voted on this bill supporting it. In addition, each of the 32 Democratic senators supported the bill, while Whigs opposed it by a margin of 10 to 1. On this vote in the Senate, members of the Democratic Party did not appear to view free land as a threat to slavery even through it promised to ease migration to the Western states. Perhaps slavery was viewed as a more stable institution in 1854 than it would be within a few years. The bill, however, was never signed, and there would be two more votes before the successful bill of 1862.

House and Senate Votes, 1859 and 1860

The 1859 and 1860 votes in the House were not even close, with homesteads winning by large margins. There remained, however, obstruction in the Senate, as well as opposition from the White House. There was nevertheless nontrivial opposition, and so information can be gained by analyzing the votes. Besides sectionalism, which continued to influence House votes on the homestead bills, partisan and economic interests also influenced legislative behavior. In the 1859 House vote, political party had the expected effect, with members of the Republican and Free Soil Parties more likely to support homesteads. Agricultural production correlated with opposition to homesteads in the House in both 1859 and 1860, consistent with my hypothesis that farmers had incentives to oppose free land because it subsidized competitors. Farmers who may have taken preemption claims may also have viewed free land as unfair: preemptioners had to pay a nominal price for land, while homesteads would have given it away. However, manufacturing composition and livestock production did not influence House votes in 1859 or 1860. As with votes on previous bills, legislators from cotton-producing districts were more likely to oppose homesteads. The results are summarized in Table 6.4.

In contrast to overwhelming support in the House, the Senate declined to consider the 1859 bill by a margin of 27 to 20. Political party and section continued to influence votes, and a Midwestern section was a bulwark of support for homesteads. Republicans supported the bill by a margin of 16 to 0 with Democrats opposing by a margin of 29 to 9. In contrast with their colleagues in the House, senators from public-land states were not as strongly supportive of homesteads, with thirteen legislators from public-land states voting for, and

TABLE 6.4. *Roll-Call Analysis of House Votes on the 1859 Homestead Bill*

	Coefficient (Standard Error)
Party (1 Whig, Free Soil Republican, Republican, or Opposition, 0 otherwise)	2.65*
	(0.68)
Public-Land State (1 Public-Land State, 0 otherwise)	1.66*
	(0.60)
District Agricultural Share	−0.03*
	(0.01)
District Manufacturing Share	−0.00
	(0.02)
District Livestock Production	0.00
	(0.02)
Cotton Production (1 if a district is cotton-producing, 0 otherwise)	−3.23*
	(1.21)
Observations	195
Likelihood Ratio Test (Chi-Square)	146.99*
Correct predictions	0.91

* Statistically significant at the 5 percent level
Logit Model: 1 for yea; 0 for nay
Dependent variable is House vote on the 1859 homestead bill

twelve against, this bill. However, Senators from Midwestern states were quite unified in support of the bill, with eleven voting in support and two against it – lending additional support to my hypothesis introduced earlier that the legislators from the Midwest were the fundamental driving force behind homestead legislation. In addition, although Democrats opposed the bill by a margin of twenty-nine to nine, eight of the nine Democratic Party legislators who defected from the preferences of their political party were from public-land states. The persistence and legacy of claim clubs in the Midwest appear to have created a divide in Democratic Party voting on both the 1852 and 1859 bills. Finally, consistent with my hypothesis regarding land and slavery institutions, legislators in the South opposed the bill, with twenty-five of twenty-six senators voting against it.

The statistical relationships between variables and votes on the 1860 bill are nearly identical to the 1859 vote (see Table 6.5). Sectional factors and political party had essentially the same consequences in 1859 and 1860: legislators from public-land states remained an important force in support of homesteads, and political parties continued to influence votes in the hypothesized direction. Similar to the finding from the 1859 vote, legislators from more productive agricultural districts were more likely to oppose homesteads. Cotton measures had to be dropped from the model because all of the cotton-producing districts opposed the homestead bill in 1860, although unanimous support from cotton-producing districts is evidence that slavery interests conflicted with free land.

TABLE 6.5. *Roll-Call Analysis of House Votes on the 1860 Homestead Bill*

	Coefficient (Standard Error)
Party (1 Whig, Free Soil Republican, Republican, or Opposition, 0 otherwise)	3.26*
	(0.84)
Public-Land State (1 Public-Land State, 0 otherwise)	4.45*
	(1.06)
District Agricultural Share	−0.08*
	(0.02)
District Manufacturing Share	−0.06
	(0.03)
District Livestock Production	0.01
	(0.02)
Observations	163
Likelihood Ratio Test (Chi-Square)	160.02*
Correct predictions	0.93

* Statistically significant at the 5 percent level
Logit Model: 1 for yea; 0 for nay
Dependent variable is House vote on the 1860 homestead bill

In 1860, manufacturing share again had no effect on votes, statistically speaking. Although economic theory suggests that manufacturers had incentives to oppose labor outmigration, the desire for a cheap labor supply did not translate into legislative influence on any of the votes. In addition, although manufacturers may have formed a coalition with Western interests, there is no statistical evidence of this effect in roll-call votes on homestead legislation.

The Senate supported the bill by a vote of 44 to 8 on May 10, 1860. Republicans supported it by a margin of 18 to 1, and Democrats supported it by a margin of 15 to 7. Southern senators supported the bill by a margin of 15 to 5. Senators from public-land states were the strongest source of support for the bill (all twenty-three senators from public-land states supported this version of the homestead bill), followed by Republicans. In this last-gasp attempt to block free land, a handful of senators from the Democratic Party and the South, consistent with partisan and slavery-based hypotheses regarding homesteads, opposed it. Thus, by 1860, political parties appear to have coordinated members in support of free land while legislators from public-land states continued to support homesteads. Whatever opposition remained was from the Democratic Party and legislators from the South, which we would expect given partisan and slavery-based interests.

Several conclusions may be drawn from the econometric analysis of roll-call votes on various versions of the homestead bill. Sectionalism exhibited the most consistent influence on homestead legislation, consistent with the hypothesis that claim clubs were a source of distributive policies. Greater legislative support for free land in the sections of the United States in which claim clubs were active suggests they influenced policy making beyond squatters' rights.

Political party had some effects on a few of the bills but it was by no means consistent, influencing votes only on homestead bills as the Civil War was imminent. Democrats were more likely to oppose free land by the late 1850s than they were in the early 1850s, perhaps because it became clear that the balance rule was in peril. However, the overall influence of political party seems at best inconclusive.

In contrast, there is consistent and strong support for my hypothesis relating free land to slavery institutions. Although Weingast's balance rule theory did not consider land in his analysis of the Civil War, free land challenged the political balance of free and slave states that made slavery a self-enforcing equilibrium. Evidence from votes on homestead bills is consistent with my hypothesis regarding the balance rule: legislators from pro-slavery regions were less likely to support homesteads, presumably because free land threatened slavery through its effect on the balance of free and slave states.

One of the limits of analysis of roll-call votes is that it cannot tell us about the desirability of homesteads as a public policy. The veto message accompanying the homestead bill of 1860 offers a clear assessment of homestead legislation from a public policy perspective that anticipates distributive perspectives on institutional change.

NATIONAL SECURITY AND THE VETO OF THE HOMESTEAD BILL

The 1860 version came closer than the rest to succeeding, succumbing after President James Buchanan returned the homestead bill with a veto on June 22, 1860.[9] The veto message is worth briefly considering because Buchanan clearly articulated the social costs of homestead legislation. It is also an excellent example of the argument against class-based legislation that would become famous in a series of Supreme Court decisions at the dawn of the twentieth century – the so-called Lochner era of Supreme Court jurisprudence, which was made famous by the willingness of the nation's highest court to strike down government legislation benefiting a particular groups of citizens because of its perceived conflict with individual liberty and autonomy.

The veto concerned both issues of fairness and public policy. One of the most salient fairness considerations was a fear that the "old class" of settlers – those who took preemption claims – would be "alienated" by a new bill giving land away. Although preemption was also a land giveaway, it nonetheless retained a positive price. Homesteads, by removing the price of land entirely, could be perceived as unfair by those who actually paid for their land by decreasing

[9] *Journal of the Senate*, June 22, 1860: 747–53. The details that follow are drawn from Buchanan's veto message unless otherwise noted.

land prices in private markets. In particular, the president was concerned the homestead bill would potentially harm soldiers who received land as payment for fighting battles for the country.

More fundamentally, the veto message articulated ideological opposition to class-based legislation, which today we might simply refer to as distributive politics. During the nineteenth century, class-based legislation referred to any law benefiting a specific class of individuals, as opposed to legislation that served the public interest more generally (Gillman 1992). Buchanan objected to public policies benefiting a specific class of citizens, a sentiment foreshadowing the famous Lochner decision of 1905, which invalidated legislation benefiting a particular class of citizens as a violation of the equal protection clause of the Constitution.[10] The case involved a New York state law restricting the hours bakers could work, presumably to improve work conditions. The Lochner majority struck down legislation, arguing that it was not in the public interest. According to the Court, "public interest" required that a law benefits all people rather than a particular class. In this case, the hours law only regulated bakers, which were in the Court's mind no different from any other occupation, and hence the regulation affected a particular class. Substantively, the court argued that the law violated "liberty of contract," which was derived from various principles in the Constitution, although the phrase itself is found nowhere in the document. The defining feature of Lochner jurisprudence to define the police powers of the states – which are a source of authority to regulate and prohibit various economic activities for the purposes of protecting health, safety, and welfare – was narrow, overruling legislation unless it had features of a pure public good.

It seems obvious that the Supreme Court was pursuing its own policy preferences in the Lochner cases (especially considering the court invented the concept of liberty of contract). However, the Court was actually applying long-standing principles in those cases. As Gillman (1992) explained in *The Constitution Besieged*, a masterful work articulating the constitutional political economy of Supreme Court decision making during the late nineteenth and early twentieth centuries, Lochner-era judges were engaged in a herculean effort to balance an institutional need to adhere to long-standing jurisprudential principles with demands ignited by unprecedented economic and class-based conflict at the dawn of the twentieth century.

Buchanan's veto message foreshadowed the Lochner principle of substantive due process in constitutional jurisprudence in arguing that homesteads were indefensible because they were transfers to a specific *class* of citizens. Indeed, it is one of the more important examples of the arguments against class-based legislation, invoked in this case to strike down a homestead bill – arguably, legislation as important in the 1850s and 1860s as a health and safety regulation in the early 1900s.

[10] *Lochner* v. *New York* 198 U.S. 45 (1905).

Philosophical opposition to class legislation aside, Buchanan offers several additional policy-relevant critiques of homestead legislation. First, free land could harm manufacturers. Reminiscent of Henry Clay, one of the most famous nationalists and mercantilists the country knew during the first half of the nineteenth century, Buchanan believed that free land threatened manufacturing interests because it created incentives for western migration. Buchanan, echoing the earlier arguments espoused by Clay, believed that government policies that encouraged migration should be avoided because they threatened business interests. Second, homesteads promised to encourage speculation. Speculators, according to Buchanan's calculus, would collude to accumulate homestead entries. This hypothesis seems entirely reasonable once the nation's experience with preemption laws is taken into account, because preemption typically benefited speculators as well as the "poor farmer." Third, free land threatened a run on American land by foreign citizens. The mining boom in California led to massive immigration of foreigners to the United States, and the California state legislature even voted to ban Chinese immigration to their state in the 1850s (Kanazawa 2005). The gold rush experience certainly seems to have influenced the veto message. However, it was not immigration per se that vexed Buchanan but rather public policies that encouraged migration simply to take advantage of free land. The President's argument was not anti-immigrant, but rather was that it was not in the country's interest to encourage people to come to American shores because they wanted free land. And as we will see in Chapter 8, legislation seeking to regulate access to the gold fields was clearly anti-immigrant legislation – compared with legislation coming out of the California legislature, there was nothing particularly offensive about the ideas expressed in the veto message.

Finally, homestead legislation had important fiscal implications. Buchanan recognized that free land undermined government revenue, backing his theory up with numbers. The Secretary of the Interior estimated that public revenue from sale of public land would be $4,000,000 without homesteads, while less than $1,000,000 would be brought in from that same source if the homestead bill passed. Buchanan himself estimated that the current system generated revenue of $10,000,000 per year while recognizing that free land threatened this important nontax revenue source ($10 million per year translates into about $270 million in today's dollars, which may not seem like much, except the size of government was much smaller back then, and so $10 million was by no means trivial). Although Buchanan did not use language of opportunity costs, the veto message clearly articulated the tradeoffs associated with free land. In addition, these numbers only include revenue from agricultural land. The fiscal implications of free mineral land, considered carefully in Chapter 7, are even more staggering.

Along with ideological opposition to distributive policies provides insight into Buchanan's decision to veto the bill, institutional incentives contributed to Buchanan's rejection of homesteads. Government debt was historically a threat to national sovereignty. The fears of inability to pay down debt, which contributed to the demise of the Articles of Confederation, remained in 1860, in part because the federal government continued to have few reliable revenue resources.

As president, Buchanan had stronger incentives to consider the welfare of the country, as opposed to members of the House and Senate, who had incentives to support public policies that were locally popular even if they undermined *national* security. The substantive content of the veto message – in particular, concern with the social costs of homesteads – reflected a president's institutional incentives to internalize the external costs of free land, in this case a fiscal externality imposed on the average voter.

Members of the Senate, evidently unconvinced by these reasonable objections, attempted to override the veto, although proponents of the homestead bill came up a vote short of the necessary two-thirds, 28 to 18. Senators from public-land states remained supportive of homesteads, with 15 of the 22 members of the Senate from public-domain states voting to override the veto. The Midwestern states remained the bulwark of support for free land, with all of the senators from the Midwestern states voting to support the override. The only senators from public-land states who supported the veto were from Southern states.

Unsurprisingly, Buchanan's veto infuriated proponents of free land. Horace Greeley, one of the most influential journalists of the time, wrote an acerbic editorial criticizing him for rejecting the tens of thousands in Iowa, Kansas, Minnesota, and similar states facing a harsh existence who were praying for a homestead bill (Robbins 1933). Nonetheless, the veto message suggests the president clearly understood the social costs of free land – costs that should be taken into account when assessing the desirability of public policies, in particular public policies as important as homesteads.

ECONOMIC ANALYSIS OF HOMESTEADS

The previous chapter suggested various reasons why squatters' rights were a source of social costs. If squatters' rights, which had a positive price of land, were a source of social costs, then homestead legislation seems like an even more obvious example of distributive politics. Yet a distributive interpretation of homestead legislation is also contingent on a welfare analysis of free land, one that considers the net benefits of these laws from society's perspective. Indeed, economic studies of homesteads, rather than seeking to understand homesteads from the perspective of institutional change, are largely confined to welfare analysis of the consequences of free land. This section considers the categories of benefits and costs of homesteads explicitly.

Welfare analyses of homesteads can be divided into two perspectives. The first perspective rationalizes free land by articulating its social benefits. The most compelling argument for benefits is the idea that free land reduces the state's costs of defending the borderlands by packing the frontier with settlers. As introduced in earlier chapters, Barzel (1989) defended homestead legislation from an economic perspective because free land potentially flooded the dangerous regions of the West with settlers, reducing the state's cost of defending that region from Indian tribes. Similarly, Allen (1991) argued that one of the virtues of homesteads was packing the Western lands with settlers who could defend the land at lower cost than the army. Each perspective suggests that the benefits from free land may have outweighed its costs.

A second general perspective on free land, which offers a less optimistic economic assessment, emphasizes its costs. According to this second perspective, free land created incentives to make socially wasteful expenditures to capture natural resources before land had sufficient value (Anderson and Hill 2002; Bohanan and Coelho 1998). Homesteads also encouraged smallholder farming when other economic activities were more appropriate, discouraged internalization of risk by reducing the price of land, and undermined incentives to invest in conservation (Hansen and Libecap 2004a,b). Free land was socially costly because it exacerbated costly conflict to establish property rights, encouraged inappropriate economic activities in Western lands, and discouraged incentives to internalize risk.

On one hand, neither of these perspectives explains why the government chose homesteads, which is what the first parts of this chapter provided. Rather, each of the aforementioned economic studies debates whether or not homesteads were efficient, rather than explaining *why* such policies were chosen. Congress may have had an interest in increasing density of settlement in the West. However, the economic defense of free land has a hard time explaining why there was often substantial opposition to homestead legislation (or why the bill failed four times). In other words, if packing the frontier with settlers was a low-cost way of defending the nation's borderlands, then it is puzzling why homesteads failed four times. More generally, economic arguments for free land do not address the following question: Why did some legislators support free land and others oppose it? The empirical study of homesteads presented in this chapter provides additional insight into these questions of institutional change.

On the other hand, existing economic studies have not provided a compelling benefit–cost analysis of homesteads. Existing studies suggest that the primary category of benefits of free land is providing security on the borderlands, while the main cost categories include undermining incentives to conserve land and farm failures. None of the economic studies above consider the benefits *and* costs of free land.

Nor have the studies that actually consider costs taken all of the relevant ones into account. For example, studies articulating the conservation costs of free land have not given much thought to the fiscal consequences of homestead legislation, focusing instead on the costs of racing to establish property rights. Indeed, none of the aforementioned studies critical of homesteads devotes much attention to the fact that land giveaways after the Civil War threatened government revenue – and perhaps even long-run security – in a period of unprecedented debt. As such, an important category of costs has been excluded from existing welfare analyses.

As a final point of contention, defenders of homesteads make a strong assumption about the security benefits of homestead legislation. Barzel and Allen each assume that settlers in borderlands were able to provide security at lower cost than the military. However, security is probably provided more effectively by a military than by pushing large numbers of settlers into harsh lands when few understood how to farm in inhospitable terrain. Settlers were not private armies, nor were they necessarily trained in security matters. Public policies that encouraged homesteaders to flock to the frontier, many with no experience in security matters or even agriculture, were unlikely to reduce substantially the federal government's need to use the army to defend borderlands, and may even have put the army in a position of having to defend inexperienced settlers from their enemies.

Once we account for settlers' inexperience with military affairs, as well as declining threat, security benefits of homesteads appear less substantial. In addition, studies articulating the costs of homesteads emphasize diminished incentives to conserve land under free land policies at the expense of the fiscal consequences of such policies, and so they understate the social costs of free land. Revenue forgone, and the potential that the army would have to defend settlers who put themselves in danger, suggest that homesteads were another example of the fruits of rent seeking rather than an example of efficient institutional change. At a minimum, a full-fledged economic analysis of homesteads should take into account all major categories of benefits and costs. The observations here merely suggest that to this point, existing studies have not done so.

LAND AND THE WELFARE STATE

The analysis of homestead legislation presented in this chapter has taken a political economy perspective, which is to say it has emphasized origins and consequences of institutions. Besides providing an example of distributive conflict over property rights, homestead legislation is important in terms of development of the American welfare state.

This interrelationship between land and welfare in the early United States has been touched on in a few previous studies. For example, small-scale grants to soldiers have been recognized as a component of social policy in the United States (Jensen 2003; Skocpol 1992). Beginning in the Revolutionary War, soldiers received land scrip for service when the government lacked a pension system for war veterans.

Land grants to veterans are an important example of the initial social policies in the United States, although one could consider these grants payment for service rather than a "social policy," which typically are determined by income status rather than in exchange for service. Regardless of what we call them, land grants to soldiers are a link between welfare policies and land policies.

Similarly, homesteads link land policy to development of the welfare state, although the link is much stronger with homesteads than with land scrip for war veteran, for two reasons: homesteads were a more extensive policy (many more people claimed homesteads than the early scrip-for-soldiers programs), as well as universalistic policies that were not tied to service. Homesteads were sufficiently extensive that they compete with pensions as a beachhead for development of social policies. As Skocpol (1992) has shown, pensions became a critical federal social-welfare program during the period from the 1890s to 1910s, with spending reaching $100 million annually after the Arrears Act of 1879 and the Dependent Pensions Act of 1890 increased eligibility. Using universalism as our criterion, which is one of the most important dimensions for assessing the extent of welfare benefits (Swank 2002; Pierson 1994; Esping-Andersen 1990), homesteads may have been much more of a pure welfare policy than land scrip for soldiers; after all, land scrip for soldiers is more like payment for a service than a social policy for reasons outlined above. Thus, homesteads were not only universal, but they also predated pensions stressed by Skocpol as the first large-scale policies seeking to benefit the poor.

These observations suggest the potential importance of considering homesteads as the first major social policies in the United States. The argument that has been presented sketches out how we might interpret homesteads as a social policy if we wanted to go in that direction. Indeed, homesteads seem like a better example of emergence of welfare policies than the actual examples used in studies of the "land welfare state," namely, land grants to war veterans.

Nonetheless, before we take this bait, it is important to reflect on such an interpretation in light of the actual operation of the homestead law. Homesteads were certainly a spending program. However, interpreting them as *social* policies requires that they actually benefited poor settlers. Social policies are generally considered policies that benefit poor people in the literature on the American welfare state. On paper, homesteads were a social policy sine qua non for poor people seeking opportunities. In practice, they were more akin to a *corporate* welfare policy, or at least forerunners to modern corporate policies. Despite possessing elements of universalistic policies benefiting the poor, homesteads were manipulated so thoroughly that it is not clear the poor settler was the beneficiary of this act. Homestead laws were de jure social policies but de facto corporate welfare programs often benefiting powerful interests and speculators. Land laws were often manipulated, and they often benefited men of means thirsting for additional land. It is certainly a stretch to interpret homesteads as social policies when they were used by ranchers, miners, and loggers to extract natural resources throughout the Midwest and Far West during the early stages of capitalist development (this corruption of the homestead principle is discussed at greater length in Chapter 7).

More generally, it is important to distinguish between the myth and reality of homesteads when interpreting these policies from the perspective of social welfare. The myth of homesteads was that they created a nation of smallholder farmers, while the reality of homesteads was that they benefited corporate interests – miners, ranchers, and loggers. There were few legitimate economic reasons to give land away in order to encourage farming in the United States during the period in which opposing sides struggled over homesteads because most of the action with respect to laying an institutional framework for agrarian development had already occurred before the debates over homesteads. Geography and effective political institutions essentially ensured agricultural development in the United States (Sokoloff and Engerman 2000). Homesteads were not necessary for agriculture to take hold; rather, the institutional matrix took shape from 1780 to 1850, rather than in the 1850s and beyond. These earlier institutional transformations, along with geography, ensured the nation would develop its agriculture without a homestead bill. Free land, rather than causing and promoting agrarian development, only exacerbated to an ever-increasing run on government land.

If one finds this interpretation of homesteads believable, then it seems reasonable to conclude that homesteads were an important component of the origins of what Anderson and Hill (1980) refer to as "the transfer society," the birth of which they located in declining protection of property rights and removal of barriers to legislative transfers during the New Deal. Yet the political economy of early land laws suggests that its origins lie much earlier. Changes of the early twentieth century documented by Anderson and Hill exacerbated a process of expansion of social and corporate welfare that was set in motion by rent-seeking squatters. Perhaps economic studies of the welfare state, as well as political ones, neglect homesteads as a welfare policy because they created private property rights. After all, private property and the welfare state are often considered in opposition to one another, as redistribution tends to involve a weakening of private property rights. In a seeming paradox, public policies creating private property institutions were also welfare policies. The paradox can be resolved once we take into account that emergence of private property institutions is a separate question from how these private property rights are allocated.

My aim in this chapter and the previous one was to articulate distributive conflict over land prices as a fundamental dimension of conflict on agricultural land during the nineteenth century. Who received land, and for what price, hung in the balance of these struggles. However, conflict over agricultural property rights was by no means the end of the story when it came to the run on government land. What remains is to consider the major resource sectors: minerals, timber, and the nation's vast pasture lands. These resource-rich lands, much like the agricultural lands, provided the government with a potentially vast revenue resource. How would the government allocate property rights to these vast riches? As we will see, the period after the Civil War witnessed a complete and unmistakable extension of rent seeking, with members of claim clubs again demonstrating their ability to take the nation's land without paying for it.

7

The Open Floodgate in the Far West

A tremendous amount of land changed hands prior to the Civil War, and the wartime Congress provided a framework for additional settlement in the midst of the nation's bloodiest conflict with the Homestead Act. Did the antebellum land rush leave the nation with any land to give away?

As it turns out, despite extensive decentralization of state ownership, the federal government still formally owned over a billion acres of land in 1865, valued in the 1870 census at $5 billion (Dunham 1941; Donaldson 1884). Nor had the government given up on competitive land auctions, as the great land giveaway to that point only technically applied to agricultural land. Thus, the federal government continued to hold on to its vast mineral, timber, and rangeland resources, a vast stock of land that continued to promise potentially vast revenues.

Despite its great potential as a revenue resource, formal federal ownership of land was in many ways chimeric as legal and illegal settlement increased in response to economic opportunities in the Western states, both real and imagined. A combination of formal federal ownership, rapid expansion of illegal and extralegal settlement, and incongruence between local norms and national laws meant that something had to give in terms of institutions. Feeling the weight of highly organized settlers, competitive auctions typically gave way to demands presented by organized interests.

This chapter considers conflict over key natural resources in the Far West: minerals, timberland, and rangeland. Dynamics of distributive politics, which surfaced during the struggle for agricultural land, continued without losing a step. Miners, loggers, and ranchers, as well as desert farmers, collectively acquired hundreds of millions of acres of land for a nominal fee or for free. Several groups on the Western frontier – in particular, miners and loggers – petitioned for, and ultimately received, bills that formally reduced the price of lands they set in their sights. By now, we should also expect that legislative change was not the only path to legal title to the nation's bountiful natural resources. Indeed, as we found in the agricultural sector, attaining legal title through coercion at government auctions was common in each of the major resource sectors. And although ranchers never secured a free-land bill allowing them to formally privatize the open range (which was probably undesirable in any event given its large geographic reach), they were able to manipulate federal land laws seemingly at will to ensure they had free access to rangeland.

Once we take account of formal legislation reducing the price of land, manipulation of land laws, and the low price paid for access to vast and valuable land, rent seeking emerges as a central theme in the process of institutional change in the Far West. After describing key developments in land laws in each of the major Western economic sectors, I conclude the discussion of federal legislation by considering why speculation persisted despite federal efforts to limit it.

THE MINING ACT OF 1866: EFFICIENT INSTITUITONAL CHANGE OR THE FRUIT OF RENT SEEKING?

During the 1850s, informal private property institutions in California and Nevada rivaled a state-enforced system of private property institutions. Even with some limitations in terms of enforcement and clarity of allocation (disorder was not unheard of in the mining districts), these informal private property regimes permitted emergence of booming sectors. Once claim clubs transformed anarchy into a situation in which production increased dramatically, all the federal government had to do was recognize these informal claims to land. However, the state was slow to change formal institutions governing mineral land despite emergence of a mining sector under its nose, waiting to reform fundamentally the property regime only in 1866, nearly two decades after gold was discovered in California. Yet when it finally came up with a legislative solution, the bill Congress produced seemed to have a number of desirable properties.

This section considers the Mining Act of 1866, which was the major piece of federal legislation regulating mineral lands to emerge after the gold rush.[1] The discussion that follows is meant to clarify certain important features of the act, features praised by economists interested in the economic history of mining in the Far West, as well as to recall some of the social costs that tend to be left out of economic defenses of this particular piece of legislation. Similar to the discussion of the homestead bill in the previous chapter, the purpose of this brief exegesis is not to offer a full-fledged economic analysis of the law, but rather to articulate important categories of social costs that have received too little attention in previous studies.

[1] *Statutes at Large*, 39th Congress, Session I, Ch. 262, 1866: 251–253.

There are several reasons to consider (and reconsider) the Mining Act. For one, Libecap (2007b, 1989) upholds this bill as an example of efficient institutional change. Several substantive features of the bill make it easy to see why it can be viewed favorably from an economic perspective. Sections 1 and 2 of the Mining Act opened mineral lands to exploration and occupation, as well as formally recognized local customs and rules of mining districts. Under federal law, an individual could acquire a legal title whenever land was claimed according to local rules. Provisions recognizing local custom are perhaps the most important evidence that the Mining Act was a Pareto-improving institutional change. Because local institutions were arguably expedient (perhaps even economically efficient), one can make the case that recognition of local institutions on the various mining frontiers enhanced efficiency.

The mining bill also formalized local institutions that emerged to regulate use of and access to water. Western water laws were typically adapted to local conditions, branching away from the Eastern water laws on which they were initially based (Kanazawa 1998). This was certainly the case in mining districts, which specified norms governing water use that were appropriate to the mining sector. In another example in favor of an efficiency perspective, the Mining Act formalized water rights recognized by local customs, laws, and decisions of miners' courts. Apparently, the federal government recognized that a centralized solution would be inappropriate to regulate access to water. From an economic perspective, it seems clear that federal procedures strengthening locally tailored institutions regulating water rights facilitated economic development of the mineral sector by reducing risk associated with new occupations.

One of the most important lessons gleaned from Libecap's various studies of contracting for property rights in American economic history is the importance of taking into account local conditions in devising formal property institutions. The Mining Act comes close to Libecap's ideal. In terms of incentive compatibility, the federal government increased chances that its rules would be self-enforcing by recognizing rules as they evolved "on the ground." Recognition of local institutions also provided the federal government with information regarding which rules were appropriate to the context at hand: rather than struggling to figure out which institutions are "efficient" for the miners, federal officials only needed to agree to enforce tried and true norms that had arisen as both a by-product of human interaction and by conscious design.

Libecap's thesis about institutional change is compelling in its own right, and it also resonates with Hayek's (1945) insights regarding utilization of knowledge in society. Hayek stressed the importance of the price mechanism and markets as providing information about what and how to produce, although the logic applies equally to institutional design: governments can improve institutional design by recognizing what institutions work locally.

In terms of taking advantage of information, the willingness of government officials in Washington, DC, to accept social norms that evolved in the West ought to be praised. In particular, these provisions in the Mining Act can be compared with legislation presiding over agricultural development in the Far West. Under federal land laws, desert farmers could claim 160 acres, a size that may have been appropriate in the Midwest but was entirely too small for the Far West (Hansen and Libecap 2004a,b). To get an idea of the challenges facing claimants seeking to till lands in the arid West, many farmers believed that "rain follows the plow" in the sense that plowing the land made it rain (Libecap and Hansen 2002). In comparison to, say, the Desert Land Act of 1877 – a bill that encouraged agricultural development in hostile and inappropriate geography by those who knew little of the demands and requirements of successful desert farming – the mining act was exceptionally well designed.

The wisdom of the Mining Act seems obvious in an era in which land laws left so much to be desired. However, there were some drawbacks to the Mining Act. Most importantly, it was a substantial land giveaway. By setting the price of land at a nominal price of $5.00 per acre, the bill represented substatial revenue forgone in an era of increasing government debt and potential fiscal insecurity. To be sure, some of the features of the bill recognize the inability of the federal government to take advantage of Hayek's "knowledge of the man on the spot." Yet the bill also had distributive features that undermined the nation's ability to pay down its unprecedented Civil War debt. Once fiscal considerations are taken into account, even a paragon of efficient institutional change during the nineteenth century had important social costs.

The distributional implications of the Mining Act come into clearer focus once we consider the context of the bill more carefully. The Mining Act preempted the possibility of nationalizing mines, which was a compelling possibility because federal debt mushroomed to an unprecedented sum of $3 billion in the wake of the Civil War. Nationalization was attractive as a revenue strategy because ore from mines was valued at over $100 million per year, which is around $2.7 billion on an annual basis in today's dollars.[2] Nationalization also had influential supporters, including President Abraham Lincoln, who at the height of the Civil War believed that California mines could be used to reduce substantially the nation's debt. Nationalization was also desirable because it raised fewer security concerns than collateralization of debt with government land, which several European banking interests proposed (Shutes 1943).

In this regard, the political economy of mineral laws was a classic example of conflict between concentrated and diffuse interests. Paying down debt is a public good that benefits the nation – the outcome preferred by the "average voter" in the United States. In contrast, Westerners preferred to acquire scarcity rent for themselves. In situations such as this, organized interests usually shape the course of institutional change, which is the logic of collective action (Olson 1965). In response to these rumblings about state control of the destiny of mineral lands, Nevada's legislature formally rejected nationalization plans in

[2] Abraham Lincoln, "Fourth Annual Message to Congress," in *Collected Works of Abraham Lincoln, Volume VIII*, R.P. Basler, editor (Rutgers, NJ: Rutgers University Press, 1953 [1864]).

1865, although the California legislature, which had already been actively regulating mining activities through taxation policy, denounced nationalization in a series of bills, also in 1865.[3]

Congress also debated conflicting proposals for free mining to promote development versus revenue-generating proposals. Nevada's Senator William Stewart, a member of the Committee on Mines and Mining, staunchly defended free mining; his leading opponent, Representative George Julian of Indiana, introduced a bill in the House to subdivide and sell mineral land to facilitate investment by large corporations (Elliott 1983). Julian's bill may have been a boon to business, but it would also have provided the government with revenue. However, the arguments presented by the proponents of free mining would eventually carry the day.

Nevada's Stewart was a key player on the side of Western interests. Yet it was Representative Cornelius Cole of California who made perhaps the most eloquent defense of free mining in the House on February 7, 1865.[4] Cole's impassioned defense began by articulating the importance of mines to the nation's economy and to society itself:

> The scope of their usefulness is absolutely unlimited. They build your houses and ships, and their agency is indispensable in all public works. They marshal armies and put fleets afloat. Cities and empires grow with their abundance and decline without them. Religion, civilization, liberty – all that men live and die for – lean upon them as upon a staff. Their withdrawal from any community operates as a dire calamity, producing distress and death. In their absence the farmer ceases his labors, the merchant closes his doors, the arms of the artisan and mechanic are unnerved, the hum of the factory is hushed, commerce folds her wings and her messengers chafe their chains in stagnant ports . . . It is somewhat remarkable, in view of these considerations, that the production of the precious metals has not been encouraged with the same fostering care and patronage which has been extended toward other pursuits.

Tellingly, Cole described this bill as *patronage*, which suggests he recognized distributive features of the bill. Nonetheless, he did not seem particularly concerned with them. Nor was he naive enough to believe his eloquent words were sufficient to convince others. Rather, one of California's greatest defenders of gold diggers backed up his words by conjuring up an image of war:

> Though we may seem secure at this time, no one can promise for any subsequent generation on that far-distant shore. If a pretense for separation was found in States interlocked as were the North and the South, how much greater would seem to be the danger when the separation is by thousands of miles, by mountain ranges and broad deserts? . . . Truly is our anxiety for the passage of this bill stimulated by our desire for a perpetual Union. The mixed population that is to inhabit these desert wilds will be instructed to look upon the Federal Government not only as the center of power, but also of light and beneficence.

[3] Legal responses at the state level are documented by Ary (1989) and Hershiser (1913).

[4] Remarks of Representative Cornelius Cole, February 7, 1865. *Appendix to the Congressional Globe*, 38th Congress, Session II, 1865: 64–65.

Cole's implicit threat was credible because his words came on the heels of the Civil War. If the value of slaves gave the South a reason to secede, as Fogel and Engerman (1974) convincingly argued, then it is certainly within the realm of imagination that federal policies that fell too far out of step with Westerners' demands would fracture the nation. Indeed, it was precisely the specter of renewed sectional conflict that gave force to Cole's demand for a bill rightly referred to as patronage.

Ultimately, proponents of free land eventually secured their preferred bill, with Stewart drafting the final bill (Elliott 1983). Even though features of the Mining Act may have been efficiency enhancing, the bill was at its core special-interest legislation. Yet we are still left with the problem of explaining why a bill with distributive features was chosen over one that might have better balanced the nation's interest in paying down debt with miners' interest in private property rights to mineral land. There are several plausible reasons why the government elected to forgo a plan that would have benefited the state more than miners.

One is the coordinating effect of nationalization plans on opposition to them. Fear of nationalization made a common enemy out of the federal government among Western mining interests, helping them to close their ranks. Successful collective action typically requires that people cooperate, although they also have to coordinate their activities (Calvert and Johnson 1999; Weingast 1997), and nothing coordinates a group like a common enemy. In this sense, the federal government's plan, by providing Westerners with a common enemy – or, in the jargon of game theory, a focal point – improved the miners' ability to overcome their collective action problem.

Another factor that cleared the path for the Mining Act was the decline in historical sources of opposition to cheap and free land. Manufacturers, who may have in an earlier period had incentives to oppose land laws that reduced constraints on migration because they benefited from a large supply of cheap labor, had less to fear from outmigration because of a large, stable population in the East. The Civil War also rendered irrelevant slavery-based opposition to free land.

Finally, and perhaps most importantly, widespread presence of claim clubs provides insight into Congressional support for a bill clothed in patronage rather than the public interest. In assessing institutional change, we must always ask: Cui bono? Distributive features of the bill certainly fit the demands issued by organized miners that they typically wrote down in their constitutions. Once mining districts occupied mineral land (perhaps colonized is a better word), the federal government had few options but to concede to their demands. Legislative support for a bill so heavily skewed toward the interests of miners as far as distribution of rents is concerned is certainly consistent with my argument that clubs were a source of such policies.

Any remaining opposition to cheap mineral land seemed to reside in the executive office. For reasons introduced in Chapter 6, a president has stronger incentives than legislators, institutionally speaking, to support land policies that contribute to national security. President Lincoln's support for nationalization to pay down debt is consistent with my hypothesis that presidents have stronger incentives to consider more carefully the full social costs of free land. A veto message by Lincoln's successor, Andrew Johnson, which was directed at a different mining bill, provides additional insight into the incentives of presidents to protect revenue-generating use of land. A brief discussion of the bill is sufficient to illustrate the social costs of mining bills that reduced substantially the price of mineral land.

In 1866, the House and Senate approved a law that allowed the New York and Montana Iron Mining and Manufacturing Company to take twenty sections of land, three of them containing iron ore and coal, provided they permanently marked boundaries and published their claim in a newspaper.[5] This bill, much smaller in scale than the mining bill, was nonetheless a substantial transfer to the mining company. Recalling that a section is 640 acres, this would have given the mining company 12,800 acres of land, to be precise.

President Johnson's veto message, presented to Congress on June 15, 1866, was motivated by a theory similar to the one espoused by President Buchanan in his veto of the homestead bill discussed in the previous chapter.[6] Johnson, like Buchanan, believed class-based legislation was inappropriate under the presumption that the public land was set apart for the welfare of *all* citizens. This bill benefited one mining company, which in the president's mind closely fit a model of particularistic rather than general-interest politics. Johnson, who viewed revenue as the first objective of public land, was more sympathetic to homesteads than Buchanan, positing that homesteads reasonably moved society closer to the worthy goals of agricultural expansion and population growth in the Western states. Nevertheless, Johnson believed land giveaways to mining, trading land, or any pursuit besides cultivation were a perversion of a preemption principle. Although the findings from earlier chapters cast some doubt on Johnson's notion that preemption and homesteads were the foundation for agrarian development, his opposition to the mineral bill at hand espoused a similar logic to Buchanan's veto of the homestead bill, as well as recognized the social costs of policies dramatically reducing the price of land.

A simple calculation demonstrates the social cost of this particular mining bill. The going price of three sections of coal land was at least $38,400 because laws of 1864 and 1865 established a minimum price of $20 an acre for mineral lands. However, under the proposed bill, the mining company would have received the land for $1.25 an acre, or a price of $2,400. The transfer was therefore $36,000 – or about $500,000 in today's dollars.[7] Johnson recognized

[5] "An Act to Enable New York and Montana Iron Mining and Manufacturing Company to Purchase a Certain Amount of Public Lands not now in the Market," *Journal of the Senate*, June 15, 1866: 536.

[6] *Journal of the Senate*, June 15, 1866: 531–535.

[7] Calculation uses 1865 as a base year.

that there was no legitimate economic reason to reduce the price of land, including the fact that Congress had recently enacted legislation that set a minimum price for these lands of $20 an acre. In addition, this law would have granted an additional seventeen sections (10,880 acres) of nonmineral land to the mining company for a minimum price, adding tens of thousands of dollars to the transfer in scarcity rent (much more than that in present value terms) because nothing would have prevented the company from selling land in private markets.

Although this particular bill died after the Senate failed in an attempt to override the veto, successful campaigns against free land in its various guises were few and far between. The Mining Act was a bill with nearly identical distributive features as the defeated bill, except for the fact that the Mining Act covered thousands of times more land than the bill that Johnson so accurately criticized as the (forbidden) fruit of rent seeking. However, the Mining Act, which was a much more massive transfer program, faced little opposition. Like squatters on agricultural land decades earlier, miners were able to acquire legal title on terms they demanded.

PROPERTY RIGHTS TO TIMBERLAND

The timber boom would eventually rival rapid expansion of the mining sector, and with it came new demands on the federal government. Although there were various ways to acquire legal title in the Eastern states, most timberland was formally a state-owned resource when logging emerged as an important economic sector in public-land states in the early to mid-nineteenth century. Widespread illegal occupation of timberland also confronted the government with a now-familiar choice between enforcing law on the books (competitive allocation of timberland) and changing course. Despite a clear interest in revenue from timberland, the state would eventually abandon competitive land auctions – also a familiar theme.

This section considers analytically the major timber legislation governing development of the western lands, again with emphasis on identifying the costs of this legislation, as well as balancing these costs against any benefits. On the whole, timber legislation in this period provides a narrative remarkably similar to the story of mineral lands, one in which the government dramatically reduced the price of land in response to widespread illegal occupation and extraction of timber.

The government ultimately abandoned land auctions, but not without a few attempts to enforce state ownership. For example, an 1860 law seeking to limit timber depredation imposed a fine on timber mills associated with illegal timber harvesting. However, a norm of evasion emerged, one in which federal bureaucrats accepted payment of $2.50 per acre for violations (Fries 1951). By informally setting the price of government land at the preemption price, these norms permitted a substantial de facto transfer of scarcity rent despite a de jure state ownership regime. Institutional weakness at the federal level led various state legislatures to attempt to control depredation, including increasing penalties for illegal cutting. Nonetheless, changes in state laws did not translate into a substantial increase in revenue from the sale of timberland or reduce unauthorized timber cutting (Hurst 1964). One of the reasons these laws did not work is obvious: penalties were small compared to the value of timber, which led loggers to view fines as a cost of doing business.

As costs of enforcing state ownership increased, decentralization of property rights became relatively more attractive. As decades of studies of management of natural resources have shown, decentralization of ownership is desirable to the extent that it promises to reduce the costs of policing access to land and related natural resources. There are two basic ways to decentralize land ownership: privatization or recognition of community-based property rights. Either can be effective in encouraging more effective management of resources. Federal officials, anticipating these economic arguments for decentralization, began privatizing ownership in response to increasing costs in the 1870s. Yet as we will see, decentralization as it was carried out had several important drawbacks.

The first major law decentralizing ownership of timberland was the Timber and Stone Act, which applied to California, Oregon, Washington, and Nevada.[8] The Timber and Stone Act allowed anyone to acquire timber and mineral lands for prices ranging from $2.50 to $5.00 an acre. Several subsequent acts also attempted to reform federal management of timberland, including the Timber Cutting Act of 1878, which permitted free cutting of timber in certain states and territories in the West for individual use. The purpose of the Timber Cutting Act, according to the text of the bill, was to benefit miners and other groups who had no legal right to cut timber at will.

These bills decentralized ownership, which is often desirable, but the devil is in the details when it comes to the political economy of land laws. In particular, the idea of decentralization in itself says nothing of the price of land; who receives the scarcity rent associated with natural resources is a separate question entirely. Despite the importance of these distributive details, existing studies of decentralization are generally unconcerned with the distribution of rents. For example, although Ostrom's (1990) argument for decentralization revolutionized our thinking about the potential for self-governance, existing studies of self-governing property regimes provide few insights into the distributive conflict inherent in the process of rights creation. More generally, existing studies of decentralization are concerned with the appropriateness of private versus common property rather than the price of land. One of the lessons from conflict over timber in American economic history is the importance of considering an additional issue: who receives scarcity rent associated with timber, and for what price.

[8] The text of these bills is found in *Appendix to the Congressional Globe*, various years.

In addition, decentralization requires that actors who acquire property rights understand the importance of conservation. On this count, decentralization was a questionable strategy because loggers were, in many regions and time periods, intent on stripping the land of all its forest cover. In 1888, for example, the secretary of the interior reported that homestead and timber cutting entries were often made to increase formal landholding for the purposes of clear-cutting timber.[9] Miners also engaged in substantial timber cutting to fuel their mining operations. Property rights are desirable to the extent that they encourage conservation, but such conclusions are based on oftentimes strong assumptions about the subjective perceptions of resource users as well as their discount rates (Bromley 2008b). More generally, differences in mental models, or subjective perceptions of the actors, ensure there will be differences between how institutions are designed and how they work in practice (North 2005; Denzau and North 1994). Various users of timberland appear to have viewed clear cutting as a more appropriate strategy than conservation, casting doubt on the appropriateness of decentralization of ownership.

These observations illustrate the importance of considering the details of decentralization, not simply the price of land but also the subjective perceptions of key users of forests. The desirability of decentralization may lead to us to simply assume these laws achieved the main goal for society, which is putting land into the hands of citizens to encourage development of new sectors. Yet on at least two counts – distribution of rent and subjective perceptions – the government's decentralization strategy should raise concern in terms of the social benefits and costs of these land laws.

Despite a general disregard for the state's interest in revenue from timberland, there were some officials in the federal government who recognized the importance of revenue from timberland. For example, Joseph A. Williamson, who took over the position of commissioner of the General Land Office in 1876, unveiled a plan for controlling timber depredation through fines, imprisonment, and confiscation. Williamson ordered a report on all sales of land from 1856 to 1877, finding that the treasury received a *total* of $154,000, which happened to be about the value of 500 acres of timber on good land (Fries 1951). Such a small return on the government's land is staggering considering this was a period of unprecedented expansion of the timber industry on the western lands.

Reform even made its way into the presidential politics. President Rutherford Hayes came into office in 1877 with a platform that included a more rational plan for disposal of timberland, federal protection of the cattle industry, and improved management of the Interior Department. Hayes's appointee to lead the Interior Department subsequently announced a plan to make settlement laws inapplicable to timberland and to fund department activities with revenue from land sales. Under the secretary of interior's plan,

[9] *Report of the Secretary of the Interior* (Washington, DC: Government Printing Office, 1888).

the government would retain legal ownership of timberland. Alternatively, the land office commissioner proposed selling government land to encourage private owners to police it (Dunham 1941).

Either of these policy proposals – the Williamson plan or the Hayes plan – would have balanced the state's interest in revenue from land with a growing demand for decentralization of ownership (or at least, either plan would have done a better job of attempting to strike such a balance than the status quo). Unfortunately for the reformers just mentioned, none of their preferred policies made it very far in terms of adoption. Rather, legislation gradually and steadily weakened competitive auctions. For one thing, none of the revenue from land sales was actually reinvested in strengthening the Interior Department (Dunham 1941). Weak bureaucratic capacity invited evasion, which was quite common on the timber frontier, as businessmen employed dummy entrymen to evade federal regulations (Libecap and Johnson 1979). In many regions, gangs of 10 to 50 men were used to make a large number of entries under existing land laws.[10] Unwillingness to levy appropriate fines for illegal cutting compounded the problem of poor funding of the land-administration bureaucracy. In fact, federal laws never imposed more than a nominal fine for violations and did little to deter collusion, and so federal policies ended up encouraging illegal cutting. Congress even passed a law granting relief to trespassers in 1880 (Fries 1951).

When all was said and done, the federal government eventually abandoned all pretense of competitive, market-based allocation of timberland. Rent seeking was again the rule, and competitive auctions the exception. To understand the magnitude of rent seeking, we need only consider the following fact from the secretary of interior's report at the request of Commissioner Williamson, mentioned above: even as hundreds of thousands of acres of timberland were being cut, *the federal government only received payment for what amounted to 500 of those acres*. Between legislation weakening competitive auctions and lack of enforcement of laws, the government essentially gave away state-owned timberland.

Economic organizations explain why the government failed to profit from its landholding, namely, power loggers' associations. In this regard, the mechanisms of institutional change contrast with those proposed by Ross (2001) during timber booms. In Ross's framework, increasing timber prices lead to political conflict over authority to allocate land, such as politicians reallocating authority from forestry agencies to the government to increase state revenue, which he refers to as rent seizing.

Ross's theory of rent *seizing* provides remarkable insight into historical conflict over resources in Southeast Asia (Ross confined attention to that region).

[10] *Secretary of the Interior Report for 1879* (Washington, DC: Government Printing Office, 1879), *Secretary of the Interior Report for 1878* (Washington, DC: Government Printing Office, 1878); *Land Office Report 1879* (Washington, DC: Government Printing Office, 1879).

However, rent *seeking* over the price of land appears to have been a more pervasive mechanism of institutional change on the American timber forntier. Specifically, if rent seizing was present in the United State, then we should see a government that profited from its landholding. In reality, the government did nothing of the sort. Rather, rent seeking by powerful groups of loggers seems to have ensured the government got little from its landholding, a finding that suggests the theory of rent seizing does not generalize all that well to the experience with timber booms in U.S. economic history.

Besides that organizational conflict is a plausible explanation for change in the property institutions, declining credibility of commitment to state ownership also helps to explain why the government failed to profit from its landholding. As the costs of maintaining state ownership increased, federal legislators had to expend more resources to police the state-ownership regime to commit credibly to competitive land auctions. By failing to make these investments, the government ensured that it would be overrun by economic organizations. Thus, organizational strength and declining credibility of commitment help us to understand why loggers secured nearly all of the scarcity rent associated with state-owned timberland.

THE POLITICS OF PROPERTY RIGHTS ON THE OPEN RANGE

Ranching was unlike other economic sectors in at least one important way: ranchers never secured large-scale changes in federal land laws granting them private ownership over the vast majority of land they used for their operations. Part of the reason is that it would not have been economically feasible, or even economically desirable, to establish private property institutions over vast stretches of land across which individual ranchers drove their cattle. Rather, all that is necessary for an open-range system to be effective is to limit the number of people using the range, with authorized users sharing access to pasture.

Despite these differences in the property regime, ranchers were as capable as individuals in the other sectors under consideration in getting what they desired, which in their case was *access* to land without paying for it. In particular, although ranchers never secured a rangeland bill comparable to the Mining Act, they never paid much if anything for access to land they used to fatten their cattle. For this reason, the institutional regime governing the open range provides yet another example of distributive politics, this time favoring cowboys and their cattle.

Before considering the distributive features of rangeland bills, it is important to acknowledge the socially desirable consequences of claim clubs in an environment of poorly designed land laws and formal institutional weakness. One problem motivating cowboys to convene claim clubs was Congress's failure to produce a rangeland bill; indeed, the federal government did not fundamentally reform institutions governing the open range until 1934 with the Taylor Grazing Act. Claim clubs provided the working rules necessary for capitalist transformation in the federal government's stead. However, lack of regulation was not the only problem; federal land laws that were adopted typically exacerbated conflict. For example, federal laws tended to encourage agriculture in the Far West despite geography that was conducive to ranching. The feelings of dislike were often mutual, as ranchers eventually began to come into conflict with farmers as they drove their cattle over long distances, while farmers had to deal with "ticky cows" that destroyed and damaged their crops (Kantor 1991). In some regions and periods, such as Georgia in the 1850s, conflict led to fence law reform (Kantor 1998, 1994). In the Far West, it just led to conflict, with very little in the way of federal regulation to remedy the situation.

In this institutional morass, claim clubs took on special significance as a source of property institutions, all the while using force to deter anyone from challenging their authority on the Great Plains and beyond. State-wide cattlemen's associations subsumed local cattlemen's associations by the 1860s, in the process attaining coordination and cooperation necessary for the growth of what had become an interstate industry by the 1870s. Through their local and state-wide associations, ranchers were able to influence politicians, lawyers, judges, and law enforcement officers, and local and state officials often formalized rules of local stock associations or various "cow customs." Eventually, the cattle industry attained substantial influence in the eleven Western states of Oregon, California, Nevada, Arizona, Utah, Idaho, Montana, Wyoming, Colorado, Washington, and New Mexico and collectively owned millions of head of cattle, estimated at four million to five million in the western states in 1870.[11]

Claim clubs were highly effective as an alternative source of property institution but their order was far from perfect, and there were calls for institutional reform. Prior to the cattle boom, official reports from Arizona, Wyoming, Utah, Dakota, Montana, and New Mexico revealed increasing business, crowded areas, and demands for federal assistance (Dunham 1941; Brockett 1881). In addition, there were appeals to the federal government to enforce laws already on the books (Webb 1931).

In response to these problems, the government was again slow to respond, but by January 1877, Congress had received a reclamation bill. The bill, which came to be known as the Desert Land Act, passed later that year.[12] Under this law, any citizen could claim a quarter-section of land (160 acres), provided he or she brought water to it and two witnesses certified that the land was irrigated according to the provisions of the law. It covered federal land in California, Oregon, and Nevada and the Territories of Washington, Idaho, Montana, Utah, Wyoming, Arizona, New Mexico, and Dakota. The price was $1.25 an acre, which is another example of a bureaucratically imposed nominal price of

[11] Dale (1960, 1942) and Osgood (1929) detail the origins and operation of the range cattle industry during the mid- to late nineteenth century.

[12] *Statutes at Large*, 44th Congress, Session II, Ch. 107, 1877: 377. It was formally called *An Act to Provide for the Sale of Desert Lands in Certain States and Territories.*

MAP 7.1. Territory covered by the Desert Land Act. *Source*: Redrawn from Donaldson (1884).

land. In essence, it was a law identical to preemption and homestead legislation, except for the requirement that individuals irrigate the land to receive a legal title. It also was one-size-fits-all, applying to a vast territory. Map 7.1 shows the coverage of the Desert Land Act, which also happened to encompass the various plains used by ranchers.

On its face, this law might seem like a good idea because it encouraged investment in irrigation in exchange for legal titles, providing opportunities to people in otherwise inhospitable areas. On closer inspection, however, it fell quite short in terms of institutional design. First (and probably foremost), the Desert Land Act did not explicitly contain any provisions regulating ranching despite the importance of the range-cattle industry in the Far West. At its core, the Desert Land Act was designed to encourage *agriculture*. This goal came into conflict with ranching, which had already become the dominant occupation in the Far West. Because it encouraged a new occupation rather than strengthening a proven one, it was an untested experiment. After all, unlike homesteads and preemption, which were adopted after land was already proven fit for cultivation, these pro-agriculture laws for the Far West invited people to try their hand at farming in land where such occupations were by no means certain.

Second, the proposed scale of landholding was far too small for economic activities in the Far West – a fact that did not go unnoticed. For example, the governor of Wyoming, believing cattlemen would pay for their access rights, proposed leasing land in large sections. In response, the Land Office Commissioner proposed, in 1876, granting land in large sections in the same manner that land was distributed to railroad companies (Dunham 1941). In 1877, the Secretary of the Interior also proposed leasing land in large sections to ranchers.[13] Perhaps most famously, Major James Wesley Powell's *Report on the Arid Lands*, published in 1878, proposed allowing nine or more individuals to secure pastoral homesteads of at least 2,560 acres each. The Public Lands Commission endorsed the plan in 1879, proposing land grants of four square miles of grazing land.

None of these proposals to increase scale of ranching operations became laws. Indeed, there was no fundamental reform to landholding scale until 1909, when Congress quadrupled the size of claims under the Homestead Act from 160 to 640 acres with the Enlarged Homestead Act – which was a better idea, but still a move to improve prospects for agriculture. The federal government would eventually "reform" the range in response to increases in the number of homesteaders and President Theodore Roosevelt's ability to mobilize support for conservation of rangeland (Alston et al. 2011).

On balance, the Enlarged Homestead Act was a minor modification of the 1862 Homestead Act. Because it did little to change the original act, it inherited many of its drawbacks. For example, the size allowance was still a fourth of what Powell proposed decades earlier, and it remained an agricultural rather than a rangeland bill. In addition, the "remedial" legislation came three decades after it was clear that changes to the major land laws governing western economic development were necessary. For these reasons, it is difficult to view the Enlarged Homestead Act as a successful policy reform. Of course, it would be another three decades after the second homestead bill until the government regulated the open range with Taylor's Act, which is another illustration of the government's slow and somewhat misguided pace of reform.

Third, the Desert Land Act ensured the federal government would receive almost no revenue from land sales in the Far West. One of the defining features of the law was its nominal price of land. Enforcement was also a problem. Although there were some efforts to limit corruption, such as repealing

[13] *Secretary of Interior Report for 1877* (Washington, DC: Government Printing Office, 1877).

the Preemption and Timber Culture Acts in 1891 and imposing a residence requirement in 1896, there was essentially no effort to create markets to allocate rights to use government land. Indeed, one of the most important pieces of evidence supporting a distributive interpretation of land laws governing the Western range is the fact that *ranchers never paid the government for use of land they used to fatten their cattle from the 1850s onward.*

The account presented here suggests a fairly clear role of claim clubs. At the same time, there remains a puzzle regarding land laws governing the range. Why were ranchers – a group that was quite strong, organizationally speaking – unable to secure a rangeland bill that gave them *exactly* what they wanted? One possibility is that they recognized that they could manipulate a politically popular homestead bill. Dunham's (1941) authoritative account of the politics of land laws in the Far West documents how ranchers had a say in the Desert Land Act in all stages of the legislative process, and that the committee marking up the bill consisted primarily of men from the West. However, the committee did not produce a bill that gave members of cattlemen's associations free land in large sections. What they received was a bill they could manipulate, which turned out to be all they needed in order to ensure they received access to the state's land without paying for it.

Before concluding this discussion of federal management of the open range in the late nineteenth century, it is important to briefly mention the implications of this period for studies of bureaucratic competence and American state development. Pisani (1996, 1992) thoroughly documented failures of government policies in the Far West (as well as some of the successes) in the latter half of the nineteenth century, attributing institutional weaknesses to features of bureaucrats themselves. Carpenter (2001) contemplates the same period analytically, explaining government failure in terms of bureaucratic competence. Yet neither considered explicitly the absence of a bill to reform management of the open range; rather, they focused on reclamation policies, as opposed to the structure of property rights. Nor did they consider explicitly how organizational conflict undermined the state's revenue aspirations in the Far West. Politically weighty cattlemen's associations provide perhaps the most insight into the inability of the federal government to profit from its landholding. More generally, the politics of rangeland management is an important case of bureaucratic weakness, one that affirms a general theme articulated by Pisani and Carpenter, yet one that suggests how bottom-up processes, such as formation of organizations, shaped and constrained bureaucratic opportunities.

REVENUE LOST: ASSESSING ALTERNATIVE EXPLANATIONS

Key features of federal land laws governing major natural resources found on the nation's Western public lands provide additional insight into distributive conflict over land allocation. Each of these bills was a distributive one that reduced the price of land. At the same time, an economic assessment of institutions from a social welfare perspective differs from an explanation of why institutions change. Although the analysis just presented suggests that major land laws were primarily distributive, it is still necessary to explain why the state chose to give away its landholding in the Far West. Four features of the political and economic environment, some of them introduced earlier, are particularly important to understanding why the state gave away its land or access to it: widespread formation of claim clubs, declining opposition to free land, a weak federal bureaucracy, and ideological commitment to cheap land.

Hopefully, the evidence presented earlier convinced readers that claim clubs were the backbone of each of sectors under consideration. It is sufficient here to observe that in each sector, clubs preceded policies that dramatically reduced the price of land. In the mining sector, mining districts contributed to "patronage" (to use Representative Cornelius Cole's fitting term) in the form of what was essentially a free mining bill. Informal occupation forced the federal government's hand despite its interest in revenue from its mineral lands. Federal officials may have given themselves more options if they had taken steps earlier to solidify state ownership of mineral lands. As things stood, however, the federal government had increasingly strong incentives to give land to miners for free (or what was essentially free) in the face of pervasive and powerful economic organizations.

Logger unions, which were remarkably cohesive economic organizations capable of imposing order on public timber land, also had important political consequences. Informal norms generally permitted loggers to take what they desired for a nominal price. Over time, formal institutions eventually shifted from competitive allocation of land to free cutting of timber. Part of the reason was the strength of logging camps.

Similarly, cattlemen's associations allowed ranchers to use government-owned land as they saw fit without paying for the right to use it. A de facto policy of free access represented a substantial transfer of scarcity rent from the federal government to ranchers because the formal property regime was state ownership. By the time the idea of reform began to work its way through Congress, the political feasibility of a bill that protected the state's interest in scarcity rent associated with Western land had declined substantially. Political capacity of cattlemen's associations ensured ranchers would continue to receive a de facto transfer from the federal government each year they used federal land without paying for it.

The apparent relationship between claim clubs and the great giveaway of resource lands is anticipated by Knight's (1992) theory of institutional change, which as explained earlier stressed informal power (or bargaining power) as an important mechanism of institutional change. A defining feature of claim clubs was their bargaining power, which repeatedly and across sectors translated into changes in the price of land. De facto control of land thoroughly and completely transformed into de jure recognition of property rights.

Claim clubs and bargaining power were perhaps the most important mechanisms of change in land laws after the Civil War. Yet there were other important factors that greased the wheels of institutional transformation, in particular changes in the structure of interest group competition. Prior to the Civil War, manufacturers and slaveholders had incentives to oppose free land. However, these hypothesized sources of opposition were no longer relevant after the Civil War. An abundant labor supply in the cities in the East quelled fear of migration. The slavery issue was also settled, although it took a war to recognize both sides were resolved in their views. It stands to reason that these economic changes made land giveaways more politically acceptable.

Finally, political factors contributed to the land giveaway in the Far West, in particular bureaucratic weakness and political ideology. The main consequence of bureaucratic weakness was declining credibility of commitment to state-owned land. Because the federal government declined to invest substantial resources to police the state-ownership regime, land giveaways became a self-fulfilling prophecy as people occupied land without much fear of being swept aside by the state. In addition, an ideological belief that free land was a source of economic prosperity, or that it was the "fair" thing to do, provides additional insight into not only the continuation of land giveaways in the Far West but also less opposition to such transfers.

Although these complementary explanations (weakening of competing interest groups and declining credibility of commitment to state ownership) are important, they pale in comparison to claim clubs, which were overwhelmingly important organizations in the Far West. Clubs were the defining feature of the organizational and political landscape, and they helped to shape the course of policy. And we should not be surprised by their influence in politics. Those who benefited from competitive land auctions – the average voters – faced a massive collective action compared to members of claim clubs. Because miners, loggers, and ranchers were concentrated interest groups, their political clout should not be particularly surprising. Nonetheless, this logic of collective action has been largely ignored in economic studies of development of western property rights, mainly because of an overwhelming focus on emergence of private property institutions rather than the price of land.

COLLATERAL EFFECTS: LAND LAWS AND SPECULATION

A final empirical dimension of federal land laws relevant to the political economy of nineteenth-century property rights is land speculation. Federal land laws, because they were often influenced by equity considerations, generally included provisions to limit speculation. For example, most of the laws discussed in Part II of this book explicitly limited landholding size and restricted trade once people entered a claim under the relevant federal law. Each of these prohibitions was designed to prevent accumulation of landholding by speculators. Nonetheless, federal laws were largely ineffective in preventing speculators from securing large quantities of desirable land.[14] In fact, federal land laws seem to have been a fountainhead for speculation.

A snapshot view of speculation is sufficient to illustrate how widespread it was during the nineteenth century. Throughout this period, timber dealers, cattle grazers, mining interests, and speculators continued to acquire lands through the use of dummy entrymen, false swearing, and often bribery of local land officers as the federal government attempted to reform land laws. A single individual with resources to pay entrymen could claim land simultaneously under several of these acts.[15] Historians and economic historians have provided many insights into the economics of speculation.[16] Rather than rehash those debates (which concern issues such as whether speculation was actually profitable, who engaged in it, and its economic and social consequences), the brief discussion that follows considers why speculation was so pervasive despite efforts to control it, based on my findings as well as theories of political economy. To this end, several features of the political and economic environment on the frontier contributed to persistence of speculation as formal rules sought to limit it.

First and foremost, an increasing array of federal land laws increased the costs of enforcing state ownership, and in the process increased opportunities for speculation. Squatters were remarkably successful in securing sympathetic bills. As a consequence, federal bureaucrats were responsible for monitoring hundreds of thousands of land transactions to ensure individuals were not exploiting the land-allocation system under a dizzying array of legislation. Thus, the proliferation of land laws was itself a source of speculation, mainly because it increased the transaction costs facing government bureaucrats seeking the process of land allocation.

Speculator wealth was a second feature of the political and economic environment that contributed to speculation. Changes in political rules may be ineffective when they fail to alter an economic balance of power or because formal rules can be manipulated by powerful groups (Acemoglu and Robinson 2008). In the United States in the nineteenth century, the economic balance of power in a region often tilted toward speculators because of their wealth. Railroads, for example, were granted nearly 130 million acres of land between 1862 and 1871 (Anderson and Martin 1987; Engerman 1972). Railroad companies charged a steep price for land near railroad tracks and many settlers who desired land near tracks could not afford this land. Speculators were often the only individuals with the resources to acquire the best land and so they

14 On the persistence of speculation, see especially Gates (1979). Speculation was one of the most important themes in Gates's many studies of development of land laws.

15 The problem of fraud is well documented. See especially Gates (1979, 1942) and Dunham (1941).

16 See especially Swierenga (1977, 1968) for a comparison of economists' and historians' perspectives on land speculation, as well as an excellent overall account of speculation in American economic history.

benefited disproportionately from railroad land grants. More generally, speculators benefited from land laws because they had the resources necessary to manipulate them.

A third reason for speculation was the federal government's failure to recognize that many squatters were actually speculators. Most notably, Bogue (1958) showed beyond doubt that claim clubs were often speculative organizations. Nonetheless, many politicians remained convinced those on the frontier were "poor squatters." As federal land laws proliferated, they encouraged and rewarded speculators because many of the members of clubs were less frontier farmer than land speculator.

Fourth, effort to put land into the hands of inexperienced farmers – poor settlers – often ended up benefiting speculators. The reason why a reduction in the price of land to substantially below market price indirectly benefits speculators lies in the incentives (or lack thereof) to carefully calculate the risk of entering a new occupation. Individuals have stronger incentives to internalize the risk of a new occupation, such as farming desert land, when they have to pay for land. Free land reduces incentives to internalize risk, and so it is reasonable to expect that free land will ultimately benefit land speculators as farm failures increase.

Finally, lack of an effective survey system contributed to speculation and fraud. Private property institutions require surveys to attain clarity of allocation. Surveys are also necessary to attain order in the process of decentralization. In particular, in order to prosecute a fraud case or to limit speculation, the government had to be fairly certain of how much land was claimed and the type of land. Nonetheless, the federal government repeatedly failed to require surveys in the West during the period in which much of the land was being allocated and appropriated (Dunham 1941). Absent surveys, prosecuting a fraud claim was nearly impossible, increasing incentives to engage in speculation. The five features of the political and economic environment that contributed to speculation are summarized in Table 7.1.

CORPORATE WELFARE AND THE ALLOCATION OF WESTERN LAND

The concluding section to the previous chapter offered a speculative interpretation of homestead laws as de facto corporate welfare policies. Federal land laws governing mineral, timber, and rangeland can be interpreted similarly. Land laws covering territory in the Far West, many of which were nominally designed to provide opportunities for poor people with few opportunities to start a new occupation, actually benefited a new and burgeoning class of capitalists on the frontier.

A corporate-welfare interpretation of federal land laws governing economic activities in the Western states flows from the fact that each of the bills considered in this chapter had unmistakable distributive features but also because the primary beneficiaries were businessmen, plain and simple. Hence, they

TABLE 7.1. *Factors Contributing to Persistence of Speculation*

Factor	Rationale
Legal complexity	Proliferation and complexity of land laws increased monitoring and enforcement costs of allocating land, yet the federal government did little to increase the ability of federal agents to police the process of decentralization of land.
Speculator wealth	Speculator wealth increased speculators' ability to manipulate public policies in their interests.
Organizational similarity	Speculators and legitimate farmers formed similar organizations, which meant that politicians supporting legislation they thought benefited farmers unwittingly benefited speculators.
Disincentives to internalize risk	Assignment of legal title to inexperienced farmers eventually benefited speculators, who could secure their titles at a reduced price after farms folded.
Lack of surveys	Lack of surveys increased the ability of settlers and speculators alike to claim land in violation of federal regulations.

were *corporate* policies. These laws were *welfare* policies because land was rarely allocated through competitive mechanisms. Even when the government conducted auctions, economic organizations often ensured claimants paid a minimal price. Collusion meant that even land that was allocated at "competitive" auctions was a de facto corporate welfare program. In addition, ranchers, although they did not receive formal rights to the open range, never had to pay to use it. Ranchers also acquired a great deal of land for their ranches even if they never divided up and privatized the entire open range. Indeed, one of the most important institutional developments on the Western range, besides the formation of claim clubs, is nonemergence of a fee to use the range.

Taken together, key empirical developments in federal land laws during the nineteenth century should be considered as part of the development of the welfare state. Despite their significance in the social history of the United States, these laws were not really social policies. They benefited the nascent seat of business political power in the United States. Rather than social welfare, the story of land laws in the Far West is one that reveals the origins of corporate welfare.

CONCLUSION: PARADISE LOST?

The notion of "revenue lost" summarizes the fiscal and social costs of land policy governing the major economic sectors of the nineteenth century. Others might suggest that a more apt description is "paradise lost," mainly because of the perceived environmental consequences of the run on government land. Indeed, Cronon (1991) articulated the transformational features of this period, one in which nature was changed fundamentally in the drive for capitalist development. Does a focus on property rights obscure this ecological revolution?

This book is not by any means a study of environmental history. Yet it provides insight into why damage to the environment was far less than it could have been. To be sure, there was resource waste and environmental damage as people stampeded over the land. However, the presence of effective property institutions ensured people had much stronger incentives to conserve resources than under conditions of open access. Indeed, if one is concerned with the environment, then the main goal is to establish private property – the price of land is less relevant than internalizing the externality. Judged by a standard of whether or not people could exclude others from the land they coveted – which typically means that those who held land had incentives to internalize externalities associated with resource overuse – the major costs during this period may have been fiscal ones, rather than environmental ones, mainly because people established private property institutions, either informally or formally. To the extent that there was resource conservation, these property systems help us understand why it was the case.

The discussion of conflict between squatters and the federal government is now complete. In conclusion to this part of the book, it is useful to consider Weaver's (2003) remarkably apt characterization of the development of property institutions in North America as "the great land rush." Although Weaver did not consider it explicitly, the defining feature of the land rush in the United States was distributive conflict over the price of land. In terms of explaining change, claim clubs help to understand who won (clubs) and lost (the state) in the rush to establish capitalism on the frontier.

Our understanding of the scope of rent-seeking remains incomplete, however, without reflecting on the consequence of claim clubs for state and local politics, which is the subject of the final empirical chapter.

8

Claim Clubs and Local Politics

Claim clubs were remarkably successful in securing land at the federal level. Yet they were also quite capable of bullying state and local legislators. This chapter considers the consequences of claim clubs for property rights at the state and local levels, using illustrative examples drawn from each of the major frontier sectors.

The first example, briefly introduced in Chapter 3, is a prolonged conflict between rival settlers over disputed territory in Pennsylvania from the late eighteenth to early nineteenth centuries, which had its roots in an English king's overlapping land grants to William Penn and people from Connecticut. This rivalry, which included a conflict that would become known as the Yankee-Pennamite War, nicely illustrates the importance of claim clubs, which were convened by settlers with ties to Connecticut as well as Pennsylvania, in an oftentimes violent struggle for legal recognition.

A second example, drawn from the gold fields of California in the 1850s, documents how discriminatory taxation policies benefited members of claim clubs at the expense of their foreign competitors. In contrast to the price of public land, which in California was controlled by Congress, state legislators controlled taxation policy. During the gold rush, members of claim clubs recognized that they could gain an advantage over their competitors – in particular, foreign-born miners – through discriminatory taxation. As key developments in state-level tax policy reveal, claim clubs and revenue-seeking state legislators formed a protection racket that increased the state's revenue while undermining opportunities of foreign miners to establish themselves in the mining occupation.

My third example is drawn from California as well, this time considering federal policies to sort out competing land claims. This federal bill is included in an analysis of state-level politics because this bill applied only to California. A case study of Gwin's Act to Ascertain Land Claims in California uncovers an important relationship between economic power and public policy implementation: claim clubs were sufficiently powerful to manipulate federal legislation designed to improve the property situation in California. One of the design flaws with Gwin's Act was offering unlimited appeals with a fee for each one. Provisions for unlimited appeals created problems because in California during this period, *physical* control of land – as opposed to *legal* representation – determined who won and lost in court. However, federal legislation did not take into account physical control of land. As a consequence, de facto economic power translated into de jure property rights in spite of federal intention to protect legal owners.

The fourth example considers the relationship between ranchers and politicians in a state-wide claim club in Montana, showing how a club could become a de facto legislative body, one in which the formal legislature typically approved norms devised by a claim club. One of the consequences of overwhelming political influence was harsh treatment of anyone not in the club. Outsiders were deemed trespassers, and they often faced strong penalties for crossing a club – punishment that was for all practical purposes sanctioned by the state. Although the state legislature had already been convened by the time the ranching sector began to boom, claim clubs rivaled the state legislature as a political organization in the late nineteenth century.

The final example considers value-added laws, which were laws that allowed squatters to reclaim from rightful owners a payment roughly equal to the value they added, through their own labor, to land while illegally occupying it. Value-added laws did not award squatters a legal title but rather forced formal owners to compensate them for improvements they made to the land while squatting. Such laws were often viewed as fair by legislators and judges during the nineteenth century, mainly because squatters invested substantial time and effort to improve land. Yet as this case illustrates, these laws also had important distributive features: under one of these laws, squatters could improve land and receive payment without assuming risk associated with land ownership, which amounted to a transfer payment from owners to squatters. Analysis of key decisions by legislators and judges involving payment for improvements made while squatting reveals that laws that on their face seemed neutral in terms of social benefits and costs had several negative consequences, including encouraging squatting, undermining investment incentives, and weakening private property rights.

As with many of the institutional transformations considered previously, the process of emergence of property rights at the state and local levels was remarkably complex. There are probably hundreds of interesting conflicts worthy of a case study. Although the cases chosen only provide a snapshot of the political consequence of claim clubs at the local level, the picture includes some of the most important examples of change in local land laws, ones that are strongly suggestive of the importance of claim clubs in the development of land laws in the states.

"WILD YANKEES" AND THE STRUGGLE FOR LEGAL RECOGNITION IN PENNSYLVANIA

During the colonial era and Revolutionary era, much of Pennsylvania was uncharted territory. There was, however, a government in place, although disputes over territory led to restrictions on settlement. Yet as we have seen, organizations such as the Fair Play System, one of the first claim clubs, imposed their own system of order on disputed lands.

The Fair Play System and other claim clubs were often effective in specifying and enforcing private property institutions informally. Yet this club and others like it had a longer-term goal, namely legal recognition. One of the most important conflicts over legal title to land occupied by competing claimants was known as the "Yankee-Pennamite War," a decades-long fight for legal recognition in the Wyoming Valley of Pennsylvania that varied in intensity from the 1760s to early 1800s.[1] The valley itself, which includes the present counties of Luzerne and Wyoming, is northeast of the location of the Fair Play System. The conflict in the Wyoming Valley differed, however, in that it was less a struggle between settlers and Indians than a competition between rival settlers. Connecticut pioneers – referred to by their enemies as Yankees – were pitted against settlers with ties to Pennsylvania because Charles II of England granted the same land to Connecticut in 1663 and then to William Penn in 1681. Specifically, settlers from Connecticut were granted from the English king *three thousand miles* of land in a fifty-mile strip stretching from sea to sea (Fisher 1897). However, conditions were initially inhospitable to settlement, and the Connecticut people left their "Western paradise" untouched, believing it was "secluded and fortified as if by the special work of god" (Fisher 1897: 43).

Nearly 100 years later, as "Western fever" spread, settlers began to venture to these same lands. Connecticut settlers, many armed with legal title from the Susquehanna Company, a landholding company that formed with the goal of developing the Wyoming Valley, first arrived in the fall of 1754 but their settlement proved impermanent. Uncertainty created by the French and Indian War (1754–63) led to a delay in any further settlement until peace was declared. The Susquehanna Company promptly began selling land once initial uncertainty caused by the French and Indian War subsided, but new conflicts with Indian tribes emerged almost immediately. The Crown subsequently suspended all further settlement in October 1763, after Indians attacked a band of Connecticut settlers, killing twenty of them. Once fear of violence subsided, the Connecticut people again ventured to lands granted to them by the English king, this time finding Indians and geography were no longer their only competitors (Fisher 1897: 43):

[1] The details of the Yankee and Pennamite war that follow draw on several voluminous historical studies: Boyd (1931), Heverly (1902), Fisher (1897), Shepherd (1896), Bradsby (1893), and Craft (1878).

> But a new enemy had appeared. The sons of the great Quaker, William Penn, believed themselves to be the owners of a vast empire of land which they called Pennsylvania. It had been given to their father in 1681 by a charter from Charles II, the same king who, nineteen years earlier, had given Connecticut her wonderland of three thousand miles from sea to sea. Pennsylvania was not such a wonderland and made no pretense of stretching from sea to sea... but she stretched northward straight across the pathway of Connecticut, cutting off her western way of empire so completely that there was nothing left but a little narrow strip on the north...

With a Quaker contingent in their way, Connecticut people faced a choice: avoid them at great cost or fight. For their part, Quakers also faced a choice between conceding and holding their ground. A fight was likely because both groups were resolved in their belief that they had a right to the land (Fisher 1897: 44):

> Each side was fully persuaded in its own mind, and it was an instance of Greek meeting Greek, for it would be hard to select two more stubborn people than a Yankee and a Quaker. They are totally unlike. The Yankee is aggressive and active; the Quaker passive and non-resistant, as he calls it. But extremes meet, and these two incongruous elements can often make what is called in certain circles a very pretty fight.

These early disputes ignited a conflict that would continue in some form or another until 1803 – nearly four decades after the first sparks began to fly. The notion of "Greek meeting Greek" connotes a drawn out battle among relatively evenly matched adversaries, and this was just such a conflict. The account that follows illustrates an important theme, one in which claim clubs were convened not simply to manage land relations but also to give settlers political voice.

In 1768, people began to take up arms to defend their claims to land. The actions of the Susquehanna Company, which was sanguine about Connecticut's right to the land in question, reignited conflict when it resolved to assign legal title to groups of forty settlers who agreed to remain on the land, man their rights, and defend each other from rival claimants. Settlers were viewed as a beachhead that would make the region safer for others – to this end, settlers' property rights were contingent on "manning their rights," a requirement that was supposed to take up some of the slack as far as enforcement was concerned.

Settlers, for their part, were more than willing to accept the challenge of manning their rights because it was an economic opportunity. The first settlement was appropriately named "Forty Fort," not simply because there were forty settlers, but because it was an actual fortification against invasion – not by Indians in this case, but rather by Quakers. An illustration of Forty Fort is included (Figure 8.1) to give an idea just what they looked like.

In response to this affront, the Pennsylvania government promised legal title to several Pennsylvania men for nominal rent on the condition they settle land

FIGURE 8.1. Forty Fort, Wyoming Valley, Northeast Pennsylvania, 1778. *Source*: Busch (1896).

and defend it from settlers from other states. Evidently, both sides could play the game of packing the state's borderlands with compatriots. Within a short time, warrant deeds (legal titles) to land were issued, the best land was surveyed, and those with ties to the Pennsylvania government acquired legal title to the best land. In addition, a well-armed Quaker contingent, led by Captain Odgen, settled the land in defiance of the claims laid by Connecticut men. Map 8.1 includes the locations of the forts along the Susquehanna River in the Wyoming Valley.

Finding their land occupied, the Connecticut men attempted to starve out garrisoned Pennsylvania claimants. The Sheriff of the region subsequently arrested all forty Connecticut settlers, who were released after paying bail. Two months later, 200 more Connecticut men arrived, establishing an outpost they called Fort Durkee, although Captain Durkee was eventually captured and all Connecticut settlers were forced to leave.

Land continued to change hands. After a new force from Connecticut compelled Ogden to abandon his fort, an undeterred Ogden returned once again, this time with a new force, and he successfully captured the fort. In response, thirty Connecticut settlers, now led by Captain Lazarus Stewart, laid siege to Ogden's garrison, capturing it. Ogden retreated and built a fort, called Fort Wyoming, and demanded Stewart surrender the land. Stewart responded that he had taken the disputed land in the name of Connecticut, promptly attacking Fort Wyoming and successfully recapturing it. The government of

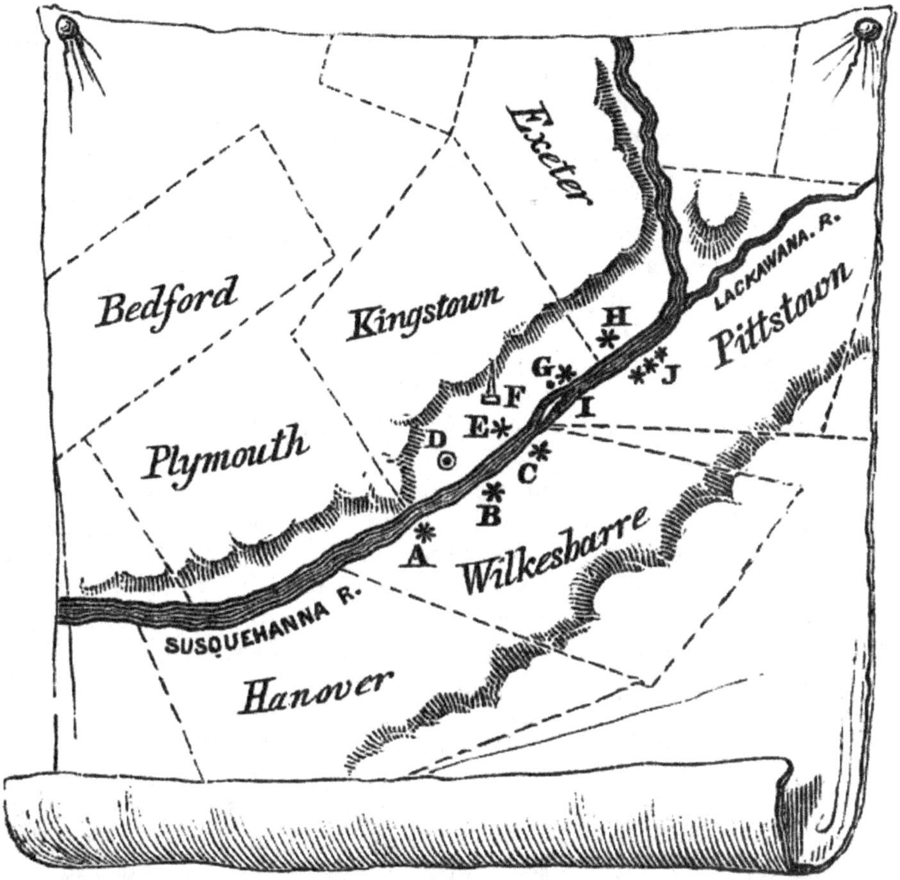

MAP 8.1. Forts of the Wyoming Valley, Pennsylvania, 1770s. (A) Fort Durkee; (B) Fort Wyoming; (C) Fort Ogden; (D) Village of Kingston; (E) Forty Fort; (G) Wintermoot's Fort; (H) Fort Jenkins; (I) Monocasy Island; (J) Pittstown Stockades; and (F) is the battleground. *Source*: Lossing (1851).

Pennsylvania, recognizing the Connecticut settlers were strongly fortified, left them in possession of the land, and in 1774, the General Assembly of Connecticut recognized their property rights. Settlers hailed the law because they viewed it as a promise of protection from the highly regarded colony of Connecticut. Formal recognition provided these men with "a sense of security and confidence that gave force to contracts and encouraged industry" (Bradsby 1893: 152).

Connecticut men seemed to have found peace as the Decree of Trenton ruled in 1782 that the State of Connecticut had no right to the lands in controversy. Connecticut's political leaders acquiesced to the treaty but Connecticut settlers, who by that time had been living in Pennsylvania for a while, rejected it. Even though they were not obligated to do so, the Commonwealth government made several concessions to Connecticut claimants in 1786, including agreeing to assign property rights to Connecticut settlers and to provide them with representation in the Council and Assembly.

A lasting peace, however, was a long way off. In 1785 and again in 1786, the Susquehanna Company reconvened and resolved to assign new legal title and support settlement on the disputed lands. The Susquehanna Company planned to "erect the Connecticut claim in Pennsylvania into a new State, and the action was as public and as bold as that of the Declaration of Independence, by brave and desperate men who stood at bay" (Bradsby 1893: 153). Connecticut settlers who secured title before laws of 1786 became known as the "old settlers" while those in possession of legal titles issued by the Susquehanna Company after 1786 were deemed "half-share men" or "Wild Yankees" by their adversaries. These so-called Wild Yankees quickly became a new thorn in the Commonwealth government's side.

A desire to profit from land sales while simultaneously quenching speculators' thirst for land led the Commonwealth government to enact intrusion legislation in 1795 that defined half-share men as squatters despite the fact that they had legal title. This law, which was the first of several intrusion laws adopted during the post-Revolutionary period, imposed fines and threatened imprisonment for anyone convicted of taking a half-share claim. The law's intent to uproot half-share men was unmistakable. For their part, half-share men denounced intrusion legislation, which they referred to as "Fire and Brimstone Laws," and they formed Wild Yankee Leagues to recount violations of their "rights" by the Commonwealth. Over 1,200 of the half-share men met in 1795, at which time they resolved to prevent surveying or seizing their lands, to provide a way for "real owners" of land to settle disputes, to secure legal title, and to recover lands possessed by their opposition. In other words, Wild Yankee Leagues were claim clubs: governance organizations arising to enforce private property institutions when the state proved unwilling to do so.

Economic organizations were necessary for the half-share men to have any hope of political representation. Once Wild Yankee Leagues congealed, it was clear that intrusion laws would not be self-executing. Perceiving the state government too weak to enforce its own laws, domestic settlers formed a counter-organization known as the "Pennsylvania Landholders' Association" to implement the intrusion laws. The Landholders' Association, whose purpose was to privately provide the public good of enforcing laws, was also a claim club, one that in this case also functioned as the strong arm of an overall weak state government.

A potential political solution was afforded by the Compromise Law of 1799, which created a mechanism for resolving disputes between old settlers and Pennsylvania claimants. In the event of conflict of claims, the state agreed to purchase Pennsylvania claimants' title and to grant a legal title to the old settlers. Connecticut settlers were thus able to acquire legal title to the land they occupied provided they submitted to the Commonwealth's laws. At the same time, compromise legislation was a false promise of peace because it did not recognize claims of new settlers; indeed, half-share men remained criminals under intrusion laws. The legislature even responded to continued occupation of land by half-share men with another intrusion act in 1801 that actually increased the penalty for selling half-share claims as well as required all persons in the territory to declare the origins of their title. Intrusion legislation criminalized half-share claims and their deeds and eliminated opportunities for half-share men to defend their claims in court. Courts also interpreted land laws as rejecting half-share claims in their entirety. In particular, the state Supreme Court interpreted the Compromise Law as designed to "cut them up by the roots," even going so far as to decree that potentially sympathetic jurors were to have no discretion in considering half-share claims.

Despite the state's intentions to forcibly uproot them, half-share men renewed their agreement to fight for their self-proclaimed property rights (as well as procedural rights) that the Compromise Law denied them. A second intrusion act led half-share men to convene another claim club at a meeting in May of 1801 in which representatives of various half-share communities wrote down their demands, developed a system for financing collective defense, and created a basic system of leadership to help them accomplish their goals. Pennsylvania landholders again responded in kind, after which with a committee of landholders sent the half-share men a letter telling them that they could purchase a legal title provided they first submitted to the demands of the Commonwealth government. According to the landholders' edict, once the half-share men submitted to the state, they would have a fair chance to purchase land but they would receive nothing until they relinquished their claims.

Half-share men were disadvantaged by superior economic and political resources of their opponents. The landholders' association represented 1,300,000 acres of land and its members agreed to share the expenses (estimated at $3,200) of putting the intrusion legislation into force. Lawyers retained by the organization also prosecuted on behalf of the state cases arising under the law and thus they effectively decided who was tried, convicted, pardoned, or set free. Quite remarkably, a private-order association specified the law, dictated penalties for noncompliance, and provided a means to enforce it.

Nonetheless, the Connecticut men were at a disadvantage in terms of resources as well as propinquity to the Commonwealth government. Perhaps realizing that they were losing ground, Wild Yankees used increasingly violent tactics but also began to take more liberty in defining who was an opponent, demonizing both government agents charged with enforcing laws and any Yankee settlers who capitulated to the Commonwealth's demands. Closing their ranks by punishing anyone "collaborating" with the government solved a collective-action problem for more militant Wild Yankees who viewed accepting government terms as cheating on an implicit pact. For example, in 1801, a group of forty settlers near Towanda Creek held a conference and agreed to renounce Connecticut titles. A government agent collected their signatures and proceeded to secure additional ones. Yankee settlers decided they could not tolerate these actions, and twenty armed men set after the agent. He attempted to elude the mob but the Yankees "followed him, and broke into his room where he was sleeping, captured his papers, burned them, and led him down to the creek, tarred and feathered him, and the leader giving him a kick told him to 'go'" (Bradsby 1893: 163).

These bold actions by half-share men led Pennsylvania settlers to again petition the government, this time to formally limit the rights of half-share men to serve on juries. In 1802, the legislature responded by prohibiting transfer of land under Connecticut title, and proscribed that no half-share men could sit on a jury involving contested claims.[2] Wild Yankees continued with their tactics of beatings and banishment in the meantime. In 1803, for example, a man from Susquehanna County was indicted under the intrusion law as an illegal settler because he was holding a half-share claim. He did not believe he could succeed against the landholders and so he bought a Commonwealth-backed land title and persuaded others to do the same. Half-share men responded by surrounding his house, tying him to a horse's tail, dragging him around Wyalusing Creek, burning him in effigy, and occasionally pushing him into the flames.

This conflict over land, which began in 1754 when the first settlers from Connecticut ventured to Pennsylvania, with roots in an English king's capricious land grants, finally subsided in 1802–3. A group of half-share men met at Athens in 1802 where they requested both parties (half-share and Pennsylvania title-holders) agree to bring a suit before the U.S. Supreme Court. The committee of landholders, however, refused to agree to any propositions until settlers agreed to relinquish Connecticut claims and submit to the Commonwealth's laws. Half-share men eventually began giving up Connecticut claims and filing submissions. By late 1803, what turned out to be a bitter, decades-long struggle came to an end, as the Wild Yankee Leagues proved unable to match the combined will of domestic economic organizations and the state.

TAXATION, IMMIGRATION, AND THE STRUGGLE FOR CONTROL ON CALIFORNIA'S GOLD FIELDS

In California, decades later, it was gold rather than agricultural land that captivated the attention of the nation. Yet much like in the agricultural sector, one of the main dimensions of conflict was the price of land. In 1850, Senators John C. Fremont, Thomas H. Benton, William H. Seward, and others debated the possibility of free access to California's mineral lands (what was often referred to as "free mining"). Fremont introduced a bill that would have

[2] *An Act to Maintain the Territorial Rights of this State* (1802).

established a system of police regulations in mining districts that included a small tax on miners to defray expenses, which succeeded in the Senate but died in the House.[3] However, miners had established their own institutions before the next session, rendering Fremont's bill somewhat irrelevant, and Congress took no further action regarding the price of mineral land until the Mining Act of 1866.

With Congress out of the picture, it is tempting to assume that most of the action occurred on the informal side of institutions. As it turns out, miners were not content to rely on their informal institutions and economic organizations between discovery of gold in 1848 and the Mining Act. They recognized, however, that the state legislature could provide them with benefits: taxing foreign miners and in the process increasing the strength of domestic miners vis-à-vis their competition.

The first major piece of legislation directed at immigrant miners was an aptly named law known as the Foreign Miner Tax, adopted in 1850, that levied a per-diem tax on any miners born outside the United States.[4] A report from the Finance Committee delivered to the California Senate stated the rationale for the bill. Supporters believed that foreigners were carrying substantial treasure from its "rightful owners," who were, according to the men who drafted the bill, the "American people" (of course, for this group, the American people meant California's miners). The Committee also viewed immigrants as criminals who would destabilize social order. Accordingly, the bill required foreigners to pay a small fee for the privilege of taking treasure from the country, presumably to defray the expenses of forging a new state. According to the committee, "strife and bloodshed which has taken place between the citizen and foreigner is mainly to be attributed to the fact that, although the latter had neither legal nor moral right to come into our country and take away the gold, they were doing nothing for the support of the Government whose protection they were looking to."[5]

The Committee emphasized that the bill would allow foreign miners an opportunity to work for domestic miners while also affording domestic gold diggers a means of controlling foreign miners by advancing them a license and holding it until a labor contract was executed. Newcomers would be able to seek a new employer at the conclusion of the contract or work on their own. In order to give force to the law, the state authorized "collectors of licenses" to enforce the bill's various provisions. Fee collectors were obligated to report anyone who failed to pay to a sheriff who was authorized to make arrests, charge violators with a misdemeanor, and imprison whoever was found guilty for a term not exceeding three months (with a fine of not more than $1,000). The bill set a fixed fee of $20 per month for the privilege of mining anywhere

[3] MacFarren (1912) thoroughly details Congressional debates over free land.
[4] *California State Assembly Journal* 1850.
[5] *California State Assembly Journal* 1850: 493.

in the state. Although $20 may seem like a small amount, it translates into around $500 in today's dollars – a substantial sum for an immigrant miner on a monthly basis.[6] The explicit rationale for this bill was increasing the state's ability to provide public goods – arguably an efficiency-enhancing rationale – yet its consequences were distributive: the tax was an entry barrier conferring bargaining advantages on domestic mining organizations in a nascent labor market.

Two years later, the government reduced the tax rate, although increasing revenue, as opposed to fairness, motivated this particular institutional calibration. Under the first tax law, the legislature extracted less revenue than anticipated because fees were sufficiently high that few could afford to pay them.[7] The economic logic of these legislative changes is straightforward when we consider the theory of optimal taxation, which, in its simplest form, states that tax revenue increases with increases in the marginal tax rate, reaches a maximum, and then decreases for further increases in the tax rate. Evidently, a $20 fee was too high, few were willing to participate in the formal tax system, and the legislature believed it could increase tax revenue by reducing the tax.

After initial discussions of a new bill, the Senate majority and minority issued reports on issues facing Chinese miners that summarized relevant points of contention. According to the *Majority Report*, Chinese miners complained that they could not participate in courts and that they were taxed without political representation. Chinese miners even proposed an *increase* in the foreign miner tax as long as the legislature formally committed to using the revenue to fund public goods at the county level.[8] Chinese miners apparently believed that an increase in taxation would improve the credibility of their promise that they were committed to California's longer-term economic development.

The sympathy of the *Majority Report* to the position of Chinese miners contrasts with the *Minority Report*, which had an explicitly anti-Chinese bias.[9] Members of the minority party included a proposal that would have explicitly allowed mining districts to discriminate based on ethnicity, rationalizing anti-immigrant policies by appealing to the "police power" of the state, which as we have seen earlier is the fundamental power of the state to protect health, safety, and welfare. In other words, opponents of Chinese immigrants believed Chinese miners were essentially a public health problem. Fortunately for Chinese miners, a majority of legislators rejected explicitly anti-Chinese provisions in an 1852 law, yet their motives were not exactly pure. Rather, the state believed the revenue lost from limiting Chinese immigration outweighed any concerns with health and welfare.

6 Calculation made using 1850 as a base year.

7 *Appendix to the California Assembly Journal* 1852: 829–35.

8 *Majority Report of the Committee on Mines and Mining Interests*, California Assembly Journal, 1852.

9 *Minority Report on Mines and Mining Interests*, California Assembly Journal, 1852.

The revised bill appears to have been self-enforcing, which refers to a situation in which all relevant parties have incentives to follow the rules.[10] In this particular case, the relevant parties were domestic miners, foreign miners, and tax collectors. As long as each had incentives to play by the rule, we would expect a political equilibrium characterized by discriminatory taxation.

As it turns out, the major groups seemed to have incentives to participate in this tax regime. Domestic miners had incentives to make sure foreign miners had licenses because they could be fined otherwise. Reducing fees increased incentives for foreign miners to pay the tax. Tax collectors received a share of revenue they brought in and so they had stronger incentives to work hard to enforce the provisions of the bill. Mining companies continued to benefit from a cheap labor supply and so they supported the bill. Adding to the incentives of foreign miners to participate in this taxation scheme, the 1852 bill specified that foreign miners could not prosecute or defend any action in the courts of California without a license. From the perspective of institutional design, it was a self-enforcing protection racket – it may not have been socially desirable, but it was self-enforcing.

Discriminatory taxation was not the only dimension of public policy governing immigrants and immigration during this period. An anti-immigration party had a political majority by the mid-1850s that was bent on utilizing the state's police power to ban Chinese immigrants from their shores. In 1855, the California legislature levied a $50 dollar tax on ships bringing immigrants ineligible for citizenship, although this particular law was ruled unconstitutional by the California Supreme Court in 1857. In 1862, the legislature again passed a law that discriminated against Chinese miners, which was also ruled unconstitutional.[11]

Kanazawa (2005) showed that domestic mining organizations were a primary source of opposition to these anti-immigration bills. Capitalists in California had an interest in cheap labor, leading them to oppose the ban, which Kanazawa interprets as an instance of market incentives combating inefficient, discriminatory public policies. Self-interest led mining districts to oppose economically inefficient constraints on immigration.

The notion that markets provided incentives against discrimination is intriguing in this context. However, it is important to keep in mind that domestic mining companies had a reason to support immigrants' rights because they had a captive labor supply in a highly distorted labor market. Kanazawa interprets these events as evidence of the power of markets to fight discrimination, with capitalist incentives conflicting with discriminatory policies imposed by political majorities. However, because mining organizations benefited from market power in the status quo, their opposition was based in part on past

[10] The concept of self-enforcing institutions was discussed at length in Chapter 2.

[11] The offending legislation was *An Act to Protect Free White Labor against Competition with Coolie Labor and to Discourage the Immigration of Chinese to the State of California.*

success in their rent-seeking endeavors (namely, in securing a tax on foreign miners), and so we must temper our enthusiasm for markets at least to an extent in this particular case. Rather, it was ability to interfere with markets that provided domestic miners with incentives to oppose a ban on immigration.

Tax policy in the early years of California also provides insight into generalized theories of the origins of property rights. For example, Olson (2000) argued that even autocratic leaders have incentives to provide private property protection (as well as to reduce taxation) to encourage production, hypothesizing that constraints on rulers are not necessary for basic property rights to emerge.

Despite the obvious contribution of Olson's theory to our understanding of origin and change in property institutions, it does not have much of a role for political institutions. As constitutional political economy teaches us, political institutions influence the quality of property institutions. Autocrats are likely to face a credibility problem in that their promises to respect private property rights will be hard to believe unless they are in some way constrained. In order for property rights to be fully effective, democracy and separation of powers are desirable.

One of the lessons from California's gold fields is that both of these theoretical perspectives – the Olsonian perspective as well as the credibility logic – provides insight into emergence and change in property institutions. Chinese miners certainly faced an autocratic government, as they had weak formal representation at best. Domestic miners, in contrast, enjoyed democratic rights – imperfect rights, but unquestionably stronger than those of Chinese miners. As anticipated by Olson, the tax rate facing Chinese miners was low enough to encourage production despite an autocratic government. At the same time, the tax rate they faced was much higher than that of domestic miners, who essentially paid no taxes for the right to extract minerals. Thus, evidence from the early legislative struggles in California supports each of the theories of property institutions described earlier: an autocrat set tax rates consistent with continued production, while groups enjoying democratic representation benefited from superior property protection, as reflected in their much lower (and perhaps zero) rate of taxation.

GWIN'S ACT, DE FACTO CONTROL OF LAND, AND DE JURE RECOGNITION OF LEGAL TITLE

Although taxation policy had important economic, social, and political implications, squatters on mineral lands were also concerned with legal recognition of their informal claims to land. The state legislature, however, was unable to do much to reform the property regime because California was a public land state, and hence much of the land in question was the responsibility of Congress. Nonetheless, in 1855, California's state legislature met with the hope of adopting a bill to reform the land-tenure system. A bill, known as the Settlers' Law, was sponsored by Senator William Shaw, head of San Francisco's most prominent settlers' association. The Settler's Law promised property rights based on peaceable possession unless a petition for ejection was made within two years of the initial application for patent. Unfortunately for squatters, the California Supreme Court rejected the 1856 Settlers' Law, and there much more in the way of settlers' conventions, court cases, and bloodshed (Pisani 1994).

Although the Settlers' Law failed to stop the bleeding as far as land conflict is concerned (mostly figuratively, and in some cases literally), the federal government had already entered the fray, believing they could do a better job of representing the interests of legal owners – namely, those who had a legal title. One of the most important attempts to resolve the land question in California was the Land Claims Act of 1851, popularly known as Gwin's Act for its champion.[12] One of the purposes of Gwin's Act was sorting out which parties held valid legal titles from the Mexican government that were constantly undermined by illegal and extralegal occupation despite a promise by the government of the United States at the end of the war to respect preexisting land claims.

Gwin's Act created a three-member panel appointed by the President to rule on land claims, with formal proceedings that could be appealed by plaintiffs or defendants to the U.S. District Court or Supreme Court. However, the bill ultimately did little to alleviate problems facing those whose land was occupied by squatters, a failure that has been documented elsewhere.[13] My interest is in one particular feature of institutional design: unlimited appeals. The following account is not meant to be a systematic test of hypotheses but rather is meant to illustrate how unlimited appeals may have contributed to the failure of Gwin's Act, as well as to suggest more generally that legislation seeking to sort out land conflict should take into account the consequences of possession of land on the ability to utilize legal rights.

A provision allowing for endless appeals may at first seem like a good idea as a means of ensuring effective judicial oversight. Yet this provision played into the hands of miners who occupied the land. In effect, the Land Claims Act institutionalized a legal war of attrition in which probability of judicial victory depended on resource control.[14] Miners had substantial advantages because they controlled land and so they had greater ability to win a war of attrition in terms of appeals that was likely to result if one of the parties (squatters or formal owners) petitioned the courts. The reason is that land was perhaps the most important input to production in California during this period.

[12] *An Act to Ascertain and Settle the Private Land Claims in the State of California*, 31st Congress, Session II, March 3, 1851.

[13] Gates (1971, 1967a,b) explains the various design flaws of the California Land Claims Act with meticulous detail.

[14] This was a war of attrition in the standard economic sense, which is that the gain to one party is exactly offset by the loss to the other party.

Mining districts ensured squatters often had greater ability than formal owners to attain judicial relief because formal owners, by virtue of having lost control of their land, were less likely to be able to continue in a long and drawn-out legal process.

Theories of de jure and de facto political power help us understand why Gwin's Act ultimately failed to represent the interests of legal owners. One of the defining features of distributive theories of institutional change is recognition that an initial distribution of economic power often translates into de facto political power. In the face of persistent economic power, formal rules may be subject to change or manipulated to the point of ineffectiveness. Claim clubs had precisely this sort of effect: they translated economic power into legal recognition because legal representation depended in part on wealth, wealth depended on control of land, and control of land was ultimately a consequence of claim clubs. For these reasons, one of the long-run consequences of failure to take into account economic power was reallocation of legal title from owners to members of clubs.

Gwin's Act leaves much to be desired from the perspective of de jure and de facto economic power. Nonetheless, Clay (1999) provides a compelling argument that it was a workable solution to the problems in California because it balanced the interests of squatters, landowners, and the government. According to Clay, the California Land Claims Act reflected a process of institutional learning between 1789 (the passage of the Northwest Ordinance) and 1851. Specifically, federal rules were viewed as an improvement over existing institutions, with incremental changes in land laws leading to a workable system of property rights.

Gwin's Act certainly seems to have been an improvement over the status quo. However, its desirable features should be balanced against its distributive shortcomings, which included increasing squatters' ability to secure legal title by virtue of their physical control of land. Possession influenced who could appeal judicial decisions, and because squatters controlled land, they had advantages in the legal process. Institutional learning would have occurred if the government limited appeals or required losing parties to pay all court costs after appeals. Changes of this sort would have adapted Gwin's Act to the circumstances of California in the early 1850s and thus reflected a process of institutional learning. Because it did not, we should probably look to the Mining Act of 1866 as a more plausible example of institutional learning in the federal government's effort to regulate mining in California. Indeed, the Mining Act is a good example of institutional learning: the federal government, recognizing that its rules could not outperform local ones as they evolved during the struggle to capture California's mineral wealth, simply formalized rules as they had developed "on the ground." In comparison to the institutional logic of the Mining Act, Gwin's Act falls far short in terms of institutional learning. This does not necessarily refute Clay's argument, but rather reminds us of an important weakness with the California Land Claims Act, as well as its weakness compared with the general Mining Act.

STATE CAPTURE: THE MONTANA STOCK GROWERS' ASSOCIATION

In the major cattle-ranching states in the American west, claim club political influence was perhaps as strong as it was in any economic sector under consideration. The political dominance of cattlemen's associations reflected their vast scale and scope. Claim clubs transformed into centralized peak associations governing ranching operations across a state or a group of states and they performed an ever-increasing number of functions. Indeed, separating informal organizations from local governments was increasingly difficult during the years of the cattle booms as associations began implementing their "laws" at the state level.[15]

The underlying reason such why large and powerful organizations were necessary was lack of federal regulation of the open range. As we have seen, federal land laws, such as the Desert Land Act of 1877, were designed to encourage agriculture in the Far West. Consequently, ranchers had to regulate the open range themselves. They also had to increase the scale of their informal property associations as they began participating in "long drives" over vast territory. Once these state-wide claim clubs were in place to enforce an informal property regime, they became instruments of political influence. A brief account of the Montana Stock Growers' Association should be sufficient to convince readers that these clubs integrated politics and business on a grand scale.

Members Montana's main claim club proclaimed that they alone had the authority to use the land and that they had the right to deal with nonmembers as they saw fit. Nonmembers had little hope of political representation because business and political leaders were intertwined in the stock associations. Granville Stuart's first-hand account (we now would call his recollections "participant observation") illustrates how business and political power congealed within cattlemen's associations. Stuart offered a particularly vivid description how stockmen dealt with rustlers (Stuart and Phillips 1925: 195–6):

> At the close of the fall roundup out tallies showed that we had suffered at least a three per cent loss from "rustling." These thieves were splendidly organized and had established headquarters and had enough friends among the ranchers to enable them to carry on their work with perfect safety... The "rustlers" were particularly active along the Missouri and Yellowstone rivers and our neighbors in the Dakota bad lands were great sufferers.

The committee decided to bring the matter up at the second annual meeting of the Montana Stock Growers' Association in 1884. There were many grievances presented but the association was able to produce a concrete plan for action (Stuart and Phillips 1925: 196–7):

> Everybody seemed to have a grievance. The members of the association that had been members of the legislature in the previous year came in for their full share of censure... The matters for consideration were overstocking the ranges... or

[15] Dale (1960, 1942) details the effectiveness of cow customs.

> Texas fever that was claiming such a heavy toll in Kansas and Nebraska and how to put a stop to "rustling." The civil laws and courts had been tried and found wanting. The Montana cattlemen were as peaceable and law-abiding a body of men as could be found anywhere but they had $35,000,000 worth of property [around $950 million in today's dollars] scattered over seventy-five thousand square miles of practically uninhabitable country and it must be protected from thieves. The only way to do it was to make the penalty for stealing so severe that it would lose its attractions. When the subject was brought up some of the members were for raising a small army of cowboys and raiding the country: but the older and more conservative men knew that would never do. I openly opposed any such move and pointed out to them that the "rustlers" were strongly fortified, each of their cabins being a miniature fortress. They were all armed with modern weapons and had an abundance of ammunition, and every man of them was a desperado and a dead shot. If we had a scrap with them the law was on the side of the "rustlers." A fight with them would result in the loss of many lives and those that were not killed would have to stand trial for murder in case they killed any of the "rustlers." My talk did not have the conciliatory effect that I expected and seemed only to add fuel to the fire. The younger men felt they had suffered enough at the hand of thieves and were for "clearing them out" no matter what the cost.

Conflict eventually broke out between members of the association and its competitors. Stuart described one of the most intense fights: "There were one hundred and sixty-five stolen horses recovered at Bates Point and one hundred and nineteen at other places. After the fight at Bates Point the vigilantes disbanded and returned to their respective homes. This clean-up of horse thieves put a stop to the horse and cattle stealing in Montana for many years" (Stuart and Phillips 1925: 198). In response, cattlemen were accused of hiring "gunmen" to drive small ranchers off the range. Stuart claimed that there "was not a grain of truth to this talk."

Although we have to take accounts offered by an "insider" with a grain of salt for obvious reasons, Stuart's words point to an intimate relationship between politics and claim clubs. This particular claim club included members ranging from state and local legislators to the future President of the United States, Theodore Roosevelt. Whether the club's actions were "just" is irrelevant. One of the most important lessons gleaned from Stuart's report is that cattlemen's associations were often indistinguishable from formal law.

Stuart's retelling of gold rush history also provides additional insight into the social construction of ownership, a dynamic that we encountered in the earlier discussion of agricultural claim clubs. Powerful ranchers with established organizations labeled their competitors as "rustlers" despite the fact that members of the state-wide association also lacked legal rights to use this land. Much like the first squatters on agricultural land who called subsequent claimants or legal purchasers "land pirates," the concept of a "rustler" appears to have depended on one's particular vantage point. In other words, ownership was socially constructed, with "rights" ultimately connected to membership in a club. Efforts to define friends and foes, which were a pervasive feature of claim clubs, appear to be an example of what Herrera (2005) refers to as "constructivist political economy," a perspective that emphasizes the social construction of economic interests. The varying notions of what constituted a rustler, speculator, and bona fide settler certainly suggest the virtue of a constructivist perspective on formation of competing interests.

Of course, history (and Hollywood) tells us that there were episodes of violence on the open range. One of the better-known fights was the Johnson County War of 1892, a conflict between organized ranchers who hired a private army to deal with their competitors. Although this conflict has been interpreted in popular accounts as vigilantism associated with a lawless period, McFerrin and Wills (2007) recognized that the real problem in the 1892 conflict was a conflict over property rights, and that such conflicts were rare. Assuming McFerrin and Wills are correct (and I have no reason to doubt their account), our problem is to understand why conflict was rare. To answer this question, we need only consider the political and economic power of cattlemen's associations. Nonmembers faced a shadow government or de facto legislature capable of implementing its own "laws" on the frontier in the 1880s. Claim clubs in Montana and Wyoming regulated economic interactions between members, rustlers, and small-scale ranchers (sometimes blurring the distinction between legitimate competitors and thieves), imposing its own "laws" on nonmembers. Because organized ranchers could raise "small armies," and because they were nearly indistinguishable from the state itself, it should not be surprising that property conflicts appear to have been rare indeed.

VALUE-ADDED RIGHTS: FAIRNESS OR WINDFALL FOR LAWBREAKERS?

Value-added rights, which were laws requiring formal owners to pay squatters for the value of improvements they made while illegally occupying land, were common in many states. These laws were often viewed as neutral from the perspective of social welfare because legal title stayed with owners and squatters were paid for improvements. For example, in searching American economic history for lessons for today's developing world, de Soto (2000) viewed these laws as an appropriate institutional response to legal uncertainty, going so far as to suggest they were among the most important institutional innovations in property relations in the early United States.

This section offers an alternative perspective on value-added laws, one that takes into account a more compelling account of their full social benefits and costs. Two of the more interesting conflicts over these provisions occurred in Kentucky in the 1820s and Wisconsin in the 1870s, each illustrating the not-so-hidden costs of these allegedly neutral laws.

Conflict over Value-Added Rights in Kentucky

Formal property relations in Kentucky at the close of the eighteenth century were a political and legal quagmire. Speculators began acquiring undeveloped frontier land in Kentucky during the revolutionary period. Squatters, who had a penchant for occupying land regardless of who owned it, soon gained the attention of landlords, many of them absentee. Landlords quickly petitioned the government to remove squatters from their land (Smith 1886). In response to speculators' demands, Virginia lawmakers moved to protect the interests of speculators who were purchasing large quantities of land in Kentucky. Squatters, who typically viewed speculation as "anti-social behavior," objected to and ignored Virginia's land laws. In one instance, when Virginia officials sent commissioners to sort out competing claims, they were sent a letter that a "combination of people" planned to seize the commissioners' books and burn them. An extralegal mob did not materialize but "land jobbers" (one of the common derogatory terms for speculators, the other being "land pirates") increasingly found themselves targeted by residents, with conflict occasionally leading to physical abuse. For example, a public meeting in Harrodsburg in 1781 ended with an assembly of informal claimants dispersing a group of investors in a forcible manner (Aron 1992).

As early as 1792, groups of legislators in the Kentucky General Assembly agitated for laws to protect settlers' interests. In the first session of the assembly, legislators of the lower house supported a bill that would have forced owners to pay squatters for improvements and freed them from past rent but it was defeated in the upper house, which was dominated by landlords who believed a compact between the states of Kentucky and Virginia that gave Virginia's legislature authority to regulate land relations in Kentucky prohibited a law favorable to squatters (Gates 1962). More generally, landlords had obvious reasons to object to laws benefiting squatters because squatters were their chief antagonists.

After the initial laws favoring squatters were defeated, the Kentucky assembly rebounded with several bills favorable to squatters. Two key principles emerged during this period: preemption rights and value added. On the preemption front, Kentucky legislators enacted several laws between 1795 and 1810 that allowed people to acquire a legal title to land as long as their claims were not challenged within a certain number of years. The price of land was cheap, usually between $40 and $60 for 200 acres of land.[16] The only requirement to acquire a legal title under these laws was that a family fenced in the land or planted a crop, and a small group was set up to enforce claims.[17]

The legislature also passed several laws granting squatters value-added rights. Many were challenged in court, and one dispute even reached the U.S. Supreme Court. The case involved John Green, a Virginia landowner, and Richard Biddle, a Kentucky squatter Green ejected from his land. Biddle petitioned Green to pay him for improvements on the land because Kentucky law

[16] *An Act for the Relief of Settlers* (1795); *An Act for Encouraging and Granting Relief to Settlers* (1797); and *An Act of 1810*. The legislation is found in William Littell (1809–19).

[17] *Acts of Kentucky*, various years.

required legal owners to pay individuals for value added to land in cases of illegal settlement. Green argued that Kentucky's occupational law was unconstitutional based on a compact between Virginia and Kentucky that imposed Virginia's contract law on Kentucky. Virginia did not require compensation for improvements; Green argued that the Kentucky law was unconstitutional because it violated the compact.

In 1821, the Supreme Court sided with Green by striking down value-added provisions of several acts.[18] The constitutional issue was not the provisions themselves but rather the compact. Kentucky lawmakers argued that the compact was inconsistent with the concept of state sovereignty under the United States Constitution. Although it may seem obvious that a sovereign state cannot be governed by land laws of another state and remain "sovereign," the Supreme Court believed that the contract clause bound states to the compacts they made, and so the majority believed that sovereignty could be limited by agreement.

A detailed discussion of contract clause jurisprudence during the early nineteenth century is unnecessary here. Rather more interesting for our purposes is the Court's assessment of value-added provisions in terms of policy. In the 1821 decision, a majority of the Court found that the law "operated unjustly and oppressively because the lawful owner is compelled to pay, not merely for the actual ameliorations in the land, not its increased value only, but the expense incurred by the occupant in making pretended improvements, whether they are merely useful or fanciful, and matter of taste or ornaments only dictated by his whim and caprice."[19] These laws, the Court reasoned, made landowners captive to squatters who would be likely to have their own men on juries and benefit from local judges sympathetic to local interests rather than the interests of investors. In other words, the Court recognized that squatters were engaged in a sort of rent-seeking – and that the Kentucky law was bad policy.

The Supreme Court's observations seem reasonable from an economic and political perspective, as well as a pragmatic one. For example, the justices took into account inability of investors to get a fair trial in squatter country. They also recognized that squatters put landholders in a precarious position as far as defending their land from unwanted improvements. Nonetheless, the decision was ignored by Kentucky courts, forcing the Supreme Court to take up the issue again only a few years later. This time, the appeal was championed by Senator Henry Clay, who argued that a compact cannot permanently undermine state sovereignty in the scheme of the federal system.[20] On appeal, the Supreme Court reversed its initial ruling, with a majority of justices upholding the authority of Kentucky to determine its own land laws.

[18] *Green* v. *Biddle* 21 U.S. 1 (1821).

[19] *Green* v. *Biddle* 21 U.S. 1 (1821).

[20] *Green* v. *Biddle* 8 Wheat. 1 (1823).

In upholding value-added provisions, the Supreme Court imposed a de facto occupancy requirement on land. Legal institutions of this sort reduce incentives to invest in land by increasing costs of policing ownership. Kentucky laws, rather than encourage investment, did the opposite: land laws privileged current consumption and penalized investment. Under the legal regime articulated by Kentucky's top jurists, investors had to occupy land or risk losing it to squatters, a requirement that undermined investment incentives ex ante.

Conflict over Value-Added Rights in Wisconsin

Another example, this one from Wisconsin, should convince readers of my argument that value-added laws undermined investment incentives and, more generally, property rights of owners. Although loggers' unions initially regulated access to natural resources informally, modern capitalism required institutions that permitted accumulation on a grand scale, which in turn required protection of legal claims from small- and large-scale trespassers. The state legislature was relatively quick to respond with laws seeking to protect legal owners. In 1844, the legislature prohibited willful theft of another's private lands, and penalties for illegal cutting were increased in 1849 and 1855. Legislation was fairly effective in stabilizing investors' expectations but weak state enforcement meant timber companies were often forced to hire local agents to protect their property rights in the 1840s and 1850s. State legislators apparently recognized the importance of protecting private property rights early in the development of the timber industry (Hurst 1964).

In contrast to legislative decisions, Wisconsin courts did not always choose rules that encouraged investment. One of the most important cases during the logging era in Wisconsin was *Single v. Schneider* (1872), one that concerned illegal timber cutting by the defendant.[21] In it, the Wisconsin Supreme Court ruled that people who cut timber illegally, *either intentionally or unintentionally*, had a right to the value added for their improvements. The decision, like the decisions made by Kentucky courts regarding such provisions, appeared neutral. However, far from having neutral consequences, these laws undermined property rights of owners. In particular, squatters on timberland reaped a windfall profit without having to assume the risk of land ownership. After all, the law did not make a distinction between intentional and unintentional cutting, and so it allowed squatters to convert land when they wanted to rather than when the owners wanted to.

Theories of judicial politics instruct us that courts rarely have last licks when it comes to statutory, or even constitutional, decision making (Eskridge 1994). The reason is that there is almost always a way to override decisions in a separated political system. This was certainly true in this case, as the legislature responded with a bill more favorable to owners, essentially reversing

[21] *Single v. Schneider* 30 Wis. 570 (1872).

the court's decision. In contrast to the state Supreme Court's decision, the state legislature prioritized long-term investment in private timberland or standing timber. A number of bills protecting timber interests were proposed and shaped by assembly men with ties to logging. Such developments suggest cronyism, yet capitalists seem to have recognized which rules increased incentives to invest in land. In this sense, the state legislature's actions are an important example of a phenomenon known as "businessmen candidates." As Gehlbach et al. (2010) have shown, businessmen often have incentives to enter politics in order to increase credibility of commitment to property rights. One of the central implications of their study is that businessmen candidates are more likely in weakly institutionalized environments, which typically suffer from credibility problems. Wisconsin courts introduced a credibility problem, with loggers entering politics in response, and in the process businessmen were able to increase the credibility of the regime's commitment to protecting private property institutions.

De Soto has shown that many people in the current developing world are forced to squat on government or private land because of outrageous regulatory burdens and poorly designed government policies. However, American land laws of the nineteenth century were not the socialist regulations de Soto (1989) masterfully criticizes in Peru and similar political and economic regimes. Rather than encouraging private enterprise, value-added provisions undermined private property institutions out of a concern for "fairness." Bromley's (2006) insight into the concept of property rights, introduced in Chapter 1, is again relevant: having property rights means not having to constantly stand guard over your possessions. De Soto, one of the most ardent defenders of private property rights, lavishes praise on institutional rules that weakened private property rights by forcing owners to make sure they continually had to stand guard over their possession.

Value-added provisions are another example of laws rewarding or encouraging rent-seeking, ones we should come to expect by now. And as we have seen throughout this book, efficiency views of squatters and their clubs – of which I count de Soto's defense of value-added rights – typically leave out important pieces of the puzzle of American land law.

CLAIM CLUBS AND COLLECTIVE ACTION IN THE STATES

The examples presented in this chapter illustrate political consequences of claim clubs in state and local politics. The Pennsylvania Landholders' Association and Wild Yankee Leagues were nothing but claim clubs locking horns over legal recognition. The Commonwealth government may have tipped the scale in favor of the Landholders' Association, yet it seems clear that claim clubs were necessary for legal recognition, if not sufficient.

Drawing on evidence from California, we found that claim clubs and a majority of state legislators forged a protection racket at the expense of foreign miners. Claim clubs also neutralized federal legislation seeking to protect legal owners because they possessed land. In a much-cited essay on inequality and legal change, Galanter (1974) observed that the "haves" – repeat players in the legal system and those with resources – often come out ahead in legal conflict. In California, Galanter's insights ring true, as the haves – the miners themselves – generally came out ahead. Indeed, the miners were not just haves in a figurative sense; they literally had the land, and it was precisely the fact of possession that benefited them in court given the structure of legal rules, in particular the possibility of unlimited appeals.

In Montana, the statewide stock association, by bringing together politicians and businessmen, provided a powerful mechanism to regulate the open range. Under the watchful eye of cattlemen's associations, which could be thought of as shadow governments because they acted with the state's sanction, anyone who violated informal norms faced harsh repercussions. Much the same story can be told in Wyoming, where there was also intimate relationship between the state legislature and the state's primary club, the Wyoming Stock Growers' Association, in the late nineteenth century (Jackson 1947).

Finally, value-added provisions, rather than illustrating efficiency in the process of institutional change, rewarded and encouraged rent-seeking by squatters. Legal decisions that seem fair on closer inspection undermined property rights of owners. In particular, value-added provisions forced owners to stand guard over their possessions, and in this regard, they weakened private property institutions.

This completes the empirical study of institutional origins and change, which has traversed economic sectors, geographic regions, time periods, and various levels of government. It is now fitting to offer a few final words on the importance of claim clubs in the political economy of the American frontier, as well as to reflect on the more general implications of this study.

9

Conclusion

This study of property relations on the American frontier is organized around two questions: Where do private property institutions come from and why do they change? *The Political Economy of the American Frontier* defended a simple thesis: claim club governed the origins and change in private property institutions throughout the nineteenth century.

Two narratives emerged, one of informal order and one of distributive conflict. In terms of informal order, claim clubs were remarkable in their ability to manage land relations in complex contracting environments. These private-order property organizations were arguably unrivaled in the economic history of the United States as far as self-governance is concerned.

As a source of social control, claim clubs contrast primarily with explanations based on spontaneous order, which have no real role for governance organizations such as clubs, and theories emphasizing the state as a source of property institutions. At the same time, it is also clear that theories of spontaneous order provide insight into certain features of human behavior on the frontier. When squatters first arrived in a region, simple first-possession norms were sufficient to allocate resources among settlers. Nobody designed these first-possession norms and there was nothing in the way of collective enforcement, yet they were often effective in the early stages of development of each sector under consideration. These simple norms were self-enforcing because settlers understood that failure to abide by them would likely lead to a fight to establish ownership even though these norms had no conscious designer or enforcer.

The remarkable property norms that arose without conscious design or enforcement nonetheless weakened as information and enforcement costs increased. A new system of governance was necessary to manage land relations effectively as the number of squatters increased, economic activities increased in scale, and conflict with variously defined "outsiders" sprang up.

As I explained, these changes in the contracting environment required consciously designed *political* institutions for *property* institutions to be effective. Spontaneously arising and decentralized personal- and community-enforcement systems, the most basic private-order systems on the frontier, were replaced by specialized organizations in the important sectors of agriculture, mining, logging, and ranching. That is, the clubs represented the basic machinery of government. Theoretically and empirically, the findings in this book suggest a much stronger role to hierarchy than economic studies of informal order allow while at the same time recognizing that property institutions specified and enforced within claim clubs were not part of the state. Rather, we required a theory of bandits *within* the state to understand the origin of property rights.

As my empirical studies showed, claim club rules substituted for legal rules as settlers migrated west, with farmers' protective associations, mining districts, logger's unions, and cattlemen's associations implementing their own property institutions in the state's shadow. In some contexts their actions were extralegal. In others they were illegal. Regardless of formal legal status, claim clubs specified working rules necessary for capitalist development. Theoretical considerations, backed up by a rich array of evidence, showed that claim clubs were one of the most important sources of economic institutions prior to development of a full-fledged capitalist economy even though they existed between spontaneous order of economics and state-backed coercion of formal politics.

With its emphasis on hierarchy, this study of clubs owes an intellectual debt to economic theories of the firm. Coase, quoting D.H. Robertson, famously characterized firms as "Islands of conscious power in this ocean of unconscious co-operation like lumps of butter coagulating in a pail of buttermilk" (1937: 386). Claim clubs were islands of conscious power in an ocean of nineteenth-century land laws that were much like the buttermilk pail, but unlike Coase's firms, clubs provided their own political and property institutions rather than relying on the state. For all Coase's insights, his theory of the firm assumed the existence of both property rights and governments without considering that organizations could provide these institutions themselves.

As far as informal order is concerned, claim clubs suggest to us some important limitations with theories of spontaneous order. In the most fundamental sense, logics of spontaneous order rely too heavily on norms of no governance, either formal or informal. On the American frontier, it was emergence of a system of governance that drove capitalist development. Indeed, claim clubs were effective as private-order sources of property institutions precisely because they were governments arising within the state. Empirically speaking, government formation, rather than spontaneous order, was the most pervasive feature of organizational and institutional development on public lands during the nineteenth century in the United States, a finding that required us to move beyond traditional theories of the firm in order to account for key features of the process of institutional emergence and transformation.

Of course, one could argue that because the clubs were not planned, they represent spontaneous order. Yet the power of spontaneous order arguments has traditionally been the ability to explain order without much in the way of governance, focusing instead on norms and conventions arising through extremely decentralized processes. Their remarkable ability to explain development in the absence of any hierarchy is also their limitation, as they have less ability to explain why people so often established what looked like governments in order to manage their property relations, or why people only relied on first-possession norms for short periods. In short, the experience of the "western lands" provides additional insight into the far-reaching applicability of logics of spontaneous order but also its limitations.

It would be a mistake to conclude they were a source of Pareto-improving institutional change simply because they established private property institutions, or because they were capable in terms of self-governance. Claim clubs had powerful distributive consequences that undermined the fiscal capacity of various levels of levels of government. After the American Revolution, the government continually faced a choice of how to assign property rights to its increasingly vast landholding. The main options were competitive auctions or first possession. The policy of the colonial governments to give land away gave way to competitive actions. As the newly independent government had unprecedented debt from war and required a means to pay it down, competitive land auctions promised revenue to the state necessary to provide public goods as well as ample opportunities for land demanders to secure a legal title. Yet claim clubs ensured the state rarely profited from its vast landholding.

This book undertook a fairly large challenge: to explain development of private property institutions in the United States through the lens of claim clubs. It is my hope that evidence convinces readers that these private-order property associations were important mechanisms of informal and formal institutional development on the American frontier, tying together issues of informal property institutions, the process of government formation, and distributive conflict over land ownership. In this conclusion chapter, I reflect on the main contributions of this study, which are to offer answers to three main questions: Where do private property institutions come from? Why do they change? And what is the relationship between land and the state?

SELF-GOVERNANCE ON THE AMERICAN FRONTIER

Existing studies of the origins of private property institutions emphasize either spontaneous order or an all-powerful state as the source of property institutions, yet neither of these perspectives provides a satisfactory account for governments arising within the state to specify and enforce property institutions. Theoretically, I argued that property institutions require governments in most situations (refining economic studies of decentralized order), yet the state is not necessarily the fundamental source of order (complementing political theories of the origins of property rights). The theoretical argument and empirical studies, which articulated claim clubs as a level of social control between decentralized order and the state, produced several key findings.

First, claim clubs created private property systems with provisions on all relevant dimensions of a property system. These private-order arrangements successfully allocated, traded, and defended claims as well as established informal judicial institutions. To the extent they had provisions on each dimension of a private property system, clubs rivaled state-backed private property rights.

Widespread success of claim clubs as a source of private property institutions led me to conclude that existing political theories of property institutions underestimate the ability of groups to form rival governments within the contours of a state. The state's competitors – these bandits within the state – are often capable of specifying and enforcing private property institutions.

Second, the method of specifying and enforcing property institutions shifted from highly decentralized norms to hierarchical organizations as the economic environment increased in "complexity," broadly defined to include increases in transaction costs, including the costs of governance. My theory of bandits within the state explained why governments are necessary and how they succeed in their endeavor to manage land relations without relying on the state. The theory produced the following hypothesis: claim clubs would substitute for the state as a source of private property institutions when spontaneously arising norms are unavailable and the state is unwilling to enforce private property rights.

This broad prediction finds support in organizational and institutional changes as the frontier economy became more complex. In each of the major economic sectors, the initial private property systems had limited vertical organization and few property provisions. Economic theories of the origins of basic private property institutions predict allocation of resources through fighting or evolutionary coordination norms, thus anticipating first-possession norms common in the early stages of each sector's development. Yet these studies provide few insights into the development of political institutions to enforce ownership norms.

Nor do theories of spontaneous order anticipate the manner in which clubs arise or how they succeed. One of the hallmarks of studies of spontaneously arising property norms is that the norms emerged (or evolved) over long periods of time – sometimes so long ago that nobody knows who designed them (or even if they had a designer at all). Claim clubs, in contrast, emerged quickly and through conscious effort. Norms arising within clubs were also consciously enforced, operating through the sword. Unlike the story told by economic studies and the vast literature on management of common-property regimes that emphasizes "covenants without swords," the threat of punishment was a defining feature of informal organizations on the frontier.

Third, it bears repeating that there is something to be said for institutional isomorphism in analyzing development of property institutions in the American case. Across time, geography, and ideology, squatters favored private property enforced through organizations that had similar political features. The search for diversity can obscure broad and profound similarities in the process of institutional emergence and change. A concern with institutional diversity has also, paradoxically, led to an overwhelming focus in some circles on common property regimes. As we have seen throughout this book, informal private property institutions can be just as important in terms of political and economic development, and in the case of the political economy of the United States, most of the action in terms of property institutions involved origins and change in private property rather than systems of co-ownership.

Fourth, claim clubs were common in all relevant frontier sectors, not simply mining. Economic approaches to informal property arrangements in the American West mainly focus on the assignment of property rights to land by miners themselves. However, mining organizations were an extension of agrarian organizations and they were also not the end of the story as far as clubs are concerned. Rather, mining districts were part of a more general profusion of private-order property associations convened by squatters, beginning with agricultural clubs and culminating with cattlemen's associations that spanned entire states. The generalizability of claim clubs as a level of social control comes into clearer focus only when we consider each of the four major frontier sectors.

Finally, settlers were not isolated individualists. Rather, they quickly formed groups to allocate land and defend claims from competitors. Indeed, organizations were necessary for private property institutions to be effective in the state's shadow because they could not achieve economies of scale through personal-enforcement systems. Individualistic settlers were thus adept at cooperating, often in large numbers. These clubs may have to steal the state's land, yet we can also appreciate their ability to establish a system of governance that rivaled that of frontier towns in order to bring their goals to fruition.

FROM SELF-GOVERNANCE TO RENT-SEEKING

On one hand, claim clubs were a source of informal property institutions. On the other hand, they were weapons in a war waged over the price of land. Competitive auctions of government-owned land promised a weak American state a source of revenue, one that would have balanced citizens' interest in legal title with the state's desire to provide public goods. Claim clubs, however, swept the state aside.

As a study of change, the main contribution of this book is to consider explicitly the political economy of sustained conflict over the *price* of land during the nineteenth century. Neoclassical theories of property rights, to the extent they consider distributive dimensions of property institutions, emphasize selective enforcement of property rights or the tendency of distributional conflict to prevent emergence of property rights. Selective enforcement and nonemergence of property rights, however, are not the only problems afflicting the process of change in property institutions. Conflict over the price of land is also a fundamental source of conflict in the process of privatization, and it was perhaps the most important dimension of conflict in land laws from 1780 to 1880.

Competitive land auctions were a potentially important source of revenue from the Articles of Confederation through the Civil War. Auctions, by putting land to its highest social value, have some quite desirable properties. Under competitive land auctions, citizens secure legal title and the government increases its capacity to provide public goods. Of course, competitive markets for state-owned land are not without problems. Markets are not inherently self-regulating and self-legitimating. Yet competitive markets remain a reasonable standard with which to assess efficiency in the choice of alternative mechanisms to allocate land.

Despite the importance of price in economics, economists interested in the implication of nineteenth-century land laws for current struggles to establish more effective property institutions have not paid much attention to the price of land. Too often, economists use the experience of squatters to infer that the federal government must have chosen the wrong policies. However, the typical defense of squatters' rights pays little attention to the price at which land changes hands. In neglecting the distributive dimension of land relations, economic defenses of squatters' rights miss one of the most important dynamics of institutional change in nineteenth-century land laws, namely the prolonged fight over scarcity rent associated with the nation's vast land empire.

One of the brightest findings from my empirical studies of formal institutional change is how clubs steadily undermined competitive markets for land. In the aggregate, squatters from every major frontier sector wrestled scarcity rent away from the state. The ability of claim clubs to establish informal institutions was rivaled only by their success in getting what they wanted politically, which was free land.

Policy conflicts over land in the early republic suggest the need to revise revenue-maximization logics of political decision making, ones that hypothesize that the state exists in order to extract revenue from citizens. As insightful as they are, theories of revenue maximization underestimate the role of economic organizations as a constraint on a state's revenue aspirations. In the particular context of development of land laws on the American frontier, a critical problem is explaining why governments *rarely pursued revenue-maximizing policies throughout the nineteenth century.*

As the empirical studies revealed, Congress began to weaken land auctions nearly as soon as it created them, eventually causing a swell of settlers by its repeated concessions. Eventually, legislators essentially gave up on competitive markets for agricultural land with the Homestead Act. Land giveaways even expanded after the Civil War despite a dramatic increase in revenue demand in the wake of the conflict. Empirical developments at the state and federal levels concerning public policies governing areas such as farmland, timberland, and the nation's mineral land demonstrate the veracity of a distributive account of claim clubs, one that provides greater insight into the process of institutional change than revenue-maximization or efficiency perspectives.

LAND AND THE STATE

The political economy of claim clubs also has important implications for our understanding of the relationship between land and the state. In particular, conflict over land laws in the nineteenth century suggests that land laws can enhance or undermine prospects for development of the state itself. It is fitting to conclude by considering briefly the implications of my study of the American frontier for state building more generally.

First, improvements in the design of institutions governing land relations can enhance prospects for a self-enforcing political system. To see this point, we need only consider experience under the Articles of Confederation. One of the design failures of the Articles of Confederation was the voluntary system of contributions to fund the federal government, a design flaw that crippled the federal government's ability to generate revenue.

Land came into play because competitive land auctions were a key source of nontax revenue during a period in which Shay's Rebellion (which was a response to a tax) weighed heavily on the minds of policy makers. Without land revenue, security could decline, perhaps by undermining the government's ability to suppress conflict between subnational governments. Bednar's (2008) foundational study of federalism has explained precisely the importance of overlapping constraints on the central government as a source of federal stability. The political economy of land policy in the early United States suggests we could add overlapping sources of revenue to the list of design principles for self-enforcing federations, with land revenue as one of the important substantive sources of federal stability.

The relationship between land and state capacity also informs studies in the scholarly tradition of American Political Development (APD). Scholars interested in APD have sought to understand the process of American state expansion during and after the Civil War, as well as to understand more generally the mechanisms governing emergence of capacity of the American state. Bensel (1991), for example, has shown how war imperatives during the Civil War were one of the primary mechanisms that led to centralization of state capacity – what he called the "Yankee Leviathan."

This study complements existing ones in the APD tradition by considering explicitly the relationship between land and state capacity. In particular, none of the major studies of APD consider explicitly how organizational conflict over land constrained expansion of American state capacity throughout the nineteenth century. Rather than being a Leviathan, the American state was in many periods overrun by claim clubs. The image conjured from this book is more like a scene from Swift's *Gulliver's Travels* – Lilliputians tying down Gulliver before allowing him the privilege of enforcing their property rights.

This perceived interrelationship between institutions governing land allocation and state capacity takes on even greater significance in the developing world. Once we accept that land relations can influence state capacity, land reform becomes a dimension of state building in the sense that improvements in property institutions can be used to enhance prospects for survival of the state itself, a point that has far-reaching implications. For one, it suggests that property institutions can make the state, rather than the conventional assumption in economic and political theories that suggests the state makes property rights. Rather, a fundamental implication of my study is that the design of property institutions can make or break the state, reversing the implied causal relationship in all major theories of the politics of property institutions. The experience of the American frontier suggests the various ways land relations can make or break states, yet it is also clear that more research, comparative in scope with emphasis on today's developing world, is necessary to better understand how particular land policies can improve prospects for strengthening the state.

Second, one of the most important aspects of orderly and effective decentralization of property rights is developing the institutional capacity to implement competitive markets for state-owned land. Land is a revenue resource that is particularly important for weak states but the state has to invest its scarce resources in bureaucratic capacity to secure future revenue streams associated with land. From an institutional design perspective, land reform first requires improving the state's administrative capacity to administer land it owns before it can reasonably hope to profit from state-owned land. In the developing world, foreign aid could be used to strengthen a nation's land-administration bureaucracy in order to increase the state's ability to allocate land through markets, with nontax revenue from land auctions improving the state's capacity to provide public goods as well as to monitor use of remaining state-owned land.

Third, credible commitment to state ownership is critical for a state to realize its interests in land. Theories of credibility of commitment provided many insights into the problem of committing credibly to private ownership. This book extends these insights by clarifying that governments also have to commit credibly to state ownership, in particular in developing countries that are likely to be characterized by substantial need for nontax revenue from land sales as well as problems with illegal occupation. In an environment characterized by widespread illegal occupation or use of land, there will typically be pressure for one-time concession to claimants or allocation through bureaucratic priorities. Concessions that may seem desirable as a one-time policy increase incentives for illegal occupation. Over time, concessions become more likely as more squatters occupy government-owned land. As the experience of the American frontier shows, there is much to be gained by committing credibly to state ownership, for revenue to provide public goods, including security, hangs in the balance.

Fourth, rules governing landholding size have implications for state strength and weakness. Just as land oligopoly is a threat to agricultural, timberland, and rangeland productivity, so too is small claim size. Small claim size can contribute to farm busts but more generally, it prevents individuals from obtaining economies of scale. It seems clear that size constraints imposed by the federal government during the nineteenth century were a source of social costs.

It is not difficult to see how landholding size can influence prospects for state development in current contexts. In many developing countries, there is not much in the way of fertile land, and so the stakes of poor land policies are high. Failure to get claim size right can exacerbate scarcity, and in response, people may have stronger incentives to fight over land. Because poorly designed property institutions can throw people into conflict, it stands to reason that improvements in the design of property institutions can improve prospects for a lasting peace.

Finally, government programs seeking to benefit the poor are likely to benefit speculators unless a government invests in administrative capacity. Many land reforms seek to benefit the poor yet alleviating poverty through these reforms depends to an extent on administrative capacity to prevent land grabs. Unfortunately, there are very few weak states that have the bureaucratic capacity and competence in key areas necessary to prevent corruption and land grabbing. For this reason, we should expect many pro-poor policies to have the opposite effect unless a state first improves is capacity to manage the process of decentralizations.

If leaders hope to provide the poor with a means of subsistence, then a more productive policy is to first establish control of state-owned land. These investments allow the state to reap its fair share of scarcity rent associated with land as well as increase the chances legal titles end up in the hands of the nation's poor. Investments in the capacity of the land-administration bureaucracy are also necessary to ensure the private property system operates smoothly in the longer term. Although the logic set forth in this book provides a historical perspective on land and the state, it will be necessary in future research to consider more carefully the extent to which property rights contributes to state strength and weakness, with emphasis on ways in which improvements in property institutions can improve prospects for fixing failed states.

In *Democracy in America*, Alexis de Tocqueville suggested agreement regarding private property was one of the defining social features of the United States: "In no other country in the world is the love of property keener or more alert than in the United States, and nowhere else does the majority display less inclination toward doctrines which in any way threaten the way property is owned." It is undeniable that most segments of American society agreed on the desirability of private property institutions in the nineteenth century. Yet Tocqueville's perspective is somewhat misleading because it says nothing about distributive conflict over the price of land within a private property system. As this book has shown, conflict – rather than consensus – was the defining feature of the political economy of the American frontier.

References

Acemoglu, Daron. 2003. "Why Not a Political Coase Theorem? Social Conflict, Commitment, and Politics," *Journal of Comparative Economics* 31: 620–52.

Acemoglu, Daron and James Robinson. 2012. *Why Nations Fail: The Origins of Power, Prosperity, and Poverty* (New York: Crown Publishers).

Acemoglu, Daron and James Robinson. 2008. "Persistence of Power, Elites and Institutions," *American Economic Review* 98 (1): 267–93.

Acemoglu, Daron and James Robinson. 2006. *The Economic Origins of Dictatorship and Democracy* (Cambridge, UK: Cambridge University Press).

Adams, Charles Kendall and William P. Trent. 1913. *A History of the United States* (Boston: Allyn and Bacon).

Adelman, Jeremy and Stephen Aron. 1999. "From Borderlands to Borders: Empires, Nation-States, and the Peoples in between in North American History," *American Historical Review* 104 (3): 814–41.

Alchian, Armen A. 1950. "Uncertainty, Evolution, and Economic Theory," *Journal of Political Economy* 58 (3): 211–21.

Alchian, Armen A. and Harold Demsetz. 1973. "The Property Right Paradigm," *Journal of Economic History* 33 (1): 16–27.

Allen, Douglas W. 1991. "Homesteading and Property Rights: Or, How the West Was Really Won," *Journal of Law and Economics* 34 (1): 1–23.

Alston, Lee J., Edwyna Harris, and Bernardo Mueller. 2011. "Property Rights, Land Settlement and Land Conflict on Frontiers: Evidence from Australia, Brazil and the U.S.," in Kenneth Ayotte and Henry E. Smith, eds., *Research Handbook on the Economics of Property Law* (Cheltenham, UK: Edward Elgar).

Alston, Lee J., Gary D. Libecap, and Bernardo Mueller. 1999. *Land Titles and Conflict in the Brazilian Amazon* (Ann Arbor: University of Michigan Press).

Anderson, Gary M. and Delores T. Martin. 1987. "The Public Domain and Nineteenth Century Transfer Policy," *Cato Journal* 6 (3): 905–23.

Anderson, George L. 1939. "The Canon City or Arkansas Valley Claim Club, 1860–1862," *The Colorado Magazine* 16: 201–10.

Anderson, George L. 1936. "The El Paso Claim Club, 1859–1862," *The Colorado Magazine* 13: 41–63.
Anderson, Terry L. and Peter J. Hill. 2004. *The Not So Wild, Wild West: Property Rights on the Frontier* (Palo Alto, CA: Stanford University Press).
Anderson, Terry L. and Peter J. Hill. 2002. "Cowboys and Contracts," *Journal of Legal Studies* 31 (Special Issue): S489–S513.
Anderson, Terry L., and Peter J. Hill. 1980. *The Birth of a Transfer Society* (Stanford, CA: Hoover Institution Press).
Arrow, Kenneth. 1951. *Social Choice and Individual Values* (New York: Wiley and Sons).
Aron, Stephen. 1992. "Pioneers and Profiteers: Land Speculation and the Homestead Ethic in Frontier Kentucky," *The Western Historical Quarterly* 23 (2): 179–98.
Ary, T.S. 1989. *Mining Law of 1872: A Legal and Historical Analysis* (Washington, DC: National Legal Center for the Public Interest).
Avant, Deborah. 2005. *The Market for Force: The Consequences of Privatizing Security* (Cambridge, UK: Cambridge University Press).
Bailey, Kenneth P. 1939. *The Ohio Company of Virginia and the Westward Movement, 1748–1792* (Glendale, CA: Arthur H. Clark Company).
Bardhan, Pranab. 1973. "Size, Production and Returns to Scale: An Analysis of Farm-Level Data in Indian Agriculture," *Journal of Political Economy* 81 (6): 1370–86.
Bardhan, Pranab and Dilip Mookherjee. 2010. "Determinants of Redistributive Politics: An Empirical Analysis of Land Reforms in West Bengal, India," *American Economic Review* 100 (4): 1572–600.
Barzel, Yoram. 2002. *A Theory of the State: Economic Rights, Legal Rights, and the Scope of the State* (Cambridge, UK: Cambridge University Press).
Barzel, Yoram. 1989. *An Economic Theory of Property Rights* (Cambridge, UK: Cambridge University Press).
Bates, Robert. 2008. *State Failure in Late-Modern Africa* (Cambridge, UK: Cambridge University Press).
Bates, Robert, Avner Greif, Margaret Levi, Jean-Laurent Rosenthal, and Barry R. Weingast, editors. 1998. *Analytic Narratives* (Princeton, NJ: Princeton University Press).
Bednar, Jenna. 2008. *The Robust Federation* (Cambridge, UK: Cambridge University Press).
Bensel, Richard F. 2000. *The Political Economy of American Industrialization, 1877–1900* (Cambridge, UK: Cambridge University Press).
Bensel, Richard F. 1991. *Yankee Leviathan: The Origins of Central State Authority in America, 1859–1877* (Cambridge, UK: Cambridge University Press).
Bogue, Allan G. 1963. *From Prairie to Corn Belt: Farming on the Illinois and Iowa Prairies in the Nineteenth Century* (Chicago, IL: University of Chicago Press).
Bogue, Allan G. 1958. "The Iowa Claim Clubs: Symbol and Substance," *The Mississippi Valley Historical Review* 45 (2): 231–53.
Bogue, Allan G. and Margaret B. Bogue. 1957. "Profits and the Frontier Land Speculator," *Journal of Economic History* 17 (1): 1–24.
Bohanan, Cecil and Philip Coelho. 1998. "The Costs of Free Land: The Case of the Oklahoma Land Rushes," *Journal of Real Estate Finance and Economics* 16 (2): 205–21.

Boyd, Julian. 1931. "The Susquehannah Company: Connecticut's Experiment in Expansion," *Journal of Economic and Business History* 4 (1): 36–69.

Bradsby, H.C. 1893. *History of Luzerne County Pennsylvania* (Chicago, IL: S. B. Nelson and Co.).

Briggs, Harold E. 1934. "The Development and Decline of Open Range Ranching in the Northwest," *Mississippi Valley Historical Review* 20 (4): 521–36.

Brockett, Linus P. 1881. *Our Western Empire* (Philadelphia, PA: Bradley, Garretson and Co.).

Bromley, Daniel W. 2008a. "The Crisis in Ocean Governance: Conceptual Confusion, Spurious Economics, Political Indifference," *MAST* 6 (2): 7–22.

Bromley, Daniel W. 2008b. "Formalizing Property Relations in the Developing World: The Wrong Prescription for the Wrong Malady," *Land Use Policy* 26 (1): 20–7.

Bromley, Daniel W. 2006. *Sufficient Reason: Volitional Pragmatism and the Meaning of Economic Institutions* (Princeton, NJ: Princeton University Press).

Bromley, Daniel W. 2005. "Purging the Frontier from Our Mind: Crafting a New Fisheries Policy," *Reviews in Fish Biology and Fisheries* 15: 217–29.

Bromley, Daniel W. 1991. *Environment and Economy* (Cambridge, MA: Blackwell).

Bromley, Daniel W. 1989. *Economic Interests and Institutions* (Cambridge, MA: Blackwell).

Busch, Clarence M. 1896. Report of the Commission to Locate the Sites of the Frontier Forts of Pennsylvania, Volumes I and II (State Printer of Pennsylvania).

Cai, Meina. 2012. *Land-Locked Development: The Local Political Economy of Institutional Change in China.* Ph.D. Dissertation, Department of Political Science, University of Wisconsin–Madison.

Cain, Michael G. and Keith Dougherty. 1999. "Suppressing Shay's Rebellion: Collective Action and Constitutional Design under the Articles of Confederation," *Journal of Theoretical Politics* 11 (2): 233–60.

Calvert, Randall L. 2006. "Deliberation as Coordination through Cheap Talk," Working Paper, Department of Political Science, Washington University in St. Louis.

Calvert, Randall L. 1995. "The Rational Choice Theory of Social Institutions: Cooperation, Coordination, and Communication," in Jeffrey S. Banks and Eric A. Hanushek, eds., *Modern Political Economy: Old Topics, New Directions* (Cambridge, UK: Cambridge University Press).

Calvert, Randall L. and James Johnson. 1999. "Interpretation and Coordination in Constitutional Politics," in Ewa Hauser and Jacek Wasilewski, eds., *Lessons in Democracy* (Rochester, NY: University of Rochester Press).

Caplan, Bryan. 2007. *The Myth of the Rational Voter: Why Democracies Choose Bad Policies* (Princeton, NJ: Princeton University Press).

Carpenter, Daniel P. 2001. *The Forging of Bureaucratic Autonomy: Reputations, Networks, and Policy Innovation in Executive Agencies, 1862–1928* (Princeton, NJ: Princeton University Press).

Carstensen, Vernon. 1958. *Farms or Forests* (Madison: University of Wisconsin Press).

Cheung, Steven N.S. 1970. "The Structure of a Contract and the Theory of a Non-Exclusive Resource," *Journal of Law and Economics* 13 (1): 49–70.

Ciriacy-Wantrup, S. V., and Richard Bishop. 1975. "Common Property as a Concept in Natural Resources Policy," *Natural Resources Journal* 15 (4): 713–27.

Clarke, John. 2001. *Land, Power, and Economics on the Frontier of Upper Canada* (Montreal and Kingston: McGill-Queen's University Press).

Clawson, Marion. 1951. *Uncle Sam's Acres* (New York: Dodd, Mead & Company).

Clay, Karen B. 2006. "Squatters, Production, and Violence," SSRN Working Paper.

Clay, Karen B. 1999. "Property Rights and Institutions: Congress and the California Land Act of 1851," *Journal of Economic History* 59 (1): 122–42.

Clay, Karen B. 1997. "Trade without Law: Private-Order Institutions in Mexican California," *Journal of Law, Economics, and Organization* 13 (1): 202–31.

Clay, Karen B. and Gavin Wright. 2010. "Gold Rush Legacy: American Minerals and the Knowledge Economy," in Ostrom and Cole, eds., *Property in Land and Other Natural Resources* (Cambridge, MA: Lincoln Institute of Land Policy).

Clay, Karen B. and Gavin Wright. 2005. "Order without Law: Property Rights during the California Gold Rush," *Explorations in Economic History* 42: 155–83.

Coase, Ronald. 1966. "The Economics of Broadcasting and Government Policy," *American Economic Review* 56 (1): 440–7.

Coase, Ronald. 1960. "The Problem of Social Cost," *Journal of Law, Economics, and Organization* 3: 1–44.

Coase, Ronald. 1959. "The Federal Communications Commission," *Journal of Law and Economics* 2: 1–40.

Coase, Ronald. 1937. "The Nature of the Firm," *Economica* 16 (4): 386–405.

Colby, Bonnie G. 1990. "Transactions Costs and Efficiency in Western Water Allocation," *American Journal of Agricultural Economics* 72 (5): 1184–92.

Commons, John R. 1924. *Legal Foundations of Capitalism* (New York: Macmillan).

Cox, Gary W. and Mathew D. McCubbins. 2005. *Setting the Agenda: Responsible Party Government in the U.S. House of Representatives* (Cambridge, UK: Cambridge University Press).

Cox, Gary W. and Mathew D. McCubbins. 1993. *Legislative Leviathan: Party Government in the House* (Berkeley: University of California Press).

Craft, David. 1878. *History of Bradford County, Pennsylvania* (Philadelphia, PA: L. H. Everts).

Cronon, William. 1991. *Nature's Metropolis: Chicago and the Great West* (New York: W. W. Norton).

Cronon, William. 1983. *Changes in the Land: Indians, Colonists, and the Ecology of New England* (New York: Hill & Wang).

Cutler, William G. 1883. *History of the State of Kansas* (Chicago, IL: A.T. Andreas).

Dahlman, Carl. 1979. "The Problem of Externality," *Journal of Law and Economics* 21 (2): 141–62.

Dal Bo, Ernesto, Pedro Dal Bo, and Jason Snyder. 2009. "Political Dynasties," *Review of Economic Studies* 76 (1).

Dale, Edward E. 1960. *The Range Cattle Industry: Ranching on the Great Plains from 1865 to 1965* (Norman: University of Oklahoma Press).

Dale, Edward E. 1942. *Cow Country* (Norman: University of Oklahoma Press).

David, Paul A. and Gavin Wright. 1997. "Increasing Returns and the Genesis of American Resources Abundance," *Industrial Change* 6: 203–45.

Davis, James E. 1998. *Frontier Illinois* (Bloomington, IN: Indiana University Press).

Day, Sherman. 1843. *Historical Collection of the State of Pennsylvania* (Philadelphia: George W. Gorton, and New Haven: Durrie and Peck).

Demsetz, Harold. 1967. "Toward a Theory of Property Rights," *American Economic Review* 57 (2): 347–59.

Dennen, R. Taylor. 1976. "Cattlemen's Associations and Property Rights in Land in the American West," *Explorations in Economic History* 13 (4): 423–36.

Denzau, Arthur T., and Douglas C. North. 1994. "Shared Mental Models: Ideologies and Institutions," *Kyklos* 47 (1): 3–31.

de Soto, Hernando. 2000. *The Mystery of Capital: Why Capitalism Triumphs in the West and Fails Everywhere Else* (New York: Basic Books).

de Soto, Hernando. 1989. *The Other Path: The Economic Answer to Terrorism* (New York: Basic Books).

Dharmapala, Dhammika. 2002. "Campaign War Chests, Entry Deterrence, and Voter Rationality," *Economics and Politics* 14 (3): 325–50.

Dick, Everett. 1970. *The Lure of the Land: A Social History of the Public Lands from the Articles of Confederation to the New Deal* (Lincoln: University of Nebraska Press).

Dick, Everett. 1954. *The Sod-House Frontier, 1854–1890: A Social History of the Northern Plains from the Creation of Kansas and Nebraska to the Admission of the Dakotas* (Lincoln: University of Nebraska Press).

Diermeier, Daniel, Steve Ericson, Timothy Frye, and Steven Lewis. 1997. "Credibility of Property Rights," in David L. Weimer, ed., *Political Economy of Property Rights: Institutional Change in Postcommunist Economies* (Cambridge, UK: Cambridge University Press).

Dimsdale, Thomas J. 1949. *The Vigilantes of Montana, or, Popular Justice in the Rocky Mountains* (Norman: University of Oklahoma Press).

Dixit, Avinash K. 2004. *Lawlessness and Economics: Alternative Modes of Governance* (Princeton, NJ: Princeton University Press).

Donaldson, Thomas. 1884. *The Public Domain: Its History, with Statistics* (Washington, DC: Govt. Printing Office).

Dougherty, Keith L. 2001. *Collective Action under the Articles of Confederation* (Cambridge, UK: Cambridge University Press).

Dougherty, Keith L. and Michael G. Cain. 1997. "Marginal Cost Sharing and the Articles of Confederation," *Public Choice* 90: 201–13.

Dunham, Harold H. 1941. *Government Handout: A Study in the Administration of the Public Lands, 1875–1891* (Ann Arbor, MI: Edwards Brothers).

Dunham, Harold H. 1937. "Some Crucial Years of the General Land Office, 1875–1890," *Agricultural History* 11 (1): 117–41.

Esping-Andersen, Gosta. 1990. *Three Worlds of Welfare Capitalism* (Princeton, NJ: Princeton University Press).

Eggertsson, Thrainn. 1990. *Economic Behavior and Institutions* (Cambridge, UK: Cambridge University Press).

Ellickson, Robert C. 1991. *Order without Law: How Neighbors Settle Disputes* (Cambridge, MA: Harvard University Press).

Elliott, Russell R. 1983. *Servant of Power: A Political Biography of Senator William M. Stewart* (Reno: University of Nevada Press).

Elster, Jon and Helene Landemore, editors. 2012. *Collective Wisdom: Principles and Mechanisms* (Cambridge, UK: Cambridge University Press).

Engerman, Stanley L. 1982. "Economic Adjustments to Emancipation in the United States and British West Indies," *Journal of Interdisciplinary History* 13 (2): 191–220.
Engerman, Stanley L. 1972. "Some Economic Issues Relating to Railroad Subsidies and the Evaluation of Land Grants," *Journal of Economic History* 32 (2): 443–63.
Eskridge, William N. 1994. *Dynamic Statutory Interpretation* (Cambridge, MA: Harvard University Press).
Feller, Daniel. 1984. *The Public Lands in Jacksonian Politics* (Madison: University of Wisconsin Press).
Fisher, Sydney G. 1897. "Historical Address," in F.C. Johnson, ed., *The Early History of Wyoming Valley* (Wilkes-Barre, PA: Press of the Wilkes-Barre Record).
Fishlow, Albert. 1965. *American Railroads and the Transformation of the Ante-bellum Economy* (Cambridge, MA: Harvard University Press).
Fiske, John. 1904. *How the United States Became a Nation* (Boston: Ginn and Company).
Fogel, Robert W. 1964. *Railroads and American Economic History: Essays in Econometric History* (Baltimore, MD: The Johns Hopkins University Press).
Fogel, Robert W. and Stanley L. Engerman. 1974. *Time on the Cross: The Economics of American Negro Slavery* (Boston: Little Brown).
Foner, Eric. 1970. *Free Land, Free Soil, Free Men: The Ideology of the Republican Party Before the Civil War* (New York: Oxford University Press).
Fries, Robert F. 1951. *Empire in Pine: The Story of Lumbering in Wisconsin, 1830–1900* (Madison: State Historical Society of Wisconsin).
Galanter, Marc. 1974. "Why the 'Haves' Come Out Ahead: Speculation on the Limits of Legal Change," *Law and Society Review* 9 (1): 95–160.
Gambetta, Diego. 2009. *Codes of the Underworld: How Criminals Communicate* (Princeton, NJ: Princeton University Press).
Gambetta, Diego. 1993. *The Sicilian Mafia: The Business of Private Protection* (Cambridge, MA: Harvard University Press, 1993).
Gard, Wayne. 1949. *Frontier Justice* (Norman: University of Oklahoma Press).
Gates, Paul Wallace. 1991. *Land and Law in California: Essays on Public Land Policies* (Ames, IA: Iowa State University Press).
Gates, Paul Wallace. 1979. *The Fruits of Land Speculation* (New York: Arno Press).
Gates, Paul Wallace. 1973. *Landlords and Tenants on the Prairie Frontier: Studies in American Land Policy* (Ithaca, NY: Cornell University Press).
Gates, Paul Wallace. 1971. "The California Land Claims Act of 1851," *California Historical Quarterly* 50 (4): 395–430.
Gates, Paul Wallace. 1968. *History of Public Land Law Development* (Washington, DC: Public Land Law Review Commission).
Gates, Paul Wallace. 1967a. *California's Ranchos and Farms, 1846–1862* (Madison: State Historical Society of Wisconsin).
Gates, Paul Wallace. 1967b. "Pre-Henry George Land Warfare in California," *California Historical Quarterly* 46 (2): 121–48.
Gates, Paul Wallace. 1962. "Tenants of the Log Cabin," *Mississippi Valley Historical Review* 49 (2): 3–31.
Gates, Paul Wallace. 1960. *The Farmer's Age: Agriculture, 1815–1860: The Economic History of the United States*, vol. 3 (New York: Holt, Rinehart and Winston).
Gates, Paul Wallace. 1954. *Fifty Million Acres: Conflicts over Kansas Land Policy, 1854–1890* (Ithaca, NY: Cornell University Press).

Gates, Paul Wallace. 1948. *Cattle Kings in the Prairies* (Cedar Rapids, Iowa: Torch Press).

Gates, Paul Wallace. 1942. "The Role of the Land Speculators in Western Development," *Pennsylvania Magazine of History* 66: 314–33.

Gates, Paul Wallace. 1936. "The Homestead Law in an Incongruous Land System," *American Historical Review* 41 (4): 562–681.

Gehlbach, Scott and Philip Keefer. 2011. "Investment without Democracy: Ruling Party Institutionalization and Credible Commitment in Autocracies," *Journal of Comparative Economics* 39 (2) 123–39.

Gehlbach, Scott, Konstantin Sonin, and Ekaterina Zhuravskaya. 2010. "Businessman Candidates," *American Journal of Political Science* 53 (3): 718–36.

Gillman, Howard. 1992. *The Constitution Besieged: The Rise and Demise of Lochner-Era Police Powers Jurisprudence* (Durham, NC: Duke University Press).

Gladstone, Thomas H. 1857. *Kansas: Squatter Life and Border Warfare in the Far West* (New York: Routledge).

Greif, Avner. 2006. *Institutions and the Path to the Modern Economy* (Cambridge, UK: Cambridge University Press).

Greif, Avner. 2005. "Commitment, Coercion, and Markets: The Nature and Dynamics of Institutions Supporting Exchange," in Claude Menand and Mary Shirley, editors, *Handbook of New Institutional Economics* (Dordrecht, the Netherlands: Springer).

Greif, Avner. 1998. "Self-enforcing Political System and Economic Growth: Late Medieval Genoa," in Barry Weingast, Avner Greif, Margaret Levi, and Jean-Laurent Rosenthal, eds., *Analytic Narratives* (Cambridge, UK: Cambridge University Press).

Greif, Avner. 1992. "Institutions and Commitment in International Trade: Lessons from the Commercial Revolution," *American Economic Review* 82 (2): 128–33.

Grossman, Herschel I. 2001. "The Creation of Effective Property Rights," *American Economic Review* 91 (2): 347–52.

Grossman, Herschel I. and Minseong Kim. 1995. "Swords or Plowshares? A Theory of the Security of Claims to Property," *Journal of Political Economy* 103 (6): 1275–88.

Grubb, Farley. 2010. "Land Policy: Founding Choices and Outcomes, 1781–1802," in Douglas A. Irwin and Richard Sylla, eds., *Founding Choices: American Economic Policy in the 1790s* (Chicago, IL: University of Chicago Press).

Grubb, Farley. 2007. "The Spoils of War: U.S. Federal Government Finance in the Aftermath of the War for Independence, 1784–1802," in Rafael Torres Sanchez, ed., *War, State and Development: Fiscal-Military States in the Eighteenth Century* (Pamplona, Spain: EUNSA).

Grubb, Farley, 2007 "The Net Worth of the US Federal Government, 1784–1802," *American Economic Review* 97 (2): 280–4.

Haber, Stephen, Armando Razo, and Noel Maurer. 2003. *The Politics of Property Rights: Political Instability, Credible Commitments, and Economic Growth in Mexico, 1876–1929* (Cambridge, UK: Cambridge University Press).

Hafer, Catherine. 2006. "On the Origins of Property Rights: Conflict and Production in the State of Nature," *Review of Economic Studies* 73 (1): 119–43.

Hall, John W. 2009. *Uncommon Defense: Indian Allies in the Blackhawk War* (Cambridge, MA: Harvard University Press).

Hamilton, Alexander, James Madison, and John Jay. 2003 [1788]. *The Federalist Papers*. Clinton Rossiter, ed. (New York: Penguin).

Hansen, Zeynep K. and Gary D. Libecap. 2004a. "The Allocation of Property Rights to Land: U.S. Land Policy and Farm Failure in the Northern Great Plains," *Explorations in Economic History* 41: 103–29.

Hansen, Zeynep K. and Gary D. Libecap. 2004b. "Small Farms, Externalities, and the Dust Bowl of the 1930s," *Journal of Political Economy* 112 (3): 665–93.

Hayek, Friedrich. 1960. *The Constitution of Liberty* (Chicago, IL: University of Chicago Press).

Hayek, Friedrich. 1948. *Individualism and Economic Order* (Chicago, IL: University of Chicago Press).

Hayek, Friedrich. 1945. "The Use of Knowledge in Society," *American Economic Review* 35 (4): 519–30.

Hayek, Friedrich. 1944. *The Road to Serfdom* (Chicago, IL: University of Chicago Press).

Herrera, Yoshiko M. 2005. *Imagined Economies: The Sources of Russian Regionalism* (Cambridge, UK: Cambridge University Press).

Hershiser, Beulah. 1913. "The Influence of Nevada on the National Mining Legislation of 1866," in *Third Biennial Report of the Nevada Historical Society, 1911–1912* (Carson City: Nevada State Printing Office).

Heverly, C. F. 1902. *History of Sheshequin 1777–1902* (Towanda, PA: The Bradford Star Print).

Hibbard, Benjamin H. 1924. *A History of the Public Land Policies* (New York: The Macmillan Company).

Hibbard, Benjamin H. 1905. *The History of Agriculture in Dane County, Wisconsin* (Madison: University of Wisconsin Press).

Ho, Peter. 2005a. *Institutions in Transition: Land Ownership, Property Rights, and Social Conflict in China* (Oxford, UK: Oxford University Press).

Ho, Peter, editor. 2005b. *Developmental Dilemmas: Land Reform and Institutional Change in China* (New York: Routledge).

Hobbes, Thomas. 1991 [1651]. *The Leviathan*. Richard Tuck, ed. (Cambridge, UK: Cambridge University Press).

Horn, Murray. 1995. *The Political Economy of Public Administration: Institutional Choice in the Public Sector* (Cambridge, UK: Cambridge University Press).

Hughes, Jonathan. 1987. "The Great Land Ordinances," in David C. Klingaman and Richard K. Vedder, eds., *Essays on the Economy of the Old Northwest* (Athens: University of Ohio Press).

Hurst, J. Willard. 1964. *Law and Economic Growth: The Legal History of the Lumber Industry in Wisconsin, 1836–1915* (Cambridge, MA: Harvard University Press).

Irwin, Douglas A. and Richard Sylla, editors. 2011. *Founding Choices: American Economic Policy in the 1790s* (Chicago, IL: University of Chicago Press).

Jackson, W. Turrentine. 1947. "The Wyoming Stock Growers' Association: Political Power in Wyoming Territory, 1873–1890," *Mississippi Valley Historical Review* 33: 571–94.

Jensen, Laura. 2003. *Patriots, Settlers, and the Origins of American Social Policy* (New York: Cambridge University Press).

Johnson, Ronald N. and Gary D. Libecap. 1994. *The Federal Civil Service System and the Problem of Bureaucracy* (Chicago, IL: University of Chicago Press).

Kanazawa, Mark T. 2005. "Immigration, Exclusion, and Taxation: Anti-Chinese Legislation in Gold Rush California," *Journal of Economic History* 65 (4): 779–805.

Kanazawa, Mark T. 1998. "Efficiency in Western Water Law: The Development of the California Doctrine, 1850–1911," *Journal of Legal Studies* 27 (1): 159–84.

Kanazawa, Mark T. 1996. "Possession is Nine Points in the Law: The Political Economy of Early Land Disposal," *Explorations in Economic History* 33 (2): 227–42.

Kandori, Michihiro. 1992. "Social Norms and Community Enforcement," *Review of Economic Studies* 59 (1): 63–80.

Kantor, Shawn Everett. 1998. *Politics and Property Rights: The Closing of the Open Range in the Postbellum South* (Chicago, IL: University of Chicago Press).

Kantor, Shawn Everett. 1994. "The Economic and Political Determinants of Fence Reform in Postbellum Georgia," *Journal of Institutional and Theoretical Economics* 150: 486–510.

Kantor, Shawn Everett. 1991. "Razorbacks, Ticky Cows, and the Closing of the Georgia Open Range: The Dynamics of Institutional Change Uncovered," *Journal of Economic History* 51: 861–86.

Karsten, Peter. 2008. "A Recognizable Law & Economics Jurisprudence?: How Much 'Wealth'- And 'Welfare'-Maximizing Took Place in the Courts, Legislatures, and Customs of Eighteenth and Nineteenth-Century Common-Law Domains?" *Australian Journal of Legal History* 8: 21–60.

Karsten, Peter. 2002. *Between Law and Custom: "High" and "Low" Legal Cultures in the Lands of the British Diaspora – The United States, Canada, Australia, and New Zealand, 1600–1900* (Cambridge, UK: Cambridge University Press).

Karsten, Peter. 1997. *Heart versus Head: Judge-Made Law in Nineteenth-Century America* (Chapel Hill: University of North Carolina Press).

Katznelson, Ira and Barry R. Weingast, editors. 2005. *Preferences and Situations: Points of Intersection between Rational Choice and Historical Institutionalism* (New York: Russell Sage).

Kilar, Jeremy W. 1987. "Great Lakes Lumber Towns and Frontier Violence: A Comparative Study," *Journal of Forest History* 31 (2): 71–85.

Klein, Daniel B. 1992. "Promise Keeping in the Great Society: A Model of Credit Information Sharing," *Economics and Politics* 4 (1): 117–36.

Klein, Daniel B. 1991. "The Voluntary Provision of Public Goods? The Turnpike Companies of Early America," *Economic Inquiry* 28 (4): 788–812.

Kluger, Richard. 2007. *Seizing Destiny: The Relentless Expansion of American Territory* (New York: Alfred A. Knopf).

Knight, Jack. 1992. *Institutions and Social Conflict* (Cambridge, UK: Cambridge University Press).

Knight, Jack and Douglass C. North. 1997. "Explaining the Complexity of Institutional Change," in David L. Weimer, ed., *The Political Economy of Property Rights* (Cambridge, UK: Cambridge University Press).

Knight, Jack and Itai Sened, editors. 1995. *Explaining Social Institutions* (Ann Arbor: University of Michigan).

Komesar, Neil K. 2001. *Law's Limits: The Rule of Law and the Demand and Supply of Rights* (Cambridge, UK: Cambridge University Press).

Komesar, Neil K. 1997. *Imperfect Alternatives: Choosing Alternatives in Law, Economic, and Public Policy* (Chicago, IL: University of Chicago Press).

Krehbiel, Keith. 1998. *Pivotal Politics: A Theory of U.S. Lawmaking* (Chicago, IL: University of Chicago Press).
Kreps, David M., Paul Milgrom, John Roberts, and Robert Wilson. 1982. "Rational Cooperation in the Finitely Repeated Prisoners' Dilemma," *Journal of Economic Theory* 27 (2): 245–52.
Kreps, David M., and Robert Wilson. 1982. "Reputation and Imperfect Information," *Journal of Economic Theory* 27 (2): 253–79.
Krueger, Anne O. 1996. "The Political Economy of Controls: American Sugar," in Lee J. Alston, Thrainn Eggertsson, and Douglass C. North, eds., *Empirical Studies in Institutional Change* (Cambridge: Cambridge University Press).
Krueger, Anne O. 1974. "The Political Economy of the Rent-Seeking Society," *American Economic Review* 64 (3): 291–303.
Kuran, Timur. 2011. *The Long Divergence: How Islamic Law Held Back the Middle East* (Princeton, NJ: Princeton University Press).
Kydland, Finn and Edward Prescott. 1977. "Rules Rather than Discretion: The Inconsistency of Optimal Plans," *Journal of Political Economy* 85: 473–91.
Langford, Nathaniel P. 1957. *Vigilante Days and Ways: The Pioneers of the Rockies, the Makers and the Makings of Montana, Idaho, Oregon, Washington and Wyoming* (Missoula: Montana State University Press).
Leeson, Peter T. 2008. "Coordination without Command: Stretching the Scope of Spontaneous Order," *Public Choice* 135: 67–78.
Leeson, Peter T. 2007a. "Better Off Stateless: Somalia Before and After Government Collapse," *Journal of Comparative Economics* 34 (4): 689–710.
Leeson, Peter T. 2007b. "Efficient Anarchy," *Public Choice* 130: 41–53.
Leeson, Peter T. 2006. "Cooperation and Conflict: Evidence on Self-Enforcing Arrangements and Heterogeneous Groups," *American Journal of Economics and Sociology* 65 (4): 891–907.
Leeson, Peter T. 2005. "Self-Enforcing Arrangements in African Political Economy," *Journal of Economic Behavior and Organization* 57 (2): 241–4.
Leeson, Peter T. and Christopher J. Coyne. 2012. "Sassywood," *Journal of Comparative Economics* 40 (4): 608–620.
Levi, Margaret. 1988. *Of Rule and Revenue* (Berkeley: University of California Press).
Libecap, Gary D. 2011. "Institutional Path Dependence in Climate Adaptation: Coman's 'Some Unsettled Problems of Irrigation.'" *American Economic Review* 111: 64–80.
Libecap, Gary D. 2007a. "Assigning Property Rights in the Common Pool: Implications of the Prevalence of First-Possession Rules for ITQs in Fisheries," *Marine Resource Economics* 22: 407–23.
Libecap, Gary D. 2007b. "The Assignment of Property Rights on the Western Frontier: Lessons for Contemporary Environmental Policy," *The Journal of Economic History* 67 (2): 257–91.
Libecap, Gary D. 1989. *Contracting for Property Rights* (Cambridge, UK: Cambridge University Press).
Libecap, Gary D. and Zeynep K. Hansen. 2002. "'Rain Follows the Plow' and Dry-farming Doctrine: The Climate Information Problem and Homestead Failure in the Upper Great Plains, 1890–1915," *Journal of Economic History* 62 (1): 86–120.

Libecap, Gary D. and Ronald N. Johnson. 1979. "Property Rights, Nineteenth-Century Timber Policy and the Conservation Movement," *Journal of Economic History* 39 (1): 129–42.
Littell, William. 1809–1819. *The Statute Law of Kentucky, Five Vols.* (Frankfort, KY: Shaw and Shoemaker).
Liu, Shouying, Michael R. Carter, and Yang Yao. 1998. "Dimensions and Diversity of Property Rights in Rural China: Dilemmas on the Road to Further Reform," *World Development* 26 (10): 1789–806.
Lloyd, Thomas W. 1929. *History of Lycoming County Pennsylvania* (Indianapolis, IN: Historical Publishing Company).
Locke, John. 1980 [1689]. *Second Treatise of Government.* C.B. Macpherson, ed. (Indianapolis, IN: Hackett Publishing Company).
Lord, Elliot. 1959 [1881]. *Comstock Mining and Miners* (Berkeley, CA: Howell-North).
Lossing, Benson John. 1851. *The Pictorial Field-book of the Revolution* (New York: Harper & Bros.).
Macaulay, Stuart. 1963. "Non-Contractual Relations in Business: A Preliminary Study," *American Sociological Review* 28 (1): 1–19.
MacFarren, H.W. 1912. "Birth of the American Mining Act," *Mining and Scientific Press* 104 (17): 592–6.
Mailath, George J. and Larry Samuelson. 2006. *Repeated Games and Reputations: Long-Run Relationships* (New York: Oxford University Press).
Marshall, Thomas M. 1920. "The Miners' Laws of Colorado," *American Historical Review* 25 (3): 426–39.
McChesney, Fred S. 1981. "Government as Definer of Property Rights: Indian Lands, Ethnic Externalities, and Bureaucratic Budgets," *Journal of Legal Studies* 19 (2): 297–335.
McConnell, William J. 1926. *Frontier Law: A Story of Vigilante Days* (New York: World Press).
McCurdy, Charles W. 1976. "Stephen J. Field and Public Land Law Development in California, 1850–1866: A Case Study of Judicial Resource Allocation in Nineteenth-Century America," *Law and Society Review* 10 (2): 235–66.
McFerrin, Randy and Douglas Wills. 2007. "High Noon on the Western Range: A Property Rights Analysis of the Johnson County War," *Journal of Economic History* 67 (1): 69–92.
Meginness, John F. 1892. *History of Lycoming County, Pennsylvania* (Bowie, MD: Heritage Books).
Mickey, Robert. 2012. *Paths out of Dixie: The Democratization of Authoritarian Enclaves in the America's Deep South* (Princeton, NJ: Princeton University Press).
Milgrom, Paul, Douglass C. North, and Barry Weingast. 1990. "The Role of Institutions in the Revival of Trade: The Law Merchant, Private Judges, and the Champaign Fairs," *Economics and Politics* 19 (2): 1–23.
Miller, Melina. 2007. "The Righteous and Reasonable Ambition to Become a Landowner: What Would Have Happened if Former Slaves Had Received Land after the Civil War?" Ph.D. Thesis, Department of Economics, University of Michigan.
Mises, Ludwig von. 1949. *Human Action* (New Haven: Yale University Press).
Mises, Ludwig von. 1944. *Omnipotent Government: The Rise of the Total State and Total War* (New Haven, CT: Yale University Press).

Mittal, Sonia, Jack N. Rakove, and Barry Weingast. 2011. "The Constitutional Choices of 1787 and Their Consequences," in Douglas A. Irwin and Richard Sylla, eds. *Founding Choices: American Economic Policy in the 1790s* (Chicago, IL: University of Chicago Press).

Monaghan, Jay. 1955. *Civil War on the Western Border, 1854–1865* (Boston, MA: Little, Brown and Company).

Muthoo, Abinay. 2004. "A Model of the Origins of Basic Property Rights," *Games and Economic Behavior* 49 (2): 288–312.

Myerson, Roger. 2004. "Justice, Institutions, and Multiple Equilibria," *Chicago Journal of International Law* 5 (1): 91–107.

Myerson, Roger. 1991. *Game Theory: Analysis of Conflict* (Cambridge, MA: Harvard University Press).

Nelson, Robert H. 1980. *Zoning and Property Rights* (Cambridge, MA: MIT Press).

Nesbit, Robert C. 1973. *Wisconsin: A History* (Madison: University of Wisconsin Press).

Nichols, Alice. 1954. *Bleeding Kansas* (New York: Oxford University Press).

North, Douglass C. 2005. *Understanding the Process of Institutional Change* (Princeton, NJ: Princeton University Press).

North, Douglass C. 1991. "Institutions," *Journal of Economic Perspectives* 5 (1): 97–112.

North, Douglass C. 1990. *Institutions, Institutional Change, and Economic Performance* (Cambridge, UK: Cambridge University Press).

North, Douglass C. 1981. *Structure and Change in Economic History* (Cambridge, UK: Cambridge University Press).

North, Douglass C. 1966. *Growth and Welfare in the American Past: A New Economic History* (Englewood Cliffs, NJ: Prentice-Hall).

North, Douglass C. and Andrew R. Rutten. 1987. "The Northwest Ordinance in Historical Perspective," in David C. Klingaman and Richard K. Vedder, eds., *Essays on the Economy of the Old Northwest* (Athens: University of Ohio Press).

North, Douglass C. and Robert Paul Thomas. 1973. *The Rise of the Western World: A New Economic History* (Cambridge, UK: Cambridge University Press).

North, Douglass C. and Barry R. Weingast. 1989. "Constitutions and Commitment: The Evolution of Institutional Governing Public Choice in Seventeenth-Century England," *Journal of Economic History* 49 (4): 803–32.

North, Douglass C., John Joseph Wallis, and Barry R. Weingast. 2009. *Violence and Social Orders: A Conceptual Framework for Interpreting Recorded Human History* (New York: Cambridge University Press).

Oates, Stephen B. 1970. *To Purge This Land with Blood: A Biography of John Brown* (New York: Harper and Row).

Ohio: History of Montgomery County. 1882. (Chicago, IL: W.H. Beers and Co.).

Olson, Mancur. 2000. *Power and Prosperity: Outgrowing Capitalist and Communist Dictatorships* (New York: Basic Books).

Olson, Mancur. 1993. "Dictatorship, Democracy, and Development," *American Political Science Review* 87 (3): 567–76.

Olson, Mancur. 1965. *The Logic of Collective Action: Public Goods and the Theory of Groups* (Cambridge, MA: Harvard University Press).

Onoma, Ato Kwamena. 2009. *The Politics of Property Rights Institutions in Africa* (New York: Cambridge University Press).

Osborne, Martin and Ariel Rubinstein. 1994. *A Course in Game Theory* (Cambridge, MA: MIT Press).
Osgood, Ernest Staples. 1929. *The Day of the Cattlemen* (Minneapolis: University of Minnesota Press).
Ostrom, Elinor. 2005. *Understanding Institutional Diversity* (Princeton, NJ: Princeton University Press).
Ostrom, Elinor. 1990. *Governing the Commons: The Evolution of Institutions for Collective Action* (Cambridge, UK: Cambridge University Press).
Parsons, Stanley B., William W. Beach, and Michael J. Dubin, 1986. *United States Congressional Districts and Data, 1843–1883* (New York: Greenwood Press).
Paul, Rodman W. 2001. *Mining Frontiers of the Far West, 1848–1880* (Albuquerque: University of New Mexico Press).
Paul, Rodman W. 1966. *The California Gold Discovery: Sources, Documents, Accounts, and Memoirs Relating to the Discovery of Gold at Sutter' Mill* (Georgetown, CA: Talisman Press).
Paul, Rodman W. 1947. *California Gold: The Beginning of Mining in the Far West* (Cambridge, MA: Harvard University Press).
Paxson, Frederic L. 1924. *History of the American Frontier, 1763–1893* (Boston: Houghton Mifflin Company).
Perrigo, Lynn I. 1941. "Law and Order in the Early Colorado Mining Camps," *Mississippi Valley Historical Review* 28 (1): 41–62.
Pierson, Paul. 2004. *Politics in Time: History, Institutions, and Social Analysis* (Princeton, NJ: Princeton University Press).
Pierson, Paul. 2000. "Increasing Returns, Path Dependence, and the Study of Politics," *American Political Science Review* 94 (2): 251–67.
Pierson, Paul. 1994. *Dismantling the Welfare State? Reagan, Thatcher, and the Politics of Retrenchment* (Cambridge, UK: Cambridge University Press).
Pisani, Donald J. 1996. *Water, Land, and Law in the West: The Limits of Public Policy, 1850–1920* (Lawrence: University Press of Kansas).
Pisani, Donald J. 1994. "Squatter Law in California, 1850–1856," *The Western Historical Quarterly* 25 (3): 277–310.
Pisani, Donald J. 1992. *To Reclaim a Divided West: Water, Law, and Public Policy, 1848–1902* (Albuquerque: University of New Mexico Press).
Pollack, Sheldon D. 2009. *War, Revenue, and State Building: Financing the Development of the American State* (Ithaca, NY: Cornell University Press).
Posner, Richard. 2002. *Economic Analysis of Law*, 5th ed. (New York: Aspen).
Powell, James Wesley. 1878. *Report on the Lands of the Arid Region of the United States* (Washington, DC: Government Printing Office).
Powers, Perry F. 1912. *A History of Northern Michigan* (Chicago, IL: Lewis Publishing Company).
Procter, James A. 1959. *The Ohio Company: Its Inner History* (Pittsburgh, PA: University of Pittsburgh Press).
Prucha, Francis Paul. 1969. *The Sword of the Republic: The United States Army on the Frontier, 1783–1846* (Bloomington: Indiana University Press).
Richmond, C. W. and H. F. Vallette. 1857. *A History of the County of Du Page, Illinois* (Chicago, IL: Scripps, Bross and Spears).

Riker, William H. and David L. Weimer. 1995. "The Political Economy of Transformation: Liberalization and Property Rights," in Jeffrey S. Banks and Eric A. Hanushek, eds., *Modern Political Economy: Old Topics, New Directions* (Cambridge, UK: Cambridge University Press).

Riker, William H. and David L. Weimer. 1993. "The Economic and Political Liberalization of Socialism: The Fundamental Problem of Property Rights," *Social Philosophy and Policy* 10 (2): 79–102.

Riker, William H. and Itai Sened. 1991. "A Political Theory of the Origin of Property Rights: Airport Slots," *American Journal of Political Science* 35 (4): 951–69.

Robbins, Roy M. 1942. *Our Landed Heritage: The Public Domain, 1776–1936* (Princeton, NJ: Princeton University Press).

Robbins, Roy M. 1933. "Horace Greeley: Land Reform and Unemployment, 1837–1862," *Agricultural History* 7: 18–41.

Robbins, Roy M. 1931. "Preemption: A Frontier Triumph," *Mississippi Valley Historical Review* 18 (3): 331–49.

Rockwell, Stephen J. 2010. *Indian Affairs and the Administrative State in the Nineteenth Century* (New York: Cambridge University Press).

Rodrik, Dani, editor. 2003. *In Search of Prosperity: Analytic Narratives on Economic Growth* (Princeton, NJ: Princeton University Press).

Rogers, James Grafton. 1949. "The Beginnings of Law in Colorado," *Dicta* 36: 111–20.

Rohe, Randall E. 1986. "The Evolution of the Great Lakes Logging Camp, 1830–1930," *Journal of Forest History* 30 (1): 17–28.

Rohrbough, Malcolm J. 1968. *The Land Office Business: The Settlement and Administration of American Public Lands, 1789–1937* (New York: Oxford University Press).

Root, Hilton L. 1994. *The Fountain of Privilege: Political Foundations for Markets in Old Regime France and England* (Berkeley: University of California Press).

Root, Hilton L. 1989. "Tying the King's Hands: Credible Commitments and Royal Fiscal Policy during the Old Regime," *Rationality and Society* 1 (2): 240–58.

Rosenthal, Jean-Laurent. 1992. *The Fruits of Revolution: Property Rights, Litigation, and French Agriculture, 1700–1860* (New York: Cambridge University Press).

Rosholt, Malcolm L. 1980. *The Wisconsin Logging Book, 1839–1939* (Rosholt, WI: Rosholt House).

Ross, Michael. 2001. *Timber Booms and Institutional Breakdown in Southeast Asia* (New York: Cambridge University Press).

Rubin, Paul H. 1977. "Why Is the Common Law Efficient?" *Journal of Legal Studies* 6 (1): 51–61.

Schelling, Thomas. 1969. "Models of Segregation," *American Economic Review* 59 (2): 488–93.

Schorr, David. 2012. *The Colorado Doctrine: Water Rights, Corporations, and Distributive Justice on the American Frontier* (New Haven, CT: Yale University Press).

Schultz, Kenneth and Barry Weingast. 2003. "The Democratic Advantage: Institutional Foundations of Financial Power in International Competition," *International Organization* 57 (1): 3–42.

Schweber, Howard. 2004. *The Creation of American Common Law, 1850 to 1880: Technology, Politics, and the Construction of Citizenship* (New York: Cambridge University Press).

Sen, Amartya. 1981. *Poverty and Famines: An Essay on Entitlement and Depression* (Oxford, UK: Oxford University Press).
Sened, Itai. 1997. *The Political Institution of Private Property* (Cambridge, UK: Cambridge University Press).
Shambaugh, Benjamin Franklin. 1894. *Constitution and Records of the Claim Association of Johnson County, Iowa* (Iowa City: The State Historical Society of Iowa).
Shepherd, William Robert. 1896. *History of Proprietary Government in Pennsylvania* (New York: Columbia University Press).
Shepsle, Kenneth A. 1978. *The Giant Jigsaw Puzzle: Democratic Committee Assignments in the Modern House* (Chicago, IL: University of Chicago Press).
Shepsle, Kenneth A. and Barry R. Weingast. 1981. "Structure-Induced Equilibrium and Legislative Choice," *Public Choice* 37: 503–19.
Shinn, Charles Howard. 1885. *Mining Camps: A Study in American Frontier Government* (New York: Scribner).
Shutes, William H. 1943. *Lincoln and California* (Stanford, CA: Stanford University Press).
Singer, Peter. 2003. *Corporate Warriors: The Rise of the Privatized Military Industry* (Ithaca, NY: Cornell University Press).
Skocpol, Theda. 1992. *Protecting Soldiers and Mothers: The Political Origins of Social Policy in the United States* (Cambridge, MA: Harvard University Press).
Skowronek, Stephen. 1982. *Building a New American State: The Expansion of National Administrative Capacities, 1877–1920* (Cambridge, UK: Cambridge University Press).
Smith, Duane A. 1973. *Rocky Mountain Mining Camps: The Urban Frontier* (Lincoln: University of Nebraska Press).
Smith, Charles. 1810. *Laws of the Commonwealth of Pennsylvania, II* (Philadelphia: John Bioren).
Smith, Zachariah. 1886. *History of Kentucky* (Louisville, KY: Prentice Press).
Sobel, Russell. 2002. "Defending the Articles of Confederation: A Reply to Dougherty," *Public Choice* 113: 287–99.
Sobel, Russell. 1999. "In Defense of the Articles of Confederation and the Contribution Mechanism as a Means of Government Finance: A General Comment on the Literature," *Public Choice* 99: 347–56.
Sokoloff, Kenneth L. and Stanley L. Engerman. 2000. "History Lessons: Institutions, Factor Endowments, and Paths of Development in the New World," *Journal of Economic Perspectives* 14 (3): 217–32.
Sorenson, Alfred. 1889. *History of Omaha* (Omaha, NE: Gibson, Miller, and Richardson).
Starr, Stephen Z. 1974. *Jennison's Jayhawker's: A Civil War Cavalry Regiment and Its Commander* (Baton Rouge: Louisiana State University Press).
Stasavage, David. 2011. *States of Credit: Size, Power, and the Development of European Polities* (Princeton, NJ: Princeton University Press).
Stasavage, David. 2003. *Public Debt and the Birth of the Democratic State: France and Great Britain, 1688–1789* (Cambridge, UK: Cambridge University Press).
Stephenson, George M. 1917. *The Political History of the Public Lands from 1840 to 1862: From Preemption to Homestead* (Boston, MA: R.G. Badger).

Stewart, James I. 2009. "Cooperation When N Is Large: Evidence from the Mining Camps of the American West," *Journal of Economic Behavior and Organization* 69 (3): 213–25.

Stewart, James B. 1976. *Holy Warriors: The Abolitionists and American Slavery* (New York: Hill and Wang).

Stuart, Granville with Paul C. Phillips. 1925. *Forty Years on the Frontier as Seen in the Journals and Reminiscences of Granville Stuart, Gold-miner, Trader, Merchant, Rancher and Politician* (Cleveland, OH: The Arthur H. Clark Company).

Swierenga, Robert P. 1977. "Land Speculation and Its Impact on Economic Growth and Welfare," *Western Historical Quarterly* 8 (3): 283–302.

Swierenga, Robert P. 1968. *Pioneers and Profit: Land Speculation on the Iowa Frontier* (Ames: Iowa State University Press).

Swierenga, Robert P. 1966. "Land Speculator 'Profits' Reconsidered: Central Iowa as a Test Case," *Journal of Economic History* 26 (1): 1–28.

Sugden, Robert. 2004. *The Economics of Rights, Co-operation, and Welfare.* 2nd ed. (New York: Palgrave Macmillan).

Sugden, Robert. 1986. "Spontaneous Order," *Journal of Economic Perspectives* 3 (4): 85–97.

Swank, Duane. 2002. *Global Capital, Political Institutions, and Policy Change in Developed Welfare States* (Cambridge, UK: Cambridge University Press).

Tocqueville, Alexis de. 2000. *Democracy in America.* Harvey C. Mansfield and Delba Winthrop, eds. (Chicago, IL: University of Chicago Press).

Tullock, Gordon. 1980. "The Transitional Gains Trap," in James M. Buchanan, Robert D. Tollison, and Gordon Tullock, eds., *Towards a Theory of the Rent Seeking Society* (College Station: Texas A&M Press).

Tuttle, Charles R. 1876. *History of Iowa* (Chicago, IL: Richard S. Peale and Company).

Umbeck, John R. 1981. *A Theory of Property Rights with Application to the California Gold Rush* (Ames: Iowa State University Press).

Umbeck, John R. 1977. "The California Gold Rush: A Study of Emerging Property Rights," *Explorations in Economic History* 14 (1): 197–226.

Von Thünen, Johann Heinrich. 1966 [1826]. *The Isolated State.* Peter Hall, ed. (Oxford, UK: Pergamon Press).

Watson, Samuel J. 2012. *Jackson's Sword: The Army Officer Corps on the American Frontier, 1810–1821* (Lawrence: University Press of Kansas).

Watson, Samuel J. 2011. *Frontier Diplomats: The Army Officer Corps in the Borderlands of the Early Republic, 1814–1846* (Lawrence: University Press of Kansas).

Weaver, John C. 2003. *The Great Land Rush and the Making of the Modern World, 1650–1900* (Montreal and Kingston: McGill-Queen's University Press).

Webb, Walter Prescott. 1931. *The Great Plains* (Boston, MA: Ginn and Company).

Weimer, David L., editor. 1997. *The Political Economy of Property Rights: Institutional Change and Credibility in the Reform of Centrally Planned Economies* (Cambridge, UK: Cambridge University Press).

Weimer, David L. and Aidan Vining. 2010. *Policy Analysis* (New York: Pearson Longman).

Weingast, Barry R. 1998. "Political Stability and Civil War: Institutions, Commitment, and American Democracy," in Robert Bates, Avner Greif, Margaret Levi, Jean-Laurent Rosenthal, and Barry R. Weingast, eds., *Analytic Narratives* (Princeton, NJ: Princeton University Press).

Weingast, Barry R. 1997. "The Political Foundations of Democracy and the Rule of Law," *American Political Science Review* 91 (2): 245–63.

Weingast, Barry R., Kenneth A. Shepsle, and Christopher Johnsen. 1981. "The Political Economy of Benefits and Costs: A Neoclassical Approach to Distributive Politics," *Journal of Political Economy* 89 (4): 642–64.

White, Richard. 2011. *Railroaded: The Transcontinental Railroad and the Making of Modern America* (New York: W.W. Norton & Company).

Williams, Francis S. 1950. "Trials and Judgments of the People's Courts of Denver," *Colorado Magazine* 27: 294–302.

Williamson, Oliver. 1996. *The Mechanisms of Governance* (Oxford, UK: Oxford University Press).

Wiseman, Alan. 2005. "Partisan Strategy and Support in State Legislative Elections: The Case of Illinois," *American Political Research* 33 (3): 376–403.

Wittman, Donald. 1995. *The Myth of Democratic Failure: Why Political Institutions are Efficient* (Chicago, IL: University of Chicago Press).

Wolfe, George D. 1969. *The Fair Play Settlers of the West Branch Valley, 1769–1784* (Harrisburg: The Pennsylvania Historical and Museum Commission).

Wyman, Mark. 1979. *Hard Rock Epic: Western Miners and the Industrial Revolution, 1860–1900* (Berkeley: University of California Press).

Young, H. Peyton. 2001. *Individual Strategy and Social Structure: An Evolutionary Theory of Institutions* (Princeton, NJ: Princeton University Press).

Zerbe, Richard O., Jr. 2000. A Foundation for Efficiency in Law and Economics (Northampton, MA: Edward Elgar).

Zerbe, Richard O. and C. Leigh Anderson. 2001. "Culture and Fairness in the Development of Institutions in the California Gold Fields," *Journal of Economic History* 61 (1): 114–43.

Zerbe, Richard O., Jr., and Howard McCurdy. 1999. "The Failure of Market Failure," *Journal of Policy Analysis and Management* 18 (4): 558–78.

Index

Other Books in the Series *(continued from page iii)*

Gary W. Cox, *The Efficient Secret: The Cabinet and the Development of Political Parties in Victorian England*
Gary W. Cox, *Making Votes Count: Strategic Coordination in the World's Electoral System*
Gary W. Cox and Jonathan N. Katz, *Elbridge Gerry's Salamander: The Electoral Consequences of the Reapportionment Revolution*
Raymond M. Duch and Randolph T. Stevenson, *The Economic Vote: How Political and Economic Institutions Condition Election Results*
Jean Ensminger, *Making a Market: The Institutional Transformation of an African Society*
David Epstein and Sharyn O'Halloran, *Delegating Powers: A Transaction Cost Politics Approach to Policy Making under Separate Powers*
Kathryn Firmin-Sellers, *The Transformation of Property Rights in the Gold Coast: An Empirical Study Applying Rational Choice Theory*
Clark C. Gibson, *Politicians and Poachers: The Political Economy of Wildlife Policy in Africa*
Avner Greif, *Institutions and the Path to the Modern Economy: Lessons from Medieval Trade*
Stephen Haber, Armando Razo, and Noel Maurer, *The Politics of Property Rights: Political Instability, Credible Commitments, and Economic Growth in Mexico, 1876–1929*
Ron Harris, *Industrializing English Law: Entrepreneurship and Business Organization, 1720–1844*
Anna L. Harvey, *Votes without Leverage: Women in American Electoral Politics, 1920–1970*
Murray Horn, *The Political Economy of Public Administration: Institutional Choice in the Public Sector*
John D. Huber, *Rationalizing Parliament: Legislative Institutions and Party Politics in France*
John E. Jackson, Jacek Klich, and Krystyna Poznanska, *The Political Economy of Poland's Transition: New Firms and Reform Governments*
Jack Knight, *Institutions and Social Conflict*
Michael Laver and Kenneth Shepsle, eds., *Cabinet Ministers and Parliamentary Government*
Michael Laver and Kenneth Shepsle, eds., *Making and Breaking Governments: Cabinets and Legislatures in Parliamentary Democracies*
Margaret Levi, *Consent, Dissent, and Patriotism*
Brian Levy and Pablo T. Spiller, eds., *Regulations, Institutions, and Commitment: Comparative Studies of Telecommunications*

Leif Lewin, *Ideology and Strategy: A Century of Swedish Politics* (English Edition)
Gary Libecap, *Contracting for Property Rights*
John Londregan, *Legislative Institutions and Ideology in Chile*
Arthur Lupia and Mathew D. McCubbins, *The Democratic Dilemma: Can Citizens Learn What They Need to Know?*
C. Mantzavinos, *Individuals, Institutions, and Markets*
Mathew D. McCubbins and Terry Sullivan, eds., *Congress: Structure and Policy*
Gary J. Miller, *Managerial Dilemmas: The Political Economy of Hierarchy*
Douglass C. North, *Institutions, Institutional Change, and Economic Performance*
Elinor Ostrom, *Governing the Commons: The Evolution of Institutions for Collective Action*
Daniel N. Posner, *Institutions and Ethnic Politics in Africa*
J. Mark Ramseyer, *Odd Markets in Japanese History: Law and Economic Growth*
J. Mark Ramseyer and Frances Rosenbluth, *The Politics of Oligarchy: Institutional Choice in Imperial Japan*
Jean-Laurent Rosenthal, *The Fruits of Revolution: Property Rights, Litigation, and French Agriculture, 1700–1860*
Michael L. Ross, *Timber Booms and Institutional Breakdown in Southeast Asia*
Shanker Satyanath, *Globalization, Politics, and Financial Turmoil: Asia's Banking Crisis*
Norman Schofield, *Architects of Political Change: Constitutional Quandaries and Social Choice Theory*
Norman Schofield and Itai Sened, *Multiparty Democracy: Elections and Legislative Politics*
Alberto Simpser, *Why Governments and Parties Manipulate Elections: Theory, Practice, and Implications*
Alastair Smith, *Election Timing*
Pablo T. Spiller and Mariano Tommasi, *The Instituional Foundations of Public Policy in Argentina: A Transactions Cost Approach*
David Stasavage, *Public Debt and the Birth of the Democratic State: France and Great Britain, 1688–1789*
Charles Stewart III, *Budget Reform Politics: The Design of the Appropriations Process in the House of Representatives, 1865–1921*
George Tsebelis and Jeannette Money, *Bicameralism*
Georg Vanberg, *The Politics of Constitutional Review in Germany*
Nicolas van de Walle, *African Economies and the Politics of Permanent Crisis, 1979–1999*

Stefanie Walter, *Financial Crises and the Politics of Macroeconomic Adjustments*

John Waterbury, *Exposed to Innumerable Delusions: Public Enterprise and State Power in Egypt, India, Mexico, and Turkey*

David L. Weimer, ed., *The Political Economy of Property Rights: Institutional Change and Credibility in the Reform of Centrally Planned Economies*